Praise for *Look for Me in th*

Listen to these voices of young men and women—from places like New Jersey or Panama or New York or Antigua—who poured their insights, courage, and creative energy into New York City's fledgling Black Panther Party that generated chapters in all five boroughs. Unlike out west, where police shot and killed Panthers to disrupt the revolutionary group, New York relied more heavily on courts, jails, and prison to sabotage the organization.

These men and women were tried in the case called the "New York 21"—a barrel full of preposterous crimes which the Panthers supposedly conspired to commit— that led to the arrest and imprisonment of all the leaders. The state fully expected that the Panthers would remain behind bars for decades after being convicted, given that a police informant had masqueraded as a Panther until their arrest. However, the powerful example of Afeni Shakur, who defended herself, other defendants who took charge of their legal representation, the fierce dedication of brilliant attorneys, and the organizing talents of Panther supporters on the outside made the trial the longest running case in New York—with a short one-hour jury deliberation before finding the 21 not guilty on all charges. The case received worldwide publicity and garnered financial support from wealthy New Yorkers to help offset the exorbitant costs of legal fees and bail.

This new edition allows a host of new readers to hear these amazing stories and gain from learning the authors' reflections and insights for today.

—Kathleen Cleaver, Black Panther Party communications secretary, 1967– 1971; senior lecturer, Emory University School of Law

In the midst of this current iteration of the Black freedom struggle, we are in constant search of reminders and sources of strength. Stresses on our time, our bodies, our Spirits, can sometimes feel overwhelming . . . and then we think about what those who struggled before us gave, and continue to give. The Black Panther Party, and the New York 21 in particular, serve a tremendous inspiration. They affirm for us that the struggle is always worth it when it contributes to the liberation of our people. We have been immensely fortunate to share space with and gain wisdom from members of the Party who have sacrificed so much for us, especially Baba Sekou Odinga and those who have served and continue to serve as political prisoners. This release of *Look for Me in the Whirlwind* challenges all of us—those who are active, and those who have yet to become activated—to step into our sacred duty to fight for our freedom and win.

—Melina Abdullah, #BlackLivesMatter leadership team; chair, California State University, Los Angeles, Department of Pan-African Studies

This book finds us teetering on the precipice of . . . What? Imperial implosion? Democracy devastated? Capitalism collapsed? The Great Society in rags? Hope?! This is a better time than most to mine our past for lessons and inspiration. And for white people to listen to Black history, Black struggle, and Black resistance. We have so much to learn if we are to be allies in building a new future. This book is the right place to start.

    —Frida Berrigan, Witness Against Torture, Plowshares, and War Resisters
        League activist; author of *It Runs in the Family: On Being Raised by Radicals*
        and Growing into Rebellious Motherhood

Look for Me in the Whirlwind: From the Panther 21 to 21st-Century Revolutions could not come at a timelier moment in history. As newly emerging grassroots movements challenge state violence against Black people in the U.S., it is essential that new generations learn anew, and that older ones are reminded, of police and FBI tools of repression deployed to demobilize Black radical activism and its growing influence on the Black working class in the '60s. These remembrances, by those framed in the Panther 21 case, are vital building blocks for reconstructing the history of one of the least understood chapters of the Black Panther Party. They are also indispensable reading for those seeking to understand how individual activists and their movements were able to hold their center in the face of harrowing government repression.

    —Johanna Fernandez, professor of history, Baruch College Department
        of Black and Latino Studies, City University of New York; co-curator,
        ¡Presente! The Young Lords in New York

LOOK FOR ME IN THE WHIRLWIND

LOOK FOR ME
IN THE WHIRLWIND

From the Panther 21 to 21st-Century Revolutions

Sekou Odinga, Dhoruba Bin Wahad, Shaba Om, and Jamal Joseph

Edited by déqui kioni-sadiki and Matt Meyer

Foreword by Imam Jamil Al-Amin

Afterword by Mumia Abu-Jamal

PMPRESS

2017

This edition © 2017 by PM Press

ISBN: 978-1-62963-389-3
Library of Congress Control Number: 2016959612

Cover by Josh MacPhee
Interior by Jonathan Rowland

10 9 8 7 6 5 4 3 2 1

PM Press
PO Box 23912
Oakland, CA 94623
www.pmpress.org

Printed in the USA by the Employee Owners of Thomson-Shore in Dexter, Michigan.
www.thomsonshore.com

"If people don't know where they have been and what they have been they don't know what they are. They don't know where they're going to have to go or where they still have to be. History is like a clock; it tells you your time of day. . . . It's like a compass that you use to locate yourself on the map of human geography: politically, culturally, financially."
—John Henrik Clarke, Carter G. Woodson Distinguished Professor of African History, Cornell University

"You are trying a political case under a criminal guise for the elite ruling class of this Babylon. . . You deny us our Constitutional rights according to the Fourth Amendment of the racist Constitution of this country and you know you are denying us those rights. . . . If I had one hundred thousand dollars, I wouldn't even bail myself out. You serve to educate Black people better than anybody in the world. . . . All we ask for is justice. That's all we ask for. Four hundred and fifty mother-fucking years we ask for justice."
—Richard Dhoruba Moore (aka Dhoruba Bin Wahad), New York Panther 21 trial transcript

Contents

Dedication to Sundiata Acoli   ix

Foreword: Look for Me in the World *by Imam Jamil Abdullah*   xi
    Al-Amin

Look for Yourselves: An Introduction *by Shaba Om*   1

Panther 21 Poetry: Newly Discovered or Rarely Seen   5

Whirlwinds All Around Us: The New York Panther 21 in   11
    21st-Century Revolutionary Context *by Matt Meyer*

The Past Catches Up to the Present *by déqui kioni-sadiki*   21

The Case of Sundiata Acoli   35

Parole 2016. Ride and Denied *by Sundiata Acoli*   37

An Updated History of the New Afrikan Prison Struggle   41
    by Sundiata Acoli

A Brief History of the Black Panther Party and Its Place in the   79
    Black Liberation Movement *by Sundiata Acoli*

Senses of Freedom *by Sundiata Acoli*   85

Still Believing in Land and Independence *by Sekou Odinga*   87

The Last of the Loud: New and Revised Commentary   95
    by Dhoruba Bin Wahad

Urban Police Repression: Criminalizing Resistance and   97
    Unraveling the FBI's Counter Intelligence Program, Timeline
    of Empire, Racial Profiling, Police Violence, and Class
    compiled and written by Dhoruba Bin Wahad and Paul Wolf

Assata Shakur, Excluding the Nightmare after the Dream: 103
    The "Terrorist" Label and the Criminalization of Revolutionary
    Black Movements in the USA *by Dhoruba Bin Wahad*

New Age Imperialism: Killing Africa Softly, with Democracy   125
    by Dhoruba Bin Wahad

Man-child in Revolution Land *by Jamal Joseph*   129

Photo Section: Original Work *by Stephen Shames*   140

Look for Me in the Whirlwind: The Collective Autobiography of the 155
    New York 21 (*full text, from 1971 edition*)

Photo Section: Original work *by David Fenton* 533

Counting to 21, Part One: Remembrances, Corrections, 543
    Biographies, and Eulogies: Overview *by Matt Meyer, with Cyril*
    Innis Jr. (Brother Bullwhip)

Poem for Sundiata *by Assata Shakur* 559

Counting to 21, Part Two: New Reflections on Members of the 21 563

Photo Section: From the Archives 571

Ready to Step Up: Lumumba Shakur and the Most Notorious 579
    Black Panthers *by Bilal Sunni-Ali*

Consciousness, Community, and the Future *by Ali Bey Hassan* 587

Capitalism Plus Dope Equals Genocide (excerpt of the classic 591
    1969 pamphlet) *by Michael "Cetewayo" Tabor*

Building a Bridge to the 21st Century (excerpt from an 597
    unpublished letter) *by Kuwasi Balagoon*

How Committed Are You? Excerpts of a Talk at Green for All's 599
    "Dream Reborn" Conference, Memphis, 2008 *by Afeni Shakur*

Look for Me in the Whirlwind (poem-lyrics from the jazz 601
    interpretation) *by Bilal Sunni-Ali*

Black Panther Party Platform and Program 603

Afterword *by Mumia Abu-Jamal* 607

Acknowledgments 609

Author/Editor Biographies 613

Index 615

DEDICATION TO SUNDIATA ACOLI

A New Afrikan political prisoner of war, mathematician, and computer analyst; former member of the Harlem branch of the Black Panther Party and the New York Panther 21

The editors and authors dedicate this book to Panther 21 member Sundiata Acoli, trapped in the dungeons of the imperial prison system that designates defense against genocide to be a crime. At eighty years old, a political prisoner of war for well over forty years, Sundiata remains a stalwart struggler for the freedom of all and the liberation of the Black/New Afrikan nation; he remains an inspiration for current, past, and future generations because of his undying love for the people, his academic brilliance, his consistency, and his all-encompassing smile in the face of torture.

Though hardly known outside a small circle of ardent supporters, Sundiata's case is surely one of the best examples of callous and heinous acts of U.S. hypocrisy: forgiving, pardoning, and embracing and funding violent perpetrators of abusive human rights policies while turning a deaf ear on Sundiata's petitions for humanitarian release.

If any word, sentence, poem, paragraph, or section of this book moves any reader even just a little bit, may it move them (*you!*) to take greater action on his behalf in the year to come. Mention him during dinner; tell a neighbor, friend, and family member; include information about him at an event; bring information about him to a concert; demonstrate; donate money; join the campaign for his immediate release.

http://www.sundiataacoli.org/

FOREWORD

Look for Me in the World

Imam Jamil Abdullah Al-Amin (formerly H. Rap Brown)

In the Name of Allah, Most Gracious, Most Merciful

1. By (the Token of) Time (through the Ages),
2. Verily Man is in loss,
3. Except such as have faith, and do Righteous Deeds, and (join together) in the mutual teaching of Truth, and of Patience and Constancy.

Qur'an 103

1. By the Token of Time through the Ages
   (I swear by the Afternoon)
2. Man is a loser.
3. Except for those who Believe and do Righteous Deeds and enjoin upon each other Truth and enjoin upon each other Patience.

Qur'an 103

Behind every Throne is an Altar—He who excuses himself Accuses himself.
Truth is The Eye of the Storm,
And I . . .

No more than a raindrop in search of
a Fertile Place to fall,
                  a scribe whose ledger is the Wind,
      a Poet who speaks to the Deaf,
      a Teardrop in the Face of Time,
      a Rainbow in the Mind of the Blind.

LOOK FOR ME IN THE WORLD, when . . .
The sharpest sword is sharpened on the Contempt of Death.
Martyrs without Borders.
Harvest from the Seeds of the Survivors of THE MIDDLE PASSAGE,
those who by my Lord's Leave, could not be broken . . . would not be broken.
The ANSWER of the Prayer of those chained and shackled,
Buried in the hulls of slave ships . . .
Made to lie in their own waste; on their necks, the scars of chains, and on their
bodies, imprinted the Indelible Evidence of an Unyielding Cruelty . . . Human
Cargo, Denied the crumbs of
Human Compassion . . . an Execrable Commerce—Commodity by
Circumstance . . .
Political by Birth.
Enduring the Blessed Curse (the Mission Placed in our Hands) . . .
Placing Our Thoughts Above understanding, in order to . . . Over-stand.
Complex Completeness Moving Together gracefully . . .
While going our own separate Way; Bound Together at Faith, thus divisible
only by the Invisible.
un-related Relationship . . . often-rarely occurring. Commonly—
un-common . . . Unique.
Complete in the Purest Heart . . . So to avoid defeat.
I have stood still and stopped the sound of d-feet.
I Brought the Heat when Heart was the Beat.
From talk'n Drums to Cyber . . . Hold'n all Hataz Libel.
Holy-Cost denial set . . . Hate'n on me cause I keep forget'n to forget!
For-Get!!! Ain't no beat for this . . . Punks Jump-up to get Beat for this!
20/20 Hindsight only Allows you to see Clearly what you Missed.
People who lose sight of the Next World become Blind in this one.
Double-Vision . . . as if seen only through one eye . . .
Only the most intelligent Fool . . . Dare give it a try.
Truth is the Cry of All . . . but, the Discipline of the few.

There is no worse Lie than . . . Truth . . . Misunderstood by those who say . . . they knew.

The Mercy of The Creator is the Door Conscious Struggle comes through.

For those who Boast about the excellence of their ancestors, we say

. . . that is True, but what about You? Truth is a trust. Falsehood is a treason.

Justice is a Master Virtue, no light matter, no nicely calculated less or more, no civil right issue:

"To respect the law in the context in which the Negro finds himself is simply to surrender . . . self-respect." —James Baldwin

Just Truth, as it Prevails over Falsehood.

Silence is no longer the Poet.

Every soul delivers itself to ruin by its own acts.

He who excuses himself Accuses himself.

The World when . . . Cubs no more . . . The Young Lions Roar . . .

World wind perfumed by the Fragrance of Bravery . . . From the cradle to the grave . . .

We became old at a young age.

In a world—when justice and law are two different conversations . . .

Justice (a product commercially registered by "Bar Codes"),

Law (Weaponized Litigation) intellectual masturbation that yields no fruitful ejaculation!

(The World When) you are at ease with Eulogies . . . tell'n lies about those who die.

"Among them is (many) a man who says: 'Grant me exemption and draw me not into trial.'

Have they not fallen into trial already?" (Qur'an 9:49).

40 Year Pause on the Cause . . . if not for the LOVE of Allah I don't care nothing about none of y'all. Tongues that stay Dry from things they don't say. The Deafening Silence!

Revolutionary High-Ate-Us . . . Battle Call . . . Sab-bat-i-Call. When the Lion kills . . . it's the jackal and the vulture who gets fat. Bullet-holes in the Minaret say the Crusades Ain't Over Yet.

We Belong to This Fight!

The World when, Step 'N to the Front from the Legion of Warriors and Warrior Queens

With "a Made-up-mind" Whirlwind Theme . . .

Look for Yourself . . . A Love Supreme!
A Fat dog makes a Poor Hunter!

Allah's Slave, Jamil Al-Amin, U.S. Penitentiary Tucson, December 2016
In Peace, Strong! In Battle, Strongest!!!

LOOK FOR YOURSELVES

AN INTRODUCTION

Shaba Om

We, the members of the New York Panther 21, were indicted for conspiracy to destroy public property, to hurt and maim police officers and other officials. It became clear after our long trial and acquittal that the real conspiracy was on the part of the police and the U.S. government—to disrupt and destroy the activities of a central branch of the Black Panther Party.

Harlem has always been a special place. From the time of the Harlem Renaissance to our time in the 1960s it was a center of powerful Black thought—of women and men working for our freedom. Dr. W.E.B. Du Bois and Congressman Adam Clayton Powell were key figures. And, of course, Minister Malcolm X was a renowned leader of the Harlem community. The U.S. government also saw Harlem as an extremely key place. They were very upset about the Panthers having a strong branch there. Harlem being Harlem, we had a very active chapter, including wide distribution of our newspaper up and down 125th Street. We covered every corner with the paper, which was filled with information on the hardships facing the Black community and the need to fight back. The Panther 10-Point Program was primarily a means of educating the community and the Panther newspaper included both the program and details of how people were dealing with it. But what I really learned while on trial with the 21 was that from the point of view of the U.S. government, educating our people was a detriment to "American society."

We were very proud of who we were as a people. As we began to learn and read about our history from renowned historians and activists, the police and the government came down really hard on the New York branch. There were at least three undercover officers in our chapter, working to weaken us at all times. There was a Bureau of Special Services (BSS, popularly known as the "Red Squad") within the New York Police Department, which was essentially a local part of the FBI's illegal Counter Intelligence Program (COINTELPRO).

My comrade Kwando Kinshasa and I were not arrested or captured on the original day of the roundup of the 21; we were caught in Columbus, Ohio, some time later. When we were brought back to New York we were connected to our other comrades on Rikers Island. Once we were all together, we were asked to write a book—the book that became *Look for Me in the Whirlwind*. We all agreed to put our stories together, to speak about ourselves personally and about our collective work as Panthers. The title centered on a speech from noted Pan-Africanist the Honorable Marcus Garvey.

What makes *Look for Me in the Whirlwind* still current today is that a lot of the same political issues that existed then are relevant even now. As you go through the original book and read the various sections, if you overlook the date you won't be able to tell whether you're reading about the 1960s or reading about today! What would be interesting to do is to continue reading—and then pick up today's newspaper. You'll find a startling series of parallels.

What touches me as a member of the 21, having real love for my comrades, is that a lot of them are with us physically while many others are not. The power of the printed word is a really beautiful thing, and here in the 21st century we are fortunate enough to be able to "hear" the members of the 21, now once again in print and thereby making a connection to the 21st century. The love and compassion that we had for the people back then we still have just as strongly today. It is an honor and a pleasure to have the baton picked up, so that proud young people today can better understand the shoulders they are standing upon.

Harlem is still a very interesting place: still very culturally significant, but with widespread gentrification. We as a people bought into the myth that we would never and could never amount to anything. We learned the myths that the schools perpetuated: that we couldn't have any sense of ownership but could only serve others. Harlem, we must remember, is very strategically located. You can get anywhere in the world from Harlem in just a matter of hours. It was a well thought-out and calculated plan to gentrify the community—to destroy us through misinformation and miseducation, through drugs, and through direct purchasing of the buildings and the land.

But the power of a whirlwind is that it comes out of nowhere and takes over everything. It has a unique beauty about itself—in the sense of ultimate transformation. Our 21 was of the 1960s, and now we all face the 21st century. As Panthers, we were always taught to have undying love for the people. That love was there then, it is here now, today, and it will remain forever. It must and will encircle and protect us all.

Read who you are, and be who you are. And look for yourselves—discover yourselves—in the whirlwinds of the 21st century.

PANTHER 21 POETRY

NEWLY DISCOVERED OR RARELY SEEN

The Lesson
Afeni Shakur

Malcolm woke up and saw what appeared to be the mountain of liberation
then he was murdered.
Martin started up that mountain and found there was beauty and lasting
peace—he was murdered.
Huey went all the way up and came down again to speak to the world of the
solidarity there—he was shot and kidnapped.
Eldridge saw my desire to go up and showed me the rugged path—he was
forced into exile.
Bobby took my hand to lead me there and I found the way rough and exhila-
rating
and of course he was gagged, beaten, and chained.
Fred overheard their directions and took to the hills for a closer look—
what he saw made him go back down to share his happiness.
When he came back in the valley, all I could hear him say was—
I am a Revolutionary.
But, it made no sense, and so I just sat and listened.

The next day I heard him repeat this melody as he prepared the morning meal
for my child.
I heard the words—and still I was quiet; Fred didn't seem to mind—he just
kept doing things and singing his song.
And then one day—the melody of his song was taken up by the evil winds of
human destruction.
They heard its message and handed to him the salary of a people's servant
KA BOOM . . .
The air that breathed his message to me was alive with urgency.
The mountains became a reality.
The tools became friends.
The curves became mere objects of jest!
I could sit still no longer.
I began to hum his song.
As I climbed, as I fell and
got up and fell again—I
Sang the song of liberation.
I AM A REVOLUTIONARY!
I AM A REVOLUTIONARY!

Truth Is a Virus
Sundiata Acoli and Walidah Imarisha

Guerrilla plague
Brought from bastard tongues
Blood from a burst blister
Blood on the legs of a sister
We are the fever that heals as it burns
Our rage purifies
Harbingers of chaos and construction.

Living virus running through your system
Resurrecting those you hit at but missed 'em
We are the war coming home
The second coming of Rome
Defeated abroad and destroyed from within
Never to terrorize or rise again.

Revolutionaries birthed and homegrown
Smeared on cheeks like ash
He smiles at all his grandchildren
He knows the inside of vaccination needles
And sterilization pills
His heart bursting with so much love
And so much fear
Hoping his strong arms
Can build a shelter
Against the coming epidemic.

He smiles at his grandchildren, loving them so,
But still must send them where angels fear to go
Grossly unprepared because they haven't been trained
Their schools long ago razed, teachers routed and cadre maimed.

Eyes so wide
You can see the future in 'em
And deep as a new york sewer drain
This child has my eyes
And they are too old for this polished apple face.

A pug nose
And a wide grin mouth
Eyes searching the landmarks for 95 south
Think you can make it thru
That's easy to do . . .
Once, twice but how about the rest of your life?

You can not hope to understand
Infinity
But 33 years starts to stretch
Farther than forever
As the blood slows
In our collective veins
In stasis
Mosquitoes in amber
With the lifeblood
Of ancestors
Suspended inside us.

33 years and more
is just a meatball
compared to foreparents
who did cradle to grave
and still stood tall.

That same blood
Yet courses our veins
Their same message drumbeats
Over and over again.

The solutions to a problem
Lie in its origin.
Human history is long
Ours goes back
To the beginning,
Before the spread of false images
That keep the world lamenting.

So the call of the Ancients

Who had the strength of 10
Will forever remind us when
Once we were free,
And that we, and the world,
Shall be
Free again.

Lock Step
Kuwasi Balagoon
Auburn Correctional Facility
(Excerpt from an unpublished letter to Meg Starr,
December 10, 1984)

They march in formation
lock step
in cadence
so that their bodies don't betray
their fear
by jerky-hesitant motions.
Head straight
on order
by order
so that the folder
cannot confirm under-certain eyes.
They make noises
"hut, two"
to think "hut, two"
and whatever they are told
instead of possible death.
And they think of dying anyway
even though they are used to thinking whatever they are told.
And they think they should be honored for this.
And they shall be
increasingly
with grenades.

WHIRLWINDS ALL AROUND US

THE NEW YORK PANTHER 21 IN 21ST-CENTURY REVOLUTIONARY CONTEXT

Matt Meyer

"It is our duty to fight for our freedom. It is our duty to win."
　　—Assata Shakur, member of the New York Black Panther Party, the
　　　　Black Liberation Army, and inspirational figure for the Movement
　　　　for Black Lives

Historians and linguists like to remind us that "radical" means "back to the roots"—and this book seeks to serve contemporary people's movements by exploring the roots of an extraordinary part of modern history that has largely been hidden from view. The Black Panther Party for Self-Defense certainly has had more than its share of attention, but the extremely active and influential New York branch—around which the essential case of the New York Panther 21 was centered—has received significantly less focus among activists or scholars. The Panther 21 case was essential in part because it served as the major launching point of the U.S. government attack on the modern Black Liberation Movement (the original, often underscored, "blm"). If we are to understand current government machinations, we must gain a deep understanding of the Panther 21. And we must do so in the context of contemporary events.

"It is our duty to fight for our freedom. It is our duty to win."

There can be little question that Black Lives Matter (BLM) has signified a burgeoning rebirth of the Black Liberation Movement (blm). With distinct chapters in close to forty locations and many, many more affiliated and connected groups and sympathetic individuals throughout the world, the naysayers have been shown that BLM is much more than just a hashtag. But it is also more than can be personified in a single organization—with related and parallel structures like the Movement for Black Lives, the Ferguson Truth Telling Project, and frontline activists, the Dream Defenders, Justice League and Gathering for Justice, and countless others. There are many clear and common goals, demands, experiences, and hopes, but one consistent thread is a militancy based in part on the mantra-like recitation of four sentences penned by Assata Shakur, who was once called "the soul of the Black Liberation Army (BLA)." Many now have heard of Assata and read her autobiography, and some wear T-shirts proclaiming, "Assata taught me."

Yet when questioned about vital historical markers—people and places barely one step away from Assata herself—confusion or ignorance too often abounds. Leaders have been asked: "Have you heard about Sundiata Acoli? Are you familiar with Sekou Odinga? Do you know the name Dhoruba Bin Wahad?" All three are closely connected to Assata both personally and politically, but their names and work—past and present—are practically unknown outside of a very small circle of mainly elder organizers. The first of these, Sundiata, remains in prison at age eighty, still doing hard time after more than forty years behind bars for activities he and Assata were involved in together. Sekou was finally paroled after more than thirty-three years in prison, convicted in part for being involved in the escape and freeing of Assata. Dhoruba, coauthor with Assata and Mumia Abu-Jamal of *Still Black, Still Strong: Survivors of the War against Black Revolutionaries*, was field secretary of the Black Panther Party in New York, the organization Assata joined in her early years. He remained a political prisoner for nineteen years until his release in 1990, after proving he was framed as part of the FBI's illegal Counter Intelligence Program (COINTELPRO).

Sundiata, Sekou, and Dhoruba have more in common than their connection to Assata, more than the fact that they serve and served substantial prison time because of their political beliefs and actions, and more than the simple fact that they were members of the Black Panther Party and allegedly part of the Black Liberation Army.

Sundiata, Sekou, and Dhoruba were all members of the infamous case of the New York Panther 21.

**

"We must love each other and support each other."

Tupac Shakur is arguably the most influential overall artist of the late 20th century—rapper, emcee, vocalist, poet, actor—and is certainly one of the era's top-selling performers even years after his death. Tupac's mystique and legacy in the areas of culture, politics, community-based economics, prison life, and more continue to shape new generations. There can be no doubt that his extensive effect on people draws in part on his own upbringing, as the son of a prominent Panther surrounded by a street survival ethic, a social commitment, and a sense of possibility using bold, creative imagery to go up against systemic injustice. The video for Tupac's smash hit "Dear Mama" has over a hundred million views on YouTube—and it's impossible to listen to the song without some awareness that Afeni Shakur was a Black Panther. It should therefore also be no surprise that one of his most consistent and supportive "uncles"—Jamal Joseph—is now a professor and former chair of Columbia University's Graduate Film Division, nominated for an Academy Award for his own artistry. But Afeni is somehow more remembered for being a crack addict than for her successful defense—while on trial and pregnant with Tupac, and against the advice of many—of herself and her comrades, ultimately getting all charges dropped against the 21 targeted and hunted defendants. She was married, at the time, to Lumumba Shakur, a founder of the Panthers in Harlem, whose brother Zayd Malik was killed in the shootout where Assata and Sundiata were captured. Lumumba himself was assassinated in New Orleans just two days before the arrest of Tupac's stepfather Mutulu Shakur, himself a Black liberation militant who has always asserted both his own innocence and that Lumumba's death was politically motivated and based on the early 1980s roundup, incarceration, and murder of militants still committed to the struggle.

Everyone knows Tupac Shakur. But how many know the history of Lumumba or Afeni Shakur, or of Jamal Joseph?

Afeni Shakur, Lumumba Shakur, and Jamal Joseph were all part of the infamous case of the New York Panther 21.

**

"We have nothing to lose but our chains."

Some leading human rights advocates have asserted that 21st-century movements for lesbian, gay, bisexual, and transgender (LGBT) liberation are the cutting edge political issues of our times. Others focus on the continuing struggles opposing militarized police violence—especially in light of heightened attacks on young people of African and Latino descent—as fundamental to understanding contemporary civil rights within the USA. On a broader scale, both LGBT and anti–police violence movements are increasingly understood within an international context, where deep-seated issues of patriarchy, capitalism, imperialism, and racism are interwoven for a holistic and "intersectional" approach toward individual and collective liberation. New organizational structures challenge old authoritarian or centrist models; consensus-informed approaches have been used in place of the leadership of a small and select group of mainly male charismatic decision-makers. But these "new" approaches have roots which can be found in attempts made during previous decades of uprising and revolt.

Kuwasi Balagoon is a little-known former Panther whose name may have been uttered once for every thousand times Huey Newton or Bobby Seale were praised during the 2016 celebrations of the fiftieth anniversary of the founding of the Oakland-headquartered Panthers. Though he was clear to some colleagues about his fluidity of political and personal practice, uniquely blending both revolutionary nationalist and anarchist beliefs, and he died in prison in 1986 due to complications from AIDS, he is held up as an important figure only among a very select group of radicals. Balagoon, in addition to being one of the team responsible for the liberation of Assata, was a member of the New York Panther 21.

At age nineteen, Joan Bird was terrorized by New York police officers who were harassing two older men while the three were in a parked car. "They dragged me out," she later testified, "and began to beat and stomp on me with heavy blackjacks, and beat and kicked me in the stomach, lungs, back, and handcuffed me." Bird had just a few months earlier become a youthful recruit of Black Panther Party; a few months later she would be formally charged as a member of the New York Panther 21.

Michael "Cetewayo" Tabor and Larry Mack traveled to Algeria to help set up the International Office of the Black Panther Party. They were early practitioners of true Pan-African solidarity: meeting and sharing resources with those struggling to free their lands of colonialism and neocolonialism from Mozambique, Angola, Zimbabwe, Namibia, Vietnam, Palestine, and elsewhere. Successful freedom fighters from Algeria, Cuba, and China discussed strategies and tactics across geographic and linguistic lines and even occasionally fought together to help liberate one another's territories. Cetewayo and Mack (along with Sekou Odinga, whose remembrances you will read about in this book) were not only part of the Panthers, they were members of the New York Panther 21.

**

Exiled in Cuba, on the FBI's Ten Most Wanted List with a $2 million bounty on her head, Assata Shakur wrote the words which are repeated nightly as a call to renewed struggle: "It is our duty to fight for our freedom. It is our duty to win. We must love each other and support each other. We have nothing to lose but our chains."

As part of that duty, as part of our collective ability to learn how to win, we must know about Sundiata and Sekou and Dhoruba, about the pitfalls and lessons of Afeni and Jamal, Lumumba and Joan, Kuwasi and Cetewayo, and Larry and all the others.

It is not merely that the case of the New York Panther 21 brought together an extraordinary group of exemplary individuals, deeply committed to the freedom of their people and of all people. It is not merely that the fiery militancy of those times forged a collective spirit and strategic approach which inspired millions and sent nervous shock waves down the corridors of state and imperial power. The story of the Panther 21 and its legacy provides essential truths which have remained largely hidden, even in the myriad of books and movies which make up the cottage industry of Black Panther nostalgia and mythology. These truths include a perspective on the need for clandestine operations during times of great repression. They include an emphasis on the role of the criminal/prison industrial complex which looks beyond the question of abolition toward a direct confrontation with existing legal structures and engagement with those on both sides of the wall. They include a unique and forgotten understanding of the ability to creatively provide both direct local services, such as the much-touted breakfast programs, while at the same time providing a concrete global vision and practice of revolutionary self-defense, fight back, and organization building.

Beyoncé, Bette Midler, and other celebrities have recently referenced the significance of the Black Panthers, sometimes even calling for the release of the more than a dozen remaining Panther political prisoners. Like their celebrity counterparts of past generations, from John Lennon to Leonard

Bernstein and beyond, the importance of these spotlights is entirely what they represent in terms of mass organizing possibilities, not in terms of negotiable support for getting anyone out of jail—much less creating lasting radical change. Possibilities must be turned into realities through the steadfast, sometimes boring, often rewarding, occasionally fun work of making phone calls, writing educational materials, reaching out to people not yet in the know, holding meetings to help unify otherwise divergent perspectives. Once in a while it means working with folks we neither agree with nor like, but who can still play a helpful role in the struggles to free Sundiata Acoli, Imam Jamil Al-Amin, Mumia Abu-Jamal, Russell Maroon Shoatz, Mutulu Shakur, Charles Sims Africa, Debbie Sims Africa, Delbert Orr Africa, Edward Goodman Africa, Merle Austin Africa, Michael Davis Africa, William Phillips Africa, Zolo Azania, Herman Bell, Jalil Muntaqim, Veronza Bowers, Kojo Bomani Sababu, Oso Blanco, Bill Dunne, Romaine Chip Fitzgerald, Patrice Lumumba Ford, David Gilbert, Robert Seth Hayes, Alvaro Luna Hernandez, Kamau Sadiki, Jaan Laaman, Mafundi Lake, Ruchell Cinque Magee, Tom Manning, Tarek Mehanna, Leonard Peltier, Ed Poindexter, Rev. Joy Powell, Gary Tyler, and others. For many of us, the publication of this book brings a special urgency to work harder for the release of Sundiata Acoli, member of the 21 who is an elder deserving of spending his eighth decade of life at home with his family.

**

In 1969, when twenty-one leading members of the New York Black Panther Party were rounded up and indicted, taking risks for some meant continuing the work to "bring the war home"—as the first U.S. troops returned from Vietnam. This was in the context of an antiwar movement, which was holding moratoriums attracting millions, with Washington, DC–based demonstrations mobilizing upwards of 500,000 people. In the wake of the assassination of Rev. Dr. Martin Luther King and the uprisings that followed, of the growing international popularity of "Black Power" and militancy on campuses and in communities, 1969 saw the inauguration of Richard Nixon as thirty-seventh president of the United States. The Chicago conspiracy trial began, bringing together eight codefendants accused of inciting riots that had taken place at the previous year's Democratic National Convention. Ultimately it seemed that Chicago's police force was more responsible for the riotous violence than any of those on trial. During the course of the trial, the judge ordered one of the eight, Black Panther cofounder Bobby Seale, bound and gagged in the courtroom—a fitting symbol to many of the treatment of vocal movement leaders.

The year 1969 is widely remembered for the Woodstock Music Festival and Jimi Hendrix, Neal Armstrong's "one giant leap for mankind" as Apollo 11 landed on the moon, and the release of the Beatles' *Abbey Road* amid rumors of their splitting up. John and Yoko staged a "bed-in" for peace, and John returned his Order of the British Empire medal in protest of the war in Biafra, West Africa. Booker T and the MGs sang "Time Is Tight" and the Fifth Dimension sang "Let the Sunshine In (Age of Aquarius)." J-Lo and Jay-Z, Sean Combs and Ice Cube, Wyclef Jean and Terrence Howard were all born in 1969.

As the year came to a close, in the wee hours of December 4, FBI undercover agent William O'Neal—who had infiltrated the Chicago chapter of the Black Panthers and become bodyguard to Illinois Party chairman and Rainbow Coalition founder Fred Hampton—slipped Hampton a powerful sedative. While Hampton slept, officers of Cook County stormed his apartment, riddling him and fellow Panther Mark Clark with rounds of automatic gunfire. Two point-blank shots to the head of the man who was bringing together youth gangs and political activists, people of all races and ideologies, made certain that Chicago's Panther leadership would be silenced—one way or another. In New York however, for 1969 at least, a different tactic was being used. Fighting for radical social change means taking real risks.

Fifty years following the founding and demise of the Black Panther Party for Self-Defense, different economic, social, and political conditions prevail—even as many of the same baseline issues and underlying causes of conflict and injustice remain. An overextended empire seems in deep crisis, while attempts to stifle popular resistance at home are carried out by ever-more-militarized police forces and agents of repression. The imperial nature of the USA's internal colonialism became clearer every day, as disenfranchised "communities of color" lived entirely separate and unequal lives even while a few Black millionaires thrived under a Black president. The U.S. presidential elections of 2016, if nothing else, showed a new level of dissatisfaction with the Washington status quo, whether evidenced by increased interest in socialistic "political revolution," in right-wing populist or fascist movements, or in a woman-led continuation of the neoliberal agenda. Whatever one's preference—including the growingly popular "none of the above"—resistance most certainly continues.

**

The radical historian's job is not, in fact, to recount the people's history in truth-telling form. As useful as that approach might sometimes be, the more urgent and revolutionary task of a people's historian is to use one's privileged positions to amplify, empower, uncover if necessary, and provide support for the voice of people themselves. Similarly, white folks struggling to be in accountable alliances with liberation movements must support anti–white supremacist, anti-imperialist, and pro–Black Power positions in many forms. Being good "interpreters" of other people's oppression—like attempting to be facilitators of other people's liberation—is ultimately a reactionary and ineffective position. Revolutionary 21st century solidarity must recognize that the oppressed of any race, ethnicity, gender, class, culture, and geographic space have much more wisdom about the nature of power and change than those of the oppressive castes (though privilege works overtime to ensure that most believe the opposite to be true). True solidarity understands that together, from different but aligned angles, we must deal strategic blows to the systems which devalue and commodify all people and things. Thus, this special book seeks to build authentic bridges between the past, present, and future—for all seeking truly revolutionary paths.

The stories and voices of the Panther 21 resonate today because they boldly confronted their own tumultuous times with creativity, candor, and directness. This anthology brings together the classic texts from their collective autobiography with contemporary commentary from the surviving Panthers on lessons learned and directions for our times. Sister déqui kioni-sadiki adds the following piece that, along with this preface, attempts to set the stage for the ideas that follow. In addition to key new pieces by former Panther 21 members Sekou Odinga, Dhoruba Bin Wahad, and Jamal Joseph—each of whom did time behind bars even after the acquittal of the 21—we also have rarely seen and never-before-published materials from Panther 21 members Afeni Shakur, Ali Bey Hassan, and Kuwasi Balagoon, as well as some key writings of Sundiata Acoli and others. With the help of Bronx Panther Cyril Innis Jr. ("Bullwhip"), we have compiled a review of the post-acquittal lives of all of the 21; photographer and communications specialist David Fenton has shared with us some never-before-seen photos from the period. Photojournalist Stephen Shames, whose recent book *Power to the People: The Black Panthers in Photographs* spectacularly chronicles the images of those times, has gifted us with some images of the 21 that do not appear in his other work. Panther leader Bilal Sunni-Ali contributes a special chapter on 21 member Lumumba Shakur and in so doing casts a light on the entire complex history of Black Panthers in New York. Panther 21 member Shaba Om provides an inspiring introduction. And finally, former Panthers and still-incarcerated political prisoners Imam Jamil Al-Amin (aka H. Rap Brown) and Mumia Abu-Jamal graciously frame the book with their foreword and afterword, strengthening our efforts to build connections between the prison walls with the force of their mighty words.

We would do well to listen carefully to them all.

More than one hundred years have passed since Pan-Africanist Marcus Garvey built the single largest organization in the history of Africans in the Americas. We would also do well to remember his admonitions, facing his own turbulent times while organizing in a period of great risk:

> If I die in Atlanta my work shall then only begin, but I shall live, in the physical or spiritual to see the day of Africa's glory. When I am dead wrap the mantle of the Red, Black and Green around me, for in the new life I shall rise with God's grace and blessing to lead the millions up the heights of triumph with the colors that you well know.
>
> Look for me in the whirlwind or the storm, look for me all around you, for, with God's grace, I shall come and bring with me countless millions of Black slaves who have died in America and the West Indies and by the millions in Africa to aid you in the fight for liberty, freedom, and life.

Let us remember well that it is our duty not simply to struggle, but to win.

THE PAST CATCHES UP TO THE PRESENT

déqui kioni-sadiki

Sankofa: go back into the past to build for the future

That Huey Newton and Bobby Seale founded the first nationally recognized chapter of the Black Panther Party for Self-Defense (BPP) is fairly well known in most progressive circles. Their October 1966 efforts centered on confronting police terror and the murder of Black people taking place in Oakland, California at that time. What isn't nearly as well known is that almost from its inception, J. Edgar Hoover (the decades-long director of the FBI) was engaged in an undeclared and clandestine Counter Intelligence Program (COINTEL-PRO) war—on the BPP in particular, and on the whole of the Black Freedom struggle in general. Though the Panthers were specially targeted, COINTEL-PRO both included and began before FBI campaigns against Malcolm X and Martin Luther King, looking to criminalize the entire Black Liberation Movement with special attempts "to expose, disrupt, misdirect, discredit, or otherwise neutralize the activities of black nationalist . . . organizations and groups, their leadership, spokesmen, membership, and supporters."

That Hoover directed the FBI to destroy this revolutionary, youth-led BPP poses a number of questions: What was it about the BPP which so challenged the capitalist power structure that it had to be neutralized?

Could it be that, as a revolutionary organization, the BPP stood firmly on the principle that Black people have the right to struggle for justice, self-determination, and liberation? That those BPP principles were firmly rooted in the Black radical tradition of self-defense and armed resistance to white-on-Black violence and murder?

Could it be that in a short span of time—in cities, towns, and states across the country—thousands of urban poor and working-class Black youth were becoming radicalized and joining the organization at a rate faster than anyone expected? Could it be that the BPP's 10-Point Platform and Program provided poor and working-class Black people with free breakfast for children programs; free health clinics; sickle cell anemia testing; food pantries; clothing drives; elder, housing, and domestic violence assistance programs; welfare rights advocacy; cultural programs; and more—all while the capitalist power structure did nothing to help people?

Could it be that the BPP articulated that the violence of poverty, hunger, homelessness, lack of decent health care, housing, and education, police terror and murder, and all manner of oppression endured by poor and working-class Black people were fundamentally a consequence and function of u.s. capitalism, imperialism, colonialism, racism, and white supremacy? Moreover, could it be that the BPP was able to politicize, inspire, awaken, and transform urban Black youth's previously reactionary dysfunctional intercommunity violence and hostility into a revolutionary commitment and practice of serving and defending the material needs of other poor and working-class Black people?

What is clear is that the deepest politics and practices of the BPP then—like its true history and legacy now—remains a source of tremendous power and potential. What is clear is that the idea that Black people, especially youth, would engage in the struggle to defend their right to justice, self-determination, and liberation—with arms if necessary—was so deeply troubling and threatening to the racist capitalist power structure that Hoover deemed the BPP "the greatest threat to the internal security" of the country.

It is in this context that the FBI, CIA, u.s. Marshals, and New York City Police Department (NYPD)—with bulletproof vests, loaded shotguns, and a shoot-to-kill attitude—conducted an early morning raid of Panther homes and offices on April 2, 1969, to serve arrest warrants on Michael "Cetewayo" Tabor, Alex "Katara" McKeiver, Curtis "Doc" Powell, Sundiata Acoli (C. Squire), Ali Bey Hassan, Lonnie Epps, Lumumba Shakur, Lee Berry, Kwando Kinshasa, Shaba Om, Walter Johnson, Richard "Dhoruba" Moore, Afeni Shakur, Jamal "Eddie" Joseph, Joan Bird, Robert "Bob" Collier, Kuwasi Balagoon, and Richard Harris, as well as Sekou Odinga, Thomas Berry, and Larry

Mack, who temporarily escaped capture. Eventually, charges were dropped against eight of them, leaving thirteen Panthers to stand trial: Joan Bird, Richard "Dhoruba" Moore, Robert "Bob" Collier, Ali Bey Hassan, Michael "Cetewayo" Tabor, Afeni Shakur, Sundiata Acoli, Lumumba Shakur, Kwando Kinshasa, Shaba Om, Abayama Katara (Alex McKeiver), Baba Odinga (Walter Johnson), and Dr. Curtis Powell. Kuwasi Balagoon and Richard Harris were already doing time in New Jersey.

The New York Panther 21, as they came to be known, were charged with 186 counts of attempted arson, attempted murder, and conspiracy to blow up police precincts, schools, department stores, and the New York Botanical Garden. If convicted, each faced the possibility of 300+ years of political imprisonment. Almost the entire Harlem-Bronx chapter of the BPP, its NYC leadership, were included in the group.

At the time, the trial against the 21 was the longest and most expensive trial in the history of New York City. It was never about justice or protecting people or places from these Panthers allegedly conspiring to harm or destroy them; and the trial was one that neither Hoover nor the powers that be had any intention of losing. As is the general case for poor and working-class Black people caught in the mangled web of an unjust criminal justice system, it was a cornucopia of injustice: perjured testimony by law enforcement, coercion of witnesses, prosecutorial misconduct, and a sitting judge (John Murtagh) who made no attempt to conceal his contempt or disdain for the Panthers, Black resistance, and the team of movement attorneys.

A visibly very pregnant Afeni Shakur functioned as her own extraordinarily effective, believable, compassionate, and capable pro se attorney. Gerald Lefcourt, William Crain, William Kunstler, Robert Bloom, Sanford Katz, Charles McKinney, and others served as the attorneys of record. The criminal charges levied against the 21 weren't just about the individuals on trial. The trial and charges were among the war strategies Hoover used to criminalize the BPP and its membership all over the country. Then and now, the arrest, trial, and political imprisonment of the 21 stands as an indictment of a centuries-old hypocrisy that amerikkka holds the promise of life, liberty, and happiness for all people regardless of race, class, or religion. In fact, as government treatment of the Panthers makes clear, amerikkka has a long trajectory of criminalizing, suppressing, and repressing Black resistance. This trajectory extends from the state-sanctioned and violence-infested slave ships and plantations during the transatlantic slave trade and Middle Passage that first brought Africans to these shores to the impunity of white-on-black violence in the post-Reconstruction era, to the one hundred years of lynchings, the storm of mass arrests, water hoses, snarling police dogs, police beat-downs, and hate-filled white mobs of Jim Crow apartheid, to the present killing of Black mothers' sons and daughters every twenty-six hours somewhere in amerikkka by white police, security guards, or vigilantes.

The Black Panthers recognized this as both a historical and contemporary reality and responded appropriately in the language of self-defense and armed resistance. It is for this reason that Hoover was so doggedly determined to maim, murder, and defeat the BPP. He didn't care how, or at what cost to life or limb, COINTELPRO was carried out; there were no legal, moral, or ethical boundaries he did not cross. All manner of overt and covert violence was used against the BPP: surveillance, illegal phone wiretapping, agents provocateurs, infiltration, coercion, fabrication of criminal charges, poisoning of the breakfast for children program, intercepting and forging mail to instigate internal and external dissension, distortions, and outright lies with the purpose of inciting hostility and violence between members and with other organizations. When all of that wasn't enough, outright assassinations were fine with the FBI.

The public was never supposed to know about COINTELPRO, or about Hoover's mission to prevent: 1) the coalition of militant Black nationalist groups; 2) the rise of a messiah who could unify and electrify the masses; 3) Black militants from gaining respectability; and 4) the long-term growth and coalition of militant Black youth. Nor were they supposed to know Hoover had the complicit support and cooperation of local, state, and federal law enforcement, politicians, the capitalist ruling class, the criminal justice system, and corporate media to manufacture the climate of fear, hysteria, and "law and order" repression to combat the BPP and militant Black youth. Our knowledge of COINTELPRO's existence is based mainly on an accidental discovery by a group of white radicals who secretly broke into a Media, Pennsylvania, FBI storage room to steal and burn draft cards. They stumbled upon the classified documents, turning those documents over to *WIN Magazine,* a biweekly associated with the War Resisters League, which dedicated its entire March 1972 issue to publishing the incriminating FBI documents. In those more radical times, in addition, the mass media was more willing to expose and spotlight the wide-scale government corruption. This eventually led to the Senate-based Church Committee hearings—named for its chair, Senator Warren Church—which ruled that COINTELPRO was an illegal operation that had committed acts violating the civil and constitutional rights of u.s. citizens.

The sole outcome of those hearings was the immediate dismantling of COINTELPRO, but no other remedies or actions were taken to punish or hold accountable any law enforcement officer or agency for the literal crimes they committed against the revolutionaries, organizations, and movements of that time. Also, although other revolutionaries and organizations were targeted by Hoover and COINTELPRO, none suffered the degree of repression, state-sanctioned violence, and political imprisonment as the unsuspecting and underprepared Panthers and their families. In a six-year period, the BPP became target number one in Hoover's vicious and unrelenting campaign of criminalization, dehumanization, distortion, demonization, and maligning that made police shoot-ins of Panther homes and offices a frequent occurrence. Across the country—even with unarmed bystanders present—dozens of Panthers were assassinated or injured. Dozens of others were driven underground or into exile, and dozens more were criminally charged, convicted, and sentenced to inordinately long terms of political imprisonment.

In the decades since the Church Committee hearings there have been sporadic grassroots calls demanding public hearings to hold the government responsible for COINTELPRO's illegal and violent acts. To date, there have been no formal investigations into the criminal convictions, and no widespread attempts to exonerate or release the dozens of Panthers and other revolutionaries targeted by COINTELPRO who are still held as political prisoners and prisoners of war (PP/POWs) in state and federal prisons across amerikkka.

On May 13, 1971, the jury in the Panther 21 case returned with its verdict: "not guilty." Although it was a tremendous victory for both the BPP and the Movement, at the same time the trial had exacted a heavy price. For two years, the NYC leadership were disappeared from the streets while BPP families and communities were disrupted and relationships and friendships became strained, with some dissolving under the duress. The work of serving and defending the people suffered. COINTELPRO had also succeeded in heightening and exploiting existing and growing contradictions between local, national, and international BPP cadre, chapters, and leadership, to the point that while fighting for their lives and freedom, the 21 were expelled by the Party's Central Committee. COINTELPRO had instigated and manipulated internal and external seeds of dissension, hostility, distrust, and paranoia within the BPP that ultimately proved too difficult for the young cadre organization to recover from. The psychological, emotional, mental, physical, spiritual, and financial toll of coping with constant police attacks, friends being killed, children and parents harassed, dangerous and pernicious stereotyping, the loss and alienation of family members, the loss of jobs and housing, the arrests and fabrication of criminal charges requiring perpetual fundraising for lawyers and bail fees eventually left the BPP fractured and splintered, a shell of its short former existence.

In the end, some members disappeared underground into the clandestine military unit of the Black Liberation Army (BLA). Some returned to their previous lives—feeling afraid, disillusioned, frustrated, disappointed, angry, and betrayed by the Party and movement they had come to love and committed their lives to. Still others found alternate means of serving the people. Fifty years later, members of the BPP are hidden in plain sight, suffering from the debilitating effects of post-traumatic stress disorder, casualties of COINTELPRO's deadly war on the BPP.

It has been four and a half decades since the trial of the 21, and the sociopolitical realities that exist today serve as a chilling reminder that the past has caught up to the present, that everything old has become new again, and that the more things change the more they stay the same. In 1966, rampant and unpunished police terror and murder of Black people led to the grassroots communal response of the BPP, with Black youth across the country being recruited in rapid-fire succession. In 2016, the persistence of unpunished police terror and murder of Black people has led to the grassroots communal response of Black Lives Matter, with once again much excitement from and recruitment of Black youth. Both are examples of organic formations that came into being as a result of the negligence and recalcitrance of a capitalist power structure, elected officials from the president of the United States to Congress, mayors, prosecutors, and grand and trial juries assiduously refusing to punish or hold police accountable for the murder of unarmed Black people.

Most troubling of all is the fact that in the 1970s, the Church Committee felt able to call COINTELPRO an illegal operation; in 2016, government criminality and violent repression have surpassed the 1970s and been made legal by Homeland Security, the Patriot Act, and the Military Defense Authorization Act. What this means for the new generation of Arab nationals, immigrants, and activists involved in a wide range of issues such as the environment and Ferguson, Baltimore, and the Black Lives Matter movement is that the criminalization, repression, demonization, arrests, dehumanization, subversion, and undermining of their ideas, principles, and organizing has not only continued but in some ways become commonplace. Criminal prosecutions, convictions, and political imprisonment imposed on the movement radicals and revolutionaries of the 1960s and '70s is now being imposed on a new generation, with less interest or attention from the mainstream media. That most people have never heard of COINTELPRO or the war it waged against the BPP and the Black Liberation Movement isn't surprising given the pervasive corporatization and commodification of history and academia. This status quo history-telling of the BPP has been fraught with revisionism, the culture of celebrity activism, and individualized Panther exceptionalism.

The residual effects of COINTELPRO's war on Black liberation continues not just in the political imprisonment of radicals and revolutionaries, but in the everyday reverberations which—over the past forty years—have led to the decimation, disintegration, and destruction of poor and working-class families and communities. The violent repression and political imprisonment of the BPP is symbolic of the notion that "when they come for you in the morning, they'll be coming for me at night." In the 1960s, the government waged war on Black liberation; twenty years later, a new draconian War on Drugs was waged on millions of poor and working-class Black men, womyn, and children. Forty years later, it's a religious xenophobic War on Terror against Muslims and Arab nationals across the globe.

The consequences and legacy of the onslaught against the Panther 21 are more than sophisticated government surveillance and disruption. That legacy continues daily as an unseen force assiduously manipulating, dictating, orchestrating, and controlling the entire Black sociopolitical landscape. It includes the lingering disorganization and sectarian disunity that plagues many activist circles and organizations today. Ultimately, what Hoover set out to accomplish has been achieved.

We see this with the glaring absence of revolutionary Black nationalist groups and coalitions between organizations and activists, while a plethora of white-funded nonprofit or not-for-profit organizations exploit the conditions created by racist capitalist policies in urban Black communities. We see this in the lack of a cohesive transformative Black agenda to halt the systematic and institutionalized police genocide of Black people, and in the overabundance of Black mis-leadership, opportunists, self- or state-anointed Black spokespersons, and Black elected officials—always ready to serve the status quo, yet unwilling to challenge and confront the institutionalized oppression that cripples Black lives. We can see this in the marginalized, misleading, and mythologized history and legacy of the Panthers, in the treatment of self-defense, armed resistance, radical grassroots political perspectives mischaracterized as "violent," "militant," or "extremist." Most perniciously, we see the overwhelming majority of misinformed and miseducated Black youth, crippled by ignorance and indifference about who they are, about the centuries and generations-old struggles waged on their behalf, distracted and obsessed by the whims of social media and technology, and consumed by hypercapitalist dreams of fame, fortune, and material possessions.

This has affected all of us: unlike the days of old, neighbors hardly speak or interact with one another, children are left to fend for themselves, people have been conditioned to be afraid of not only the power structure but their neighbors, Black children, and everyone else. Each one of these wars has been waged on Black people in particular, but they have also targeted Brown, immigrant, Arab, and Muslim people, and have led to the further disintegration and destruction of poor and working-class families, kinship communities, and nations around the world. u.s. history is replete with perpetual wars meant to repress and control those who dare to struggle against the violence of capitalism, imperialism, colonialism, racism, and white supremacy. Unbeknownst to many, these wars have helped usher amerikkka into the police state we live in today. They have consolidated law enforcement into the most militarized police force in the world. It is against this backdrop that, radical or not, activists must heed the collective histories and herstories of the 21, the Black Panther Party, and past movements—to better understand and prepare themselves for the virulent state repression and potential political imprisonment that awaits them.

For all these reasons and more, this updated version of *Look for Me in the Whirlwind* is a book whose time has come. Hoover is long gone, as is the covert version of the COINTELPRO. For the most part, the public's perception and understanding of the BPP/BLA and what the organization represented within the Black freedom struggle is based upon an anti-Black, mythological, demonized, or criminalized idea of Black resistance—especially armed resistance. And while much has been written about the West Coast membership of the BPP, the East Coast stories have yet to be told. In many ways, the perspectives in this book will be an introduction for some, and a reintroduction for others, not only of the historic case of the 21 as members of the East Coast NYC chapter of the BPP, but about the who, what, and why regarding every level of the u.s.a.'s continuing war against the BPP/BLA and Black resistance movements. Like the original edition, it is presented in the first-person narrative of the once-younger members of the BPP. They are now becoming older, some departing this earthly realm, taking with them a litany of untold and valiant histories and herstories from one of the most significant revolutionary organizations and movements of the 20th century.

Dhoruba Bin Wahad, Jamal Joseph, Sundiata Acoli, Shaba Om, and Sekou Odinga, underground at the time of the original publication, are among the surviving members of the 21, and of the rarely presented East Coast membership of the BPP. They are survivors of Hoover's war on the Black Liberation Movement. They offer here their fifty-year post-perspective on the significance of the 21, on Hoover's COINTELPRO war, on the BPP/BLA and Black Liberation Movement, and on the still alarming rate of police genocide against unarmed Black men, womyn, and children. Here they expose the forty-year-old lies told about them and their comrades; here they make visible the often invisible existence of their fellow Panthers and dozens of other radicals and revolutionaries from the Movements of the 1960s and '70s, held as PP/POWs in this purported land of "freedom and democracy." Their collective histories as revolutionaries and former PP/POWs will counter the narrative of the BPP/BLA as anything but revolutionary—showing that they are nothing like the reactionary hate group or militant violent extremists conspiring to blow people up while they shopped for Easter outfits, as the case against the 21 tried to present them.

With COINTELPRO waging war against the BPP, being a revolutionary was a matter of life and death. Surviving COINTELPRO has left deep scars, and means that to varying degrees every member of the BPP has gained, lost, and suffered from their involvement in the Black Liberation Movement. For Dhoruba, Jamal, and Sekou—and their families—this is especially true given that as former PP/POWs, they endured being underground and hunted down by law enforcement, prison isolation and separation from family, and torture and police beat-downs. What they share on these pages will challenge the vilification, denigration, and falsehoods that permeate any mainstream discussion about the BPP/BLA, their contributions to the Black Freedom struggle, and the presumptive denunciations of them and their comrades as "violent," "cop killers," "convicted felons," or "domestic terrorists" for taking up arms to defend themselves, their families, community, and a nation of poor and working-class Black people against extreme state violence. As revolutionaries who stood up to this vile, hundreds-of-years-old system of oppression, repression, and suppression of Black people's lives they can speak best to what they believe is their legacy in the movement for Black liberation.

They tackle some of the questions most on people's mind: Is there anything any of them would have done differently if given a chance? What challenges did they face then, and what challenges do they face now? What were the lessons learned? What has it meant to leave their still imprisoned comrades behind the wall thirty, twenty, or two years after their own release from prison? Most importantly, what messages of hope, resistance, and vision do they have for current and future generations of revolutionaries?

It has now been more than forty-five years since the acquittal of the 21 and each of their lives has taken a different political, spiritual, personal, and professional path. Sundiata Acoli has spent well over forty years as a POW; he has been repeatedly denied parole based on pressure from the New Jersey law enforcement apparatus. Sekou Odinga was a POW thirty-four years until his release in November 2014. Dhoruba Bin Wahad served nineteen years as a POW until his conviction was overturned following a court appeal that released details of the COINTELPRO conspiracy against him. Jamal Joseph served five and a half years behind bars and is now a well-known filmmaker, college professor, and arts educator.

The 21 and the BPP, like Malcolm X and so many Black folks before them, upheld the principle and tactic of self-defense and armed resistance, born out of the historical reality of Black people's lived experiences resisting centuries and generations of white-on-Black terror, violence, and murder. Self-defense and armed resistance neither began nor ended with the BPP; both are a matter of Black survival in an amerikkka built on the violence and genocide against millions of indigenous people and the enslavement of millions of kidnapped Afrikans. Both are an ideology and practice firmly rooted in the Black radical tradition of justice, self-determination, and liberation—as aptly suggested by recent book titles such as *This Nonviolent Stuff'll Get You Killed: How Guns Made the Civil Rights Movement Possible* and *We Will Shoot Back: Armed Resistance in the Mississippi Freedom Movement*. Self-defense and armed resistance are calls to action, to Black self-determination—to not be unarmed victims and witnesses of police genocide or any other form of white-on-Black terror and violence. For this reason, the BPP fighters were not and are not criminals, dangerous villains, "domestic terrorists," "the greatest threat," murderous people intent on killing police, or any of the other pejorative name-calling phrases ascribed to them by Hoover, police officers, judges, prison administrators, the corporate media, prison parole boards, history books, and Hollywood movies.

And while all this is important, and a great deal of attention has been given to the Panther's focus on the gun (with some also to the larger strategy of armed resistance), it isn't the most significant aspect of the BPP legacy. The BPP's primary objective was serving and defending the material needs of poor and working-class Black people. Keeping this in mind, the 21 and the BPP are Black heroes and sheroes, servants of the people, freedom fighters in the pantheon of the Black freedom struggle concerned about poor and working-class Black children living in a system that denied their humanity, dignity, justice, and most basic material needs. That millions of poor and working-class people of all races and ages—in cities, rural or suburban towns, and states across this country—now have access to free breakfast/lunch programs, free health clinics, food pantries, soup kitchens, a "patients' bill of rights," coats, shoes, and clothing drives—all this is a reflection of the work of the BPP.

These survival programs initiated by the BPP made them targets of Hoover's destructive, racist obsessions. The programs have since been co-opted by the u.s. government, to be administered as disempowering social service programs. Rather than speaking this truth to power about the legacy and work of the BPP, white amerikkka, reactionary academics, conservative political pundits, the corporate media, and bourgeois Blacks consistently demonize and misrepresent the role of the BPP as revolutionaries in the Black freedom struggle. These same forces clamor to glorify the highly fictitious "nonviolent" civil rights movement—which always had significant self-deter-mination and self-defense elements built into it. Sadly, this dichotomy persists today. Whenever another unarmed Black man, womyn, or child has been mur-dered by the police, and Black people who must confront the reality of trying to live and breathe safely while Black in amerikkka make the obvious choice to rebel, we are all treated to the guardians of the status quo insisting on the need for calm, "nonviolent," and "peaceful" protests.

This hypocritical cry is antithetical to the historic realities of resistance and change; it is a patronizing and reactionary response to the contemporary paradox of state-sanctioned white-on-Black terror, violence, and murder. How are victims to remain calm, nonviolent, and peaceful in the face of intentional and unpunished violence and murder? In the 1960s, the BPP denounced the power structure's sanctioning of police murder of Black people, and declared that Black lives matter in word and in deed. Today, that same Black lives matter declaration speaks just as profoundly to the souls of Black folk, because we still live in a nation of anti-Black laws and policies.

That said, the reissue of the original book included here is a praise song to the 21 and to all those members of the BPP/BLA—inside and outside the prison walls, here and gone—who gave their hands, bodies, hearts, minds, and spirits to answer the Black freedom call; who woke up at 3:00 A.M. to cook breakfast for hungry children not their own; who escorted poor and working-class mothers into the bowels of housing court and welfare offices; who held slum landlords accountable for rats, roaches, and peeling paint; who faced down marshals attempting to evict mothers with children; who confronted drug dealers on street corners and playgrounds; who placed their bodies and lives in the police line of fire to stop them from shooting down other people's sons and daughters; who served and defended poor people not because they were asked to but because necessity has always been the mother and fatherhood of Black resistance.

The BPP didn't just inspire this nation of Black youth to join the people's movement for liberation—it inspired nations of young freedom dreamers and freedom fighters the world over to do the same. In their lives and the lives of their families, being a Panther cadre meant wanting other people's children to live in a better world. And this commitment has come at an incredibly heavy intergenerational cost.

At the time of the fiftieth anniversary celebrations of the founding of the BPP, there could have been no more fitting a tribute than inclusion of the decades-long Panther political prisoners. The sacrifices which have been made are incredible, as is the ongoing commitment of Anthony "Jalil Muntaqim" Bottom, Veronza Bowers, Herman Bell, Sundiata Acoli, Robert Seth Hayes, Ed Poindexter, Kamau Sadiki, Imam Jamil Al-Amin (formerly H. Rap Brown), Mutulu Shakur, Mumia Abu-Jamal, Kenny "Zulu" Whitmore, Joseph Bowen, Russell Maroon Shoatz, and Romaine "Chip" Fitzgerald. We must also never forget Assata Shakur (with a $2 million bounty, "terrorist" label), Pete O'Neal, Nehanda Abiodun, and others living in forced exile throughout Afrika, the Caribbean, and South America. We remember Albert "Nuh" Washington, Teddy "Jah" Heath, Bashir Hameed, Mondo we Langa, Kuwasi Balagoon, Warren Wells, Herman Wallace, and Abdullah Majid—martyred as POWs from the state-sanctioned medical neglect inside amerikkka's prison death camps. Can we also think about the dozens of unnamed and long-forgotten members of the BPP, mercilessly shot down by killer cops in the streets across amerikkka? For them and their families, the moments of nostalgia, reunions of former comrades/revolutionaries not seen in years, commemorations, praise for and reveling in the courage, bravery, strengths, triumphs, and tenacity of the BPP is not so much an anticipated event as it is a painful reminder of the revolution that didn't happen in their lifetime. It is a reminder of the deafening silence that pervades their loss, separation, trauma, pain, disappointment, and betrayal by all those claiming to love the BPP, to love Assata, but too busy to lift a finger for these freedom fighters. In honor of their lives, let there be an anniversary commemoration that softens the calloused apathy, disregard, dismissal, and indifference to their ongoing exile and political imprisonment, that brings more BPP voices, solidarity, dollars, and support into the work of building national and international campaigns to release these BPP PP/POWs from behind the prison walls.

While the BPP/BLA of the 1960s and '70s no longer exists, the spirit of the BPP lives on in the freedom dreams of Black folk—young and older—who rebel, agitate, organize, and resist. It doesn't mean that the BPP is without fault or not in need of constructive critique. Certainly, the passage of time and history will absolve them of their so-called crimes and forgive them their mistakes, weaknesses, youthful ignorance, arrogance, and shortcomings. In the meantime, there are valuable lessons and insights to be learned by the example, resilience, strengths, triumphs, good, and not-so-good Panther practices, as they carried us forward in the Black freedom struggle. Whatever their shortcomings, both the 21 and the BPP in general represent the tie that binds our collective histories to the lives and legacies of Nat Turner, Harriet Tubman, the Afrikan Blood Brotherhood, Republic of New Afrika, Revolutionary Action Movement, Rosa Parks, Deacons for Defense and Justice, Malcolm X, Robert and Mabel Williams, and a long list of unnamed Black men and womyn who recognized their human rights, political rights—rights as defined by international law to arm and defend themselves, family, community, and nation against the tyranny and oppression of white-on-Black violence, state-sanctioned or not—to every past, present, and future movement of radical Black resistance.

In closing, the great revolutionary Ernesto "Che" Guevara said revolutionaries are guided by great love for the people. And so it is with great love that this *Look for Me in the Whirlwind* edition goes out—as a love letter to a much older generation of Black men and womyn who joined the East and West Coast chapters of the BPP, fought and won the historic 21 case, sacrificed their lives on the battlefield of the Black Liberation Movement, unwillingly relinquished their freedom for ours, were murdered as PP/POWs in the dungeons of amerikkka's prison death camps. It is a love letter to say "job well done." A new generation must now seize the time to carry forward the Black struggle for justice, self-determination, and liberation. It is time to undo the far-reaching disinformation campaigns, with their oversimplification of the BPP's role in the Black freedom struggle.

In the simple and clear words of our beloved Abdullah Majid, a BLA political prisoner who died while incarcerated in 2016, "Let's get to work."

In the meantime, *asante sana* to the New York Panther 21 and all those who resist, resist, resist—with the understanding that "freedom ain't free."

THE CASE OF SUNDIATA ACOLI

At eighty years of age, Sundiata Acoli—beloved Black liberation community elder, revered mathematician and former NASA employee, and close comrade of Assata Shakur—remains behind bars as one of the USA's most-respected and least-known political prisoners. If contemporary tributes to the movements of the 1960s and '70s are to mean anything; if apparent official commitments to restorative justice, reconciliation regarding past injustices, and a rule of law based on prevention and not revenge are to appear even slightly true; if this book is to be more than merely an academic exercise in nostalgia—then Sundiata Acoli must be set free. The movement to free Sundiata Acoli (and all U.S. political prisoners) must reach beyond a small, dedicated cadre of his family and friends. It must be based on more than simply a devotion to the politics and tactics which he and his comrades espoused. At eighty years of age, Sundiata Acoli's continued imprisonment serves nothing other than to show—in a most direct, cruel, unusual, heinous, torturous, vindictive, and callous fashion—that the U.S. government and all those who support his current incarceration have not moved beyond the racist notions of Hoover, McCarthy, Jim Crow, or Old Dixie. Check out the important writings below by Sundiata, but also urgently check out his website and help build the movement for his freedom: sundiataacoli.org.

Free Sundiata Now!

PAROLE 2016: RIDE AND DENIED

Sundiata Acoli

This is a brief recap of my July 2016 parole hearing and denial.

Almost two years prior, on September 29, 2014, the New Jersey Appellate Court ordered the New Jersey Parole Board to "expeditiously set conditions" for my parole. The parole board appealed the order on grounds that I had not undergone a hearing before the full parole board prior to securing the order for release.

The New Jersey Supreme Court reversed the Appellate Court's order and remanded the case to the full parole board for completion of the administrative process, which, for a convicted murderer like me, requires a full hearing before the parole board prior to securing release from incarceration.

The process further requires that the victim be given the opportunity to address the board and to witness the full board's interaction with the incarcerated murderer prior to his or her release.

The Ride

On June 6, 2016, I was transported by van from the federal prison in Maryland where I am "housed," to Trenton, NJ, for a parole hearing—without my attorney present—before the full New Jersey State Parole Board. Upon arrival at New Jersey State Prison (NJSP), formerly Trenton State Prison, the driver of the van reported that he had "inadvertently" left my legal valise, containing *all* my legal material, at FCI Cumberland, Maryland.

New Jersey and the FBI are caught in a time warp and can see me only as a cop killer, not the mathematician, computer analyst, intellectual, and humanitarian known and loved by the rest of the world, who registered voters in Mississippi in 1964, worked in Harlem with the Panthers, and has educated, mentored, and counseled countless younger prisoners over the years. My supporters say I am their hero. Imagine the term "killer cop" branding someone and burying him behind bars for life [the way the words "cop killer" are currently used —Ed.].

Most importantly, the valise contained my speech, "Why I Should Be Paroled," cowritten by my dear comrade-daughter Fayemi Shakur and me, which I planned to deliver before the full board two days hence. I asked the driver to call R&D at FCI Cumberland and have them mail my valise overnight.

NJSP immediately mug-shot me, gave me a Sundiata Acoli NJSP photo ID with my height reset from 5 feet 9 inches to 5 feet 5 inches by a spiteful guard, took me to lockdown, and cut off all communications and contact between me and the outside world: *no* incoming or outgoing mail, telephone, telegram, e-mail, visitor, money transfer, commissary, pen, paper, pencil, eraser, stamps, envelopes, towel, face cloth, or pillow.

I told them I was from a medium security federal prison with no reason to be locked down. They ignored me. My attorney, Bruce Afran, was scheduled to visit me the next day; the cell was freezing cold; it was near sundown, so I called it a night and slept in my jumpsuit.

Next day I arose at sunup, stiff-necked, showered and shook myself dry like a wet dog. I was given two-thirds of my normal medication dosage at FCI Cumberland and when I asked why, I was given no reason but simply told "No."

I told them I was from a medium security federal prison with no reason to be locked down. They ignored me.

I was four-man escorted to Health Services for a Hep-C blood test and returned to my cell when I noticed they had written "PC" and "NO-CON" (i.e., "Protective Custody" and "NO CONTACT") on my cell ID card. I told the escort sergeant that I was not PC, had not requested PC, and would sign any release form necessary to remove myself from that status.

He said "No" and would not summon a lieutenant or the captain, so I resigned to put my attorney on the matter when we met. A prisoner overheard my complaint to the sergeant and sent me a stub pencil with no eraser. I was most thankful and sat down to write what I could remember of my "parole" speech when the guard called out that my attorney was here.

Bruce's father had died the previous week, but he was holding up well. He shared some youthful photos of his father and family with me, I expressed my condolences, and we got into the work.

I told him they had lost my legal material, they have me in "total" lockdown, have a "PC" sign on my cell door, and have cut my meds to two-thirds of the dosage I received at FCI Cumberland. Bruce said he'd look into it and that meanwhile we needed to focus on the parole hearing tomorrow.

Hearing Day

On June 8, 2016, I arose and told the guard I had no clean clothes and no (safety) razor but I did have a parole hearing today and I was *not* going to the hearing unless I got a shower, razor, and clean clothes. He produced all three within the hour, except he substituted a barber for the razor.

The U.S. Cold War with Cuba is thawing, whetting the appetite of New Jersey and the FBI to throw Assata Shakur back in a U.S. prison. They've labeled her a "terrorist"—she's the first woman on the FBI's terrorist list—and raised the price on her head to $2 million. That is a measure of the same officials' attitude toward her codefendant, Sundiata Acoli.

I noticed that my ankles had begun to swell from water accumulation, due most likely to the change in my medication. I was escorted to take a TB x-ray and returned to put the finishing touches on my speech when the guard said, "Parole board's calling!"

The hearing lasted from about 9:00 A.M. until about 4:00 or 5:00 P.M. It reached a new level of examination, cross-examination, and recrimination.

Again, they questioned me primarily about the events on the turnpike with almost nothing about my many positive accomplishments. They also asked, "Aren't you angry that they broke Assata out of prison instead of you?" My response was, "No, I don't or wouldn't wish prison on anyone."

At the end they again denied parole and went outside the guidelines to give me a longer than usual "hit" (time until next parole hearing). Since Blacks, others of color, and the oppressed are the overwhelming majority of people in prison, we need to seriously think about creating parole boards that mirror the people in prison, that is, "people's parole boards."

My remaining two weeks at NJSP were spent in almost complete isolation from the outside world, except that on my last night there the Inmate Legal

Association (ILA) sent me a free permit for an outgoing legal letter. By then my ankles were almost continually swollen from excess water buildup. I wrote my favorite attorney, and next morning they packed me out for the return trip to FCI Cumberland.

AN UPDATED HISTORY OF THE NEW AFRIKAN PRISON STRUGGLE

Sundiata Acoli

Sundiata's preface: This article was first written at the request of the New Afri-
kan People's Organization (NAPO) [in the late 1980s —Ed.]. Its original title
was "The Rise and Development of the New Afrikan Liberation Struggle Behind
the Walls." It was first published, in 1992, as "A Brief History of the New Afrikan
Prison Struggle," and then updated in 1998 to its present form. Although this work
focuses almost exclusively on New Afrikan prisoners and their struggle, it is by no
means intended to discount the many long heroic prison struggles and sacrifices by
all other nationalities—the Puerto Ricans, Native Americans, Mexicans, whites,
Asians, and others. Raphael Cancel Miranda, who led the work stoppage of the
United States Penitentiary in Marion, Illinois, in 1972 in response to the beating of
a Mexican prisoner, has been one of my heroes and role models since I first became
aware of him long ago. The same can be said of Lolita Lebrón, with whom Assata
Shakur did time at the Alderson Women's Penitentiary—and of numerous other
prisoners of different nationalities whom I've done time with and struggled together
with during the long years of my imprisonment. There are so many deserving pris-
oners of all nationalities that it would extend this article indefinitely to include them
all—and I did not feel justified in including some if I couldn't include all. Nor did
I feel presumptuous enough to write a prison history of other nationalities who are
best suited to record their own history. My main intent is to chronicle the history of

the New Afrikan prison struggle which, for too long, has been written by others who often took it upon themselves to read out of history those Black prisoners and Black prison organizations which did not conform to their preconceived notions of what was fit to include. The updated 1998 edition expressed appreciation to Zakiyyah Rashada, Nancy Kurshan, Steve Whitman, Joan McCarty, and Walee Shakur for providing prison source data. Any incorrect interpretations of the data are strictly mine. Also my warm gratitude to Mtumwa Iimani for her typing, editing, and helpful suggestions in the updating of the original version.

The "New Afrikan liberation struggle behind the walls" refers to the struggle of Black prisoners, "behind the walls" of U.S. penal institutions, to gain liberation for ourselves, our people, and all oppressed people. We of the New Afrikan Independence Movement spell "Afrikan" with a "k" as an indicator of or cultural identification with the Afrikan continent and because Afrikan linguists originally used "k" to indicate the "c" sound in the English language. We use the term "New Afrikan" instead of Black, to define ourselves as an Afrikan people who have been forcibly transplanted to a new land and formed into a "New Afrikan" nation in North America. But our struggle behind the walls did not begin in America.

The 16th Century through the Civil War

The Afrikan prison struggle began on the shores of Afrika, behind the walls of medieval pens that held captives for ships bound west into slavery. It continues today behind the walls of modern U.S. penitentiaries where all prisoners are held as legal slaves—a blatant violation of international law, as is the present U.S. policy of executing minors and the mentally impaired.

The conception of prison ideology began to take form as far back as the reign of Louis XIV of France (1643–1715) when the Benedictine monk Mabillon wrote: "Penitents might be secluded in cells like those of Carthusian monks and there being employed in various sorts of labor." In 1790, on April 5th, the Pennsylvania Quakers actualized this concept as the capstone of their fourteen-year struggle to reform Philadelphia's Walnut Street Jail. No longer would corporal punishment be administered. Henceforth, prisoners would be locked away in their cells with a Bible and forced to do penitence in order to rehabilitate themselves. Thus was born the "penitentiary."

The first prison physically designed to achieve total isolation of each prisoner was the Eastern State Penitentiary, better known as Cherry Hill, in Philadelphia, constructed in 1829 with cells laid out so that no prisoner ever saw any person other than his guards. This "separate system" represented by Cherry Hill was being rivaled by an alternative, the "silent system," which was designed specifically for exploiting mass convict labor. Under the latter system, prisoners were housed in solitary cells but worked together all day as an ideal source of cheap reliable labor, under rigorous enforcement of the rule that all convicts must maintain total silence. The model for this system was set up at Auburn, New York, in 1825, where they initiated the "lock step" so that guards could maintain strict control as the prisoners marched back and forth between their cells and their industrial workshops.

By 1850, approximately 6,700 people were found in the nation's newly emerging prison system. Almost none of the prisoners were Black. They were more valuable economically outside the prison system because there were other means of racial control. During this time most New Afrikan (Black) men, women, and children were already imprisoned for life on plantations as chattel slaves. Accordingly, the Afrikan struggle behind the walls was carried on primarily behind the walls of slave quarters through conspiracies, revolts, insurrections, arson, sabotage, work slowdowns, poisoning of the slave master, self-maiming, and runaways. If slaves were recaptured, they continued the struggle behind the walls of the local jails, many of which were first built to hold captured runaways. Later they were also used for local citizens.

Even before the end of the Civil War, a new system had been emerging to take the place of the older form of slavery: the convict lease system. Thus, shortly after 1850 the imprisonment rate increased, then remained fairly stable with a rate of between 75 and 125 prisoners per 100,000 population. The Afrikan struggle continued primarily behind the slave quarters' walls down through the issuance of the Emancipation Proclamation. This was a declaration issued by President Lincoln on January 1, 1863, during the height of the Civil War. It declared the slaves free only in those states still in rebellion and had little actual liberating effect on the slaves in question. Their slave masters, still engaged in war against the Union, simply ignored the declaration and continued to hold their slaves in bondage. Some slave masters kept the declaration secret after the war ended following Lee's surrender on April 9, 1865. As a result, news of the Emancipation Proclamation did not reach slaves in Texas until June 19, 1865. This date, called "Juneteenth," is celebrated annually by New Afrikans in Texas and outlying states as "Black Independence Day."

Post–Civil War to the 20th Century

Immediately after the Civil War and at the end of slavery, vast numbers of Black males were imprisoned for everything from not signing slave-like labor contracts with plantation owners to looking the "wrong" way at some white person or for some similar "petty crime." Any "transgression" perceived by whites to be of a more serious nature was normally dealt with on the spot with a gun or rope—provided the Black was outnumbered and out-armed. "Black-on-Black" crime was then, as now, considered to be "petty crime" by the U.S. justice system. But petty or not, upon arrest most New Afrikans were given long, harsh sentences at hard labor.

Within five years after the end of the Civil War, the Black percentages of the prison population went from close to zero to 33 percent. Many of these prisoners were hired out to whites at less than slave wages. This new convict-lease system appeared to have great advantages for the landowners: they did not own the convicts, and hence could afford to work them to death. (The movie *Gone with the Wind* actually uses this new form to glorify the older system by comparison.) The president of the Board of Dawson discovered that in 1869 the death rate among leased Alabama Black convicts was 41 percent. Some restraints were obviously necessary; Mississippi managed to reduce its annual death rate for leased Black convicts between 1882 and 1887 to a mere 15 percent. Overnight prisons had become the new slave quarters for many New Afrikans. Likewise, the Afrikan prison struggle changed from a struggle behind the walls of slave quarters to a struggle behind the walls of county workhouses, chain gang camps, and the plantations and factories that used leased convicts as slave laborers.

The 20th Century through World War II

From 1910 through 1950, Blacks made up 23 to 34 percent of the prisoners in the U.S. prison system. Most people conditioned by prison movies like *The Defiant Ones* (starring Sidney Poitier, a Black, and Tony Curtis, a white) or *I Am a Fugitive from a Chain Gang* (starring Paul Muni, a white in an integrated chain gang), or *Cool Hand Luke* (starring Paul Newman, a white, in a southern chain gang) erroneously assume that earlier U.S. prison populations were basically integrated. This is not so. The U.S. was a segregated society prior to 1950, including the prisons—even the northern ones. Roger Benton's 1936 overview of Louisiana's Angola prison and its historical background states:

There were actually six camps at Angola, five of which were composed of men and one for women. Only in the women's camp were whites and coloreds mixed. Camps A, B, C, and D were all colored and constituted by far the bulk of the population, furnishing the state with the cheap convict labor so sorely needed to raise and harvest the mammoth sugar cane crop necessary to satisfy the hungry maws of the gigantic and profitable grinding and refining plant. Once you saw the operation of the plant—the terrific busyness of everybody during grinding time—once you learned what the plant meant to the state in dollars-and-cents profit, you understood why it was so easy to convict and imprison a Negro in the South, and gained a new understanding of the whole basis for the subjugation of the Negroes. Although only 40 percent of the entire population of Louisiana at this time was colored, 83 percent of the prison population was made up of Negroes.

Blacks were always, at least from the time of Emancipation, the majority population in the southern state prisons. But elsewhere the early populations of the more well-known or "mainline" state and federal prisons—Attica, Auburn, Alcatraz, and Atlanta—were predominantly white and male. Whenever New Afrikans were sent to these "mainline" prisons they found themselves grossly outnumbered, relegated to the back of the lines, to separate lines, or to no lines at all. They were often denied outright what meager amenities existed within the prisons. Racism was rampant. New Afrikans were racially suppressed by both white prisoners and guards. All of the guards were white; there were no Black guards or prison officials at the time.

In the period between the Civil War and World War II, the forms of convict labor spilled over and intermingled with "free" labor. Thus, we find Virginia convicts being worked by a canal company. Tennessee worked a part of its convicts within the prison walls, a part on farms, and the rest were leased to railway companies and coal mines. North Carolina and South Carolina employed a portion of their convicts within the walls. The rest were scattered under various lessees. Much of the tunneling of the Western Carolina Railroad through the Blue Ridge was accomplished by convict labor. Georgia convicts were leased to lumber camps and brickyards. Alabama employed hers in railroad building, in mines, and sawmills. Mississippi convicts were leased to railway contractors and planters. Until 1883, the lessees of Texas convicts employed a portion of them in a cotton mill and at other times within the walls of the penitentiary, and placed the remainder in railway construction camps. Arkansas convicts were leased to plantation owners and coal mines. In

Florida, the majority of the convicts were leased to turpentine farms. A smaller number were employed in phosphate mines.

The Afrikan prisoners continued to struggle behind the walls of these segregated convict-lease systems, county workhouses, chain gang camps, and state and federal prisons, yet prison conditions for them remained much the same through World War II. Inside conditions accurately reflected conditions in the larger society outside the walls, except by then the state's electric chair had mostly supplanted the lynch mob's rope.

Post–World War II to the Civil Rights Era

Things began to change in the wake of World War II. Four factors flowing together ushered in these changes. They were the ghetto population explosion, the drug influx, the emergence of independent Afrikan nations, and the civil rights movement.

The Ghetto Population Explosion
Plentiful jobs during the war, coupled with a severe shortage of white workers, caused U.S. war industries to hire New Afrikans in droves. Southern New Afrikans poured north to fill these unheard of job opportunities, and the already crowded ghetto populations mushroomed.

Drug Influx
New Afrikan soldiers fought during the war to preserve European democracies. They returned home eager to join the fight to make segregated America democratic too. But the U.S. had witnessed Marcus Garvey organize similar sentiments following World War I into one of the greatest Black movements in the western hemisphere. This time the U.S. was more prepared to contain the new and expected New Afrikan assertiveness. Their weapon was "King Heroin."

The U.S. employed the services of the Mafia during World War II to gather intelligence in Italy to defeat fascist Mussolini. Before the war, Mussolini embarked on a major campaign against the Mafia, which enraged the group's leaders. (Fascism was a big Mafia itself so it couldn't allow another Mafia to exist.) Mussolini's activities turned Mafiosi into vigorous anti-fascists, and the American government cooperated with the Mafia both in the United States and in Sicily. In the eyes of many Sicilians, the United States helped restore the Mafia's lost power. The Americans had to win the war, so they couldn't pay much attention to these things. "They thought the Mafia could help them, and perhaps they did," said Leonardo Sciascia, perhaps the best-known living Sicilian novelist and student of the Mafia.

During World War II, the Office of Strategic Service (OSS), the fore-runner of the Central Intelligence Agency (CIA), helped to commute Lucky Luciano's sentence in federal prison and arrange for his repatriation to Sicily. Luciano was among the top dons in the Mafia syndicate and the leading orga-nizer of prostitution and drug trafficking. The OSS knew that Luciano had excellent ties to the Sicilian Mafia and wanted the support of that organization for the Allied landing in Sicily in 1943. When Luciano left the U.S., numerous politicians and Mafia dons gathered together at the Brooklyn docks to wave him goodbye in what was the first of many occasions that international drug dealers were recruited by the U.S. government to advance its foreign policy interests.

After the war, in return for "services rendered," the U.S. looked the other way as the Mafia flooded the major U.S. ghettos with heroin. Within six years after World War II, due to the Mafia's marketing strategy, over 100,000 people were addicts, many of them Black.

The Emergence of Independent Afrikan Nations

Afrikans from Afrika, having fought to save European independence, returned to the Afrikan continent and began fighting for the independence of their own colonized nations. Rather than fight losing Afrikan colonial wars, most Euro-pean nations opted to grant "phased" independence to their Afrikan colonies. The U.S. now faced the prospect of thousands of Afrikan diplomatic person-nel, their staffs and families coming to the UN and wandering into a minefield of racial incidents, particularly on state visits to the rigidly segregated capital, Washington, D.C. That alone could push each newly emerging independent Afrikan nation into the socialist column. To counteract this possibility, the U.S. decided to desegregate. As a result, on May 17, 1954, the Supreme Court declared school segregation illegal.

In its landmark *Brown vs. Board of Education* case, which heralded the beginning of the end of official segregation in the United States, the Supreme Court had been made fully aware of the relations between America's domestic policies and her foreign policy interest by the federal government's amicus curiae (i.e., friend of the court) brief, which read:

> It is in the context of the present world struggle between freedom and tyranny that the problem of racial discrimination must be viewed ... [for] discrimina-tion against minority groups in the United States has an adverse effect upon

our relations with other countries. Racial discrimination furnishes grist for the communist propaganda mills, and it raises doubts even among friendly nations as to the intensity of our devotion to the democratic faith.

Malcolm X provides similar insight into the reasoning behind the U.S. decision to desegregate. During his February 16, 1965, speech at Corn Hill Methodist Church in Rochester, New York, he said:

> From 1954 to 1964 can be easily looked upon as the era of the emerging African state. And as the African state emerged . . . [w]hat effect did it have on the Black American?
>
> When he saw the Black man on the [African] continent taking a stand, it made him become filled with the desire to also take a stand. . . . Just as [the rulers of the U.S.] had to change their approach with our people on this continent. As they used tokenism . . . on the African continent . . . they began to do the same thing with us here in the States: . . . tokenism. . . . Every move they made was a token move. . . . They came up with a Supreme Court desegregation decision that they haven't put into practice yet, not even in Rochester much less in Mississippi. [Applause.]

Origin of the Civil Rights Movement

On December 1, 1955, Ms. Rosa Parks defied Montgomery, Alabama's bus segregation laws by refusing to give her seat to a white man. Her subsequent arrest and the ensuing mass bus boycott by the Montgomery New Afrikan community kicked off the civil rights movement. Martin Luther King Jr., a young college-educated Baptist minister, was chosen to coordinate and lead this boycott primarily because he was a new arrival in town, intelligent, respected, and had not accumulated a list of grudge enemies as had the old guard. His selection for leadership catapulted him upon the stage of history. The 381-day boycott toppled Montgomery's bus segregation codes.

Reverend Joseph E. Lowery was part of a group of young activist ministers who had begun to test segregated public transportation laws, in addition to Martin Luther King Jr.—and Ralph Abernathy in Montgomery, Alabama; Fred Shuttlesworth in Birmingham, Alabama; Theodore "T.J." Jemison in Baton Rouge, Louisiana; and Charles K. Steel in Tallahassee, Florida. "The earliest boycotts were in Baton Rouge and Tallahassee, but they were unsuccessful," says Lowery. "We used to meet monthly in Montgomery to share our pain." After the success of the Montgomery bus boycott, the ministers met in New Orleans in February 1957 and formed the Southern Christian Leadership Conference (SCLC), with Martin Luther King Jr. later nominated as chairman of the board. A month later, in March 1957, Ghana became the first of a string of sub-Saharan Afrikan nations to be granted independence.

As northern discrimination, bulging ghettos, and the drug influx were setting off a rise in New Afrikan numbers behind the walls, southern segregation, the emergence of Independent Afrikan nations, and the resulting civil rights movement provided those increasing numbers with the general political agenda: equality and antidiscrimination.

Civil Rights through the Black Power Era

Religious Struggles in Prison

Meanwhile, behind the walls, smart segments of New Afrikans began rejecting Western Christianity. They turned to Islam as preached by Elijah Muhammad's Nation of Islam (NOI) and by Noble Drew Ali's Moorish Science Temple of America (MST). The NOI preached that Islam was the true religion of Black people, that Blacks were the original people on earth, and that Blacks in America were a nation needing land and independence. The MST preached that the Asiatic Black people in America must proclaim their nationality as members of the ancient Moors of Northern Africa. These new religions produced significant success rates in helping New Afrikan prisoners rehabilitate themselves by instilling them with a newfound sense of pride, dignity, piety, and industriousness. Yet these religions seemed strange and thus threatening to prison officials. They moved forthwith to suppress these religions, and many early Muslims were viciously persecuted, beaten, and even killed for practicing their beliefs. The Muslims fought back fiercely.

Civil Rights Struggles in Prison

Like American society, the prisons were rigidly segregated. New Afrikans were relegated to perform the heaviest and dirtiest jobs—farm work, laundry work, dishwashing, garbage disposal—and were restricted from jobs as clerks, straw bosses, electricians, or any position traditionally reserved for white prisoners. Similar discriminatory rules applied to all other areas of prison life. New Afrikans were restricted to live in certain cell blocks or tiers, eat in certain areas of the mess hall, and sit in the back at the movies, TV room, and other recreational facilities.

Influenced by the anti-discrimination aspect of the civil rights movement, a growing number of New Afrikans behind the walls began stepping up their struggle against discrimination in prison. Audacious New Afrikans began violating longstanding segregation codes by sitting in the front seats at the movies, mess hall, or TV areas—and more than a few died from shanks in the back. Others gave as good as they got, and better. Additionally, New Afrikans began contesting discriminatory job and housing policies and other biased conditions. Many were set up for attack and sent to the hole for years, or worse. Those who were viewed as leaders were dealt with most harshly. Most of this violence came from prison officials and white prisoners protecting their privileged positions; other violence came from New Afrikans and Muslims protecting their lives, taking stands and fighting back. From these silent, unheralded battles against racial and religious discrimination in prisons emerged the New Afrikan liberation struggle behind the walls during the civil rights era of the 1950s. Eventually the courts, influenced by the "equality/anti-discrimination" aspect of the civil rights movement, would rule that prisons must recognize the Muslims' religion on an "equal" footing with other accepted religions, and that prison racial discrimination codes must be outlawed.

Black Power through the Black Liberation Era

As the civil rights movement advanced into the '60s, New Afrikan college students waded into the struggle with innovative lunch counter sit-ins, freedom rides, and voter registration projects. On April 15, 1960, a student conference was called under the auspices of Ms. Ella Baker, a field worker for the SCLC. The Student Nonviolent Coordinating Committee (SNCC) was formed during this period to coordinate and instruct student volunteers in nonviolent methods of organizing voter registration projects and other civil rights work. These energetic young students, and the youth in general, served as the foot soldiers of the movement. They provided indispensable services, support, and protection to local community leaders such as Fannie Lou Hamer, Ella Baker, Septima Clark, Bob Moses, Amzie Moore, Daisy Bates, and other heroines and heroes of the civil rights movement. Although they met with measured success; white racist atrocities mounted daily on defenseless civil rights workers.

Young New Afrikans in general began to grow increasingly disenchanted with the nonviolent philosophy of Martin Luther King. Many began to look increasingly toward Malcolm X, the fiery young minister of NOI Temple No. 7 in Harlem, New York. He called for "self-defense, freedom by any means necessary, and land and independence." As Malcolm Little, he had been introduced to the NOI doctrine while imprisoned in Massachusetts. Upon release, he traveled to Detroit to meet Elijah Muhammad, converted to Islam, and was given the surname "X" to replace his discarded slave-master's name. The X symbolized his original surname lost to history when his fore-parents were kidnapped from Afrika, stripped of their names, language, and identity, and enslaved in the Americas. As Malcolm X he became one of Elijah Muhammad's most dedicated disciples and rose to National Minister and spokesperson for the NOI. His keen intellect, incorruptible integrity, staunch courage, clear resonant oratory, sharp debating skills, and superb organizing abilities soon brought the NOI to a position of prominence within the Black ghetto colonies across the U.S.

Origin of the Revolutionary Action Movement

During the fall of 1961, an off-campus chapter of the Students for a Democratic Society (SDS) formed at Ohio's Central State College, called Challenge. Challenge was a black radical formation having no basic ideology. Part of its membership was students who had been expelled from southern schools for sit-in demonstrations. Others were students who had taken freedom rides or from the North, some of whom had been members of the NOI and Afrikan nationalist organizations. Challenge's main emphasis was struggling for more students' rights on campus and bringing a Black political awareness to the student body. In the yearlong battle with the college's administration over student rights, members of Challenge became more radicalized. Challenge members attended student conferences in the South and participated in demonstrations in the North. Donald Freeman, a Black student at Ohio's Case Western Reserve University maintained correspondence with Challenge's cadre discussing the ideological aspects of the civil rights movement.

In the spring of 1962, *Studies on the Left,* a radical quarterly, published Harold Cruse's article "Revolutionary Nationalism and the Afro-American." Freeman wrote a letter to Challenge cadre telling them to seriously study the article. He also said Black radicals elsewhere were studying the article and that a movement had to be created in the North similar to the NOI, using the tactics of SNCC but outside of the NAACP and CORE.

After much discussion, the cadre decided to form a broad coalition to take over student government at Central State. Meetings were held with representatives from each class, fraternity, and sorority. A slate was drafted and a name for the party was selected. It was called "RAM," later to be known as the Revolutionary Action Movement. The Challenge cadre met and decided to dissolve itself into RAM and become the RAM leadership. RAM won all student government offices. After the election, the inner RAM core discussed what to do next. Some said that all that could be done at Central State had already been done, while other disagreed. Some of the inner core decided to stay at Central State and run the student government, while a few decided to return to their communities and attempt to organize around Freeman's basic outline. Two of the returning students were Wanda Marshall and Max Stanford, now named Akbar Muhammad Ahmad, who transplanted RAM from Cleveland to the ghettos of Philadelphia, New York, and other urban areas.

The March on Washington

In 1963, Malcolm X openly called the March on Washington a farce. He explained that the desire for a mass march on the nation's capital originally sprang from the Black grassroots: the average Black man and woman in the streets. It was their way of demonstrating a mass Black demand for jobs and freedom. As momentum grew for the march, President Kennedy called a meeting of the leaders of the six largest civil rights organizations, dubbed the "Big Six"—NAACP, SCLC, CORE, National Urban League (NUL), SNCC, and the National Brotherhood of Sleeping Car Porters (NBSCP)—asking them to stop the proposed march. They answered that they couldn't stop it because they weren't leading it, didn't start it, and that it had sprung from the masses of Black people.

Since they weren't leading the march, the president decided to make them the leaders by distributing huge sums of money to each of the Big Six, publicizing their leading roles in the mass media, and providing them with a script to follow regarding the staging of the event. The script planned the march down to the smallest detail. Malcolm explained that government officials told the Big Six what time to begin the march, where to march, who could speak at the march and who could not, generally what could be said and what could not, what signs to carry, where to go to the toilets (provided by the government), and what time to end—and most of the 200,000 marchers were never the wiser. By then SNCC's membership was also criticizing the march as too moderate and decrying the violence sweeping the South. History ultimately proved Malcolm's claim of "farce" correct, through books published by participants in the planning of the march and through exposure of government documents on the matter.

Origin of the Five Percenters

Clarence 13X (Clarence Smith) was expelled from Harlem's Nation of Islam Temple No. 7 in 1963 because he wouldn't conform to NOI practices. He frequently associated with the numerous street gangs that abounded in New York City at the time and felt that the NOI didn't put enough effort into recruiting among these street gangs and other wayward youth. By '64 he had established his own "movement" called the "Five Percenters." The name comes from their belief that 85 percent of Black people are like cattle, who continue to eat the poisoned animal (the pig), are blind to the truth of God, and continue to give their allegiance to people who don't have their best interests at heart; that 10 percent of Black people are bloodsuckers—the politicians, preachers, and other parasitic individuals who get rich off the labor and ignorance of the docile exploited 85 percent; and that the remaining 5 percent are the poor righteous teachers of freedom, justice, and equality who know the truth of the "Black" God and are not deceived by the practices of the bloodsucking 10 percent. The Five Percenters movement spread throughout the New York State prison system and the Black ghettos of the New York metropolitan area. Meanwhile the New York City Police Department's Bureau of Special Services (BSS), who kept their eyes on radicals and dissidents, put Clarence 13X at the top of their list of "Black militants."

Origin of the New World Nation of Islam

In December 1965, Newark's Mayor Hugh Addonizio witnessed a getaway car pulling away from a bank robbery and ordered his chauffeur to follow with siren blasting. The fleeing robbers crashed into a telephone pole, sprang from their car and fired a shot through the mayor's windshield. He screeched to a halt, and police cars racing to the scene captured Muhammad Ali Hassan (known as Albert Dickens) and James Washington. Both were regular attendees of Newark's NOI Temple No. 25, headed by Minister James 3X Shabazz. Ali Hassan and Washington were members of the New World Nation of Islam (NWI). Ali Hassan, its leader and Supreme Field Commander, dates the birth of the New World Nation of Islam as February 26, 1960. He states that on that date Elijah Muhammad authorized the New World Nation of Islam under the leadership of Field Supreme Minister Fard Savior and declared that the Field Minister had authority over all the NOI Muslims. Ali Hassan and Washington were convicted for the bank robbery and sent to Trenton State Prison.

The NWI's belief in the supreme authority of Fard Savior was rejected by NOI Minister Shabazz, and thereafter an uneasy peace prevailed between the followers of Shabazz, who remained in control of Newark's NOI Temple No. 25, and the followers the NWI who sought to gain control of it.

Meanwhile, Ali Hassan published a book titled *Uncle Yah Yah* and ran the NWI from his prison cell. Along with the more established and influential NOI, the influence of the NWI spread throughout the New Jersey state prison system and the metropolitan Jersey ghettos. The NWI began setting up food

co-ops, barbershops, houses to teach Islam, and printing presses; and purchased land in South Carolina, all in furtherance of creating an independent
Black nation.

The Black Liberation Era

Black Power

James Meredith was shot on June 6, 1966, while on his march against fear
in Mississippi. A civil rights group decided to complete the march. One
night during a rally connected to the march, SNCC organizer Willie Ricks
("Mukassa") raised the cry of "Black Power." Stokely Carmichael, SNCC
chairman, repeated the slogan the next night at a mass rally and the Black
Power movement began to sweep the country.

Black Panthers Usher in the Black Liberation Movement

Midstride the '60s, on February 21, 1965, Malcolm was assassinated, but
his star continued to rise and his seeds fell on fertile soil. The following year,
October 1966, in Oakland, California, Huey P. Newton and a handful of
armed youths founded the Black Panther Party for Self-Defense on principles
that Malcolm had preached—and the Black Liberation Movement (BLM)
was born. Subsequently the name was shortened to the Black Panther Party
(BPP) and a 10-Point Program was created which stated:

1. We want freedom. We want power to determine the destiny of our
   Black community.
2. We want full employment for our people.
3. We want an end to the robbery by the CAPITALISTS of our Black
   community.
4. We want decent housing, fit for the shelter of human beings.
5. We want education for our people that exposes the true nature of
   this decadent American society. We want education that teaches us
   our true history and our role in the present-day society.
6. We want all Black men to be exempt from military service.
7. We want an immediate end to POLICE BRUTALITY and MURDER of
   Black people.
8. We want freedom for all Black men held in federal, state, county and
   city prisons and jails.
9. We want all Black people when brought to trial to be tried in
   court by a jury of their peer group or people from their Black

communities, as defined by the Constitution of the United States.

10. We want land, bread, housing, education, clothing, justice and peace. And as our major political objective, a United Nations–supervised plebiscite to be held throughout the Black colony in which only Black colonial subjects will be allowed to participate for the purpose of determining the will of Black people as to their national destiny.

(See full 10-Point Program later in this volume, pp. 603–606)

The Panthers established numerous programs to serve the Oakland ghetto—free breakfasts for children, free health care, free daycare, and free political education classes. The program that riveted the ghetto's attention was their campaign to "stop police murder of and brutality against Blacks." Huey, a community college pre-law student, discovered that it was legal for citizens to openly carry arms in California. With that assurance, the Black Panther Party began armed car patrols of the police cruisers that patrolled Oakland's Black colony. When a cruiser stopped to make an arrest, the Panther car stopped. They fanned out around the scene, arms at the ready, and observed, tape recorded, and recommended a lawyer to the arrest victim. It didn't take long for the police to retaliate. They confronted Huey late one night near his home. Gunfire erupted, leaving Huey critically wounded, a policeman dead, and another wounded. The Panthers and the Oakland/Bay community responded with a massive campaign to save Huey from the gas chamber. The California Senate began a hearing to rescind the law permitting citizens to openly carry arms within city limits. The Panthers staged an armed demonstration during the hearing at the Sacramento Capitol to protest the Senate's action, which gained national publicity. That publicity, together with the Panthers' philosophy of revolutionary nationalism and self-defense combined with the "Free Huey" campaign, catapulted the BPP to nationwide prominence.

But it was not without cost. On August 25, 1967, J. Edgar Hoover issued his infamous Counter Intelligence Program (COINTELPRO) memorandum, which directed the FBI (and local police officials) to disrupt specified Black organizations and neutralize their leaders so as to prevent "the rise of a Black messiah."

Attacks Increase on Revolutionaries

The Panthers rolled eastward, establishing offices in each major northern ghetto. As they went, they set up revolutionary programs in each community that were geared to provide community control of schools, tenant control of slum housing, free breakfast for schoolchildren, free health care, daycare, and legal clinics, and free political education classes for the community. They also initiated campaigns to drive dope pushers and drugs from the community, and campaigns to stop police murder and brutalization of Blacks. As they went about the community organizing these various programs they were frequently confronted, attacked, or arrested by the police, and some were even killed during these encounters.

Other revolutionary organizers suffered similar entrapments. The Revolutionary Action Movement's Herman Ferguson and Max Stanford were arrested in 1967 on spurious charges of conspiring to kill civil rights leaders. In the same year the poet and playwright Amiri Baraka—aka LeRoi Jones—was arrested for transporting weapons in a van during the Newark riots and did a brief stint in Trenton State Prison until a successful appeal overturned his conviction. SNCC's Rap Brown, Stokely Carmichael, and other orators were constantly threatened or charged with "inciting to riot" as they crisscrossed the country speaking to mass audiences. Congress passed "Rap Brown laws" to deter speakers from crossing state lines to address mass audiences lest a disturbance break out leaving them vulnerable to federal charges and imprisonment. And numerous revolutionary organizers and orators *were* being imprisoned.

This initial flow of revolutionaries into the jails and prisons began to spread a revolutionary nationalist buzz through New Afrikans behind the walls. New Afrikan prisoners were also influenced by the domestic revolutionary atmosphere and the liberation struggles in Afrika, Asia, and South America. Small groups began studying on their own, or in collectives, the works of Malcolm X, Huey P. Newton, *The Black Panther* newspaper, *The Militant* newspaper, contemporary national liberation struggle leaders Kwame Nkrumah, Jomo Kenyatta, Frantz Fanon, Che Guevara, Fidel Castro, Ho Chi Minh, and Mao Tse-tung, plus Marx, Lenin, and Bakunin too. The numbers of New Afrikan and Third World prisoners increased while the number of white prisoners decreased throughout U.S. prisons. Under this onslaught of rising national liberation consciousness, increased percentages of New Afrikan and Third World prisoners, and decreased numbers of white prisoners, the last of the prisons' overt segregation policies fell by the wayside.

The New Afrikan Independence Movement

The seeds of Malcolm took further root on March 29, 1968. On that date the Provisional Government of the Republic of New Afrika (RNA) was founded at a convention held at the Black-owned Twenty Grand Motel in Detroit. Over five hundred grassroots activists came together to issue a Declaration of

Independence on behalf of the oppressed Black nation inside North America, and the New Afrikan Independence Movement (NAIM) was born. Since then Blacks desiring an independent Black nation have referred to themselves and other Blacks in the U.S. as "New Afrikans."

That same month, March '68, during Martin Luther King's march in Memphis, angry youths on the fringes of the march broke away and began breaking store windows, looting, and firebombing. A sixteen-year-old-boy was killed and fifty people were injured in the ensuing violence. This left Martin profoundly shaken and questioning whether his philosophy was still able to hold the youth to a nonviolent commitment. On April 4th, he returned to Memphis, seeking the answer through one more march, and found an assassin's bullet. Ghettos exploded in flames one after another across the face of America. The philosophy of Black liberation surged to the forefront among the youth.

But not the youth alone; following a series of police provocations in Cleveland, on July 23, 1968, New Libya Movement activists there set an ambush that killed several policemen. A "fortyish" Ahmed Evans was convicted of the killings and died of "cancer" in prison ten years later.

More CIA dope surged into the ghettos from the Golden Triangle of Southeast Asia. Revolutionaries stepped up their organizing activities on both sides of the walls. Behind the walls the New Afrikan percentage steadily increased.

The Street Gangs

There were numerous Black, white, Puerto Ricans, and Asian street organizations, i.e., "gangs," in New York City during the 1950s. Among the more notorious Black street gangs of the era were the Chaplains, Bishops, Sinners, and Corsair Lords; also there were the equally violent Puerto Rican Dragons. All warred against each other and any gangs that crossed their paths.

By the 1960s, the post–World War II heroin influx had taken its toll. Most of the New York street gangs faded away. Their youthful members had succumbed to drugs, either through death by overdose, by ceasing gang activities in order to pursue full-time criminal activities to feed their drug habits, or because they were in prison for drug crimes or youth-gang assaults and killings.

Lumumba Shakur, warlord of the Bishops, and Sekou Odinga, leader of the Sinners, were two such youths who had been sent to the reformatory for youth-gang assaults. They graduated up through the "Gladiator Prisons"—Woodburn and Comstock—to mainline Attica, became politicized by the stark brutal racism in each prison, and at age twenty-one were spit back upon the streets. When the Panthers reached the East Coast in 1968, Lumumba and

Sekou were among the first youths to sign up. Lumumba opened the Harlem chapter of the Black Panther Party as its Defense Captain. Sekou opened the Queens chapter as a lieutenant and later transferred to Harlem to co-head it with his boyhood pal, Lumumba.

Origin of the Gangster Disciples Street Gang

The Gangster Disciples were founded in the 1960s in Chicago by the late David Barksdale, known historically in gang circles as "King David," under the name "Black Disciples." The group's name was later changed to "Black Gangster Disciples," and later still the name was shortened to "Gangster Disciples," or simply "GD." Its gang colors are blue and black.

COINTELPRO Attacks

In 1969, COINTELPRO launched its main attack on the Black Liberation Movement in earnest. It began with the mass arrest of Lumumba Shakur and the New York Panther 21. It followed with a series of military raids on Black Panther Party offices in Philadelphia, Baltimore, New Haven, Jersey City, Detroit, Chicago, Denver, Omaha, Sacramento, and San Diego, and was capped off with an early-morning four-hour siege that poured thousands of rounds into the Los Angeles BPP office. By mid-morning, hundreds of angry Black residents gathered at the scene and demanded that the police cease-fire. Fortunately, Geronimo ji Jaga, decorated Vietnam vet, had earlier fortified the office to withstand an assault and no Panthers were seriously injured. However, repercussions from the outcome eventually drove him underground. The widespread attacks left Panthers dead all across the country—Fred Hampton, Mark Clark, Bunchy Carter, John Huggins, John Savage, Walter Toure Pope, Bobby Hutton, Sylvester Bell, Frank "Capt. Franco" Diggs, Fred Bennett, James Carr, Larry Robeson, Spurgeon "Jake" Winters, Alex Rackley, Arthur Morris, Steve Bartholomew, Robert Lawrence, Tommy Lewis, Nathaniel Clark, Welton Armstead, Sidney Miller, Sterling Jones, Babatunde Omawali, Samuel Napier, Harold Russell, and Robert Webb, among others. In the three years after J. Edgar Hoover's infamous COINTELPRO memorandum, [two dozen —Ed] members of the BPP were killed. Nearly a thousand were arrested and key leaders were sent to jail. Others were driven underground. Still others, like BPP field marshal Donald "DC" Cox, were driven into exile overseas.

The RNA was similarly attacked that year. During its second annual convention in March '69, held at Reverend C.L. Franklin's New Bethel Church in Detroit, a police provocation sparked a siege that poured 800 rounds into the church. Several convention participants were wounded; one policeman was killed, another wounded, and the entire convention (140 people) arrested en masse. When Reverend Franklin (father of "The Queen of Soul" singer Aretha Franklin) and Black state representative James Del Rio were informed of the incident they called Black judge George Crockett, who proceeded to the police station where he found total legal chaos. Almost 150 people were being held incommunicado. They were being questioned, fingerprinted, and given nitrate tests to determine if they had fired guns—in total disregard of fundamental constitutional procedures. Hours after the roundup, there wasn't so much as a list of persons being held and no one had been formally arrested. An indignant Judge Crockett set up court right in the station house and demanded that the police either press charges or release their captives. He had handled about fifty cases when the Wayne County prosecutor, called in by the police, intervened. The prosecutor promised that the use of all irregular methods would be halted. Crockett adjourned the impromptu court and by noon the following day the police had released all but a few individuals who were held on specific charges. Chaka Fuller, Rafael Vierra, and Alfred Hibbit (Alfred 2X) were charged with the killing of the police officer. All three were subsequently tried and acquitted. Chaka Fuller was mysteriously assassinated a few months afterwards.

On Friday, the 13th of June 1969, Clarence 13X , founder of the Five Percenters, was mysteriously assassinated in the elevator of a Harlem project building by three male Negroes. His killers were never discovered but his adherents suspect government complicity in his death. News reports at the time hinted that BSS instigated the assassination to try to foment a war between the NOI and the Five Percenters. Revolutionaries nationwide were attacked and/or arrested—Tyari Uhuru, Maka, Askufo, and the Smyrna Brothers in Delaware; JoJo Muhammad Bowens and Fred Burton in Philadelphia; and Panthers Mondo we Langa, Ed Poindexter, and Veronza Daoud Bowers Jr. in Omaha.

Police mounted an assault on the Panther office in the Desiree Projects of New Orleans, which resulted in several arrests. A similar attack was made on the People's Party office in Houston. One of their leaders, Carl Hampton, was killed by the police, and another, Lee Otis Johnson, was arrested later on an unrelated charge and sentenced to forty-one years in prison for alleged possession of one marijuana cigarette.

The Rise of Prison Struggles

Like the Panthers, most of those arrested brought their philosophies with them into the prisons. Likewise, most had outside support committees to one degree or another so that this influx of political prisoners linked the struggle behind the walls with the struggles in local communities on the outside. The combination set off a beehive of political activity behind the walls, and prisoners stepped up their struggle for political, Afrikan, Islamic, and academic studies, access to political literature, community access to prisons, an end to arbitrary punishments, access to attorneys, adequate law libraries, relevant vocational training, contact visits, better food, health care, housing, and a myriad of other struggles. The forms of prison struggle ranged from face-to-face negotiations to mass petitioning, letter writing, and call-in campaigns, outside demonstrations, class-action lawsuits, hunger strikes, work strikes, rebellions, and more drastic actions. Overall, all forms of struggle served to roll back draconian prison policies that had stood for centuries, and to further the development of the New Afrikan liberation struggle behind the walls.

These struggles would not have been as successful, or would have been much more costly in terms of lives lost or brutality endured, had it not been for the links to the community and the community support—and legal support—that political prisoners brought with them into the prisons. Although that support was not always sufficient in quantity or quality, and was sometimes nonexistent or came with hidden agendas, or was marked by frequent conflicts, on the whole it was this combination of resolute prisoners, community support, and legal support which was most often successful in prison struggles.

The Changing Complexion of Prisons

As the '60s drew to a close New Afrikan and Third World nationalities made up nearly 50 percent of the prison population. National liberation consciousness became the dominant influence behind the walls as the overall complexion neared the changeover from white to Black, brown, and red. The decade-long general decrease in prisoners, particularly whites, brought a drop of between 16,000 and 23,000, while the total number of New Afrikan prisoners increased slightly or changed insignificantly over the same period. Yet the next decade would begin the period of unprecedented new prison construction, as the primary role of U.S. prisons changed from "suppression of the working classes" to suppression of domestic Black and Third World liberation struggles inside the U.S.

Origin of CRIP

There existed street organizations in South Central Los Angeles before the rise of the Black Panther Party. These groups, criminal in essence, were indeed the wells from which the Panthers would recruit their most stalwart members. Alprentice "Bunchy" Carter, who chartered the first L.A. chapter of the Party, was the leader of perhaps the most violent street organization of that time—The Slausons. James Carr, former cellmate of comrade George Jackson and author of *BAD*, was a member of the Farmers. There were the Gladiators, the Businessmen, the Avenues, Blood Alley, and the Rebel Rousers, to name but a few.

After the 1965 rebellion in Watts, there came an unsteady truce of sorts that caused the street organizations to focus on a larger, more deadly enemy— the Los Angeles Police Department. So, by the time the Black Panther Party came to L.A. in 1968 a shaky peace existed among them in which they could vent their anger, respond to injustice, and represent their neighborhoods.

By and large, the Party usurped the youthful rage and brought the street organizations of that time to an end. Of course, the U.S. government also did its share by drafting young brothers into the Vietnam War.

These, however, were the storm years of COINTELPRO, and the Party was the focal point. Thus, by late '69, the aboveground infrastructure of the BPP was in shambles due to its own internal contradictions and the weight of the state. Confusion set in among the people, creating, if you will, a window of opportunity—of which both the criminals and the counterrevolutionists in the government took advantage.

Community Relations for an Independent People (CRIP) was a city-funded team post (meeting place) on the east side of L.A. that played host to some of the area's most rowdy youth. One such brother was Raymond Washington, who at the time belonged to a young upstart clique called the Baby Avenues. The team post became center ground to an ever-widening group of youth who eventually took its title, CRIP, as a name and moved westward with it. With the vanguard in shambles and the local pigs turning a deliberate deaf ear, the CRIPs flourished rapidly. In its formative years, the Party's influence was evident within it, for the same uniform/dress code of the Party's was that of the CRIPs. Yet a sinister twist developed in which New Afrikan people became targets of the young hoodlums. And with no vanguard forces readily available to teach and train these youth, they spiraled out of control, taking as their nemesis the Brims, who later developed into the citywide Bloods. The founding of the CRIPs is established as 1969. Their gang color is blue, and sometimes also the color white.

Enter the '70s

A California guard, rated as an expert marksman, opened the decade of the '70s with the January 13th shooting at close range of W.L. Nolen, Cleveland Edwards, and Alvin "Jug" Miller in the Soledad prison yard. They were left lying where they fell until it was too late for them to be saved by medical treatment. Nolen, in particular, had been instrumental in organizing recent demonstrations at Soledad Prison in protest of killings by guards of two other Black prisoners—Clarence Causey and William Powell. He was consequently both a thorn in the side of prison officials and a hero to the Black prison populations. When the guard was exonerated two weeks later of the triple killings of Nolen and two others, the prisoners retaliated by throwing a guard off the tier.

George Jackson, Fleeta Drumgo, and John Clutchette were charged with the guard's death and came to be known as the Soledad Brothers. California's Black prisoners solidified around the Soledad Brothers case and the chain of events led to the formation of the Black Guerrilla Family (BGF). The Panthers spearheaded a massive campaign to save the Soledad Brothers from the gas chamber. The nationwide coalescence of prisoners and support groups around the case converted the scattered, disparate prison struggles into a national prison movement.

On August 7, 1970, Jonathan Jackson, younger brother of George, attempted to liberate Ruchell Cinque Magee, William Christmas, and James McClain from the Marin County courthouse in California. Jonathan, McClain, Christmas, and the trial judge were killed by SWAT teams, who also wounded the prosecutor and paralyzed him for life. Miraculously, Ruchell and three wounded jurors survived the fusillade. Jonathan frequently served as Angela Davis's bodyguard. She had purchased weapons for that purpose, but Jonathan used those same weapons in the breakout attempt. Immediately afterward she became the object of an international "woman hunt." On October 13, Angela was captured in New York City and was subsequently returned to California to undergo a very acrimonious trial with Magee. She was acquitted on all charges. Magee was tried separately and convicted on lesser charges. He remains imprisoned to date—over three decades in all [four decades at the time of publication of this edition —Ed.]—and is our longest-held political prisoner.

Origin of the Bloods

Most South Central street organizations, commonly called "gangs," "sets," or "orgs," take their names from prominent streets: Slauson, Denver Lane, Piru, Hoover, etc., that run through their neighborhood. The CRIPs had already formed, were massed up and rolling together. Their strength attracted other sets to become CRIPs. As they moved into territories occupied by other South Central organizations they met stiff resistance from those neighborhood sets who did not want to align with or be taken over by them.

Among those gang leaders resisting the CRIP invasion were Peabody of the Denver Lanes, Puddin of the Westside Pirus, Rooster of the 30 Pirus, and the Westside Brims—perhaps the most well-known and respected of the lot, although their leader is unknown today. The Brims families used their prestige and influence to recruit other sets to join their side in opposition to the CRIPs. As the various sets began hooking up with each other to start other Brim families and to recruit other sets to join their side in opposition to the CRIPs in the early 1970s, the federation solidified and formally united into the citywide Bloods. They adopted the color red as their banner; they also use the colors green or brown.

Prison is a normal next stop for many gang members. The first Bloods sent to Chino, a mainline California prison, are commonly referred to in Blood circles as the "First Bloods to walk the line at Chino." To increase their prison membership and recruitment, they created a "Bloodline (BL) Constitution" patterned after the constitution of the BGF: a Panther-influenced group already established in the California prison system at the time. The BL Constitution contained the Blood's code of conduct, history, and bylaws and was required reading for each new recruit. To speed up recruitment, the older "First Bloods" made reading the constitution an automatic induction into their ranks and thereafter began tricking young prisoners into reading it. Once read, the new recruit could only reject membership at the risk of serious bodily harm.

The press-ganging of young recruits at Chino set off ripples of dissatisfaction and breakaways among Bloods in other California prisons. Those disaffected centered around Peabody at Old Folsom Prison who took parts from the BL and the BGF constitutions and created a new United Blood Nation (UBN) Constitution designed to unify all Bloods in prison. Since then, Bloods have chosen which constitution they would come under. If they choose either the BL or UBN Constitution they are held to a higher standard than other members; they hold positions and are similar to the officers' corps of a military organization. Those Bloods not under a constitution are the foot soldiers. The BL and UBN organization spread throughout the California prison system, and they are strictly prison organizations. Once a Blood leaves prison he returns to his old neighborhood set. From South Central the Bloods spread to Pasadena, Gardenia, San Diego, Sacramento, Bakersfield, and throughout the state and its prison system.

San Francisco Bay Area Gangs
San Francisco Bay Area gangs or "cliques" can be traced back to the early 1960s and are usually identified by, or named after, their neighborhoods or

communities. Most of those functioning today came from splinter groups of the BPP after it broke up.

In Oakland, the 69th Street Mob, founded by Felix Mitchell in the early 1970s, still exists despite the government's best efforts to derail it. In East Oakland the Rolling 20s and the 700 Club, along with the Acorn Gang in West Oakland, are the powerhouse cliques on the streets.

In San Francisco, there is Sunnydale and Hunters Point, the city's largest street gang which is divided into several cliques—Oakdale, Harbor Road, West Point, etc. East Palo Alto is the home of the Professional Low Riders (PLR), who are a major influence in the South Bay Area—and in Vallejo there are the North Bay Gangsters and Crestview. Most Bay Area gangs don't have colors but align primarily on the basis of money and hustling endeavors. Many are associated with the rap music industry and with various prison groups—the 415 Kumi, BGF, or Ansar El Muhammed Muslims.

Growth of the Gangster Disciples

In 1970, Gangster Disciple (GD) Larry Hoover was convicted for a gang-related murder and sentenced to a 150 to 200–year state sentence. He's the current leader of the GDs and runs the syndicate from an Illinois prison cell.

As drugs flooded into the Chicago ghettos, young black men flooded into the Illinois prisons where they were given GD application forms to fill out. If their references proved solid, they were indoctrinated into the gang. Everyone who joined had to memorize the GD's sixteen-rule code. The GDs spread throughout the Illinois and Midwest prison systems. The flow of GDs back into the streets enabled them to expand their street network which is an intricate command and control structure, similar to a military organization.

Comrade George Assassinated

On August 21, 1971, a guard shot and killed George Jackson as he bolted from a control unit and ran for the San Quentin wall. Inside the unit lay three guards and two trustees dead. The circumstances surrounding George Jackson's legendary life and death, and the astuteness of his published writings, left a legacy that inspires and instructs the New Afrikan liberation struggle on both sides of the wall even today, and will for years to come. September 13, 1971, became the bloodiest day in U.S. prison history when New York's Governor Nelson Rockefeller ordered the retaking of Attica prison. The previous several years had seen a number of prison rebellions flare up across the country as prisoners protested widespread maltreatment and inhumane conditions. Most had been settled peaceably with little or no loss of human life after face-to-face negotiation between prisoners and state and prison officials. At Attica Black, brown, white, red, and yellow prisoners took over one block of the prison and stood together for five days seeking to negotiate an end to their inhumane conditions. Their now-famous dictum declared: "We are men, not beasts, and will not be driven as such." But Rockefeller had presidential ambitions. The rebelling prisoners' demands included a political request for asylum in a non-imperialistic country. Rockefeller's refusal to negotiate foreshadowed a macabre replay of his father John D.'s slaughter of striking Colorado miners and their families decades earlier. Altogether forty-three people died at Attica. New York State troopers' bullets killed thirty-nine people—twenty-nine prisoners and ten guards—in retaking Attica and shocked the world by the naked barbarity of the U.S. prison system. Yet the Attica rebellion too remains a milestone in the development of the New Afrikan liberation struggle behind the walls, a symbol of the highest development of prisoner multinational solidarity to date.

New World Clashes with the Nation of Islam

In 1973, the simmering struggle for control of Newark's NOI Temple No. 25 erupted into the open. Warren Marcello, a New World member, assassinated NOI Temple No. 25 Minister Shabazz. In retaliation several NWI members were attacked and killed within the confines of the New Jersey prison system, and before the year was out the bodies of Marcello and a companion were found beheaded In Newark's Weequahic Park. Ali Hassan, still in prison, was tried as one of the coconspirators in the death of Shabazz and was found innocent.

The Black Liberation Army

COINTELPRO's destruction of the BPP forced many members underground and gave rise to the Black Liberation Army (BLA)—a New Afrikan guerrilla organization. The BLA continued the struggle by waging urban guerrilla war across the U.S. through highly mobile strike teams. The government's intensified search for the BLA during the early 1970s resulted in the capture of Geronimo ji Jaga in Dallas, Dhoruba Bin Wahad and Jamal Joseph in New York, Sha Sha Brown and Blood McCreary in St. Louis, Nuh Washington and Jalil Muntaqim in Los Angeles, Herman Bell in New Orleans, Francisco and Gabriel Torres in New York, Russell Maroon Shoatz in Philadelphia, Chango Monges, Mark Holder, and Kamau Hilton in New York, Assata Shakur and Sundiata Acoli in New Jersey, Ashanti Alston, Tarik, and Walid in New Haven, Safiya Bukhari and Masai Gibson in Virginia, and others. Left dead during the government's search and destroy missions were Sandra Pratt (wife of Geronimo ji Jaga, assassinated while visibly pregnant), Mark Essex, Woody Changa Green, Twyman Kakuyan Olugbala Meyers, Frank "Heavy" Fields, Anthony Kimu White, Zayd Shakur, Melvin Rema Kerney, Alfred Kambui Butler, Ron Carter, Rory Hithe, and John Thomas, among others. Red Adams, left paralyzed from the neck down by police bullets, would die from the effects a few years later.

Other New Afrikan freedom fighters, not directly a part of BLA, were also attacked, hounded, and captured during the same general era. These included Imari Obadele and the RNA-11 in Jackson, Mississippi; Don Taylor and De Mau Mau of Chicago; Hanif Shabazz, Abdul Aziz, and the VI-5 in the Virgin Islands; Mark Cook of the George Jackson Brigade (GJB) in Seattle; Ahmed Obafemi of the RNA in Florida; Atiba Shanna in Chicago; Mafundi Lake in Alabama; Sekou Kambui and Imani Harris in Alabama; Robert Aswad Duren in California; Kojo Bomani Sababu and Dharuba Cinque in Trenton; John Partee and Tommie Lee Hodges of Alkebulan in Memphis; Gary Tyler in Los Angeles; Kareem Saif Allah and the Five Percenter–BLA–Islamic Brothers in New York; Ben Chavis and the Wilmington 10 in North Carolina; Delbert Africa and MOVE members in Philadelphia; and others doubtless too numerous to name.

Political Converts in Prison

Not everyone was political before incarceration. John Andaliwa Clark became so, and a freedom fighter par excellence, only after being sent behind the walls. He paid the supreme sacrifice during a hail of gunfire from Trenton State Prison guards. Hugo Dahariki Pinell also became political after being sent behind the California walls in 1964. He has been in prison ever since. [Pinell was murdered in California State Prison–Sacramento in 2015. —Ed.] Joan Little took an ice pick from a white North Carolina guard who had used it to force her to perform oral sex on him. She killed him, escaped to New York, was captured and forced to return to the same North Carolina camp where she feared for her life. Massive public vigilance and support enabled her to complete the sentence in relative safety and obtain her release.

Dessie Woods and Cheryl Todd, hitchhiking through Georgia, were given a ride by a white man who tried to rape them. Woods took his gun, killed him, and was sent to prison where officials drugged and brutalized her. Todd was also imprisoned and subsequently released upon completion of the sentence. Woods was denied parole several times then finally released.

Political or not, each arrest was met with highly sensationalized prejudicial publicity that continued unabated to and throughout the trial. The negative publicity blitz was designed to guarantee a conviction, smokescreen the real issues involved, and justify immediate placement in the harshest prison conditions possible. For men this usually means the federal penitentiary at Marion, Illinois. For women it has meant the control unit in the federal penitentiary at Alderson, West Virginia, or Lexington, Kentucky.

Effect of Captured Freedom Fighters on Prisons

In 1988 political prisoners Silvia Baraldini, Alejandrina Torres, and Susan Rosenberg won a D.C. District Court lawsuit brought by attorneys Adjoa Aiyetoro, Jan Susler, and others. The legal victory temporarily halted the practice of sending prisoners to control units strictly because of their political status. The ruling was reversed by the D.C. Appellate Court a year later. Those political prisoners not sent to Marion, Alderson, or Lexington control units are sent to other control units modeled after Marion/Lexington but located within maximum security state prisons. Normally this means twenty-three-hour-a-day lockdown in long-term units located in remote hinterlands far from family, friends, and attorneys, with heavy censorship and restrictions on communications, visits, and outside contacts, combined with constant harassment, provocation, and brutality by prison guards.

The influx of so many captured freedom fighters (i.e., prisoners of war—POWs) with varying degrees of guerrilla experience added a valuable dimension to the New Afrikan liberation struggle behind the walls. In the first place it accelerated the prison struggles already in process, particularly the attack on control units. One attack was spearheaded by Michael Deutsch and Jeffrey Haas of the People's Law Office, Chicago, which challenged Marion's H-Unit boxcar cells. Another was spearheaded by Assata Shakur and the Center for Constitutional Rights, which challenged her out-of-state placement in the Alderson, West Virginia control unit.

Second, it stimulated a thoroughgoing investigation and exposure of COINTELPRO's hand in waging low intensity warfare on New Afrikan and Third World nationalities in the U.S. This was spearheaded by Geronimo ji Jaga with Stuart Hanlon's law office in the West and by Dhoruba Bin Wahad with attorneys Liz Fink, Robert Boyle, and Jonathan Lubell in the East. These COINTELPRO investigations resulted in the overturn of Bin Wahad's conviction and his release from prison in March 1990 after he had been imprisoned nineteen years for a crime he did not commit.

Third, it broadened the scope of the prison movement to the international arena by producing the initial presentation of the U.S. political prisoner and prisoner of war (PP/POW) issue before the UN's Human Rights Commission. This approach originated with Jalil Muntaqim, and was spearheaded by him and attorney Kathryn Burke on the West Coast and by Sundiata Acoli and attorney Lennox Hinds of the National Conference of Black Lawyers on the East Coast. This petition sought relief from human rights violations in U.S. prisons and subsequently asserted a colonized people's right to fight against alien domination and racist regimes as codified in the Geneva Convention.

Fourth, it intensified, clarified, and broke new ground on political issues and debates of particular concern to the New Afrikan community, i.e., the "national question," spearheaded by Atiba Shanna in the Midwest. All these struggles, plus those already in process, were carried out with the combination in one form or another of resolute prisoners and community-legal support. Community support when present came from various sources—family, comrades, friends; political, student, religious, and prisoner rights groups; workers, professionals, and progressive newspapers and radio stations. Some of those involved over the years were or are: the National Committee for Defense of Political Prisoners, the Black Community News Service, the African Peoples Party, the Republic of New Afrika, the African Peoples Socialist Party, The East, the Bliss Chord Communication Network, Liberation Book Store, WDAS Radio Philadelphia, WBLS Radio New York, Radio New York, Third World Newsreel, *Libertad* (political journal of the Puerto Rican Movimiento de Liberación Nacional [MLN]), the Prairie Fire Organizing Committee, the May 19th Communist Organization, the Madame Binh Graphics Collective, The Midnight Express, the Northwest Iowa Socialist Party, the National Black United Front, the Nation of Islam, *Arm the Spirit*, *Black News*, International Class Labor Defense, the Real Dragon Project, the John Brown Anti-Klan Committee, the National Prison Project, the House of the Lord Church, the American Friends Service Committee, attorneys Chuck Jones and Harold Ferguson of Rutgers Legal Clinic, the *Jackson Advocate* newspaper, Rutgers law students, the Committee to End the Marion Lockdown, the American Indian Movement, and others.

The End of the '70s

As the decade wound down, the late '70s saw the demise of the NOI following the death of Elijah Muhammad and the rise of orthodox Islam among significant segments of New Afrikans on both sides of the wall. By 1979, the prison population stood at 300,000, a whopping 100,000 increase within a single decade. The previous 100,000 increase—from 100,000 to 200,000—had taken thirty-one years, from 1927 to 1958. The initial increase to 100,000 had taken hundreds of years. Since America's original colonial times. The '60s were the transition decade of white flight that saw a significant decrease in both prison population and white prisoners. And since the total Black prison population increased only slightly or changed insignificantly over the decade of the insurgent '60s through 1973, it indicates that New Afrikans are imprisoned least when they fight hardest.

The decade ended on a masterstroke by the BLA's Multinational Task Force, with the November 2, 1979, prison liberation of Assata Shakur—"Soul of the BLA" and preeminent political prisoner of the era. The Task Force then whisked her away to the safety of political asylum in Cuba where she remains to date.

The Decade of the '80s

In June 1980, Ali Hassan was released after sixteen years in the New Jersey state prisons. Two months later, five New World Nation of Islam (NWI) members were arrested after a North Brunswick, New Jersey, bank robbery in a car with stolen plates. The car belonged to the recently released Ali Hassan, who had loaned it to a friend. Ali Hassan and fifteen other NWI members refused to participate in the resulting mass trial, which charged them in a Racketeer Influenced and Corrupt Organization (RICO) indictment with conspiracy to rob banks for the purpose of financing various NWI enterprises in the furtherance of creating an independent Black Nation. All defendants were convicted and sent behind the walls.

The '80s brought another round of BLA freedom fighters behind walls—Bashir Hameed and Abdul Majid in 1980; Sekou Odinga, Kuwasi Balagoon, Chui Ferguson-El, Jamal Joseph again, Mutulu Shakur, and numerous BLA Multinational Task Force supporters in 1981; and Terry Khalid Long, Leroy Ojore Bunting, and others in 1982. The government's sweep left Mtyari Sundiata dead, Kuwasi Balagoon subsequently dead in prison from AIDS, and Sekou Odinga brutally tortured upon capture—torture that included pulling out his toenails and rupturing his pancreas during long sadistic beatings that left him hospitalized for six months. But this second round of captured BLA freedom fighters brought forth, perhaps for the first time, a battery of young, politically astute New Afrikan lawyers: Chokwe Lumumba, Jill Soffiyah Elijah, Nkechi Taifa, Adjoa Aiyetoro, Ashanti Chimurenga, Michael Tarif Warren, and others. They are not only skilled in representing New Afrikan POWs but the New Afrikan Independence Movement too, all of which added to the further development of the New Afrikan liberation struggle behind the walls.

The decade also brought behind the walls Mumia Abu-Jamal, the widely respected Philadelphia radio announcer, popularly known as the "Voice of the Voiceless." He maintained a steady drumbeat of radio support for MOVE prisoners. While moonlighting as a taxi driver on the night of December 9, 1981, he discovered a policeman beating his younger brother. Mumia was shot and seriously wounded, the policeman was killed. Mumia now sits on death row in greatest need of mass support from every sector, if he's to be saved from the state's electric chair. [After a widespread international campaign and legal battle, Abu-Jamal was removed from death row and eventually resentenced to life in prison without parole. —Ed.]

Kazi Toure of the United Freedom Front (UFF) was sent behind the walls in 1982. He was released in 1991.

The New York 8—Coltrane Chimurenga, Viola Plummer and her son Robert "R.T." Taylor, Roger Wareham, Omowale Clay, Lateefah Carter, Colette Pean, and Yvette Kelly were arrested on October 17, 1984, and charged with conspiring to commit prison breakouts and armed robberies, and to possess weapons and explosives. However, the New York 8 was actually the New York 8+ because another eight or nine persons were jailed as grand jury resisters in connection with the case. The New York 8 were acquitted on August 5, 1985.

That same year Ramona Africa joined other MOVE comrades already behind the walls. Her only crime was that she survived Philadelphia Mayor Goode's May 13, 1985, bombing which cremated eleven MOVE members, their families (including their babies), home, and neighborhood.

The following year, November 19, 1986, a twenty-year-old Bronx, New York youth, Larry Davis (now Adam Abdul Hakeem) would make a dramatic escape during a shootout with police who had come to assassinate him for absconding with drug-sales money that some cops had appropriated for themselves. Several policemen were wounded in the shootout. Adam escaped unscathed but surrendered weeks later in the presence of the media, his family, and a mass of neighborhood supporters. After numerous charges, trials, and acquittals in which he exposed the existence of a New York police–controlled drug ring that coerced Black and Puerto Rican youths to push police-supplied drugs, he was sent behind the walls on weapon possession convictions. Since incarceration, numerous beatings by guards have paralyzed him from the waist down and confined him to a wheelchair.

On July 16, 1987, Abdul Haqq Muhammad, Arthur Majeed Barnes, and Robert "R.T." Taylor, all members of the Black Men's Movement Against Crack, were pulled over by state troopers in upstate New York, arrested, and subsequently sent to prison on a variety of weapon possession convictions.

Herman Ferguson at sixty-eight years old voluntarily returned to the U.S. on April 6, 1989, after twenty years exile in Ghana, Afrika, and Guyana, South America. He had fled the U.S. during the late '60s after the appeal was denied on his sentence of three and a half to seven years following a conviction for conspiring to murder civil rights leaders. Upon return he was arrested at the airport and was moved constantly from prison to prison for several years as a form of harassment.

The '80s brought the Reagan era's rollback of progressive trends on a wide front and a steep rise in racist incidents, white vigilantism, and police murder of New Afrikan and Third World people. It also brought the rebirth and re-establishment of the NOI, a number of New Afrikan POWs adopting orthodox Islam in lieu of revolutionary nationalism, the New Afrikan People's Organization's (NAPO) and its chairman Chokwe Lumumba's emergence. From the RNA as banner carrier for the New Afrikan Independence Movement (NAIM), the New Orleans assassination of Lumumba Shakur of the Panther 21, and an upsurge in mass political demonstrations known as the "Days of Outrage" in New York City spearheaded by the December 12th Movement and others.

The end of the decade brought the death of Huey P. Newton, founder of the Black Panther Party, allegedly killed by a young Black Guerrilla Family adherent on August 22, 1989, during a dispute over "crack." Huey taught the Black masses socialism and popularized it through the slogan "Power to the People!" He armed the Black struggle and popularized it through the slogan "Political power grows out of the barrel of a gun." For that, and despite his human shortcomings, he was a true giant of the Black struggle, because his particular contribution is comparable to that of other modern-day giants, Marcus Garvey, Elijah Muhammad, Malcolm X, and Martin Luther King.

AIDS, crack, street crime, gang violence, homelessness, and arrest rates have all exploded throughout the Black colonies. The nation's prison population on June 30, 1989, topped 673,000, an incredible 372,000 increase in less than a decade, causing the tripling and doubling of prison populations in thirty-four states and sizable increases in most others. New York City prisons became so overcrowded they began using ships as jails. William Bennett, former U.S. secretary of education and so-called drug czar, announced plans to convert closed military bases into concentration camps.

The prison-building spree and escalated imprisonment rates continue unabated. The new prisoners are younger, more volatile, have long prison sentences, and are overwhelmingly of New Afrikan and Third World nationalities. It is estimated that by the year 1994 the U.S. will have over one million prisoners. Projections suggest that over 75 percent of them will be Black and other people of color. More are women than previously. Their percentage rose to 5 percent in 1980 from a low of 3 percent in 1970. Whites are arrested at about the same rate as in Western Europe while the New Afrikan arrest rate has surpassed that of Blacks in South Africa. In fact, the U.S. Black imprisonment rate is now the highest in the world. Ten times as many Blacks as whites are incarcerated per 100,000 population.

The '90s and Beyond

As we began to move through the '90s, the New Afrikan liberation struggle behind the walls found itself coalescing around campaigns to free political prisoners and prisoners of war, helping to build a national PP/POW organization, strengthening its links on the domestic front, and building solidarity in the international arena. 1991 brought the collapse of the Soviet Union and the end of the Cold War. It freed many of the CIA's Eastern Europe personnel for redeployment back to America to focus on the domestic war against people of color. In the same manner that COINTELPRO perfected techniques developed in the infamous Palmer raids at the end of World War I and used them against Communist Party USA, SCLC, NCC, BPP, NOI, RNA, and other domestic movements, repatriated CIA operatives used destabilization techniques developed in Eastern Europe, South Africa, Southeast Asia, etc., to wreak havoc in New Afrikan and other domestic communities of color today.

Although the established media concentrated on the sensationalism of ghetto crack epidemics, street crime, drive-by shootings, and gang violence, there was a parallel long, quiet period of consciousness-raising in the New Afrikan colonies by the committed independence forces. The heightened consciousness of the colonies began to manifest itself through apparent random sparks of rebellion and the rise of innovative cultural trends, i.e., rap/hip-hop "message" music, culturally designed hairstyles, dissemination of political/cultural video cassettes, re-sprouting of insurgent periodicals, and the resurrection of forgotten heroes; all of which presaged an oppressed people getting ready to push forward again. Meanwhile, the U.S. began building the Administrative Maximum Facility (ADX) control unit prison at Florence, Colorado, which would both supersede and augment USP Marion, Illinois. ADX at Florence combined, in a single hi-tech control prison complex, all the repressive features and techniques that had been perfected at USP Marion.

In 1992, Fred Hampton Jr., son of the martyred Panther hero Fred Sr., was sent behind the walls. He was convicted of firebombing of a Korean "deli" in

Chicago in the aftermath of the Simi Valley, California, verdict that acquitted four policemen of the Rodney King beating, setting off the Los Angeles riots.

In 1994, Shiriki Uganisha responded to the call of POWs Jalil Muntaqim, Sekou Odinga, Geronimo ji Jaga, and Mutulu Shakur, by hosting a national conference in Kansas City, Missouri, where various NAIM organizations discussed forming themselves into a national front. After a year of holding periodic negotiations in various cities, the discussion bore fruit in Atlanta, Georgia. On August 18, 1995, NAPO, the December 12th Movement, Malcolm X Grassroots Movement, the Malcolm X Commemoration Committee, the Black Cat Collective, International Campaign to Free Geronimo, the Sundiata Acoli Freedom Campaign, and various other POW and grassroots organizations formally unified under the banner of the New Afrikan Liberation Front, headed by Herman Ferguson.

The mid-90s brought the World Trade Center bombing which marked the beginning of the U.S. strategy to substitute Islam for the former Soviet Union as the world's new bogeyman. It produced the first foreign Islamic PP/POWs—Amir Abdelgani, Rasheed Clement El, Sheik Omar Eahman, and others.

The mid-decade also brought forth a growing right-wing white militia movement that had obviously studied the guerrilla tactics and political language of the '60s left-wing movements but not its philosophy of avoiding innocent deaths—and which culminated in the bombing of the Oklahoma City Federal Building causing 168 deaths. Upon arrest, Timothy McVeigh, a right-winger and by then the chief suspect, usurped the language of the left by claiming POW status. He was subsequently convicted. But largely overlooked in the media coverage of his case was McVeigh's firsthand verification of the U.S. government's involvement in bringing drugs into this country (and the ghettos) and its use of the police in carrying out assassinations, notable because the overwhelming majority of people killed or assassinated by police in this country are people of color.

Timothy McVeigh had been an All-American boy—a longhaired, blue-eyed patriot who enlisted in the army to defend the American way of life that he so fervently believed in. He rose rapidly through the military ranks (private to sergeant) in two years, and was accepted into the Special Forces: the elite, top 4 percent of the military's forces. There he learned something that average thinking persons of color have known most of their lives but found difficult to prove. McVeigh's own words provide the proof.

In an October 1991 letter to his sister and confidant, Jennifer, McVeigh disclosed his revulsion at being told that he and nine other Special Forces commanders might be ordered to help the CIA, "fly drugs into the U.S. to fund covert operations" and "work hand in hand with civilian police agencies" as "government paid assassins." Disillusioned and embittered with the U.S. government, McVeigh soon left military service, gravitated deeper into the right-wing militia service, and surfaced four years later upon his arrest in the Oklahoma City bombing case.

The mid-90s found white anarchists Neil Batelli and Mathias Bolton collaborating with Black POWs Ojore Lutalo, Sekou Odinga, and Sundiata Acoli, which resulted in the transformation of their local New Jersey Anarchist Black Cross into an ABC Federation (ABCF) which now serves as a role model of the proper way for organizations to provide political and financial support to PP/POWs of all nationalities. The period also witnessed the re-sprouting of Black revolutionary organizations patterned after the BPP (the Black Panther Collective, the Black Panther Militia)—along with the NOI Minster Louis Farrakhan's emergence at the October 16, 1995, Million Man March (MMM) in Washington, D.C., as an undeniable force on the New Afrikan, Islamic, and world stage. In the meantime, the U.S. moved further to the right with the passage of a series of racist, anti-worker legislation. The government ratified the NAFTA treaty to legitimize the policy of private corporations sending U.S. jobs overseas. California passed Proposition 209, which killed affirmative action programs throughout the state. Then, it floated Proposition 187, whose purpose was to implement statewide racist anti-immigration legislation. But this failed to pass. The federal government killed Black voting districts and passed Clinton's Omnibus Crime Bill, which greatly increased the number of crime statutes, death penalty statutes, policemen and armaments, arrests of people of color, youths tried as adults, three-strike convictions, and prison expansion projects.

The so-called War on Drugs sent Blacks and other people of color, more commonly associated with crack cocaine, to prison in droves while allowing white offenders to go free. Five grams of crack worth a few hundred dollars is punishable by a mandatory five-year prison sentence, but it takes 500 grams, or $50,000 worth of powdered cocaine, more commonly associated with wealthier whites, before facing the same five years. In the mid-90s, 1,600 people were sent to prison each week. Three out of every four were Black or Latino, with the rate of Afrikan women imprisonment growing faster than that of Afrikan men.

Blacks were 90 percent of the federal crack convictions in 1994. The normal assumption follows that Blacks are the majority of crack users. Wrong! Whites are the majority of crack users but were less than 4 percent of the crack convictions, and no white person had been convicted of a federal crack offense in the Los Angeles area since 1986—or ever in Chicago, Miami, Denver, or sixteen states according to the 1992 survey. As a result, there are now more Afrikan men in prison than in college, and one out of every three Afrikan men aged twenty to twenty-nine is in prison, jail, or on probation or parole. Most of the convictions were obtained by an informant's tainted testimony only, no hard evidence, in exchange for the informant's freedom from prosecution or prison.

After lobbying Congress for a few years, Families Against Mandatory Minimums (FAMM), a predominately white lobby group, succeeded in getting harsh mandatory sentences lowered for marijuana and LSD convictions. Both drugs are more commonly associated with white offenders, and FAMM's success resulted in the release of numerous white offenders from long prison sentences.

Blacks and other prisoners of color patiently waited for similar corrections to be made to the gross disparity between crack and powdered cocaine sentences. Several years passed before the answer came during a 1995 C-SPAN TV live broadcast of the congressional session debating the disparity in sentencing. Congressional Black Caucus (CBC) member Maxine Waters's summation speech, typical of those made by congresspersons in favor of correcting the disparity, included the following:

> Mr. Chairman, we have been before this body this evening pointing out the disparity, pointing out the inequality, pointing out the injustice of the system as it operates now. I am surprised at much of the rhetoric and all of these so-called conversations that my friends on the other side of the aisle have been having in minority communities. I am glad to know that my colleagues are going there. I am glad to know that they are communicating. But let me tell my colleagues what the mothers in my community say where I live.
>
> They say: Ms. Waters, why do they not get the big drug dealers? What is this business under Bush that stopped resources going to interdiction? Why is it large amounts of drugs keep flowing into inner cities? Where do they come from and why don't they get the real criminals, Ms. Waters, why is it 19-year-olds who wander out into the community and get a few rocks of crack cocaine? Why is it they end up in the Federal system? Why is it they end up with these 5-year minimum mandatory, up to 10-year mandatory sentences? Why can't you get the big guys?
>
> They say: We believe there is a conspiracy. This is what mothers in these communities say. We believe there is a conspiracy against our children and against our communities. They do not understand it when policymakers get

up and say, Oh, it is not interdiction that we should be concerned about. As long as there is a desire for drugs they are going to continue to flow, and what we have to do is just concentrate on telling them, Just say no.

They say: Ms. Waters, we do not understand that and we do not know why a first time offender, who happens to be black or Latino, ends up with a 5-year sentence. And why is the Federal Government targeting our communities? They are not targeting white communities who are the major drug abusers. They are targeting our communities from the Federal level. Thus, our kids go into the Federal system and the whites who are drug abusers and traffickers go into the state systems. They get off with their fancy lawyers with probation, with 1 year, with no time, and our kids are locked up.

Mr. Chairman, for those of my colleagues who say, Well we know it is unfair, but just keep letting it go on for a while and we will take a look at it— are they out of their minds? How can they stand on the floor of Congress pretending to support a Constitution and a democracy and say, "We know it is not fair, but just let it continue and we may take another look at it"?

When I give them the facts they know them to be true, and I will say it again. In Los Angeles, the U.S. District Court prosecuted no whites, none, for crack offense, between 1988 and 1994. And my colleagues tell me that they think it may be applied unequally? This is despite the fact that two-thirds of those who have tried crack are white and over one-half of crack regular users are white. This is a fairness issue and it is a race issue.

Mr. Chairman, I do not care how they try and paint it. I do not care what they say. This is patently unfair. It is blatant and my colleagues ought to be ashamed of themselves. It is racist, because their little white sons are not getting up in the system. They are not targeted. Our children are.

Mr. Chairman, they are going into the Federal system with mandatory sentences and it is a race issue. It is a racist policy.

Despite the best arguments and passionate pleas of CBC members Waters, Jackson-Lee, Conyers, Watts, Fattah, Flukes, Lewis, Mfume, Payne, Rush, Stokes, Scott, and similar speeches by non-CBC members Clayton, Baker, Frank, Schroeder and Traficant, Congress voted 316 to 96 to continue the same 100 to 1 disparity between crack and powder cocaine sentences. Instantly, prison exploded in riots, 28 in all, although most were whited-out of the news media, while across the country prison officials instituted a nationwide federal prisons lock down. The disparity in crack/powder cocaine sentencing laws remains to date; the only change made was the removal of the C-SPAN TV channel from all federal prisons' TVs.

Only two prison elements grew faster than the Afrikan prison population. One was the number of jobs for prison guards and the other was prison slave labor industries. A California guard with a high school diploma makes $44,000 after seven years, which is more than the state pays its PhD public university associate professors and is $10,000 more than its average public school teacher's salary. The national ratio for prisons is one guard for every 4.38 prisoners. And although the prisoners are usually Black or others of color, the guard hired is most often white, since most prisons are built in depressed, rural white areas to provide jobs to poor, unemployed white populations.

After decades of the U.S. loudly accusing China of using prison labor in their export products, the U.S. sells prison products to the public. It set off a stampede by Wall Street and private corporations—Smith Barney, INM, AT&T, TWA, Texas Instruments, Dell, Honda, Lexus, Spaulding, Eddie Bauer, Brill Manufacturing Co., and many others—to shamelessly invest in prisons, set up slave labor factories in prisons to exploit every facet of the prison slave labor industry for super profits, while callously discarding civilian workers for prison slave laborers.

From 1980 to 1994, prisoners increased 221 percent, prison industries jumped an astonishing 358 percent, and prison sales skyrocketed from $392 million to $1.31 billion. By the year 2000, it is predicted that 30 percent of prisoners (or 500,000) will be industry workers producing $8.9 billion in goods and services.

Although crime has been decreasing for five straight years, as we approach the new millennium we find that prison expansion has continued at a record pace and that the prison population has mushroomed over the last decade to an astonishing 1.75 million souls—the majority of whom are Black, period—not counting the 675,000 on parole and the 3,400,000 on probation for a grand sum of six million people under the jurisdiction of the criminal "justice" system. The prisons/jails have been majority Black since 1993 when Blacks ascended to 55 percent. Other prisoners of color made up 18 percent and whites shrank to 27 percent of the prison population. There are now over two Blacks for every white prisoner, and the ratio increases daily.

The incarceration of women continues to accelerate. There are over 90,000 women in prison today; 54 percent are women of color, and 90 percent of women in prison are single mothers. Upon imprisonment they lose contact with their children, sometimes forever. There are 167,000 children in the U.S. whose mothers are incarcerated. [*Editor's note: Though specific contemporary statistics are hard to ascertain on a federal level, an August 2008 Bureau of Justice Statistics special report determined that from 1991 to 2007—ten years after the latest version of this article was published—the number of children whose mother was incarcerated rose by a staggering 131 percent. At that time, the number of U.S. children with a parent behind bars had risen to a record 1.7 million (at least).*]

The term "crime" has become a code word for "Black and other people of color." The cry for "law and order," "lock 'em up and throw away the key," and for "harsher prisons" is heard everywhere. Nothing is too cruel to be done to prisoners. Control units and control prisons abound across the landscape and prison brutality and torture is the order of the day. The "war on drugs" continues apace, by now transparent to all as a "war, actually a preemptive strike, on people of color" to knock out our youth—our warrior class—and to decrease our birth rate, destabilize our families, re-enslave us through mass imprisonment, and ultimately to eliminate us. The threat is serious and real. We ignore it at our own peril.

Despite the government massively imprisoning our youth and covertly fomenting deadly internecine wars among Black street gangs, the abhorrence of the Afrikan community and persistent "Peace Summits" sponsored by Afrikan spiritual, community, and prison leaders have produced, somewhat positive, although checkered results.

The New Afrikan liberation struggle behind the walls now follows the laws of its own development, paid for in its own blood, intrinsically linked to the struggle of its own people, and rooted deeply in the ebb and flow of its own history. To know that history is already to know its future development and direction.

A BRIEF HISTORY OF THE BLACK PANTHER PARTY AND ITS PLACE IN THE BLACK LIBERATION MOVEMENT

Sundiata Acoli

The Black Panther Party for Self-Defense was founded in October 1966, in Oakland, California, by Huey P. Newton and Bobby Seale. The name was shortened to the Black Panther Party (BPP), and it began spreading eastward through the Black urban ghetto colonies across the country.

In the summer of '68, David Brothers established a BPP branch in Brooklyn, New York, and a few months later Lumumba Shakur set up a branch in Harlem, New York. I joined the Harlem BPP in the fall of '68 and served as its finance officer until arrested on April 2, 1969, in the Panther 21 conspiracy case, which was the opening shot in the government's nationwide attack on the BPP. Moving westward, police departments made military raids on BPP offices or homes in Philadelphia, Chicago, Newark, Omaha, Denver, New Haven, San Diego, Los Angeles, and other cities, murdering some Panthers and arresting others.

After most other Panther 21 members and I were held in jail and on trial for two years, we were acquitted of all charges and released. Most of us returned to the community and to the BPP, but by then COINTELPRO had taken its toll. The BPP was rife with dissension, both internal and external. The internal strife, division, intrigue, and paranoia had become so ingrained that eventually most members drifted or were driven away. Some continued the struggle on other fronts and some basically cooled out altogether. The BPP limped on for several more years, then died what seemed a natural death.

History will be the ultimate judge of the BPP's place in the Black Liberation Movement (BLM). But in these troubled times Afrikan people in the U.S. need to investigate both the positive and negative aspects of the BPP's history in order to learn from those hard lessons already paid for in blood. In particular, we need to learn the reasons for the BPP's rapid rise to prominence, the reason for its ability to move so many Afrikans and other nationalities, and the reason for its demise during its brief sojourn across the American scene. It is not possible in this short paper, on short notice, to provide much of what is necessary, so this paper will confine itself to pointing out some of the broader aspects of the BPP's positive and negative contributions to the BLM.

The Positive Aspects of the BPP's Contributions

1. Self-defense: This is one of the fundamental areas in which the BPP contributed to the BLM. It's also one of the fundamental things that set the BPP apart from most previous Black organizations and which attracted members (particularly the youth), mass support, and a mass following. The concept is not only sound, it's also common sense. But it must be implemented correctly, otherwise it can prove more detrimental than beneficial. The self-defense policies of the BPP need to be analyzed in this light by present-day Afrikan organizations. All history has shown that this government will bring its police and military powers to bear on any group which truly seeks to free Afrikan people. Any Black "freedom" organization which ignores self-defense does so at its own peril.

2. Revolutionary nationalist ideology: The BPP was a nationalist organization. Its main goal was the national liberation of Afrikan people in the U.S., and it restricted its membership to Blacks only. It was also revolutionary. The BPP's theories and practices were based on socialist principles. It was anti-capitalist and struggled for a socialist revolution of U.S. society. On the national level, the BPP widely disseminated socialist-based programs to the Afrikan masses. Internationally, it provided Afrikans in the U.S. with a broader understanding of our relationship to the Afrikan continent, the emerging independent Afrikan nations, Third World nations, socialist nations, and all the liberation movements associated with these nations. Overall the ideology provided Afrikans here with a more concrete way of looking at and analyzing the world. Heretofore much of Black analysis of the world and the society in which we live was based on making ourselves

acceptable to white society, proving to whites that we were human, proving to whites that we were ready for equality, proving we were equal to whites, disproving racist ideas held by whites, struggling for integration or equal status with whites, theories of "loving the enemy," "hating the enemy," "they're all devils," spook-ism, and other fuzzy images of how the real world worked.

3. Mass organizing techniques: Another fundamental thing that attracted members and mass support to the BPP was its policy of "serving the people." This was a policy of going to the masses, living among them, sharing their burdens and organizing the masses to implement their own solutions to the day-to-day problems that were of great concern to them. By organizing and implementing the desires of the masses, the BPP organized community programs ranging from free breakfast for children to free health clinics, to rent strikes resulting in tenant ownership of their buildings, to liberation school for grade-schoolers, to free clothing drives, to campaigns for community control of schools, community control of police, and campaigns to stop drugs, crime, and police murder and brutality in the various Black colonies across America. For these reasons, and others, the influence of the BPP spread far beyond its actual membership. Not only did the BPP programs teach self-reliance, but years later the government established similar programs such as free school lunch, expanded medicare and daycare facilities, and liberalized court procedures for tenant takeovers of poorly maintained housing—partly if not primarily in order to snuff out the memory of previous similar BPP programs and the principle of self-reliance.

4. Practice of women's equality: Another positive contribution of the BPP was its advocating and practice of equality for women throughout all levels of the organization and in society itself. This occurred at a time when most Black nationalist organizations were demanding that the woman's role be in the home and/or one step behind the Black man, and at a time when the whole country was going through a great debate on the women's liberation issue.

5. Propaganda techniques: The BPP made significant contributions to the art of propaganda. It was very adept at spreading its message and ideas through its newspaper *The Black Panther*, mass rallies, speaking tours, slogans, posters, leaflets, cartoons, buttons, symbols (e.g., the clenched fist), graffiti, political trials, and even funerals. The BPP also spread its ideas through very skillful use of the establishment's TV, radio, and print media. One singular indication, although there are others, of the effectiveness of

BPP propaganda techniques is that even today, over a decade later, a large part of the programs shown on TV are still "police stories," and many of the roles available to Black actors are limited to police roles. A lot of this has to do with the overall process of still trying to rehabilitate the image of the police from its devastating exposure during the Panther era, and to prevent the true role of the police in this society from being exposed again.

The Negative Aspects of the BPP's Contributions

1. Leadership corrupted: COINTELPRO eventually intimidated and corrupted all three of the BPP's top leaders: Huey P. Newton, Bobby Seale, and Eldridge Cleaver. Each, in his own way, caved in to the pressures and began acting in a manner that was designed deliberately to destroy the BPP and to disillusion not only Party members but Afrikan people in America for years to come. COINTELPRO's hopes were that Afrikans in America would be so disillusioned that never again would they trust or follow any Afrikan leader or organization which advocated real solutions to Black oppression.

2. Combined above and underground: This was the most serious structural flaw in the BPP. Party members who functioned openly in the BPP offices, or organized openly in the community by day, might very well have been the same people who carried out armed operations at night. This provided the police with a convenient excuse to make raids on any and all BPP offices or on members' homes, under the pretext that they were looking for suspects, fugitives, weapons, or explosives. It also sucked the BPP into the unwinnable position of making stationary defenses of BPP offices. There should have been a clear separation between the aboveground Party and the underground armed apparatus. Also, small military forces should never adopt, as a general tactic, the position of making stationary defenses of offices, homes, buildings, etc.

3. Rhetoric outstripped capabilities: Although the BPP was adept at the art of propaganda and made very good use of its own and the establishment's media, still too many Panthers fell into the habit of making boisterous claims in the public media, or selling "wolf tickets" that they couldn't back up. Eventually, they weren't taken seriously anymore. The press, some of whom were police agents, often had only to stick a microphone under a Panther's nose to make him or her begin spouting rhetoric. This often played into the hands of those who were simply looking for slanderous

material to air or to provide possible intelligence information to the police.

4. Lumpen tendencies: It can be safely said that the largest segment of the New York City BPP membership (and probably nationwide) were workers who held everyday jobs. Other segments of the membership were semi-proletariat, students, youths, and lumpen-proletariat. The lumpen tendencies within some members were what the establishment's media (and some party members) played up the most. Lumpen tendencies are associated with lack of discipline, liberal use of alcohol, marijuana, and curse words, loose sexual morals, a criminal mentality, and rash actions. These tendencies in some Party members provided the media with better opportunities than they would otherwise have had to play up this aspect, and to slander the Party, which diverted public attention from much of the positive work done by the BPP.

5. Dogmatism: Early successes made some Panthers feel that they were the only possessors of absolute truths. Some became arrogant and dogmatic in their dealings with Party members, other organizations, and even the community. This turned people off.

6. Failure to organize economic foundations in the community: The BPP preached socialist politics. It was anti-capitalist and this skewed its concept of building economic foundations in the community. The Party often gave the impression that to engage in any business enterprise was to engage in capitalism and it too frequently looked with disdain upon the small business people in the community. As a result, the BPP built few businesses which generated income other than *The Black Panther* newspaper, or which could provide self-employment to its membership and to people in the community. The BPP failed to encourage the Black community to set up its own businesses as a means of building an independent economic foundation which could help break "outsiders'" control of the Black community's economics and move it toward economic self-reliance.

7. TV mentality: The '60s were times of great flux. A significant segment of the U.S. population engaged in mass struggle. The Black Liberation, Native American, Puerto Rican, Asian, Chicano, anti-war, white revolutionary, and women's liberation movements were all occurring more or less simultaneously during this era. It appears that this sizable flux caused some Panthers to think that a seizure of state power was imminent or that a revolutionary struggle is like a quick-paced TV program. That is, it comes on at 9:00 P.M., builds to a crescendo by 9:45, and by 9:55 victory! All in time to make the 10 o'clock news. When it didn't happen after a

few years—that is, Afrikans in the U.S. still were not free, no revolution occurred, and worse the BPP was everywhere on the defensive, taking losses, and riddled with dissension—many members became demoralized, disillusioned, and walked away or went back to old lifestyles. They were not psychologically prepared for a long struggle. In hindsight, it appears that the BPP didn't do enough to root out this TV mentality in some members. But it did in others, which is an aspect to ponder on.

Although the BPP made serious errors it also gained a considerable measure of success and made several significant new contributions to the BLM. The final judgment of history may very well show that in its own way the BPP added the final ingredient to the Black agenda necessary to attain real freedom—armed struggle—and that this was the great turning point which ultimately set the Black Liberation Movement on the final road to victory.

SENSES OF FREEDOM

Sundiata Acoli

August 31, 2014, FCI Cumberland, Maryland

Freedom FEELS sublime
like a slow Sunday morn in the springtime
of your lover.
The kids are outside
delighting in the new turn of the tide
and each other.
Children are priceless again,
women are liberated.
All races are respected
and the people placated.
SOUNDS of a Sax Supreme,
riffs of laughter, Salsa and Country themes
all syncopate with the Trane.
Indigenous drums toll:
"The Long War's Over" as soft wind chimes knell
in matching refrain.
No "Shots fired!" today.
No mother crying for her child.
No stroll thru the morgue tonight.

Just the best night's sleep in a long while.
Aromas of fine wines
and SCENTS of baked breads draw the masses to dine
outdoors in the street.
The Haves share freely
with the Nots now as both have equally
when they meet.
No need for snatching, grabbing
or fighting to be first.
There's enough for all now
in this wisely-shared universe.
A TASTE of honey
on earth, sweeter than the sweetest pastry,
milk, or sugar tea.
People living free,
controlling their own lives and destiny,
as it should be.
Looking back, SIGHTING
ahead to a legacy of lightings
delayed by theft.
But back on path at last,
seeking keys from the present past
to the age-old mysteries of LOVE & JOY, LIFE and DEATH.

STILL BELIEVING IN LAND
AND INDEPENDENCE

Sekou Odinga

In the name of Allah, the Beneficent, the Merciful.

I bear witness that there is no God but Allah, Creator and Sustainer of all the Universe. He alone deserves the worship and He alone deserves the praise. And I bear witness that Muhammad ibn Abdullah is His last Prophet and slave servant.

From the early summer of 1970 and onward I was in Algeria. I was there to help open the Black Panther Party's International Section. Our responsibility was the accumulation and dissemination of information. Eldridge and Kathleen Cleaver were there, Donald Cox (Field Marshall D.C.), Larry Mack, and a few others were there, but it was a fairly small group at that time. We wanted to gather information from various political formations, front line anti-colonial struggles, such as the MPLA of Angola, ANC of South Africa, ZANU and ZAPU of Zimbabwe, and the Palestinians (PLO). There were also representatives of progressive and revolutionary governments—the Chinese government was there, and the North Vietnamese were as well—almost all progressive or left-leaning governments were there.

Algeria had opened its doors and invited all progressive movements to come, gather, and work together. Initially, the Algerian government was very active in supporting the work. Not only did it give us a building where we could open our office, it also gave us a little stipend to help us maintain that office. We were able to have conversations, to build international relations just by being there with each other in the capital.

We were reading all the information coming from the liberation movements and progressive governments and sharing the Black Panther news with other oppressed peoples. Most reported on the ways in which their struggles were going, how their struggles were proceeding, what their goals were. Most of them today, other than the Palestinians, are independent states. The Palestinians and New Afrikans in America are about the only ones who have not yet achieved self-determination: land and independence. We initially were able to do a lot of things; we traveled a lot—we went to the Congo, North Korea, China, Egypt, and other places.

I went to Kuwait for the Second International Symposium on Palestine, held in February 1971. We worked with Palestinian student groups there. I went to Egypt and Lebanon a number of times, and the International Section was able to send representatives to a number of other places. I remember meeting a Palestinian comrade named Abu, who was based in Egypt. He provided all kinds of help to us. He was a relatively young man, mid-thirties, who had been on the front lines and was wanted in Israel. He was a real good comrade who invited us to meet his people in Egypt and in a number of other countries. He was a revolutionary who believed in international solidarity. He believed that our struggle was part and parcel of his struggle. Abu approached us with open arms and wanted to help in any way that he could. We also met with PLO leader Yasser Arafat.

After a couple of years in Algeria the U.S. government, represented by Robert McNamara (then president of the World Bank and former U.S. secretary of defense), made a political and financial deal with the Algerian government to help them develop their natural gas. When Algeria actually signed the contract, one of the conditions that the U.S. asked for was that we be turned over to them. A number of us had cases pending against us—Larry Mack, Cetewayo (Michael Tabor), and myself of the Panther 21, Donald Cox, or D.C. as we called him, and Pete O'Neal from Kansas City.

Algeria refused to give us up, but McNamara came up with a compromise: at the very least, he wanted the Algerians to shut us up. He told them: "You can't let them keep putting out all this negative information about the U.S. government." The Algerians did agree to that, and at one point they actually put us under house arrest, demanding that we give up any arms that we might have. They interrupted our telex service, which was the main way we were able to easily communicate with the outside world.

Some of us decided that it was time to leave. We no longer felt completely safe in Algeria. Some of us decided to go to France, others to Tanzania, still others to Zambia. And some of us continued the work in Algeria. Larry Mack and I came back to the U.S. We decided to come back because Amerikkka is where our struggle was, where we felt we could be most effective. This was after the acquittal of the Panther 21 on all charges (May 13, 1971), but we thought that—because the FBI's and police attacks, and because of renegade Panthers—our lives were still in danger.

Although I don't really remember how I felt upon hearing of the acquittal of the NY 21, I'm sure I was very happy. Because it was a clear victory; I definitely felt that. It was a clear-cut political victory. The government had pulled out a lot of stops to try to get a conviction and had failed. I always felt that if the jury was not totally right-wing dogs they would find us not guilty because the charges were so outrageous. They didn't make sense—that we were these hardcore revolutionaries, trying to blow up department stores and the Botanical Gardens with our own people in them!

The Panther 21 arrest was a very strategically important one for the state, and for our movement as well. The powers that be wanted to interrupt the revolutionary work that the New York Black Panther Party was doing. They identified the more radical leaders within New York and were able to disrupt our activities—the children's programs, the clothing drives, the food drives, the welfare program, the free health clinics, etc. Instead of those programs moving forward, now we would have to concentrate on getting our Black Panther Party leadership out of jail. A lot of people at that time came to prominence through the Panther 21 case. That's when people nationally first heard of Jamal Joseph and Afeni Shakur, during their public speaking. The 21 case was important because of the many ways it helped shape our movement. Even though a lot of people still don't know about it, I think this is important history.

I always felt like the charges against the Panther 21 were more of a ploy to get us off the streets and to bankrupt us, rather than to actually find us guilty. But I also always knew that there was a possibility that we could be found guilty even though the charges were outrageous. It wasn't beyond the pale, since so many other people were found guilty of outrageous acts that we thought people should have known were bullshit. The U.S. government did achieve the goal of getting a lot of the leadership of the NY Black Panther Party off of the street. It did even more than they thought it would do—it probably precipitated the split within the Party.

One of the big issues which came up at that time was how the funds that were being raised specifically for the NY 21 were being used. The BPP Central

Committee (CC) in California was insisting that all funds collected by any Panthers come to them. Whatever we collected was to go straight to them, and then they'd send back whatever they deemed necessary. And they didn't seem to deem anything necessary! Huey Newton was in jail when we first started to complain about this. Huey initially was sympathetic to the plight of the NY 21 while he was in jail. BPP Chief of Staff David Hilliard was the main one who insisted that the money go through him.

Once Huey got out, however, he too adopted David's position, and they weren't sending any money back to New York. We had people in jail with large bail, and much of the money had been specifically raised for their bail. Being in Algeria at the time, Cetewayo, Larry and I insisted that our section, the International Section, take up our plight. We were able to get the International Section to demand that the money raised for the bail—at least a major part of it—go toward what it was raised for. That demand precipitated a contradiction between the International Section "led by" Eldridge Cleaver and the BPP Central Committee. I put the words "led by" in quotes because it wasn't actually only led by Eldridge; we operated more under democratic conditions, so we made collective decisions.

We consistently voted to support the NY 21 position at a time when divisions were beginning. The first big difference arose when the NY 21 put out a statement, a January 1971 "Open Letter to the Weather Underground"—the "mother country" radical organization that had grown out of Students for a Democratic Society. The statement was critical of the racism we saw in all white movements, and—while wishing them revolutionary victory—it cautioned them to remember that "the degree of racial co-existence greatly depends on your successes." The West Coast didn't like that we were critically supportive of Weather, and especially didn't like that we asserted our criticism without asking them first. Our position was that we didn't need to ask them; we reserved the right to have our own opinions.

There were a lot of issues between East and West that were coming to a head. There were issues about where Huey was living and how much rent he was paying while so many rank-and-file Panthers were living collectively in virtual poverty. There were concerns about how Huey was treating people and many other things that bothered us. But the issues around the NY 21 brought it all to a splitting point. The period was very tumultuous, but it wasn't just about the times. We felt that the more power and money Huey got the softer he got. We read this as Huey becoming more reformist, developing bourgeois tendencies which weren't compatible with what we had been taught and were teaching. He was becoming very dictatorial, demanding that he be called the

"Supreme Commander." At this time, it seemed like Huey was mainly thinking about and talking about himself: "I did this, and I did that: I, I, I."

But the straw that broke the camel's back was the money issue regarding the NY 21. The CC began by expelling one of us, then another. Finally, they said that everyone from the NY 21 was expelled. We in Algeria disagreed with that and put out a written statement supporting fully the NY 21 position. Huey took that as insubordination and expelled the entire International Section. We were supposed to have a public coming together over the radio—between Huey and those of us in Algeria. Actually, we blindsided him. He thought we were coming on to reconcile, but we came on with our criticisms and he was mad as hell. Ultimately, we just brought the split—which was clearly already there—out into the open.

In 1973, the BPP in New York City was still officially in existence, but was dying. The Harlem office closed. After the death of Sam Napier, a leader from the West Coast who was working in NY, everything just became an armed struggle among ourselves. Some of us at this time began shifting into the Black Liberation Army (BLA). It was a time of war. Those who were inclined to rumble went (or were already) underground. I thought that building a clandestine, underground capacity was necessary.

Although I was still underground, I would have surfaced if I believed with any confidence that I could have done so without being captured and imprisoned. I had a family, and though I did see them occasionally I couldn't see them on any regular basis. I wanted to. The illegal Counter Intelligence Program (COINTELPRO) of the U.S. government seemed so effective that work above ground was no longer strategic. We couldn't work under the banner of the Black Panther Party, which was at war with itself. A clandestine movement could bring about political consequences when the people were attacked by the state. Much like it is today, the state apparatus (federal, state, and local police and sheriff departments, etc.) were constantly brutalizing and murdering people of color, especially radical Black people. Leading members of the BPP were primary targets, like Chicago's Fred Hampton, Los Angeles's John Huggins and Bunchy Carter, and many others around the country. The police and all the press gloated over the murder of Panthers. We were under siege.

The BLA units that I worked with were semiautonomous or completely autonomous. Some of them had members from out of the Party; actually, most of those I worked with had at least one or two members who had been in the Party. But all of them also had members who hadn't been in the Party. All of us believed in the need to build a clandestine response; in fact, the BLA was just one response. Some units, especially from the South, weren't BLA at all. All of

us had a political consciousness around the need for the potential for retaliation—that there should be some consequences to the actions of the police and
the government. Some folks just wanted to fight back. Police say that their own
violence is justifiable homicide. We said, "It's not justifiable to kill unarmed
schoolchildren like Clifford Glover, or grandmothers a bit late on their rent
like Eleanor Bumpurs." We said, "It's not justifiable to kill unarmed civilians."
We said, "There would be consequences for that kind of state murder."

As for me, I believed in land and independence. And I still believe that
freedom is based on land and independence!

**

The case of the Panther 21 has always been important as a historical factor in
New Afrikan people's movement for land and independence. Our case was
one of the first major political cases that had a large number of Black radical
political prisoners. Twenty-one were indicted, thirteen actually locked up for
a long period of time. It was important to understand why the state did it and
some of the effects of locking us up. It was a prelude to the split in the BPP
itself; a lot of contradictions were brought forward from people in the NY 21
when they talked about where money was going. As I said before, I think the
government knew that they didn't have much of a case, but that we'd have to
fight the case. To do that, they knew we'd have to take people off the streets
who were very effective organizing on the streets.

The 21 was a collection of revolutionary Black men and women, and
most of these radicals continued to work in radical politics, radical struggle.
Some of us went underground and took up arms to defend the community. In
that sense, there was a continuum; it never stopped. Maybe it got quiet; some
people had been forgotten. Sometimes we didn't want things to be in the limelight; the less people thought about them, the more the people underground
were able to do.

One thing we know is that Assata Shakur was liberated. What some might
not know is that I was convicted of aiding in Assata's liberation. I was accused
of going into the Clinton Correctional Facility in New Jersey and bringing her
out. That probably wouldn't have been possible if my picture had been flashed
around in the media, with my name ringing out. But the continuity of struggle
never stopped—even though most people didn't know what was going on.

The work I'm trying to do today is to legally help free those still in prison
for their political beliefs and activities—political prisoners and prisoners of
war. It's not just personal—those inside are part of our movement. We are all

part of the same movement. Our movement, although crippled, is still alive. People are still struggling; Black/New Afrikan people are still oppressed. We are still at the bottom of the system: All the negatives that were there in the 1960s still are here today. It's important that those of us who are part of the movement, who are no longer dealing with armed struggle, continue to deal with our struggle on whatever level we can. We can deal with, and I choose to deal with, the work to free political prisoners.

The work to free political prisoners is especially important work for all those who were a part of the Black Panther Party/Black Liberation Movement. It's important for those both inside and out to know that people haven't forgotten, that there is a struggle still going on. Our struggle to get the Panther political prisoners and others out is a struggle to keep the movement moving. It must remain a priority.

Young people need to know that they can't do it alone. They need to be organized, and they need to be clear about what their goals are. They need to be goal-oriented, and to have long-term and short-term goals. Short-terms goals, of course, need to be conducive to accomplishing the long-term goals. Black and New Afrikan people in particular need to know who we are—where we came from, where we're at, but also where we want to go. We need to be clear about what freedom means. Does freedom mean a $60,000–100,000 a year job? Does freedom mean being able to go to any school we want? Does freedom mean land and independence? I think a cultural revolution is needed to help us identify what freedom means. When we talk about Black people, African people, and New Afrikan people, we need to know who we are. If I asked any of my white allies what's their nationality, they probably would tell me exactly what it is. But if you ask ten Black people what their nationality is, you probably will get four or five answers—if not more. I think we need a cultural revolution; a cultural revolution should be able to make that clear—how we're going to get to where we need to be.

I talk about a cultural revolution in part because it's widely "acceptable." It's something that I can talk to the preacher about, I can talk to the Rabbi about, I can talk to the Imam about, I can talk to the social worker about, I can talk to the policeman about—because anybody who has any interest in the people, in Black/New Afrikan people, won't have a problem with a cultural revolution. Plus, culture is what binds a people together—what makes a people a people: same language, same history, same land, etc. So it is in fact not just acceptable, but I think necessary.

What do I say to young people today? Organize, organize, organize! I say that again and again. And to study: study your history—ancient and modern.

Too many of us don't know who Lumumba Shakur was, who Zayd Shakur was. It's a shame, but most of our youth don't even really know who Malcolm X was, other than that he was someone who stood against the system. But if you ask them, "What did he stand for?" very few of them can tell you. And there aren't that many who can tell you what Martin Luther King really stood for, if you ask them, "What did he do that makes you like him?" We don't study our history. We have other people teaching us who we are, people who don't have our interests at heart. If people don't know who they are, it's easy for them to destroy one another. That's why you see our kids killing each other and laughing about it, not even caring. They don't recognize that they're beefing with themselves; they're fighting themselves; they're killing themselves. They don't know that that's their brother—for real, that's their brother. With study and organization, with widespread cultural revolution, it becomes clear that we can't get freedom without land and independence.

THE LAST OF THE LOUD

NEW AND REVISED COMMENTARY

Dhoruba Bin Wahad

Comrades Sekou Odinga and Dhoruba Bin Wahad gave tribute and thanks at the 2016 New York memorial service for Panther 21 member Afeni Shakur, held at Brooklyn's House of the Lord Church and organized by Senior Minister Rev. Dr. Herbert Daughtry, NYC City Councilman Charles Barron, and fellow 21 defendant Jamal Joseph. Both devout Muslims, Sekou and Dhoruba began their remarks giving praise; Dhoruba went on to address the assembled crowd, characterizing their intergenerational differences and common points. This excerpt of Dhoruba's remarks provides an introduction to three recently written essays by Dhoruba revised or excerpted for this publication.

All praise to Allah. There is no God but Allah. I am a servant of Allah. I thank Allah for giving me life, for giving me strength. And most of all, I thank Allah for giving me people like you as comrades, as brothers and sisters who have fought beside us, who have died for our cause, and who stand today in strength and in solidarity.

We were the last of the loud. We got in crackers' faces. We told them what our rights were. We demanded respect. But most of all, we were the last of the loud. It was in the struggle that we gained our identity. We remember Afeni

Shakur, but we know also that Afeni was a product of our tradition, a product of our struggle: of our blood, of our tears, of our pain.

We are the last of the loud. We stand on the shoulders of those of went before us, who suffered for us, who died for us, and who fought for us. So when we have a memorial, it's not just a celebration of who passed; it's a celebration of the generation that is coming as well because we are the last of the loud but they are the first of the bold, of a new generation. And I want to say here, on behalf of my Comrade Afeni, that her spirit resides in those young people whom she nurtured, whom she touched. And they will take her to the next step, to the next level.

Our revolutionary Black women have stood at the forefront of struggle since the days of slavery, since the bullwhip days . . . Comrade Afeni stood in the courtroom and nurtured all of our spirits every day with that effervescent smile. She's not gone; she's not forgotten; she lives every time we mention her name. I honor my sister and I'm very grateful for the opportunity to be here. I get to remember those times when we stood against the power of the state, and we prevailed. We won . . . We never thought that we'd get this far, have the children that we have and the blessings that we have.

This fight ain't over yet, and it won't be over until we are free, until we are liberated, until those enemies of the sun are driven down and subjugated . . . We will be free in this place, in this time, and in this age.

We were the last of the loud, but we got children, and our children are going to have children, and it ain't over until it's over. Power to the people.

URBAN POLICE REPRESSION

CRIMINALIZING RESISTANCE AND UNRAVELING THE FBI'S COUNTER INTELLIGENCE PROGRAM, TIMELINE OF EMPIRE, RACIAL PROFILING, POLICE VIOLENCE, AND CLASS

Compiled and written by Dhoruba Bin Wahad and Paul Wolf, with contributions from Attorney Robert Boyle, Bob Brown, Tom Burghardt, Noam Chomsky, Ward Churchill, Jim Vander Wall, Kathleen Cleaver, Bruce Ellison, Cynthia McKinney, Nkechi Taifa, Laura Whitehorn, Nicholas Wilson, and Howard Zinn

In 1966, the New York City Police Department commenced its own investigation of the Black Panther Party. Detective Ralph White of the NYPD was directed to infiltrate the Black Panther Party and submit daily reports on the Party and its members. The NYPD regularly communicated with police departments throughout the country, sharing information on the BPP, its members and activities.

The NYPD was also working with the FBI on a daily basis. On August 29, 1968, FBI Special Agent Henry Naehle reported on his meeting with a member of an NYPD "Special Unit" investigating the BPP. SA Naehle acknowledged that the FBI's New York Field Office (NYO) "has been working closely with BSS in exchanging information of mutual interest and to our mutual advantage."

An FBI "Inspector's Review" for the first quarter of 1969 shows that the NYPD, in conjunction with the FBI, had an "interview" and "arrest" program as part of their campaign to neutralize and disrupt the BPP. The NYPD advised the FBI that these programs have severely hampered and disrupted the BPP, particularly in Brooklyn where, for a while, BPP operations were at a complete standstill and in fact have never recovered sufficiently to operate effectively.

A series of FBI documents reveal a joint FBI/NYPD plan to gather information on BPP members and their supporters in late 1968. During an unprovoked attack by off-duty members of the NYPD on BPP members attending a court appearance in Brooklyn, the briefcase of BPP leader David Brothers was stolen by the NYPD, its contents photocopied and given to the FBI. Rather than seeking to prosecute the police officers for this theft, the FBI ordered "a review of these names and telephone numbers [so that] appropriate action will be taken."

That "appropriate action" included an effort to label Brothers and two other BPP leaders (Jorge Aponte and Robert Collier) as police informants. On December 12, 1968, the FBI's New York Office proposed circulating fliers warning the community of the "DANGER" posed by Brothers, Collier, and Aponte. The NYO proposed that the fliers "be left in restaurants that Negroes are known to frequent (Chock Full O'Nuts, etc.)." BSS later told the FBI that its proposal was successful in that David Brothers had come under suspicion by the BPP. An FBI memorandum dated December 2, 1968, captioned "Counterintelligence Program," lists several operations during the previous two-week period. It closes by stating that "every effort is being made in the NYO to misdirect the operations of the BPP on a daily basis."

In August 1968, Dhoruba Bin Wahad, then known as Richard Dhoruba Moore, joined the BPP and within a few months was promoted to a position of leadership. He was soon identified by the Bureau and by the NYPD as a "key agitator" and placed in the FBI's "Security Index," "Agitator Index," and "Black Nationalist Photograph Album." FBI supervisors instructed the NYO to "develop better liaison and closer working relationship with the NYPD" in their investigation of Dhoruba Bin Wahad.

On April 2, 1969, Bin Wahad and twenty other members of the Black Panther Party were indicted on charges of conspiracy in the so-called Panther 21 case. An NYPD memorandum notes that the Panther 21 arrests were considered a "summation" of the overt and covert investigation commenced in 1966. In a biweekly report to FBI Headquarters listing several counterintelligence operations, the FBI reported: "To date, the NYO has conducted over 500 interviews with BPP members and sympathizers. Additionally, arrests of BPP members have been made by Bureau agents and the NYPD. These interviews and arrests have helped disrupt and cripple the activities of the BPP in the NYC area. Every effort will be made to continue pressure on the BPP."

In July 1969, the NYPD sent officers to Oakland, California, to monitor the Black Panther Party's nationwide conference calling for community control of police departments. An NYPD memorandum candidly acknowledged that community control of the police "may not be in the interests of the department."

Through its warrantless wiretaps of BPP telephones, the FBI learned that the BPP was trying to raise the $100,000 bail that had been set for Bin Wahad, whose release was considered by the BPP to be a priority over the other twenty defendants due to his leadership role in the organization. Fundraising efforts were impeded by FBI/NYPD counterintelligence operations. For example, following a fundraiser at the home of conductor Leonard Bernstein, the FBI sent falsified letters to those in attendance in order to "thwart the aims and efforts of the BPP in their attempt to solicit money from socially prominent groups." Unable to raise bail, Dhoruba Bin Wahad spent the next year incarcerated.

The FBI continued to target BPP community programs. For example, the FBI pressured several churches not to institute the BPP's free breakfast for children program in their parishes. In September 1969, an NYPD BSS representative told the FBI that the BPP was disintegrating in New York.

By March 1970, the BPP had raised enough money to post bail for the most articulate leaders and chose Mr. Bin Wahad for release. The FBI ordered that he be immediately and continuously surveilled and that donors of bail money be identified. Director Hoover reminded his New York Office that the activities of Panther 21 defendants were of "vital interest" to the "seat of government."

Through their warrantless eavesdropping on BPP offices and residences, the FBI became aware in May 1970 of dissatisfaction among New York BPP members, including Bin Wahad, with West Coast BPP members. A COINTELPRO operation prepared by the New Haven Field Office and submitted to the FBI's New York Office consisted of an FBI-fabricated note wherein Bin Wahad accused BPP leader Robert Bay of being an informant.

This successful operation resulted in Dhoruba Bin Wahad's demotion within the BPP. Aware of his disillusionment, the FBI disseminated information regarding BPP strife to the media and participated in a plan to either recruit Bin Wahad as an informant or have BPP members believe he was an agent for the FBI.

In August 1970, BPP leader Huey P. Newton was released from prison. A plethora of counterintelligence actions followed which sought to make Newton suspicious of fellow BPP members, particularly those, like Bin Wahad, who were on the East Coast.

By early 1971, the plan bore fruit. On January 28, 1971, FBI Director Hoover reported that Newton had become increasingly paranoid and had expelled several loyal BPP members:

Newton responds violently. . . . The Bureau feels that this near-hysterical
reaction by the egotistical Newton is triggered by any criticism of his activities, policies, or leadership qualities, and some of this criticism undoubtedly
is a result of our counterintelligence projects now in operation.

This operation was enormously successful, resulting in a split within the
BPP with violent repercussions. In early January 1971, Fred Bennett, a BPP
member affiliated with the New York chapter, was shot and killed, allegedly
by Newton supporters. Newton came to believe that Bin Wahad was plotting
to kill him. Bin Wahad, in turn, was told by Connie Matthews, Newton's secretary, that Newton was planning to have Bin Wahad and Panther 21 codefendants Edward Joseph and Michael Tabor killed during Newton's upcoming
East Coast speaking tour. As a result of the split and fearing for his life, Bin
Wahad, along with Tabor and Joseph, was forced to flee during the Panther
21 trial.

On May 13, 1971, the Panther 21, including Dhoruba Bin Wahad, were
acquitted of all charges in the less than one hour of jury deliberations, following what was at that time the longest trial in New York City history. BSS
Detective Edwin Cooper begrudgingly reported to defendant Michael Codd
that the case "was not proven to the jury's satisfaction." Alarmed and embarrassed by the acquittal, Director Hoover ordered an "intensification" of the
investigations of acquitted Panther 21 members with special emphasis on
those, like Bin Wahad, who were fugitives.

On May 19, 1971, NYPD Officers Thomas Curry and Nicholas Binetti
were shot on Riverside Drive in Manhattan. Two nights later, two other officers, Waverly Jones and Joseph Piagentini, were shot and killed in Harlem.
In separate communiqués delivered to the media, the Black Liberation Army
claimed responsibility for both attacks.

Immediately after these shootings, the FBI made the investigation of
these incidents—called "Newkill"—a part of their long-standing program
against the BPP. Before any evidence had been collected, BPP members—in
particular those acquitted in the Panther 21 case—were targeted as suspects.
Hoover instructed the New York FBI Office to consider the possibility that
both attacks may be the result of revenge taken against NYC police by the
Black Panther Party (BPP) as a result of its arrest of BPP members in April
1969 (i.e., the Panther 21 case).

On May 26, 1971, J. Edgar Hoover met with then-president Richard
Nixon, who told Hoover that he wanted to make sure that the FBI did not
"pull any punches in going all out in gathering information . . . on the situation

in New York." Hoover informed his subordinates that Nixon's interest and the FBI's involvement were to be kept strictly confidential.

"Newkill" was a joint FBI/NYPD operation involving total cooperation and sharing of information. The FBI made all its facilities and resources, including its laboratory, available to the NYPD. In turn, NYPD Chief of Detectives Albert Seedman, who coordinated the NYPD's investigation, ordered his subordinates to give the FBI "all available information developed to date, as well as in future investigations."

On June 5, 1971, Bin Wahad was arrested during a robbery of a Bronx after hours "social club," a hangout for local drug merchants. Seized from inside the social club was a .45 caliber machine gun. Although the initial ballistics test on the weapon failed to link it with the Curry-Binetti shooting, the NYPD publicly declared they had seized the weapon used in May 19. The NYPD now had in custody a well-known and vocal Black Panther leader and the alleged weapon linked to a police shooting. His prosecution and conviction would both neutralize an effective leader and justify the failed Panther 21 case. But there was no direct evidence linking Bin Wahad to the shooting.

Pauline Joseph, a diagnosed paranoid schizophrenic, became the prosecution's star witness. Ms. Joseph first surfaced when she made a phone call to the NYPD on June 12, 1971, supplying her name and address and stating that Bin Wahad and Edward Joseph (a Panther 21 defendant who jumped bail with Bin Wahad) were innocent of the Curry-Binetti shooting. She told the police that Bin Wahad "did not do it, either the Riverside Drive [Curry-Binetti] shooting or the 32nd precinct [Piagentini-Jones] shooting."

The first person to arrive at Ms. Joseph's apartment was NYPD Lieutenant Kenneth Sauer, the head of the 24th Precinct detective squad. Contrary to her testimony at trial, Ms. Joseph continued to maintain that Bin Wahad was innocent of the Curry-Binetti shooting. Later that day she was interviewed by BSS Detective Edwin Cooper. Joseph repeated that Bin Wahad was innocent.

Ms. Joseph was arrested, and committed as a material witness. For nearly two years she remained in the exclusive custody of the New York County District Attorney's Office. She was repeatedly interviewed by state and federal authorities. While in the custody of the district attorney, Joseph was recruited as a "racial informant" for the FBI. She was paid for her services and housed first in a hotel and then in a furnished apartment, paid for by the district attorney. Despite her mental health issues, Pauline Joseph became the prosecution's star witness in the case.

Dhoruba Bin Wahad was indicted for the attempted murder of Officers Curry and Binetti on July 30, 1971. Although the NYPD and FBI continuously interviewed Ms. Joseph, and prepared written memoranda of those interviews, the assistant district attorney represented that, except for a one paragraph statement made on the night of her commitment and her grand jury testimony, there were no prior statements. The text of Ms. Joseph's initial phone call was withheld by the prosecution through two trials. No notes of memoranda of the initial, exculpatory interviews by Lieutenant Sauer and Detective Cooper were ever provided to Bin Wahad. Neither were reports of subsequent interviews during the two years she was in custody. After three trials, Dhoruba Bin Wahad was convicted of attempted murder and sentenced by Justice Martinisto to the maximum penalty, twenty-five years to life.

In December 1975, after learning of Congressional hearings which disclosed the FBI's covert operations against the BPP, Dhoruba Bin Wahad filed a lawsuit in Federal District Court, charging that he had been the victim of numerous illegal and unconstitutional actions designed to "neutralize" him, including the frame-up in the Curry-Binetti case.

In 1980, the FBI and NYPD were ordered by the Court to produce their massive files on Mr. Bin Wahad and the BPP, that they had claimed did not exist. The FBI and NYPD documents revealed that Mr. Bin Wahad was indeed a target of FBI/NYPD covert operations and, for the first time, depicted the FBI's intimate involvement in the Curry-Binetti investigation. The "Newkill" file, which was finally produced in unredacted form in 1987, after twelve years of litigation, contains numerous reports which should have been provided to Dhoruba Bin Wahad during his trial.

In a decision announced December 20, 1992, Justice Bruce Allen of the New York State Supreme Court ordered a new trial. The court exhaustively analyzed the prosecution's circumstantial case, particularly the testimony of Pauline Joseph. The court found that the inconsistencies and omissions in the prior statements contradicted testimony "crucial to establishing the People's theory of the case." The inconsistencies, said the Court, "went beyond mere details" and involve "what one would expect to have been the most memorable aspects of [the night of the shooting]." On January 19, 1995, the District Attorney moved to dismiss the indictment, acknowledging that the prosecution could not prove its case. The indictment was dismissed. After more than twenty years in prison, Mr. Bin Wahad is at liberty today, residing in Accra, Ghana, and Atlanta, Georgia.

ASSATA SHAKUR, EXCLUDING THE NIGHTMARE AFTER THE DREAM

THE "TERRORIST" LABEL AND THE CRIMINALIZATION OF REVOLUTIONARY BLACK MOVEMENTS IN THE USA

Dhoruba Bin Wahad

Americans live at a time when the history of those who have been cheated, murdered, or excluded is being destroyed. Eliminated from this history are the collective narratives of struggle, resistance, and rebellion against various forms of authoritarianism.

— Henry Giroux, *The Ghost of Authoritarianism in the Age of the Shutdown*

At a press conference in May 2013, the Federal Bureau of Investigation (FBI) announced that it was designating Assata Shakur (JoAnne Chesimard) as one of its top ten most-wanted "terrorists." Assata escaped from a New Jersey prison in 1979 and thereafter surfaced in Cuba where she was granted political asylum. The "terrorist" designation, and the media hoopla surrounding it, has significant historical and political implications. While numerous progressive individuals and organizations correctly denounced that designation, recognizing that it was, in part, an attack on Cuba, far too many progressive and civil rights advocates have missed the greater and more pernicious historical revisionism and racist political implications behind the rebranding of Assata Shakur as a "terrorist."

Many people fighting for human rights, who oppose President Barack Obama's policies of "rendition," torture (which is euphemistically termed "enhanced interrogation technique"), indefinite detention, state sponsored murder by remote control vehicles (drones), have simultaneously called upon Obama to remove Shakur's "terrorist" designation, arguing that Assata is innocent of the murder charges that resulted from her 1973 arrest. Many of these same people opposed Obama's illegally conducted "war on terror" and oppose the murder and detention of so-called militants and jihadists without according them legal due process, recognizing that those targeted by the U.S. are in fact members of "movements" targeted more generally by the U.S. government who would not be otherwise targeted as individuals. Yet notably missing from most public statements decrying Assata's designation as a "terrorist," and unlike the connections made in terms of foreign policy, were attempts to place Assata's case, and the "terrorist" designation, in the political and cultural context of the Black Liberation Movement in the United States.

By contrast, officials at the highest level of government have little trouble placing the movements of the sixties in a different context. President Obama, during his speech commemorating the 1963 March on Washington, recounted his version of the sixties, claiming Black people lost their way when "legitimate grievances against police brutality tipped into excuse-making for criminal behavior." What was Obama talking about? Who was he referring to? What Blacks used police brutality to somehow mask criminal activity? Though he never said it directly, clearly Obama was referring to the Black Panther Party. But his comments speak volumes when juxtaposed to the actions of his own Justice Department. In an effort to appease domestic law enforcement, Obama sanctioned his Justice Department's targeting of Assata Shakur, intensifying the designation of her and her movement as "terrorists."

Rather than open up a discussion on the excesses of the sixties and seventies to discern who were the real criminals and assassins—the architects of COINTELPRO or the movements they illegally infiltrated and destroyed—both supporters and detractors of Assata distort, exclude, and ignore the movement from which she emerged. This essay is an attempt to place the "terrorist" designation and Assata's case in a historical and political context—a context that also significantly impacts the status of Black political prisoners in the United States today.

The Black Liberation (Nationalist), Civil Right (Integrationist), and Pan-African Movements circa 1960–1975

To begin, it is necessary to step into a time capsule and head back to the 1960s. The following history is not intended to be definitive or complete. But this is a history that is relatively unknown—or, if known, deliberately twisted by some who may have benefited from the distortion of Black '60s activism. That is why it is important to review the era now defined as a watershed period in American racial and political history, the tumultuous sixties.

The 1960s and early 1970s was a period of significant social upheaval. Globally, former European colonial powers (all members of North Atlantic Treaty Organization) were locked in the false dichotomy of the Cold War and the struggle to reassert their control over the resources of Africa, Asia, and Latin America. The Cold War geopolitically divided the world into two hostile camps: the Euro-Russian and Sino-Communist East (led by Moscow and Beijing) versus the West led by the USA and its NATO allies. The front line of this global contest after the Korean War (1950–1954) and the French expulsion from its colonial position in Southeast Asia was Vietnam. The U.S. pursuing a policy of "containment of communism" took on the "white man's burden" of the French in Vietnam and introduced a massive military presence to thwart the Vietnamese Independence movement. By 1965, the Vietnamese people were winning a war of liberation against the most powerful military force in history. (We note the 2013 passing of the liberation movement's great leader Võ Nguyên Giáp). Movements within the United States—Black, Native American, Puerto Rican, Mexican—were waging similar struggles that, over time, took on an increasingly anti-imperialist character. This inspired masses of white people, primarily youth, to question the very foundations of United States society. The women's liberation and LGBT movements also grew out of this context. Indeed, it was militant nationalist organizations such as the RNA, BPP, SNCC, which vocally opposed U.S. militarism abroad and the Vietnam War, prior to Dr. Martin Luther King's denunciation of American involvement in Vietnam as amoral and capitalism as exploitive. These were the forces and events that, by 1966, defined the historical and geopolitical conditions that shaped the great civil and human rights movements of middle 20th century.

Inspired by the example of the martyred El-Hajj Malik El-Shabazz (Malcolm X), Robert Williams,[1] and the original Black Panthers of Lowndes

---

1   Robert F. Williams was president of the Monroe, North Carolina, NAACP, which was working to integrate the public swimming pools. They organized peaceful demonstrations, but some drew gunfire. No one was arrested or punished, although law enforcement officers were present. Williams had already started a Black Armed Guard to defend the local Black community from racist activity. KKK membership numbered some 15,000 locally. Black residents fortified their homes with sandbags and trained to use rifles in the event of night raids by the Klan. In *Negroes with Guns*, Williams writes: "[R]acists consider themselves superior beings and are not willing to

County Alabama,[2] the Black Panther Party for Self-Defense was founded in October 1966 in Oakland, California, by Huey P. Newton and Bobby Seale. In just a few months after its inception the Black Panther Party for Self-Defense emerged as a significant influence on "New Left" and radical politics in America and as one of the most popular organizations, and romanticized groups, in the Black community. The BPP developed a ten-point political program based on the conditions of African American and poor people in the Bay Area of San Francisco, California, and across the nation. However, the BPP's emphasis on community control of institutions within the Black community, including education, health care, and housing, resonated with urban Blacks everywhere because institutional racism lay at the very basis of racial and political inequality nationally, not only in the Bay Area. Blacks in Oakland and its adjacent communities had migrated from the South and Southwest, to serve as labor battalions during World War II. The naval base adjacent to Oakland and the Port of San Francisco played a primary logistical role in the U.S. war effort against Imperial Japan during World War II (1941–45). Black workers, arriving from the South to work as laborers for the war effort, were red-lined into specific residential areas. These Black worker communities were policed by racist and brutal police officers—themselves recent migrants from the deep South, mainly from Texas, Arkansas, and Louisiana. It should surprise no one

---

exchange their superior lives for our inferior ones. They are most vicious and violent when they can practice violence with impunity.... It has always been an accepted right of Americans, as the history of our Western states proves, that where the law is unable, or unwilling, to enforce order the citizens can and must act in self-defense against lawless violence." Followers attested to Williams's advocating the use of advanced powerful weaponry rather than more traditional firearms. Williams insisted his position was defensive, as opposed to a declaration of war. He called it "armed self-reliance" in the face of white terrorism. Threats against Williams's life and his family became more frequent. In 1959, Williams debated the merits of nonviolence with Martin Luther King Jr. at the NAACP convention. The national NAACP office suspended his local chapter presidency for six months because of his outspoken disagreements with the national leadership. He said his wife would take over his position and he would continue his leadership through her.

2   The Lowndes County Freedom Organization, or Black Panther Party, was a short-lived political party that formed in 1966 to represent African Americans in the central Alabama Black Belt counties. Though the organization failed to win any election, its influence was felt far beyond Alabama by providing the foundation for the better-known Black Panther Party for Self-Defense that arose in Oakland, California. Although the population was roughly 80 percent African American, no Black resident had successfully registered to vote in more than 60 years, as the county was controlled by 86 white families which owned 90 percent of the land.

then that the BPP 10-Point Program and Platform addressed the existential reality of Black people as workers and as "cannon fodder" for U.S. militarism. One point of the BPP program called for the end to the military draft of all Black men. Another point called for a plebiscite in the Black community to determine whether Black people wished to remain part of the United States. This point directly addressed the conditional and ambivalent nature of African American perennial second-class "citizenship" that seems up for review every decade or so whenever the contradictions of civil and economic reforms placed undue pressure on white skin privilege. Challenging the conventional dichotomy of race relations in the U.S., the BPP reasoned that if Black people must struggle to reaffirm their "civil rights" every decade and constantly secure new legislation protecting their right to vote, then maybe "citizenship," e.g. integration, is not synonymous with freedom or empowerment—and national self-determination (community control/decentralization of institutional controls) does in fact mean empowerment. This was the essential reason for proposing a UN-supervised plebiscite in the BPP 10-Point Platform of "What We Want; What We Believe." Understanding that the right of self-determination for all peoples is part of the Universal Declaration of Human Rights as well as articles condemning racial repression and genocide, the BPP proclaimed its internationalist tendency from its very inception.

Nonetheless the most controversial, vilified, and misrepresented point of the BPP's 10-Point Program was its recognition of Black people's inherent right to self-defense, including armed self-defense against racist attack by civilians or the police. In Oakland, California, armed BPP members engaged in the original "cop-watch," establishing regular armed patrols that followed the police, intervening at a legal distance when the police violated someone's rights. Fully appreciating how short-lived their right to bear arms in public would be, and instinctively sensing how the power structure of white supremacy would attempt to disconnect the rights of Black self-defense from nonviolent movements for broader civil rights and assimilation—the bread and butter of "responsible Negro leaders"—the BPP embarked on a publicity campaign to emphasize the racist political character and purpose of law enforcement and the legislative process. The BPP's instincts were verified when, in 1967, in direct response to the BPP, the State of California sought to amend its gun laws to eliminate the right to carry a firearm in open view. (Ironically, the bill was supported by gun rights advocates: the NRA and then Governor Ronald Reagan. After all, it was about taking firearms from Black people!) Indeed, the Bill was called the "Black Panther" Bill. Racially motivated reform from the right threatened to eat its own! On May 2, 1967, the BPP responded by sending an armed delegation to the Legislative Office Building in Sacramento challenging the new gun law.[3] The image of armed young Black women and men marching in formation on a state capitol circulated like wildfire around the world.

Dozens of Black community activists, mainly from the Black and brown ghettos, and from the streets across America, were galvanized by the BPP's response to the perceived denial of Black people's right to openly carry arms. Those who were the daily victims of police harassment, violence, and intimidation were attracted to the BPP. These were not just the "criminal minded" or sociopaths as the media and later blaxploitation movies would portray, but in most cases serious activists and organizers in their respective communities. It is not generally understood that the membership and leadership of BPP in cities across the U.S. was comprised of local activists who were involved in their community before 1967. The organizational character of the BPP was also shaped by its ideological and organizational structure. A creation of its era, the BPP was not a "faith-based" messianic movement, or mass-based organization like Garvey's UNIA, but a cadre-based revolutionary formation that introduced a disparate membership to principles of revolutionary nationalism and internationalism. These characteristics permitted the BPP to become the first Black organization to establish functional relations with liberation movements in Africa, the Middle East, and Latin America. It is the legacy of those fraternal relationships that serves to protect Assata Shakur in Cuba today. This is one of the reasons why the FBI publicity stunt classifying Assata as a terrorist blatantly attempts to rewrite this history and disparage legitimate movements.

When BPP Chapters sprang up throughout the country, the FBI, along with state and local law enforcement agencies, realized that unless the ideas of Black self-defense were completely discredited, demonized, and rejected by the African American populace, it could lead to a sustained uprising of America's most marginalized and maligned national minority—Africans in America. Barely ten months old in August 1967, the BPP became the FBI's major target in its expanding COINTELPRO operation against the Black Liberation Movement. The stated purpose of the program according to an August 25, 1967, document was to "expose, disrupt, misdirect, discredit, or otherwise neutralize" Black organizations and their leadership. In March 1968, the pro-

---

3   See Adam Winkler, "The Secret History of Guns," *The Atlantic*, September 2011, accessed at http://www.theatlantic.com/magazine/archive/2011/09/the-secret-history-of-guns/308608/.

gram was further expanded to 43 FBI field offices. Those offices were ordered to develop counterintelligence operations designed to prevent the "coalition" of Black groups as well as the rise of a "messiah" who would unify the movement.[4] The FBI was also very concerned about the spread of revolutionary ideology among youth. As candidly put by the FBI's San Francisco field office in April 1968, COINTELPRO must convince youth to buy into the system:

> The Negro youth and moderate must be made to understand that if they succumb to revolutionary teaching they will be dead revolutionaries. Is it not better to be a sports hero, a well-paid professional athlete or entertainer, or a regularly paid white or blue collar worker, a peaceful human being with a family, or a person who is at least being accepted than a Negro who may have gotten even with the establishment by burning it down, but who along with this burned down his own home and gained for him and all his people the hatred and distrust of the whites for years to come?[5]

What started out as a general repressive and surveillance program in 1967, by mid-1968 became a campaign to destroy the BPP and its ideology of armed resistance to racist violence. The Black Panther Party was the chief target of COINTELPRO.[6] According to a 1976 Senate Report (the Church Committee), the Black Panther Party was targeted in 90 percent of all COINTELPRO actions directed at the Black Liberation Movement. Some of the actions included forcing churches and schools to evict the breakfast program, sending spurious notes to contributors threatening violence, placing false stories in newspapers, manipulating fund raising, using informants to spread false rumors, and other disinformation machinations. BPP members were arrested on the street for selling the newspaper. Police conducted interrogations with no legal basis. In all of this, local police played an integral role.[7] As noted in an

---

4   See FBI airtel from Director to 43 Field Offices, March 4, 1968, captioned "Counterintelligence Program."

5   See FBI airtel from San Francisco to Director and 42 field offices, April 3, 1968, captioned "Counterintelligence Program."

6   On December 2, 1968, FBI Director Hoover ordered all field offices to submit bi-weekly memoranda "containing counterintelligence measures aimed against the BPP. The biweekly letter must also contain accomplishments obtained during the two-week period under captioned program." See FBI Memorandum from Director to 43 field offices, December 2, 1968 captioned "Counterintelligence Program."

7   As noted in an FBI Report in early 1969, the FBI had a "program of arresting BPP members. . . . According to the Bureau of Special Services, New York City Police Department (BSS, NYPD) and other sources, these programs have severely hampered

FBI airtel on December 2, 1968, "every effort is being made to misdirect the activities of the BPP on a daily basis." Apartments and offices were regularly subjected to search. There were spurious arrests. All BPP offices, and many homes, were subjected to warrantless (and illegal) wiretaps. The organization was flooded by the FBI with informants and police agents who worked as provocateurs. A few days later the BPP office in Los Angeles was attacked by police.

False criminal charges were also lodged against BPP local and regional leaders. In April 1969, 21 leading cadre members of the New York City Chapter of the Black Panther Party (author included) were indicted and arrested on conspiracy charges. The so-called Panther 21 case was based solely on the allegations of three undercover NYPD officers who posed as Panther members. One of these undercover Black "BOSSI" (aka BSS) operatives, Detective Gene Roberts, had years earlier infiltrated Malcolm X's Organization of Afro-American Unity (OAAU) and was on Malcolm's security detail at the Audubon Ballroom when Malcolm was gunned downed and killed. The entire Harlem chapter leadership and its regional field secretary, Dhoruba Bin Wahad, were incarcerated. It was at this juncture in the covert and overt repression of the BPP that Assata Shakur, then a student at City College of New York, became active in BPP programs as a National Committees to Combat Fascism (NCCF) medical cadre in Harlem's Washington Heights.[8]

Despite escalating state repression and attacks by various Black groups and Black intelligentsia the BPP's influence continued to grow with each police and reactionary attack on its members and programs. What was once a local BPP newsletter became the "Black Community News Service" and the voice, as well as the revolutionary image, of the BPP. Sales of the BPP newspaper skyrocketed becoming the primary funding source for BPP operations.[9] After the armed Sacramento BPP demonstration, the Party dropped

---

and disrupted the BPP."

8   In May 1971, the Panther 21 defendants that actually went to trial were acquitted of all charges.

9   The FBI quickly understood this. In an August 19, 1970, airtel to the Director captioned "Counterintelligence Program" the FBI's New York Field Office stated that the New York FBI Office "realizes that one of the most effective Black nationalist propaganda operations is the sale and distribution of the BPP newspaper, *The Black Panther* in the New York City area. . . . The NYO realizes the importance of negating the financial benefits coming to the BPP through the sale of its newspaper. Continued efforts will be made to derive logical and practical plans to thwart this crucial BPP operation."

the hyphenated "for self-defense." The BPP began national organizing efforts to unify the radical left in America in a common "front" against police brutality, in early 1968.

Despite the race and class analysis that drove BPP activities, the organization and the Black Liberation Movement were ill prepared to cope with the historic moment. The BPP's strategic vision by late 1968 became increasingly focused on the burgeoning corporate police state and what its leading members saw as the precipitous consolidation of corporate, military, and police power that would criminalize and crush future civil unrest, and politically redirect popular antiwar sentiment into more "institutional" avenues of reform. The slogan and war cry of the BPP, "Power to the People, Black Power to Black People," had distilled in a few words, accompanied by a clenched fist, the sentiments of millions of people who felt controlled and exploited by the white-supremacist state, culture, and political system. But slogans only reflect reality; they do not change it. The BPP, and all progressive movements of the period, were living on the cusp of the historic reformation of two systems of economic and political control: corporate/capitalist democracy and authoritarian state socialism. Both systems, fundamentally hierarchal and elitist, would ultimately coalesce into variations of national security state model that typify both so-called "democratic" (Western) and "authoritarian" (Eastern) states today.

Creating a New Generation of Black Reformers

Before stepping down as president, Lyndon B. Johnson (after consultation with "Black leaders": businessmen, and politicians) launched his "War on Poverty," opening up the coffers of the government to anyone who could calm the Ghetto Fires (rebellions) that each year consumed urban America and tarnished the image of the U.S. as a democracy. Employing government and corporate largess to capital-starved Black inner-city communities had immediate political consequences. Radical change was out—and liberal reformism was in. The class nature of many Black institutions became the determining factor in race politics. The dividing of the Black liberation/civil rights movement along class lines would mean that the Panthers faced immediate and imminent class opposition from newly minted "anti-poverty pimps" and apolitical organizations eager for government funding. The launching of the War on Poverty significantly affected the grassroots Black narrative of "Black Power" versus integration politics and African American subservience to the two-party system. The money and "access" to white corporate America provided under the War on Poverty was just what the doctor ordered to wean marginal middle-class Blacks off any radical notions of collective empowerment rather than selfish individualism. But the BPP was not reformist. Alongside its community programs for radical reform was a genuine commitment to revolution, an advocacy of and preparation for a radical transformation of U.S. Society. Unlike many leading "civil rights" organizations of the time, the BPP believed that only with a revolution of values and radical change of political power in the dominant white society could Black political self-determination occur. In the politically expedient embrace of Johnson's "Great Society" and civil rights legislation, Richard Nixon ascended to the U.S. presidency and immediately pushed the "1968 Omnibus Crime Bill" through a compliant Congress, thereby providing law enforcement with additional tools for containment of racial unrest under the pretext of the "war on crime."

There was also police murder and violence. For example, on December 4, 1969, Chicago police, aided by information provided by an FBI informant, fired hundreds of rounds into the apartment of Chairman Fred Hampton, killing him and BPP member Mark Clark. Fred Hampton was killed as he lay in his bed, drugged from the Seconal secretly given to him. The U.S. government understood that the Panthers, unlike the majority of African American civil and human rights organizations, clearly understood the crucial and pivotal issue of racist violence in America and its deep connection to the state and its "criminal justice system." Consequently, the Panthers' perception of organized armed resistance to state repression, terrorism, and criminalization of Black youth as essentially a strategy of "imposition of political consequences" for state-sponsored terrorism. It was as necessary to any people's struggle for freedom from a powerfully entrenched and violent adversary as nonviolent mass protests. History supported the Panthers' perception. Whenever people—the lower classes, exploited, and disenfranchised—rise up against their rulers inevitably the police/military apparatus of the state violently represses any popular uprising, movement, civil disobedience that threatens the existing order.

The attempt by the State of California to execute the leader of the BPP marked the beginning of an escalated and coordinated national police campaign to eliminate the Panthers' local and regional leadership. By 1969 the popularity of the BPP extended far beyond inner-city neighborhoods. Functional alliances were formed that were based on professed principles derived from anti-imperialist and Afrocentric liberation movements (the latter an ongoing radicalization of Malcolm X's internationalist concepts) accompanied with a class analysis based on the African American experience. The

BPP's radicalism affected other national minorities who formed cadre-like community defense formations: the Brown Berets (Chicano/Mexicana), the Young Lords Party (Puerto Rican), the Young Patriot Party (working-class/ student white youth) are the more commonly known. By mid-1969, the BPP put out a national call for a "United Front Against Fascism" that challenged the radical left in general and the Black nationalist movement in particular to build in their communities democratic and institutional frameworks to combat the militarization of police and state repression. Police decentralization and community control of public safety were the ascendant features of this consolidation effort.

But the BPP had to respond to the infiltration, police raids on its offices, targeted assassination of its leaders, prosecution of its leaders, and suppression of its major source of income: *The Black Panther* newspaper. Its first response to state repression was to "close the Party" to new membership. This would be organizational anathema for a "mass-based political party," but the BPP was no ordinary "mass political party" or left radical formation. The BPP, circa 1966–1971, was a paramilitary political as well as socio-cultural formation that, by default, represented the historical Black armed resistance to violent white supremacy in America. Understood in these terms, it is self-evident that the BPP was not armed merely for revolutionary theater, macho posturing, or publicity, but to assert in the most direct terms possible Black people's right to resist racist attacks and police repression.

Given the huge disparity between the power of the state and a small civilian organization, the BPP's survival required and generated an underground component, a clandestine capability to achieve and underscore the political and strategic objectives of the Party. Although the BPP was popular it could be physically eradicated and isolated if it did not expand its influence and support base. Emerging from the BPP's call for radical unity against the burgeoning power of the militarized police state were local coalitions designated "National Committees to Combat Fascism." NCCF chapters sprang up across the U.S. in places where BPP chapters had either been depleted by police attack or had never existed. The timeliness of the call to political arms against rising police state–style repression was evident by the fact that radical whites, progressive students, organized their own NCCF chapters in communities where they struggled and lived. This BPP strategy—to build a broader radical "United Front Against Fascism" and consolidate the prevailing anti-establishment youth culture behind its leadership, (i.e., a Black Liberation Movement and a politically insurgent "Black Power" movement)—was only partially successful. But it nonetheless alarmed law enforcement authorities and discomfited their Black collaborators.[10] The NYPD, in particular, noted the BPP/NCCF-led effort to decentralize police departments in major cities with alarm.[11]

The FBI's fear index of the BPP increased in geometrical proportion to the effectiveness of the BPP's political influence over a broad spectrum of America's antiwar movement and the New Left. The public adulation by a significant segment of African American people was at an all-time high. BPP international solidarity with the Cuban Revolution, Palestinian people's struggle for self-determination, and direct relations with anti-imperialist liberation movements on the African continent were equally alarming, and the Party's penetration of the U.S. military as well as its connection to European left and student movements elicited the scrutiny of agencies outside of domestic law enforcement. U.S. military intelligence units, the CIA, U.S. State Department all targeted and monitored BPP international activities.

Achieving Legal and Moral Legitimacy by Rewriting and Ignoring the History of Black Self-Defense

By May of 1971, despite the considerable amount of money and support the Panther 21 and similar cases had raised for the Party, and the international success of the "Free Huey" campaign that resulted in Newton's acquittal and release from jail, BPP resources were depleted and programs cut back due to the relentless overt and covert police attacks and prosecutions. COINTEL-PRO operations continued and escalated. To exacerbate regional, personal, and political differences, the FBI had embarked upon a plan (eventually successful) to split the Black Panther Party into two factions: one on the West Coast which they called the "Newton" faction, and one of the East Coast termed the "Cleaver" faction, after Eldridge Cleaver.[12] While many may debate whether the split would have occurred even without FBI instigation, it is

10   Sensing the threat posed by such coalitions, the NYPD dispatched detectives to attend the founding conference 3,000 miles away in Oakland. They filed a detailed report listing all speakers and the topics that they addressed. See NYPD document, from Detective Gene Roberts to the Commanding Officer, July 21, 1969.

11   See NYPD document from the Commanding Officer, BSS, August 6, 1969, entitled "The Black Panther Party and the United Front Against Fascism," discussing in detail the proposal to decentralize police departments.

12   In late 1968 Eldridge Cleaver, facing incarceration resulting from a police shootout, fled the United States. He eventually made it to Algeria where he and others founded the BPP's International Section. Many of the COINTELPRO operations focused on creating dissention between Cleaver in Algeria and Newton who, after his release, remained in Oakland, California.

beyond dispute that the FBI and local law enforcement played a central role in making the split violently irreconcilable. Using information gleaned from their wiretaps and informants, some highly placed in BPP national headquarters, the FBI created a mindset within the BPP that leaders of one faction were intent on killing the other. As one FBI document noted:

> It appears that Newton responds violently to any questioning of his actions or policies or reluctance to do his bidding. He obviously responds hastily without getting all the facts or consulting with others.
>
> The Bureau feels that this near hysterical reaction by the egotistical Newton is triggered by any criticism of his activity, policies or leadership qualities and some of this criticism undoubtedly is the result of our counter-intelligence projects now in operation. The present chaotic situation within the BPP must be exploited and recipients must maintain the present high level of counterintelligence activity.[13]

FBI COINTELPRO machinations did result in deaths. Fred Bennett, Robert Webb, and Sam Napier were three of those victims. In an April 5, 1971, FBI memorandum, the New York office gleefully reported that the "dichotomy" in the BPP created by COINTELPRO had resulted in the death of Webb, apparently by Newton supporters. After the retaliatory killing of Sam Napier for Webb's assassination in New York, the FBI lamented that with the confusion in the BPP many East Coast members chose to go underground, making it difficult to engage in COINTELPRO-like activities.[14] They noted that it would obviously be "detrimental to the continuing efforts" of COINTELPRO should the two factions reach a détente.[15]

The BPP's principled stand on the right of Blacks to defend themselves led them to respond to legalized racist repression by deepening and resourcing the BPP's clandestine organization. Self-defense in face of violent state repression could not remain reactionary, passive. Self-defense had become proactive, retaliatory, a political consequence, "illegal" resistance to "legal injustice." Armed struggle against state and rightwing racist violence and criminal elements that profited from the debilitation of the Black community—e.g., heroin, cocaine, dealers and street-sets terrorizing Black neighborhoods—devel-

---

13   See FBI airtel from Director to New York, Los Angeles, San Francisco, and Boston, January 28, 1971, captioned "COINTELPRO."

14   Napier was the West Coast distribution manager for the *Panther* newspaper

15   See FBI airtel from New York to Director, April 5, 1971, captioned "COINTEL-PRO."

oped as the distinct adaptation of East Coast Panthers to COINTELRPO targeting the New York 21, Geronimo Pratt, and the International Section of the BPP led by Eldridge Cleaver. The Black Liberation Army (BLA) was the conscious response of those targeted by COINTELPRO for police-style assassination or imprisonment. Some BPP members fled underground to avoid the COINTELPRO-inspired violence. Two examples were Zayd Malik Shakur, former NY Chapter Deputy Minister of Information, and Sundiata Acoli, a Panther 21 member. Both Zayd (who was killed) and Sundiata (captured) were with Assata Shakur when she was shot and wounded on the New Jersey Turnpike. Others chose to go underground to further revolutionary activity; many of today's Black political prisoners with their activism rooted in the BPP/BLA are from this group.

It must be noted that the choice of clandestine armed resistance in response to increased militarization of the police and effective COINTEL-PRO-orchestrated state repression of the BPP had an even broader historical basis in white-supremacist subjugation of African people in the U.S. Like all of white America's racist stereotypical fears, white supremacy evolves to encompass the times and the shifts in class and race relations. When the BPP sent an armed delegation to the California state capital to protest changes in then-existing California gun laws aimed at curtailing armed "Panther Patrols" monitoring police conduct in the Bay Area's Black community, it intensified the simmering debate over gun control, specifically whether the Second Amendment actually applies to the descendants of slaves. Of course, the debate wasn't worded that way. Then as now the controversy over modern gun control is coded, designed to conceal white-majority population fears of Blacks and peoples of color. Gun regulations are more related to abridging the rights of Black Americans to armed self-defense against the organized police terror of the state than to keeping guns out of the hands of crazy apolitical criminals who, regardless of legal gun restrictions, acquire guns illegally.

When the FBI embarked on its sixties-era disinformation campaign to criminalize Black radicalism it resorted to the time-honored white American practice of demonizing Black people, a practice still employed today with descriptive terms like "thug" and "super-predators" to characterize Black protesters and rebellious Black youth. In white America's mind-set the word "criminal" has replaced "Black" as the bogeyman behind the call for stiffer gun control regulation. While right-wing gun advocates drape themselves in the Second Amendment and cloak racist vigilantism with the euphemism of "a well-regulated militia" (as stated in the Constitution), it is clear to any objective student of history that policing of Blacks in southern states was the rationale for ratification of the Second Amendment. The establishment of a "well-regulated militia" was a concession not only to states' rights, but also to the institutionalization of armed slave patrols. The institutions of modern law enforcement, especially across the South, derive their origins from these slave patrols and slave codes. The generic term "law-abiding citizens" used by gun control advocates and gun lobbies to delineate those who can legally own guns only serves to underscore the historical criminalization of Black life. This is one reason why recent mass murderers had little problem acquiring legal firearms—they weren't Black and threatening, i.e. did not have a menacing criminal persona. Cosmetic gun control reforms only attempt to address this anomaly by identifying domestic violence, mental illness, and pathological social behavior as "enlightened" reasons for non-issuance of gun licenses. These are categories many of today's armed white law-enforcement personnel themselves fit into without similar vetting.

Debate surrounding gun ownership laws presently in effect revolves around "criminal background checks" to legally proscribe access to firearms. It is a bit of legal artifice, based at least partly on universal police practices of criminalizing Blacks by employing a plethora of seemingly innocuous "stop and frisk" tactics and unwritten codes governing officer's "discretionary" suspicion of "criminal" behavior—ranging from "driving while Black" to the absurdity of "suspicion of being suspicious" (as in the Freddie Gray case). These practices obscure the racial motive behind criminal background checks that seldom apply to the majority of whites, who are less likely to experience run-ins with the law and therefore more likely to be considered "law-abiding" and eligible. Racist law enforcement along with mass incarceration, another legal device for racial and social control, further reinforces a "whites only" access to gun ownership, use of weapons for self-defense, and the overall societal militarization. Codifying "gang-related activity" as essentially a crime-by-association, for example, virtually ensures that five out of ten Black males living in economically marginalized communities—those that are subject to political gerrymandering, housing discrimination, and high unemployment—are legally ineligible for gun ownership, merely by living in close proximity to each other. Entire Black communities are thereby unable to defend themselves against armed attacks either by predominantly white police forces or armed white vigilantes. These Black communities are not only unable to organize themselves against racial violence from without, but are incapable of organizing themselves against criminal violence from within, and therefore must rely on racist institutional law enforcement for protection. This obviously contrived paradigm of Black defenselessness is so pervasive that supposedly "law-abiding" Black people who "legally" qualify for gun ownership are afraid to pursue their "right to bear arms" for fear of being mistaken for a criminal by Eurocentric law enforcement!

In the final analysis, fear of armed Blacks was the driving force transforming white America's gun culture into an "inalienable" right to bear arms—right up there with Mom's cherry pie and Disneyland. When the U.S. Constitution was ratified, hundreds of substantial slave uprisings had occurred across the South. Black freedom dreams had always agitated the captive Africans' waking nightmare of chattel servitude. As mentioned earlier, Blacks outnumbered whites in many areas, requiring state "militias" to both prevent and put down slave rebellions. Torturing and lynching our ancestors was the slaveholders' class war on self-radicalized African slaves who dared take up arms against their rightful "owners."

The BPP, in 1967, understood this history on a very fundamental level. It was imprinted on our DNA. We clearly comprehended, if only spiritually, that racist police violence and the suppression of Black human rights, like the institution of chattel slavery itself, could only exist and function in a police state. To stand against the "pigs of the power structure" was to reaffirm the freedom dreams of our ancestors, to reclaim our humanity. For the BPP, and Black radicals generally, Malcolm X's statement that "if you are Black and born in America, you were born in prison" meant Blacks in America lived and died at the whim of white supremacist power, and therefore existed as inmates of a police state. What "warden" would protect us from the bullets and mace of the police?

Today, the racist militarized police have replaced the institutional function of the state "militias" that enforced the slave codes of 18th and 19th century America. The routine and cavalier police murders of peoples of color can only occur in a police state. The violent repression of minorities, and racist, sexist violence so endemic to American society only finds expression through the historical continuum of white male supremacy and the sociopolitical Frankenstein of America's corporate two-party system of electoral "democratic fascism." In the 21st century the "national security state" that evolved from the loins of America's slaveholding propertied classes has reduced all American citizens, Black and white workers, the poor and the middle class, to the category of potential "criminals" and self-radicalizing "terrorists." It has classified anti-racist protest and anti-establishment expression as distortions of "freedom of speech" and thereby subversive, subjecting unarmed marginalized communities to vigilante violence and state repression. In 1967, the BPP revealed that America's gun rights advocates had only got it half twisted. It was not the unbridled capitalist state they feared; it was all of us not endowed with white skin male privilege, wealth, and the human right to self-defense. This became self-evident when the State of California passed its anti-Panther gun laws with hardly a peep out of the National Rifle Association in 1967.

Black Liberation Army—Striking Back

After the killings of several Black youth by the NYPD in 1970 and '71, there were shootings of police in New York City in the spring of 1971. Other armed attacks occurred in California and elsewhere. In communiqués to the media, the "Black Liberation Army" claimed responsibility for those attacks. In response, President Richard Nixon   at a White House meeting with FBI Director J. Edgar Hoover, John Ehrlichman, and others—ordered a "full-out" law enforcement effort to capture former BPP members who might have been involved in the attacks. The initial investigation, called "Newkill" by the FBI, would become a joint FBI-NYPD effort that would serve as a model for later police-federal collaborations such as the Joint Terrorism Task Force.[16] FBI agents who were involved in COINTELPRO became part of the Newkill task force. BPP members who were then underground—and many who were not—were considered "logical suspects" and targeted for arrest. The FBI director ordered the New York FBI Office to review appropriate files of "Black extremist" organizations, including those of so-called Third World groups to develop additional "logical suspects" and include those organizations and their leaders in target assignments given to outside agency sources. Even known Black drug dealers were leaned on for information and their networks threatened with shutdown if they failed to cooperate. Hoover instructed his minions "to consider the possibility that both attacks might be the result of revenge taken against New York City police by the Black Panther Party as a result of its arrest of BPP members in April 1969."[17]

---

16   The creation of "Newkill" was ordered by President Richard Nixon. In an FBI memorandum authored and signed by J. Edgar Hoover himself, he states to senior officials that he had "just left a long conference with the President . . . [and assured him] that we had offered the full facilities of the Bureau" to the NYPD. See Memorandum for Mr. [Clyde] Tolson and others, May 26, 1971. In a memorandum created a day later the FBI had alerted "all of its confidential sources in the racial, criminal, and security fields" to target possible suspects in the shootings.

17   See FBI teletype from the director to New York, May 25, 1971. The "arrest of BPP members in April 1969" is a reference to the Panther 21 conspiracy case. All of those that had gone to trial were acquitted on May 13, 1971.

Assata Shakur, who was recruited into the medical cadre of the Harlem chapter of the BPP, aligned herself with the East Coast "Cleaver" faction, and though never initially a COINTELRPO target she became a primary target of the FBI's post-COINTRELPRO anti-urban guerrilla terrorism investigations—collectively labeled under her slave name (JoAnne Chesimard) as "Chesrob." Chesrob became a national anti-urban guerrilla investigation in disguise, aimed directly at destroying BLA soldiers and their clandestine infrastructure. By early 1972, the media labeled her the "soul" of the Black Liberation Army. She was labeled a suspect in virtually every New York City bank robbery where a woman was thought to have participated. Although "Chesrob" was nominally an FBI bank robbery investigation, it was really another coordinated NYPD-FBI effort to capture or kill underground BPP members and BLA members.

In a few short years, former BPP members and BLA soldiers Harold Russell, Woody Green, Anthony Kimu White, and Twyman Meyers were killed during armed confrontations with the police. Others were arrested, tried, and convicted for incidents claimed by or thought to have been committed by the BLA.[18] It mattered not to prosecuting agencies whether those arrested were legally "guilty" or "not guilty." What was important was that the counterinsurgency begun under COINTELPRO, and continued under programs such as Newkill and Chesrob, effectively covered their ongoing racist repression of former BPP members and their supporters with criminal charges and prosecutions. Conspiracy trials of the sixties were emotional and cumbersome affairs that often resulted in acquittals of the defendants and creation of liberal "cause célèbre" figures, such as the Panther 21, Bobby Seale, and Dhoruba Bin Wahad.

It is in the context of the post–Panther 21 acquittal, the fiasco of the Chicago 7 conspiracy trial, and the framing of Bobby Seale in New Haven for murder, that Assata Shakur's May 2, 1973, arrest on the New Jersey Turnpike must be viewed. Along with BPP members Zayd Malik Shakur and Sundiata Acoli (an acquitted Panther 21 defendant, former NASA employee, and computer genius), she was stopped on the New Jersey Turnpike for "driving while Black." It is more likely that the troopers learned the identities of those in the car shortly before it was stopped. In any event, a shootout erupted. Zayd Malik

---

18 These include Albert "Nuh" Washington, Anthony Jalil Bottom, Herman Bell, Henry "Sha Sha" Brown, Teddy Jah Heath, Robert "Seth" Hayes, Safiya Bukhari, Ashanti Alston, Victor Cumberbatch, Oscar Washington, and Dhoruba Bin Wahad, author of this article.

Shakur and one trooper were killed. Assata was shot while her hands were in the air attempting to surrender. She was arrested. Sundiata Acoli, though injured, managed to escape but was captured a few days later in the woods like a runaway slave.

Assata was then tried for the numerous acts in which she was suspected of participating. Each trial resulted in acquittals or dismissals. It was the May 2, 1973, incident that gave rise to her only conviction and life sentence. Sundiata Acoli was also convicted in a separate trial and sentenced to life. Assata was liberated from her New Jersey prison in November 1979 and eventually surfaced in Cuba, where she was granted political asylum.

Given the rapprochement of America's relations with Cuba, Assata and her legal advisors can and should use any available means and arguments to keep her safe and free. But everyone else—supporters and those interested in justice and in an end to racist and political repression—should, as a matter of principle, place her case, and the "terrorist" designation placed on her by the FBI, in its proper context: as the continuation of a criminalization and demonization of the Black Liberation Movement. Assata's guilt or innocence in relation to the actual charges is totally and absolutely irrelevant. Assata was part of a movement that sustained and suffered massive police and state repression under COINTELPRO, Newkill, and Chesrob. This movement for Black self-determination, the right to control institutions within the Black community and the right to self-defense, was declared "terrorist" by the U.S. government's law enforcement agencies charged with executing its racist political destruction. With its recent posting of Assata Shakur on the FBI's Most Wanted Terrorists list, U.S. law enforcement and the U.S. Justice Department under Barack Obama reaffirmed its past illegal policies of domestic repression of political dissent, racial and the religious demonization of minority and immigrant populations. This is the political message that the "terrorist" label carries. It is our job to flatly reject that argument and to re-affirm the right of Black people and all people of color to self-determination. While it is true Assata Shakur is the victim of an injustice, that injustice is not only administered by the state but also by her so-called supporters: progressive civil libertarians and Black cultural figures who proclaim her "innocence" and dismiss the movement from which she emerged as a mere "law enforcement fantasy" propounded to rationalize their illegal police actions and give them the cover of law. Assata Shakur, in a so-called post-racial era that boasted a "Black" man in the White House, is made into a Black Madonna of abstract resistance by "millennial" activists—disconnected as an activist, freedom fighter, and soldier of a legitimate anti-racist and anti-imperialist movement. Clearly such a disconnect is in the political eye of the beholders and not derived from the actual history of the movement or the Black radical tradition.

Progressives and civil libertarians must understand that what happened to Assata was but one part of a series of episodes during a systemic and coordinated campaign to crush a domestic revolutionary movement. A state of war existed between the state and that movement. The state succeeded in smashing the movement, and its absence today should not serve as a license for political opportunism, to exploit and misinterpret the past to suit individual agendas or develop one's politics of "intersectional" oppression. Most of the political prisoners in American jails come from the BPP/BLA and Black nationalist movement. The system of visible and hidden racist control of African Americans that brought that movement into existence still persists, and because it still persists rebranding the Black political prisoner is unprincipled, leaving their movements up for opportunist reinterpretation. All Black political prisoners should be supported, not based on their guilt or innocence but based on the historical reality that their actions and current conditions of confinement were, and are, premised on their past relationship to a movement targeted by law enforcement and various agencies of the state—a targeting that was illegal, violent, and permanent.

It is for this reason that we should not become mired in a debate over legal "guilt" or "innocence." Was Nelson Mandela less a political prisoner worthy of freedom because he engaged in armed actions? In this country, the successful campaign to free the Puerto Rican political prisoners who were granted clemency by Bill Clinton provides an example. The campaign to free them did not admit or deny that they were "guilty" of seditious conspiracy or committed the acts attributed to them. Rather it emphasized that they are not "criminals" or "terrorists" but partisans in the struggle over Puerto Rico's destiny.

Although there are historical nuances to be considered, the political characterization of Assata as a "terrorist" by law enforcement and the cases of the Black political prisoners (her comrades) serve only one purpose—to criminalize the Black radical resistance to racist police repression: they were/ are part of a legitimate political movement for human rights and self-determination. Many of the BPP political prisoners from that era remain in jail: Anthony Jalil Bottom, 42 years; Sundiata Acoli, 40 years; Robert "Seth" Hayes, 41 years; Herman Bell, 40 years; Russell "Maroon" Shoatz, 40 years, and others. Albert "Nuh" Washington, Teddy Jah Heath, Bashir Hameed, and Abdul Majid died in prison after serving decades. Many of the arrested BPP/ BLA members had trials characterized by gross violations of due process at a time when COINTELPRO disclosures had not yet been made. But only two,

Dhoruba Bin Wahad (the author) and the late Geronimo Pratt, were able to secure reversals of their criminal convictions and freedom from imprisonment based on COINTELPRO files.

But once again, the issue after more than forty years is not guilt or innocence or whether the trials of Black activists were fair. These prisoners were and are part of a movement and after all of this time should be freed irrespective of their legal guilt or innocence. Is "restorative justice" possible after all these years? If so, to achieve it the "terrorist" label attached to our freedom fighters must be challenged not on an individual basis but politically and in correct historical context. Reconciling the so-called excesses of the past with the reality of post–Patriot Act America is a specious proposition at best. But to forthrightly declare that all political prisoners must be set free as one of many democratic principles of a mass campaign to curtail the political power of militarized law enforcement would seem more likely to succeed in freeing all political prisoners and changing Assata's status from "most-wanted terrorist" to that of a refugee from American racial and political repression.

The author wishes to acknowledge Robert J. Boyle, Esq., who contributed research and documents for this article.

NEW AGE IMPERIALISM

Killing Africa Softly, with Democracy
An excerpt from *The Pale Face Behind Finance Capital Speaks with a Forked Tongue* (an unpublished work)

Dhoruba Bin Wahad

New age imperialism has its own modern-day "moral" crusade and ethical artifice of "respect for human rights" to conceal its ignoble agenda and capitalist greed. Unlike the "old school" imperialism which relied on the ethical artifice of biblical white supremacy and "Christianizing the African heathen" to rationalize cold-blooded exploitation, new age imperialism's moral cloak is an unbelievably transparent and phony humanism and a cynical respect for "rule of law" (see note at end of article). This phony "humanism"—though not religiously based—nonetheless appeals to universal religious ethics of tolerance, and thereby distorts most people's perception of its racist and imperialistic political objectives. Likewise, the developed nations which practice this new age imperialism are endlessly lecturing poorer nations on the need to respect the rule of law while themselves employing "legal" artifice to justify military assassination of heads of state they disfavor, or to rationalize amoral economic embargoes of poorer nations and secure unimpeded access to Third World resources.

The new age imperialists consume an inordinate amount of the world's resources and are the major source of global pollution and toxic waste. Their ideals of "free market economy" and morality of conspicuous consumption are masked by the propaganda of "environmentally friendly" multinational corporations. But despite their rhetoric, the corporate managers of new age imperialism do not respect even the rule of "natural law" and derive maximum profits in a manner which pollutes the planet and depletes its ecosystem. New age imperialists encourage greed, individualism, and selfish acquisition of power. Their ethos of conspicuous consumption appeals not just to the rich and famous but to the down and out, who are encouraged to fantasize about becoming wealthy themselves even though the dichotomy between rich and poor benefits only the rich.

Finally, new age imperialism seeks to neutralize the need for Pan-African unity by further consolidating the political influence of capital over Africa's incomplete decolonization process. With this perspective in mind the current upsurge of "democratic reforms" in Africa takes on a more sinister role, revealing the hand of new age imperialism at work on the African continent along with the nature of its political agenda.

We can see that finance capital (read "dividends from colonialism") now requires a new integrated global marketing system based on consistent recirculation of perpetual debts. This integrated (or organic) global system is meant to supplant the old imperialist economic order and alleviate the economic anomalies of Cold War rivalry between competing capitalists and socialist systems. Since the end of the Cold War, the introduction of "free market" measures on the individual "socialist" economies of Africa, were accompanied by shifts in the political policies of those African states toward a "voluntary" form of new age imperial controls and away from Pan-African interdependence. That is to say, what is supported by the major industrial and financial centers of global commerce is not "democracy" or promotion of human rights per se but promotion of those Africans who support policies of "liberal investment opportunities" and "free market development."

Only by promoting Eurocentric "political democracy" as the sole atmosphere conducive for "investment" can the integration of Third World resources into a global marketing system that fully (organically) services the needs of U.S. and European finance capital be accomplished. Colonialism integrated Africa into European economic development while under-developing Africa. New age imperialism does the same thing, but with a different twist: it integrates African "development" into European economic supremacy by regulating Africa's markets, reinvesting African debt payments, and restricting Africa's access to capital.

It is my opinion that global economic integration, as defined by the developed industrial economies, represents the highest form of neocolonialism to date. It is imperialist by definition because of its wholesale incorporation and co-optation of post-colonial progressive ideas. Having said all this, it is also important to emphasize that this paper is not an attempt to discredit or subvert any particular African government or negate the achievements of progressive African regimes, especially those regimes which developed from the anti-colonial liberation movements of the sixties and seventies. The fact that this clarification is necessary in the first place indicates the relatively low level of support among African heads of state for bold and revolutionary Pan-African initiatives and their deliberate marginalization of serious Pan-African proposals made by non-governmental organizations as "utopian" whenever such proposals do not coincide with their parochial "national" interests.

Perhaps one possible explanation for this hostility to Pan-African political practice is the fact that many of today's African leaders did not emerge from anti-colonial struggles as revolutionary nationalists, but instead assumed state power as a consequence of military coups, tribal based power struggles, European meddling in regional politics, or a combination of all of these factors. For many such persons, "African unity" is a concept best left in the realm of theory because only in a disunited Africa do they achieve political relevancy. Indeed, this paper questions the very proposition that the European archetype of government, the nation-state, can provide for the empowerment of the African masses absent Afro-centric social, political, and cultural foundations—let alone express the genuine interest of the African peoples. This in itself may present a conceptual problem for some progressive brothers and sisters. After all, who wouldn't be somewhat skeptical of an Afro-centric paradigm emerging from Africa's current political quagmire?

Unwarranted optimism aside, there undoubtedly are individual African leaders of good intent; therefore, the question needs to be asked: Is Africa's destiny a matter of subjective leadership and personality alone, or is it a matter of seizing the historical moment before the historical moment seizes all of us?

I fully understand that inevitably, whenever a Black person is critical of a political modality such as the European nation-state, he or she runs the risk of being marginalized by most African politicians—especially those who enjoy the class/caste privileges derived from administration of the postcolonial European-style state so cunningly grafted onto the African political mentality. Should opportunism, political or otherwise, persist as the raison d'être of African state power, it would not give anyone much hope for radical change in the conduct of African affairs. But should Africans genuinely interested in Africa's total empowerment transcend their own petty differences and privileges, the conduct of African affairs will be transformed literally overnight. First, we must understand that Africans and Africa are not the primary enemy even though there surely exist African enemies of the African race. We must learn to give each other the benefit of doubt, rather than the certainty of condemnation. History is indeed the best subject to reward all research. We need to apply our history to the problems confronting Africa and act accordingly.

Note: The "rule of law" vis-à-vis the European nation-state as a Western concept is relatively new, dating essentially back to the Magna Carta. However, it is—from an Afrocentric perspective—*an artifice by which to institutionalize and regularize territorial conquest or racial subjugation.* This is a historically accurate view and can be verified in exhaustive detail by examining British, French, Belgian, and Portuguese colonial records in Africa. For example, the annexation of West Africa by the British as the "Gold Coast Territory" is a classic case of a carefully devised matrix of legal definitions justifying crimes of British military aggression, fraudulent commercial dealings, religious persecution, chattel slavery, as well as the usurpation of a sovereign people's right to self-determination, theft of their land, and castration of their political institutions—actions which are still considered unacceptable behavior for national governments. Indeed, the USA, Britain, and their allies currently embargo a number of nations for supposedly practicing similar activity (e.g. Iraq, Iran, Cuba, Libya) and criticize others for employing varying degrees of "human rights" abuse.

MAN-CHILD IN REVOLUTION LAND

Jamal Joseph

On June 15, 2016, Kathleen Cleaver and I were in Harlem as the guest speakers at an event called "Black Power 50" at the Schomburg Center for Research in Black Culture. Sister Kathleen—now an attorney and law professor at Emory University—and myself—now a writer, director, youth mentor, and film professor at Columbia University—had an hour-long conversation about "Black Power" as first proclaimed in 1966 by the brilliant Stokely Carmichael, leader of the Student Nonviolent Coordinating Committee (SNCC), and its explosion to "All Power to the People" as demanded by Huey P. Newton, Bobby Seale, and the Black Panther Party on the streets of Oakland, California. I tried to frame it as a journey from pride and anger to awareness and revolution. There is no one correct narrative for political struggle and revolution—just as there is no one individual journey that speaks to how everyone in the struggle became active. In fact, there is no one struggle or one kind of activist.

There were people fighting the three major evils of poverty, racism, and war that Dr. King outlined in the seminal speech he gave at Riverside Church exactly one year before he was assassinated. There were people who felt they were fighting against the repressive capitalist system with the possible tools of armed struggle that Malcolm X talked about in a pivotal speech given at Oxford University six months before he was murdered. In between those great men and our times is a complex history of people, ideas, struggles, losses, and victories. The causes were just and many: women's rights, gay rights, children's rights, housing, antiwar, police brutality, hunger, medical care, prisons, political prisoners, education, immigration, labor, and more. Some called themselves revolutionaries, others activists, freedom fighters, nationalists, Pan-Africanists, feminists, socialists, communists, anarchists, humanists—or as poet, activist, and professor Sonia Sanchez calls it, "being a human being."

But the writer/director in me honors the spirit of the African griot—the storyteller who sat in the shade of the large baobab tree and wove tales that needed to both educate and entertain. If the griot was really academic and informative, the young people in the village might say, "You don't want to miss that griot, unless you're ignorant and want to take a nap cause you think he (or she) is boring as hell. Let's go to the next village cause their griot is popping and all the young folks are there." On the other hand, if you were a really entertaining griot who could sing, dance, do poetry, and play instruments, but your facts were wrong, people would call you out. "Yo, man, I know that griot is saying that Mustafa killed the lion on the hunt, but I was there and it was his little sister Keisha. Yep, seen it with my own eyes."

So, I started my "Black Power 50" remarks to a crowd of three hundred or so at the Schomburg with a griot-like story—a true story about an experience I had as a twelve-year-old boy with Pa Baltimore, my adoptive grandfather. His wife Noonie had raised me since I was five. Noonie was a domestic worker who cleaned houses and cared for other people's children (both Black and white). Pa had done everything—boxer, merchant marine, street vendor, numbers runner—a street hustler (but always hardworking and honest). Both Noonie and Pa's parents and older siblings had been slaves. I heard stories about slavery and firsthand accounts of lynching and the Klan. They were both proud Negroes. They had been followers of Marcus Garvey, members of the NAACP, and also Republicans because Lincoln and the Republicans had literally freed their families. Beyond being proud, Pa was what you called a "race man"—not only did he not fear white people, he didn't give a damn about white people. At a time when there were no Black studies programs and no mention of any Negroes in any of my history books, Pa (a man with a sixth-grade education) would home-school me about Crispus Attucks (a Negro who was the first to die in the American revolution), Benjamin Banneker (who designed clocks and also the layout of Washington, DC), Frederick Douglass, Harriet Tubman, and the abolitionist movement. His history lessons were informal, conversational, and impromptu, often held in the living room while I was trying to watch Grandma's old black-and-white TV. Here's the story I told the Schomburg audience:

Pa and I were watching a Tarzan movie—Pa in his favorite chair, me on the couch allegedly doing math homework. Tarzan swings across the screen on a vine doing his famous Tarzan yell. He lands to confront some evil white hunters who are holding a damsel in distress at rifle point. Africans (many of them white actors in black body paint) stand nearby looking fearful, bug-eyed, and ignorant. Tarzan calls out to the jungle in "Tarzaneze," and elephants, lions, tigers, and a cute chimp with an IQ far superior to the Africans charge in from all directions to help Tarzan defeat the evil hunters and rescue the damsel. Pa Baltimore watched the scene with great intensity before interrogating the TV (and me) with a "What the fuck is that? Tell me how in the hell a little cracker-assed baby fall out a plane and run the jungle! He can speak lion, tiger, monkey, and the Africans standing around like they crazy. Boy, change the damn channel!"

This was my introduction to critical media theory through the lens of race and class. I laughed because Pa's delivery was perfect and he had a PhD in cussing and talking smack. But he made me aware that racism was everywhere and that white America was shady.

After the audience had a good laugh I quoted an H. Rap Brown (now known as Imam Jamil Al-Amin) speech about cultural brainwashing. Rap's timing and delivery was on par with Pa Baltimore. "You wear black to funerals and white to weddings," Rap scowled. "In cowboy movies, the good guys wear the white hats, the villains wear black. Angel food cake is white cake, devil's food cake is black. Black magic is bad, white magic is good. Even Santa Claus!" Rap would then deliver the punchline. "Tell me how in hell a fat, redneck, camel-breath honkey can slide down a black chimney and still come out white! I'm telling you—you've been brainwashed!"

Kathleen and I talked about the rapid evolution of "Black Power" from the "Black is Beautiful" pride of Afros and dashikis to the direct action of campus take-overs and armed patrols of police by Black Panthers. We also talked about the Panthers' ideological expansion of "Black Power" to "All Power to the People" and the famous Panther breakdown of the greeting: "That means Black power to Black people!" Great Panther orators like Bobby Seale, Fred Hampton, or Kathleen herself would explain, "white power to white people, brown power to brown people, red power to red people, yellow power to yellow people, and Panther power to the vanguard!" For all those shocked that the Black Panthers would give a shout-out to white power, the Panthers would explain that "white power" and the oppression by the white power structure were not the same thing. In fact, most white people in the country were poor or working poor and being ripped off and stomped down by the same capitalist system that is oppressing people of color. Organizing the "masses" around the idea of revolutionary class struggle is what caused the Panthers to be attacked overtly by the police and covertly by the FBI's Counter Intelligence Program (COINTELPRO).

Kathleen and I went on to point out that Dr. King and Malcolm X were also killed when they started talking about capitalism and class struggle. Yes, people fighting for racial equality have been imprisoned and killed throughout U.S. history—but calling for class struggle and organizing the many into a progressive coalition is guaranteed to evoke fury from the ruling class.

Huey Newton and Bobby Seale, the founders of the Black Panther Party, understood that Black Power had to evolve beyond the affirming culture and fashion of "Black is Beautiful," the educational demands for Black studies, the co-op capitalist's demand for Black jobs and Black businesses, a Black exodus to the African motherland, or the Black nationalist's demand for a separate nation-state. A struggle that understood race and class oppression needed to fight for all oppressed people and demand "All power to (all) the people."

Then, from the stage of the Schomburg, I got to channel Bobby Seale and Fred Hampton, who sounded like preacher-poets when they would say, "That means Black power for Black people, white power for white people, brown power for brown people, red power for red people and Panther power to the vanguard!" The crowd applauded. Kathleen talked brilliantly about her evolution from a SNCC organizer to a member of the Black Panther Party's governing central committee. Stokely Carmichael (known later in life as Kwame Ture) was the first to give popular voice to "Black Power" as a response to the frustrations of nonviolent students and civil rights workers in the face of an increasingly brutal and violent white America. H. Rap Brown, another charismatic SNCC leader who followed Carmichael as chair of that organization, talked about self-defense and the revolutionary face of "Black Power" by saying that "violence is as American as cherry pie"—so why not be willing to shed blood and die for our liberation? When Rap got arrested on a gun charge in Louisiana, he told the press gathered as he was released on bail, "If you thought my rifle was bad, wait till you see my atom bomb!" Rap and Stokely both brought their brilliance, boldness, and swagger to the Black Panther Party and respectively served as minister of justice and prime minister. It was a high point in Panther history, when chapters were opening in some thirty-plus cities across the USA and all of the Panthers and rainbow supporters were united around freeing one major political prisoner: cofounder and minister of defense Huey P. Newton.

As a new young Panther who proudly and constantly wore my crisp new black beret and the black leather jacket that my grandma had given me for

Christmas, I thought all we had to do was free Huey and he would lead to us to the revolutionary promised land. Of course, we had to get the community ready for revolution so I worked with Afeni, Lumumba, Dhoruba, Sekou, Cetewayo, and other Harlem and Bronx Panthers organizing tenants, students, and health care workers. We stopped city marshals from throwing families out into the cold, took over hospitals and turned them into "people's clinics," kept schools open and taught classes during teachers' strikes that we felt were anti-community, escorted and brought food to the elderly, settled countless fights and disputes in the community without the help or the invitation of the police.

Being a Panther meant working in the community everyday—concrete action programs, not just words and slogans. "Freedom to a hungry person is a meal," I told the Schomburg audience; "liberation to a homeless person is a safe, warm, dry place to sleep." It's why the Panther free breakfast program remains one of the Party's greatest achievements. It was Bobby Seale's vision—he pointed out that young children can't be expected to understand that three apples plus two apples equals five apples when their stomachs are growling. Without funding or permission from anyone, the Panthers set about to address this problem and at the same time used the breakfast program to raise awareness by pointing out the "capitalist pigs'" lack of desire or interest in feeding our children—even though we are living in the richest nation in the world. We identified our communities as colonies that suffer the same exploitation and oppression as Third World colonies around the world. We identified the wealthy, privileged, and government zones as the mother country, and even called our beloved white comrades outside of the hood "white mother country radicals." My good buddy Neil, a white high school student from New Jersey, would drive his beat-up, peace-sign-covered Volkswagen van around to help me and other Harlem Panthers make our food pick-ups for the breakfast program. The breakfast program was all vision and dedication—no money. Panthers would ask churches and community centers to donate their kitchens and dining rooms. Many said no, but enough said yes. Then we would ask store owners in the neighborhood for weekly food donations. A case of milk and cereal here, a case of pancake mix and eggs there. Fliers would be handed to kids and their parents by enthusiastic young Panthers. And yes, we were young. I was one of the youngest at age fifteen, but most Panthers were in their teens and early twenties. The average age of a rank-and-file Panther member was nineteen or twenty. The first week at a location, ten or fifteen kids would show up for breakfast. By the end of the month, it would be between seventy-five and a hundred. It's estimated that the Panthers fed about thirty thousand kids nationally each week.

Kathleen and I used the breakfast program, health clinics, food baskets, clothing programs, and liberation schools as examples of revolutionary community organizing. My oldest son, Jamal Jr., a Columbia University MFA in film, has sickle cell anemia and bravely fought through some tough and near-fatal sickle cell episodes. He is an activist and one of the organizers of an annual sickle cell conference held at Mount Sinai Hospital. Last year, a white doctor who is a leader in sickle cell research opened his speech by giving credit to the Black Panther Party for having the first national program of sickle cell testing, and for raising awareness about sickle cell anemia.

There are community programs across the country (clinics, schools, clothing programs) that say they were inspired by Panther programs. Ericka Huggins (professor, Panther, former political prisoner) points out that the breakfast program shamed the government into funding food programs across the country—funding that Republicans are now trying to cut.

**

As a fifteen-year-old high school student, a choir boy, and a member of the National Association for the Advancement of Colored People (NAACP) youth council, my American dream was of college, becoming a lawyer, or in moments of liberated imagination, a star ship commander like Captain Kirk of *Star Trek,* my favorite TV show. My adoptive grandmother "Noonie" did her best as a single parent to instill her Baptist Church–rooted values of "love thy neighbor." My Black American reality was that Dr. King had been murdered, ghettos across America were going up in riots and flames, and I was a fatherless, angry man-child who had been called "nigger" and smacked around by white cops a few too many times.

After Pa Baltimore passed away from a stroke in a crowded, dirty hospital ward, I worked part-time as a stock and delivery boy at the supermarket so that Noonie wouldn't have to give me an allowance from her tight income—a combination of social security and part-time housekeeping work. I would sweep, mop, and vacuum so that Noonie would not have to do any more bending or scrubbing when she pulled her tired body up the stairs to our second floor apartment.

Noonie and I were close, I loved and respected her, but she was seventy and I was fifteen—and a hip, cool path to manhood was on the streets. The Bronx and Harlem street corners I passed and sometimes hung out on had gangs, drugs, craps games, fights, hustlers, foxy ladies, and patrolling cops that had to be eluded even when you were doing no wrong. The teens and men who held court there were living examples of how to walk, talk, swagger, and fight your way into the manhood ranking system of being a "cool," "bad," or "crazy" dude—which was the highest honor. The corners also had "warrior prophets" who talked about Black pride, progress, and revolution. Some would be respected "bad" and "crazy" dudes who had gone to prison or to the Vietnam War and came back with something they called "Black consciousness." They critiqued drugs, hustling, and violence as tools of oppression. They not only gave the corner contrast—they gave it context, and I was fascinated!

The evening news was filled with images of civil rights marchers and antiwar protesters being beaten and tear-gassed by cops and National Guard troops. Black militant leaders uttering phrases like "burn baby burn!"—not quite neo-Marxist revolution, but definitely a raised fist on the angry pulse of a lot of Black folks. The Afros, dashikis, and denim jackets the militants wore became the style of the day from schools to the street corners. We wore our Afros and dashikis to church, to marches, and to NAACP meetings. The elders frowned but tolerated us with memories of the "wild styles" they wore when they were young.

Then Dr. King was killed and style became ideology. A generation of Black youth became instantly radicalized. I went down to 125th Street where riots were happening and almost got shot by cops. A group of men I later found out were Panthers saved me and sent me home. A few days later I saw a news story about Black Panthers on TV.

In Oakland, California, Panthers would patrol the streets at night with legally owned shotguns and law books. Police brutality and false arrests dropped dramatically. The response of the state legislature was to change the gun laws so that Black Panthers could no longer do armed patrols. The Panther's response was to interrupt the hearings with guns and proclamations in hand. Panther leaders told the press that Black people had a constitutional right to bear arms to defend themselves.

Now I was more than fascinated—I was blown away! That night, as I watched *Star Trek*, I realized that Captain Kirk punched somebody out or used his phaser on damn near every mission. I may not be able to get on a star ship to promote justice in the universe, but I was boldly going to seek out the Black Panthers!

During the long subway ride to the Panther office, two of my older friends told me that I might have to kill a white dude or maybe even a cop to prove myself to the Panthers. I sat in the back of my first Panther meeting psyching myself with the courage to prove I was a "bad-assed, crazy dude."

In the middle of a discussion about better education, I jumped up and said that I was ready to get a gun and kill a white dude. The Panther running the meeting called me up and handed me a stack of books. He "armed me," but not the way I had anticipated.

In the coming weeks, the Panthers sent me on a number of missions. I had to make and serve pancakes to children in the Panthers breakfast program. I had to help tenants paint and make repairs to run down buildings that were on rent strike. I tutored first and second graders in the community-run Liberation Schools.

"Organize people around their needs," Afeni Shakur once told me. "A true revolutionary is motivated by love."

There were a couple of rifles in the Panther office and at Panther apartments. Fred Hampton had been murdered in his sleep during a raid by Chicago police. Panther homes and offices had been raided and even bombed around the country. Young Panthers took turns standing guard at night, waiting for the squad cars and tanks to come.

I was arrested at sixteen and indicted as part of the Panther 21 conspiracy case. Although acquitted of those charges, I would spend nine years in prison for leading raids on drug dens and hiding out people wanted by the authorities. "Hey, Scotty, beam me up!" No transporter beam came.

I instead received the wise advice from an old convict not to serve my time but to let my time serve me. I earned two college degrees, organized a theater company, and became a writer in prison.

But let's beam back to the Schomburg!

The public conversation with Kathleen and me turned to J. Edgar Hoover and the FBI's Counter Intelligence Program infamously codenamed COINTEL-PRO. With approval and funding from Congress, the FBI wiretapped, photographed, and filmed Panthers and other activists and organizations from Dr. King and SNCC to Students for a Democratic Society (SDS), the American Indian Movement (AIM), and the Young Lords, a Puerto Rican Street gang that evolved into a revolutionary party that believed in class struggle and Puerto Rican independence. Beyond gathering intelligence, the FBI launched a vicious campaign of disinformation which included writing and sending letters to Panthers and supporters designed to create suspicion and paranoia, using informers and undercover cops to provoke and frame Panthers, and providing false "intelligence" that incited local police to arrest, attack, and murder Panthers.

After an hour of conversation between Kathleen and me, we opened up for questions from the audience. "What do you think of Black Lives Matter compared to the Panthers?"

"They're different," Kathleen responded. "The Panthers talked about armed struggle and political organizing in the community. Now we go on protests over police killings and policy, as compared to a movement that wanted to dismantle state power and institutionalized racism and repression."

"What do you think about the New Black Panther Party?"

"Nothing!" Kathleen snapped. "Next question!" Most original Panthers feel that the New Black Panther Party is not worthy of discussion or recognition—especially after their brutal gang beat-down of Panther 21 icon Dhoruba Bin Wahad at one of their rallies in Atlanta. Besides berets and leather coats, nothing about the New Black Panthers resembles the Black Panther Party.

Then a twelve-year-old Black man-child named Phoenix stepped to the Q&A microphone.

"I want to be an activist but I don't want to go to prison or be killed," he stated in a voice filled with innocence and hope. If the room didn't stop, my own heart, mind, and spirit certainly did. Phoenix would not have to ask this question at a career and educational panel filled with doctors, lawyers, teachers, or alumni of great colleges and universities. But on considering activism as a calling, as a noble profession, young Phoenix had studied enough and learned enough to be rightfully afraid for his life. In that moment, I was reminded of how little had changed in fifty years since the founding of the Black Panther Party. If you read the 10-Point Program of the BPP, you'll be amazed at how unflinching and on-point it was about taking on critical issues facing the community.

> Point 2—We want full employment for our people.
> Point 3—We want decent housing fit for shelter for human beings.
> Point 7—We want an immediate end to police brutality.
> Point 8—We want all Black men and women freed from federal, state, city and county prisons.

You will also be saddened that none of the points in the 10-Point Program have been realized. In fact, prison populations have jumped from a few hundred thousand to 2.3 million people. Police terror continues. And our communities are impoverished and underserved.

But a twelve-year-old boy named Phoenix, brought to a Panther event by his educated and progressive mother, had the courage to stand up and express both his desire to make a difference and his fear of the price America imposes on those seeking change.

We assured Phoenix that not every activist winds up in prison or dead. I asked him to meet me after the event so I could tell him about a creative arts and youth activist program I cofounded with producing legend Voza Rivers and my wife Joyce. Our sons, Jamal Jr. and Jad, and daughter Jindai spent formative years in the program and are still passionate about arts and activism in their post-college years.

Later that week I spoke at a Harlem high school graduation. It was a celebratory event with many of the graduates in this dedicated school heading to college. I was caught off guard when the African American male principal presented the last diploma to the parents of an eighteen-year-old Black manchild who had been killed a few weeks earlier. For the second time in a week my world stopped. The same night I walked with my wife and daughter to a cool millennial restaurant on Malcolm X Boulevard in Harlem. French bistros, Italian cafés, and sushi lounges now line the former Lenox Avenue that had been home to collapsing tenements, liquor stores, and fish-and-chip joints. New wave Harlemites can walk from their million-dollar condominiums and multimillion-dollar brownstones to dozens of eateries and social gathering spots. A few feet away from one restaurant destination was a crowd of about fifty young people standing around a sidewalk altar of candles and flowers for another young Black man who had been killed: gang violence of rage turned inward—young men and women relegated to the Harlem apartheid zones of housing projects and sub-ghettoized blocks and buildings in the "New Harlem." These young men and women will never live in those condos or eat in those restaurants. The young men will have a one-in-eight chance of going to college but a one-in-three guarantee of going to prison. The young women will be the mostly likely to suffer physical and sexual abuse and to be infected with HIV. As they catch bits and pieces of Black Lives Matter protests on their cell phones, will there be any context, person, or movement that is in their communities, in their faces—in their hearts and spirit—letting them know that their lives matter?

The Black Panther community programs weren't just staffed by Panthers. There were men, women, teens, and elders from the block side by side with Panthers, giving out the food and clothing. Some became Panthers; others radicalized in different ways. Some just continued to be "good folk from the block who loved the community." Ask any Panther what our number one principal or belief was, and the guaranteed answer will be "to have an undying love for the people."

One of the points I made at the Schomburg that seemed to surprise the audience was something I was taught in an early political education class: that the goal of the Black Panther Party was not to have everybody in the Black community become a Panther, but rather to show the community—by example—the possibility of struggle and thereby make the Black Panther Party obsolete.

As my Panther teachers would say, "Freedom *Is*—we all know we're free; you dig?"

It has been forty-eight years since a skinny, fifteen-year-old had the courage and audacity to walk into a Panther office and ask for a gun. I am now a professor of professional practice of film at Columbia University, founder and executive director of Impact Repertory Youth Theater in Harlem, husband, and dad to three kids who attended Columbia and Brown. At many events, I am introduced as a former Black Panther. Many of us have cast the "former" aside and just say "Panther."

There are organizations that claim to be inspired by the Black Panthers, putting bounties on people and calling for armed rebellion. Members of the original Black Panther Party (many now in their '60s and '70s) cringe at this. In the sixties, the Panthers moved from guns and law books to service and community programs. Original Panthers would be patrolling the streets, this time with cell phone cameras as many young activists are doing. We would still be organizing and serving, in community-based free food, health, and education programs.

As Mao Zedong said in the *Red Book* which all Panthers carried, "Pay more attention to the condition of the masses and less attention to the methods of work." As my beloved Panther big sister Afeni said at the funeral of young Yafeu Akiyele Fula Odinga (aka Yaki Kadafi)—Panther Sekou Odinga and Yaasmyn Fula's son—choking back the pain at the loss of her godson Yafeu and the recent loss of her birth son Tupac: "As we cry for Yafeu and Tupac, look around at all these young people standing in the back of this church and the hundreds of others standing outside because they couldn't get in. They're alive and they need us!"

I walked into my youth program the Saturday following the Schomburg event, the high school graduation, and passing the Harlem street altar, feeling the weight of all I haven't done as a Panther, artist, educator, or activist. And there, among a group of twenty teens and tweens waiting to join the Impact Program, was young Phoenix and his brother Indigo. I breathed, I smiled, I gathered my young staff who had grown up in the program who now had returned as mentors and teachers.

And I said, "All power to the people. Let's begin."

Unidentified Panther 21 supporter, New York, circa 1970.

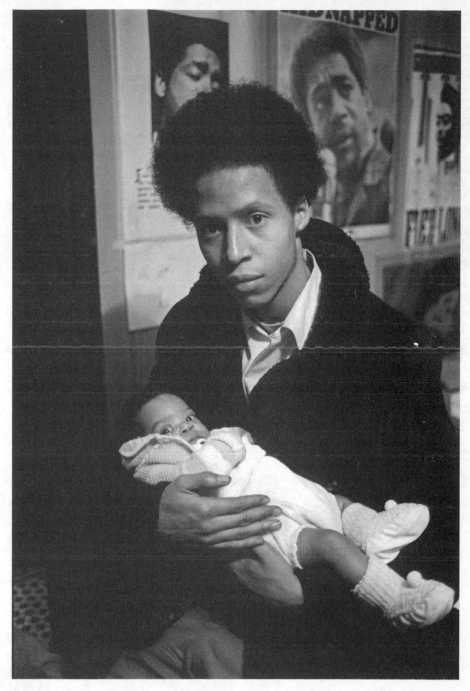

Jamal Joseph with unidentified baby.

Panther 21 codefendants Michael "Cetewayo" Tabor, Joan Bird, and Dhoruba Bin Wahad.

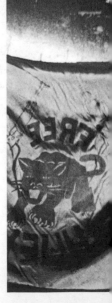

Panther activist Ila Mason and Panther 21 codefendant Jamal Joseph in political education class.

New York Black Panther Party Harlem office front, circa 1970.

Assata Shakur in Panther political education class.

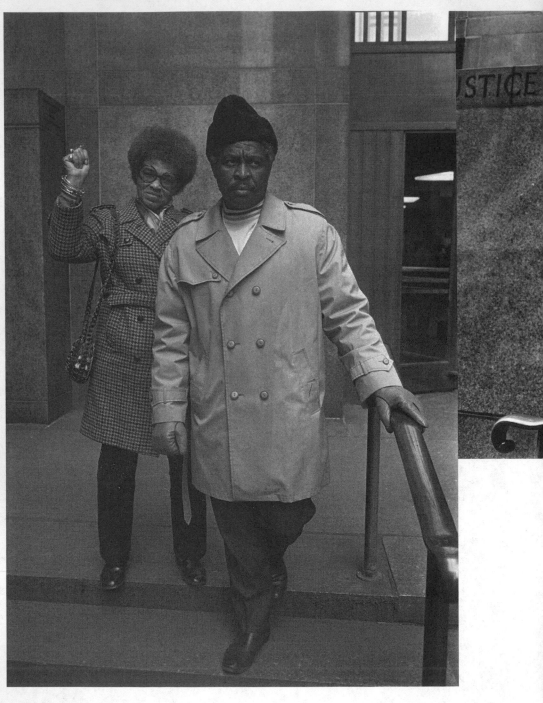

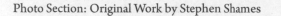

Haji *Abba* Salahdeen Shakur (with Mariyama Shakur), father of Panther 21 codefendant Lumumba Shakur and New York Panther activist Zayd Shakur, in front of the Manhattan courthouse during the trial.

Panther 21 codefendant Michael "Cetewayo" Tabor and Panther activist
Connie Matthews.

Dhoruba Bin Wahad.

Zayd Malik Shakur.

Jamal Joseph.

Unidentified Panther 21 supporters.

Panther picket line at the courthouse during the Panther 21 trial.

Unidentified Panther 21 supporter.

LOOK FOR ME IN THE WHIRLWIND

The Collective Autobiography of the New York 21

Kuwasi Balagoon
Joan Bird
Cetewayo
Robert Collier
Dharuba
Richard Harris
Ali Bey Hassan
Jamal
Abayama Katara
Kwando Kinshasa
Baba Odinga
Shaba Om
Curtis Powell
Afeni Shakur
Lumumba Shakur
Clark Squire

with an Introduction by
Haywood Burns

Look for me in the whirlwind or the storm, look for me all around you, for, with God's grace, I shall come and bring with me countless millions of black slaves who have died in America and the West Indies and the millions in Africa to aid you in the fight for Liberty, Freedom and Life.

MARCUS GARVEY, *writing from Atlanta Prison, February 10, 1925*

INTRODUCTION

I

In the processing, packaging and presenting of news involving group political trials, the mass media so often, perhaps inevitably, squeeze out the personal and human aspects of the defendants and they become numbers—Presidio 27, Chicago 8, Panther 21—cardboard, stereotyped one-dimensional composites. In these pages the defendants in the New York Panther trial reclaim their personalities, and we get to see them as individual people. In their own voices they trace in poignant detail their lives from early childhood down to their cells in the houses of detention. Despite any distortion that might be expected in tales told to the outside world through prison walls, the writers open themselves and their pasts, the autobiographies ring true, and we come to feel we know the defendants as people—in their differences and in their similarities. They are not to be dealt with as abstractions but as persons with families, with triumphs, with defeats, with different educational and occupational attainments. Some are from the rural South, some from the ghetto North, one from the West Indies. Some have received their higher education in colleges and universities, some in prisons and some in the streets. They come from family settings of varying degrees of stability. They are loved—some not enough perhaps, others perhaps indulged. But it is impossible to lump them in the cold isolation of the grand jury's indictment "People of the State of New York v. . . ." They are part of "the people," members of a community that swirls around them, protects them, beleaguers them, fortifies them, debilitates them, spurs them on to action. We cannot but be struck by the tenacity with which, on the whole, members of this community are able to carry on the survival fight in the face of appalling odds; the fierce independence of spirit and will shown by so many of the defendants' families; how, despite the vortex that would suck them down, they scuffle and scrape and reach out for some small branch of dignity to which they can cling, upon which they can clamber. We see families, with great effort, trying to give their children some of the opportunities for a "normal" childhood—though, of course, few of the larger society's norms ever apply in the ghetto. No one thinks of Panther defendant Eddie Joseph as Eddie Joseph, let alone as an ex-Cub Scout, choir boy and Junior NAACP member, or asks the question of how he came from the Junior NAACP to the Black Panther Party. (But few asked that question about Fred Hampton either.) No one thinks of Shaba as the friendly neighborhood paperboy or of Kinshasa or Joan Bird rehearsing for their Carnegie Hall piano or dance recitals. Their contributions to this book impress upon us their individual humanity, despite their common goals and common plight.

II

Though each has his or her individual story to tell, the authors have given us here the chronicle of a generation. It is the story of my own generation. Taken as a whole, the authors' experience is very representative of that of millions of young black men and women born around the time of World War II and growing up in the urban ghettos of the fifties. Throughout this period the Great Migration of blacks out of the South into the North, out of the country into the city, was in full swing. For decades blacks had been "going up the road," out of the canebrakes, cotton and tobacco fields, streaming into the Northern and Western industrialized metropolises, brimming with hope—only to have that hope shrivel and finally die, while in the suffocating urban slum it became clear that the journey had only succeeded in replacing one form of racism and exploitation with another. Many of the authors here came to the Big Apple (New York) from small Southern towns—like Vernon, Texas; Lumberton, North Carolina; McCellonsville, South Carolina—and from their earliest days knew American racism in its most overt form. Others, though born in Harlem, had Southern roots. All had to learn to survive in that black world north of 110th Street.

Harlem of the early and mid-fifties, despite its perennial desperation, preserved in many ways a convivial communal spirit. Cool was in. Black music was providing the fuel for a national rock 'n roll explosion. Street-wise finger-popping diddy bops, well togged, crooned in doorways, working to get the heavy bass part right and the right number of background "ooo-wahs." The spirit up and down the avenue was, in general, good. But among young blacks there was the destructive scourge of gang warfare, responsible for the maiming and death of myriad youth. The gang for many became the primary social institution (Jolly Stompers, Bishops, Chaplains, Sportsmen, etc.). With their romantic names and women's auxiliaries (debs), gangs held sway over their sections of the ghetto (turf) and rumbled (warred) with rival gangs over real or imagined insults or incursions. Gangs provided a social home for many black youth. In the culture, gang membership and active participation in gang activity—counting coups against the enemy—was a way to register and to win peer-group recognition. It was an opportunity for showing *machismo* in a setting where many other ways of registering were not available. It was a way as well of giving vent to the pent-up fury that raged in young black breasts. In gangs, young blacks stabbed, stomped and shot other blacks. It was a long while before some gang members realized that their violence might be the product of self-hate and directed at targets which were not the true source of their outrage. Some of the authors lived through and were a part of the gang scene. Given their time and place in history, it would have been hard for them to have avoided it.

Gang warfare began to fade away late in the fifties not so

much because of a greater political awareness on the part of
gang members (or, as some have said, because social workers
stopped trying to break up youth gangs and to redirect their
energies) but, rather, gang activity ceased to claim many
black youth because an even worse plague was upon them
—dope, smack, horse, heroin. As Harlem youths in this period,
the authors could not escape contact with the evil stuff. Shaba
for a while peddled it, Michael Tabor for a while was hooked
on it, Afeni Shakur saw her "only friend" die from it at age
eighteen. The pall that dope has cast over the entire community hangs heavy on these pages.

III

This book was written in jail by men and women who face
literally hundreds of years' imprisonment for their supposed
crimes against society. Their accounts of their lives, however,
told in simple straightforward narrative, amount to a damn-
ing indictment of this society for its crimes against a people.
In their young lives they have seen just about all of it: the
violence done to a people who are put or held in degradation
and denied the most elemental requirements for a decent and
wholesome life. The authors' faithful recording, without turning up the volume or throwing in adjectives, makes their
case for them. You smell the smells, see the sights, hear the
sounds, and feel the horror. It is no coincidence that several
of the writers remark upon the poor hospital services provided
in their community, or look upon the local hospital as "the
butcher shop." Many of the medical problems they describe
are ghetto medical problems: a roach in a child's ear, a baby
bitten by a rat, a small child dying of lead poisoning. In
these descriptions of lives in the ghetto there is much talk
about death—deaths from violence, from medical neglect,
deaths of teen-agers, of babies. For the writers, it is more than
a statistical fact that black folk do not live as long as white
folk in this country. In the ghetto there is death and dying
all around. It is part of the daily reality.

In the American land of plenty, several of these writers tell us how they cried for food. They tell us of being forced to live in wretched run-down hovels—as with Ali Bey Hassan's family home, where the kitchen was a hotplate and the toilet a five-gallon can; of being packed to overcrowding—as with Michael Tabor, forced to sleep with his crippled sister and being perpetually bruised and battered by her braces. They tell us of the mistreatment and dehumanizing process they went through in the name of education. They went to Northern schools, Southern schools, segregated schools, newly integrated schools; but most of their experiences as blacks in American schools were not greatly dissimilar. Most of the authors seem personally to have experienced some of the abuse and humiliation meted out to blacks during their "socialization" through American education. One or two found out that white teachers in the North, in the New York City school system, knew the word "nigger," and that the treatment you received in school if you were not white just might depend on how light your complexion was. Bob Collier learned that he would have his share of troubles at school because he had only ragged patched-up clothes to wear; Curtis Powell, that he was not going to get the scholarship to go away to college even though he did score higher on the scholarship test than the white students in his high school; Lumumba Shakur, that his third-grade teacher did not have time for students who stuttered.

All were to learn that the job market was not open to blacks in the same way as it was to whites and that survival for the black man—a marginal man—often meant having a hassle of some kind. This increased the likelihood of ghetto dwellers coming in contact with the law. Long before their arrests in this case, the authors, either through observation or direct personal experience, were familiar with police abuses in the minority community—discourtesy, harassment arrests, beatings. Many in the courts had observed the workings of the criminal justice system, a system that often seemed more criminal than just. Some had had experience with prisons. Of course, all have had such experience now, after their lengthy pretrial detention. The descriptions of prison practices and regimen, the Women's House of Detention and the 1970 prison uprisings are especially vivid and add a further count to the already long catalog of the state's crimes against the people.

IV

Most black youth of our generation knew from an early age that something was wrong, but we could not always tell what or perceive why. The authors' growth to consciousness closely parallels that of so many others of our generation. There are events which take place in childhood that leave their indelible mark. Many recall how as children they were stoned or otherwise set upon by racist whites. What a trauma it must have been for Clark Squire to realize that his mother, tough and ready to take on all comers in her own community, was absolutely powerless to come to his aid when a Southern white housewife focused her venom upon him. Early in their lives, many of the Panthers experienced the reality of Jim Crow firsthand. Kinshasa, for example, when visiting the nation's monuments in Washington, D.C., with his father, was turned away from a restaurant; when crossing the Delaware by ferry, saw the sign ALL DOGS AND NEGROES TO THE REAR; and at another time learned that his summer friend who had discovered new courage and a new sense of himself during a visit to Harlem had returned to Georgia to be castrated and lynched by a mob. Kuwasi, in a segregated court decorated with WHITE and COLORED signs, watched as his friend was summarily tried, convicted on little or no evidence and sentenced to life for raping a white girl. Afeni Shakur experienced firsthand the terrorizing of the local Ku Klux Klan when she saw her grandfather tied to the back of a wagon and dragged through a North Carolina town. Several had direct confrontations with racist whites in which they stood up armed and ready for self-defense and, in some cases, were put in situations where they fought back against white attacks.

The Southern Freedom movement influenced many lives. It was part of what brought Clark Squire to Panola County, Mississippi, to register voters during the summer of 1964. Though in retrospect some now look with disfavor on some of its tactics and philosophical underpinnings, the movement was at the time a source of inspiration to those who knew firsthand the ugliness of Southern white racism. Blacks standing up en masse, saying no and taking direct action in their own behalf, was an encouragement to other blacks.

Through the military and to a lesser extent through study, blacks of our generation have traveled and been exposed to other ideas and ways of doing things which have a broadening effect. In this age of mobility, various of the authors here have visited Europe, Africa and Central America. They have seen racism in other corners of the globe, but they have also seen that things do not have to be the way they are in this country and the way they always have been as far as the black man is concerned.

The rise of black nationalism, black pride and black self-awareness has been one of the greatest of all influences on black youth of this period, as partly evidenced here by the number of writers who have dropped their slave names in favor of African names. The upsurge of the Black Muslim movement in the late fifties probably had the greatest impact on the Northern black urban ghetto dweller of any movement since Garvey's. The chief spark to this heightened consciousness, both in his life and in his death, has been Malcolm X— a fearless man from off the block who gave tongue to the hidden hurt and the hidden hate that few before him could synthesize or articulate. By the time of his assassination Malcolm had moved away from the narrow confines of religious doctrine and, through his Organization of Afro-American Unity (OAAU), was becoming more political, building an urban grass-roots movement based on community advancement and an active program of self-defense. Although Malcolm's organization did not survive long after his death, it had attracted many to it, including some of the authors, and was in many aspects of its program and focus a forerunner of the Black Panther Party.

As black activism moved North, it, too, played its part in educating and involving young blacks. From the mid-sixties on, Northern cities were the scene of direct group action concerned with the basic needs of the community—housing, education, employment, health. Rent strikes, picketing, chain-ins, sit-ins, all represented the community's attempt to deal effectively with its ills. The writers were exposed to this. They were also exposed to the fire and blood of ghetto rebellions. Ali Bey Hassan, and others in other ghettos around the country, witnessed the gunning-down of unarmed blacks by police during the Newark rebellion of 1967. Such a social climate was but one of a number of factors that drew individuals from consciousness to action.

The Black Panther Party came to New York at a time when feelings were running unusually high over a teachers' strike and the drive for community control of the schools. New York was fertile ground for a party which had as one of its main tenets control by blacks of their own communities. This, coupled with the dramatic and bold image projected by the West Coast Panthers, held a national attraction for young black men and women who had been tempered in the crucible of ghetto life, politically educated to the value of self-help and direct action and now ready to struggle collectively to bring about the social change they so deeply desired.

Joining the Black Panther Party was not the culmination of this growth to consciousness and then to action. Rather, it was just part of an ongoing process—a process that, in one form or another, will involve more and more people. It is the natural outgrowth of our situation here in America. Internal political dissension within the Black Panther Party is of no consequence to this process; with or without the Party, the process will go on. The authors are creatures of this society. Their commitment to change will be unyielding, no matter

what banner they decide to walk under. America is creating
more and more "Panthers" all the time. Not all will choose to
act in the same way, but all will see the necessity of action.
The authors represent not only where our generation has been
but also where it is going.

More power to us!

HAYWOOD BURNS, *National Director*
National Conference of Black Lawyers

part 1

SHABA OM; born September 14, 1949, New York City: I was born in the Big Apple—the city so wild they named it twice—in the butcher shop called Harlem Hospital. (The reason we black people call Harlem Hospital the butcher shop is that so many of the people who go into that hospital don't come out alive.) About four years after I was born, my brother David and I went down South, to our grandma's house in North Carolina. The house she lived in was not her own house. She rented it from a capitalist.

We went down for a family visit, along with my mother's sister, and then David and I liked it, and stayed. We both dug the sight; it was the first time we'd seen real sheep, cows, and big trees, that sort of thing—and I, especially, really related. Grandma would tell me and David about the trees, flowers, birds; she told me about Mother Nature and Father Time, how they are in love with one another—Grandma would say one could not live without the other. David and I played all day long. Grandma at one point had a lot of cats—all colors: black, brown, gray, you name it, they were there. I would sit on the little back porch or steps and dig on the kittens and cats, creeping up and jumping. I remember one big black cat Grandma had was the coolest cat I ever saw in my life.

He came in the house and ransacked it—pulled down everything—and he could fight: when you cornered him he fought back like a big lion.

Grandma's rented house had three rooms. David and I slept in what was called the front room, Grandma and my mad grandfather slept in the middle room, and the last room was the kitchen, then the bathroom. We slept on a pull-out sofa that could be made into a fairly nice-sized bed. Right up and across the street from Grandma's house was Walltown Elementary School, and when it came time, we were enrolled. I wanted to play, and Grandma was out working and didn't have time to know much about it, so I played a lot—and I stayed in the first grade two years straight. I did anything at all in school until one day Grandma put big fire—and I mean big fire —to my little ass. Then I began to say my ABCs backward and forward, crossways and upside down, and count, too, after the beating.

But Mother Nature and Father Time roll on. I made it out of Walltown Elementary School. My brother David had gone back to the Big Apple by then, so I was the only grandson down there with Grandma. I had to cut wood and bring in coal for the stoves in the house. Man, I dug cutting wood, it made me feel like a real grown man. The swing of the ax against the big old plank sounded good to me. Then I began to dig on other people cutting wood too, and dug on the skill and art of how to really swing the ax to make every blow count. I liked cutting wood but I liked playing too, so I would cut more wood in less time and have more time to play. We played with old car tires, rolled the tires up and down the street. I caught grasshoppers, bumblebees, snakes and everything, because I really dug Nature; that was my thing. Grandma soon gave all of the cats and kitties away that I and my friend didn't kill. We would do a job on the poor cats. I still liked them, but it was something to do and it was exciting. Also, I was only about eight or nine at the time.

My grandma slaved for some racist honky—cooking, washing, in other words domestic work. She was always crying and praying on my shoulder about getting a good education so I could grow up and get a decent job, be somebody in this world. She said she didn't want me slaving and saying No ma'am, Yes ma'am, and Yes sir, No sir, to some wild-acting honky.

My grandma is very well put together. I remember she would tell me always be independent; once you have it upstairs no one can take it from you. She would make herself an example by asking me what I am going to do when her head is cold. And this, man, would like blow my little mind. After Grandma said something like that I would be nice and helpful for days. She taught me how to cook, wash, sew, and iron. She is more than beautiful, and she is the only black woman I ever really loved. Like, she was really slaving to send me to school and buy me things I wanted—it was hard, I mean hard, she being old in age, and we being poor black people in the racist South. But Grandma had a very sharp mind. She read over my homework—that meant no TV until it was correct, and she was for no jive at all.

At my birthday and Christmas, I got new clothes. Christmas was the best time of my life. Every year for about five years straight I received a different kind of gun or rifle—all kinds of pistols, revolvers, automatics. Some shot just plain newspaper strips, some popped and some shot caps or water. As I became older I saw why she was giving me all of that advice with toys.

ROBERT COLLIER;   born January 27, 1937, Boston:
My mother and father, Elizabeth and Robert, had wanted
a son, and so they gave me my father's name. I was born
with a shoulder deformity as a result of a difficult forceps
delivery, and my mother had to roll me back and forth
to strengthen my back—or else I would grow up disfigured
for life, or so the doctor said. But then I've never had
much faith in doctors. For a little while I had a baby sister, Audrey. She died at the age of three because no one
of the medical people in Boston City Hospital's emergency room cared enough to look at an injured child in a
black woman's arms until too late, when she was beyond
help.

I hated going to school, and I used to spend as much
time as I could eating tea and toast in the morning before
leaving for school. My mother didn't eat with me in the
morning, but I didn't think that was strange; I didn't
know what the word "Depression" meant, I only knew
that most of the kids I knew were always hungry. One
morning Mom asked me to go to the store for milk and
bread, and when I got there the store was still closed.
I looked around and saw that the streets weren't too busy,
and I took the milk and bread that the deliverymen had
left in cases in front of the store. I ran home and gave
Mom the food and gave her back the money. I told her
the "store man" forgot to charge me. That morning for
the first time Mom ate when I did. It was a wonderful
feeling for me, being able to eat with my mother, and
I stole milk and bread whenever I could after that because it made me happy to see my mother happy. Sometimes I kept a nickel or a dime out of the "change" so I
could go to the movies. That storekeeper made an awful
lot of mistakes, but I guess my mother just didn't want
to make a fuss.

I didn't know my "real" father, and I asked my mother a lot of questions about him. He'd been going to a school to learn electrical engineering when the Depression started—he had completed an associate degree, but he found it almost impossible to get any kind of work, much less the kind he was trained for. The Depression—and discrimination—kept him from using the education he had fought so hard to acquire. He started drinking and staying away from the house, and finally he and Mom had to separate.

CETEWAYO (Michael Tabor); born December 13, 1946, New York City: As kids we'd ask each other, "Hey, man, what hospital were you born in?" and if the dude was born in New York more often than not he'd say, "I was born in Harlem Hospital," and you'd sharply shoot back, with an air of put-on amazement, "What! You were born in that butcher shop? No wonder your face is so fucked up." After a while dudes would get uptight, and you couldn't get anybody to say they had even been inside Harlem Hospital. I was born in the Big Apple— New York City—in Columbia Presbyterian Hospital. Being born in Columbia Presbyterian was damn-near considered a status symbol.

CURTIS POWELL; born October 25, 1935, South Orange, New Jersey: South Orange had "the Hill," where the rich whites lived, and "the Bottom," starting with Church Street, where the blacks and Italians lived. Most of the women from the Bottom, especially the blacks, were maids for the Hill people. Some of the men were chauffeurs, the rest ran taxicabs, garbage trucks, became cops, or worked in some service for the benefit of the rich. For instance, the best money the taxi drivers received was for hustling the "pot hustlers" (maids) up to the Hill.

My father split when I was one year old. I have since heard that he died a few years later. My mother was very independent, but although she had enough education to do secretarial work and things of that nature, she couldn't find enough work to support us doing that, so she became a maid. Even then she could hardly make it. I remember sometimes in the winter we used to burn old shoes to keep warm.

After my father left, my mother took solace—fanatical solace—in religion. She went from Episcopalian to Baptist to where she has been ever since I was in my early teens —The Sanctified Church. Of all the people I have ever met, my mother has the greatest capacity to love people. When I was seven, a friend of my mother's who had three daughters died, and I acquired three sisters, even though we were poor as hell. They were a lot older than I was and I was still in secondary school when they were grown up and ready to leave. Just about that time a cousin of ours with two children—a boy and a girl—had some calamity, and so I got another brother and sister. They were younger, and we grew up together just as real brothers and sisters. My mother has had to retire. Right now, at this writing, she is sick—very sick. My sister, a divorcee with three children, is at home taking care of her. I used to send money and help out, but since I'm in jail they're on welfare. I hardly ever saw the boy, Billy, since childhood, but Carol and I are still very close, and she and I discuss many things together, and share our opinions. As with my mother, my sister and I each have our own lives, and we understand and respect those lives.

I never really fit in; I was always into something. After I was seven or eight I used to run away from home approximately once a week. I wasn't sure where I wanted to go, but I felt that South Orange wasn't the place.

I have been a troublemaker and a rebel all my life. I never dug authority, and I couldn't give anybody automatic respect because they had power. Ever since I was small I have respected someone because they respected me or because they *deserved* respect, not just because I was told I should respect someone—or something. My mother says that part of that attitude came from my godmother, Sis Ida, who is a real groove. I remember when I was very young, a Chinese cat wanted to sell out his hand laundry and my mother and godmother borrowed some money and bought the place. They went bankrupt in just a little while, and I don't know all the details, but I know part of it was my godmother's attitude. The customers were the rich whites from the Hill, and when my godmother brought their clothes from the back, she used to drop them on the counter and say to my mother, real loud, "I think these are *her* rags." It really blew those rich bitches' minds. My godmother didn't like any people too much—she checked everybody out before she would even talk to them—but she *hated* white people.

The cops, along with the white people and the conservative Negroes, didn't like my attitude. I had a lot of petty encounters with them. No record—just harassment busts. Once I was coming out of the station house, and one of the white town merchants said the fuzz should build me a lab in a cave somewhere, give me a woman of my choice, and seal me off from humanity. When I asked him why, he said because of my attitude.

ABAYAMA KATARA (Alex McKeiver); **born September 30, 1951, New York City:** My mother, Mary Alexander, was born in Georgia and my father, Fred Mitchell McKeiver, in South Carolina. My one brother, Fred, is two years older than I. I was born in 1951 in Harlem. We lived in the average tenement house that you find in ghettos around America, but my mother had a special knack as so many black mothers have to make that hole seem like heaven.

My mother always tried to teach me and my brother how to take care of ourselves and always told us she would be leaving us someday and we'd have to look after ourselves. I remember she was sort of the mother for the whole block. All the young kids were over at our place a lot, and Moms used to feed everybody she could. One blood became a kind of unofficial brother: everything Fred and I were into, this friend was there—from shoveling snow and playing baseball to drinking wine and getting fucked up. When times were bad Moms would bake brownies or cookies and send the three of us down to the stoop to try to sell them. But Moms had to come down because mostly we ate them. If some of the kids didn't have money, Moms told us to give the cookies away, so we didn't make much. I found out recently that our friend is a junkie now—caught up in the plague that is really a smooth form of genocide.

Fred and I dug each other when we were young, but as time went on I could tell we weren't going to see eye-to-eye on a lot of things. He was a street-crossing guard in school, and I was head of the jaywalkers. When my mother died (when I was twelve), Fred went to live with my uncle upstate. Later he joined the army and became an M.P., and I joined the Black Panther Party and became a political prisoner.

I spent most of my summers on my Uncle Gussie's farm in upstate New York when I was a kid. We loved it up there and went to visit every chance we got, sometimes just for weekends. The nearest neighbors were white, but we treated them like human beings and they treated us the same. One family of whites up there was just barely doing it. They had about eight children. Even though I'd lived in Harlem all my life and saw poverty every day, whenever I think about dirt-poor I think of them. The thing that really blew my mind was that the tables were what you might call turned around; some of the younger kids used to ask if they could mow our grass and they got our hand-me-down clothes and the handy work around the house. It was kind of hard for me to believe that there were poor whites that had it worse than black families so I thought they were just lazy, but when I saw the father and his two oldest sons going into town every day trying to get a job and not getting it, I dug that the cats with the money didn't like black people because they were black and didn't even care about their own poor people. When that family moved out another white family moved in that was poor and we got along with them too, so then I decided that there were some good white people and there were some bad, so if a dude treated me right I'd treat him as a friend.

Near my uncle's bungalow was a camp for the mentally retarded, and two of my older cousins worked there in the summer as counselors. The cat who ran the camp was one white man who was no good! He had five Dobermans and some apple trees; the reason I mention the two together is that every time we went to hit the apple trees the dogs would be hot on our asses. He even used to set the dogs on us when we weren't on his property, just standing on a bridge nearby. We learned to

get up and quick; when it's 70 pounds times 5 of Dober-
man pinscher coming after you if you're slow you blow.

In the summer of 1964 we were up there for a family
get-together and my mother wasn't feeling so well so she
stayed upstairs, and the rest of us were downstairs dancing. I was dancing and playing and then I got a funny
feeling about my mother and went upstairs. When I got
to the door of her room my hand started shaking and I
started to run away but she had always told me to be
a man so I went in. She was lying there, and it looked
like she was staring at the ceiling with a small smile on
her face. I thought she might still be alive but when I
shook her I knew she was dead. I wanted to cry, but
Moms was a very religious woman and used to tell me
that when she died not to cry because she was going to
a better place where she wouldn't get cold and hungry
any more, so I left and started downstairs. I remember
I was mad. I was really mad; mad at God for taking her,
mad at the whole world. I saw one of my aunts at the
bottom of the stairs, and told her; she said, "Don't play
like that." I screamed at her that she was stupid and to
go up and see for herself. When she came back she was
crying, and I knew Moms was really dead.

After the funeral Fred went to live at Uncle Gussie's
place, but I didn't want to see that house for a while so
I stayed with my father. I remember the summer of
1964 well, not just because of the death of my mother
but because that was the time I became aware that the
"American dream" was really a nightmare as far as black
people were concerned. I dug how in that summer there
were ghetto rebellions all over the country. In Harlem
I saw people I had known all my life, the same people
that broke up the fights around the block, that screamed
and called cop when rumbles started, these same people

that had stopped us from killing ourselves in our futile attempts at gaining manhood by gang wars—they were out in the streets with bricks and bottles in their hands. Housewives, young bloods, pimps, pushers, whores, bloods with so-called "good" jobs, were all in the streets telling the man in the only way they knew how that black people had started to awaken from the "American dream."

With my mother's death I was forced to relate to the outside world apart from Harlem. I began to check out what was going on down South. I started thinking about some of the things I'd seen on TV and read in the news-paper—George Wallace had stopped those students from going to school; the church where four young black girls were blown to bits while praying; big, fat Bull Connor and the rest of those cops beating, kicking, and training dogs on all those black people. I remember thinking if President Kennedy wanted to help black people in the South he should give them all submachine guns to pro-tect themselves. My father used to show me his army discharge papers and a medal he got, and I knew all my uncles had fought too. Pops said he fought the Germans because they were killing people who hadn't done any-thing to them and I saw those white people as being just like the Germans and I wished that they would come up to Harlem and try that stuff on 135th Street, because I knew if they did we would have something for them.

AFENI SHAKUR; born January 10, 1947, Lumber-ton, North Carolina: I was born in Lumberton even though my mother and my father and my sister were living in Norfolk, Virginia, at the time, but my grand-mother who lived in Lumberton got sick, so my mother went to Lumberton to see about my grandmother and I was born while she was there. A midwife delivered me. My mother almost died when I got here because the midwife didn't want to take the afterbirth out. I think I went back to Virginia, I'm not sure. I know I spent most of my early childhood between North Carolina and Norfolk, Virginia—there wasn't anything different about it, it was fucked up like everybody else's is, all the rest of my comrades and all the rest of my friends, their lives and my life are not really that different.

JAMAL (Eddie Joseph); born January 17, 1953, New York City: My mother's name was Gladys Joseph and on my birth certificate it said that my father's name was Chico Joseph, but that wasn't his real name. I can't tell you his real name simply because I don't know it. I never knew my father and barely knew my real mother. After my mother was discharged from the hospital, she got in contact with a Mrs. Anna Jackson and Mr. Alexander Jackson, two people who had a reputation for raising foster children with loving care and a whole lot of tenderness. Gladys just wanted Anna to keep me until she could get back on her feet—she had to get a job. On the seventeenth day of my life she brought me uptown to Anna Jackson's house, a two-family house in the Bronx. This is where I spent the majority of my life.

At the time the Jacksons were responsible for raising four other foster children, and the one real daughter they'd brought into the world. When I came into the household the oldest boys were thirteen and twelve years old, the two girls were both fifteen, one boy was nine, and one was about six. I can't recall too much of what went on at that time, because it's behind the point of my memory. Most of what I know is from coming in contact with them later on in life, because when I reached the age where I begin to remember things specifically, where I can paint clear pictures in my mind of things that happened, they weren't around. They were nowhere to be found, for that matter.

My foster parents originally came from Virginia, although they didn't know each other when they were still in the State of Virginia. Alexander Jackson worked his way to the North doing all types of things: riding horses for money, driving other people's cars, chauffeuring, various types of domestic labor—he finally came to New York and began working with a bedding company and then for the Singer Mirror Company, and he worked there for thirty-six years, until a few years before his death. Anna worked her way up North primarily doing industrial work. At the time I was young, they were both very religious. Both were members of the Baptist church. Anna and I had many hours together, because no one else was home. My foster brothers and sisters had all left by this time, and Alexander was always at work. His work day was very long: he left the house at six in the morning and didn't come back until eight or nine at night. Every night he was weary and very tired from the type of work he did. He was a carpenter; he built frames for the mirror glass to be put in once that glass was processed.

I know I was a very mischievous child when I was little. I used to crawl around and investigate the different closets and doors in the house—the way the house was built, there were many doors and many turns in the hallways, all of which amazed me when I was young. I loved to go into the closets. I thought the mothballs I found in the pockets of coats I pulled down on top of my head were candy, and I would eat mothballs until someone came and found me to take me out of the closet and put me back in my playpen. As soon as they let me out of the playpen, I'd go to another closet and do it all over again. I must've had Anna worried to death. She probably thought that I would die of mothball poisoning before I reached the age of two.

And I used to grab newspapers like the *Daily News* —that's the type of newspaper my foster father read— and I'd look through the newspaper, look at all the pictures, and when I finally got to the last page, I'd pick the newspaper up and rip it to shreds. No matter what time it was, no matter where I was at, if I found some paper I had enough strength to tear, it was guaranteed that I would tear it up.

Gladys would slip away from her job and her two-room apartment in Brooklyn about once a month in order to come to the Bronx and see how I was doing. One of the things she did for me when I was young was send a check for about $16 or $17 every week until the time of her death to make sure that the Jacksons were able to give me diapers, milk, and whatever else they needed to raise me.

Very early in my life, Anna became ill. She had to go to the hospital, and then other people began babysitting during the day. My first babysitter, Mrs. Jones, had children of her own, a little older than I was, and it seemed to me that she didn't like me very much. I remember crying for food a lot of times. When I got into scrapes with her son, I would wind up taking the punishment. I didn't have enough understanding to tell my foster father what was going on. It wasn't too long, though, before he saw that I was underweight—then he began to question Mrs. Jones, and after that I didn't have to go to Mrs. Jones's house any more.

Anna came home again, but her health was still failing her and she wasn't able to take care of me properly. So one Sunday my foster father had the preacher make an announcement during the service that someone was needed to come to his house, and soon Jessie Mae Baltimore and Charles Baltimore moved in uptown and Jessie —who I called Noonie—began cleaning up the house and watching out for me and for Anna. It took a little while, but when I grew accustomed to Noonie I loved her, because in spite of the strictness and all the hard rules she laid down for me (they seemed hard at that time), she was very kind. She took time to play with me and to teach me in her own way. I began to learn how to read and write. She wasn't an intellectual. She had dropped out of junior high school, but everything she knew she passed on to me.

Anna's condition worsened and she went back into the hospital once again, so it was just Noonie and me in the house throughout the day. When I was five years old, Noonie registered me in PS 21. I didn't have a birth certificate—the only name that people knew me by until that time was Chico. Gladys was becoming increasingly hard to get in touch with. Noonie and the secretary from the school, Mrs. Bower, went down to the Health Department and jammed the officials until they finally took the trouble to look through the records and find my birth certificate. One day Mrs. Bower came into the schoolroom and called me outside along with the teacher, and she said, "I'm now christening you Edward Joseph." After school, when Noonie came to pick me up, I told her what happened. And she went back down to school and hugged Mrs. Bower. She was very happy about the whole thing. I didn't really understand the significance—that for five years I had really been a child without a name—but the name Edward seemed noble to me, a respected name, and I immediately put in a demand with all my friends that they stop calling me Chico and call me Eddie. People had a hard time dealing with that. I even remember that I got into a couple of fights over people wanting to be funny and calling me Chico when I'd said I wanted to be called Eddie.

ALI BEY HASSAN;   born December 29, 1937, Newark, New Jersey: I was born in the Third Ward—which was and still is where the majority of black people in Newark live. As far as I know, I am an only child.

My mother and father separated a little while after I was born. I don't know the exact reasons for the separation, but I know they had mainly to do with him running around with different women and not buying any milk or food for me. When I was about two, he was put into a mental institution up around Morristown, New Jersey, called Greystone Park. Later on I found out that he stayed in that institution fifteen years. Nobody could sign him out but my mother, and I guess she couldn't see her way to doing that for a long time. Up till when I was ten or twelve, my mother used to speak of my father when she was angry. I never knew my father and never developed any father-and-son relationship with anyone else. No one ever talked about him to me—except Moms in anger—and so the word "father" had no real meaning.

When I was three, my mother, Maxie Lee Ross, left me with some first cousins who had a small house on Rutgers Street in Newark so she could look for work. They fed

and clothed me along with the rest of their children
without charging my mother anything. The youngest,
Andy, used to crawl up onto the piano to play from the
time he was about two. His two sisters, Jerry and Salome,
were the singers. When they were old enough they started
making records, which they are doing now under the
name of Andy and the Bey Sisters.

When I was five or six years old my mother took me to
New York. We lived on 117th Street, between Park Avenue and Lexington, a few doors down from a big Catholic
church. We lived in a three-room apartment with another
woman and her two small boys. I used to call her Aunt
BeeBee, and still do today. They both worked, one in the
daytime and the other at night. My mother worked at a
plant near Morristown, making ammunition for World
War Two (this was in 1943–44). Then after a while my
mother sent me to Newark to stay with my uncle. We
lived on South Street in the Ironbound section, which at
that time was an Irish community. The war blackouts
were a regular thing, and much of the time we were without lights and had to use kerosene lamps. While I was
staying there, my aunt gave me a black kitten, which I
named Blackout, and my uncle gave me a table-model
radio to listen to. I slept in the living room on the couch
next to my radio. One day in 1945, my mother came to
pick me up, and the next thing I knew I was staying with
different people—still in Newark, this time in a basement
on Charlton Street. I don't remember their names any
more. Anyway, moving from place to place became a regular thing to me. I didn't know at the time what all that
moving meant, how hard it was to make money, how
hard it was to survive—but that's what my mother was
doing, trying to survive and keep me fed, clothed, and
sheltered as best she could. I also know now that all the

people I was staying with were "just surviving"—and still are, up to the present day.

From Charlton Street my mother and I moved down one block to Hillside Place—from ghetto block to ghetto block. At Hillside Place we lived with Aunt BeeBee and her two boys again. I was happy to see them, and had somebody to play with again. I learned later that my mother and Aunt BeeBee were having pretty rough times holding jobs, and that was why Aunt BeeBee had left New York. I also learned why my mother and aunt kept getting apartments together. If one was out of work, the other would take on all the responsibility of getting to-gether food, clothes, and rent. This was in the 1940s, so you can imagine what they were making, as black work-ing women. The "apartment" on Charlton Street was nothing but an attic. The kitchen was a hot plate, and the toilet was a five-gallon can, which we dumped daily. There were three tiny rooms that served for living, sleep-ing, and eating, and an old storeroom full of junk, where we played. One summer we managed to set that store-room on fire, and so we had to move again. There were a lot more moves to come, all in Newark:

—To stay with Mother's second oldest brother and his family (only for a little while after the fire);

—To Avon Place, to live with Will Bishop and his wife Pearl—we used to call her Mommer Pearl—Aunt BeeBee and her two boys, Irene and her son Charlie, and Mother and me;

—To live with Mom's oldest sister, Dorothy Evans, and her son Gene Rountree (my mother was living somewhere else in New York at the time),

—To 214 Court Street, with my Uncle Eugene and Aunt Lillian, and their two sons Earl and Joe. Things were pretty bad there. We all went to school with worn-out and patched-up clothes, although Aunt Lillian did manage to teach me my ABCs and how to count. I remember my mother and Aunt Lillian getting into an argument when my mother tried to take me back to New York. Mother finally said, "This is my son and I'll be back for him." Then she left. One morning on the way to school (Mother had been gone for months) I heard someone calling me. I stopped and looked around and there was my mother standing around the corner. The next thing I knew, we were at Penn Station getting on the train for New York.

In 1967 my mother died, after a nightmare of pain, lousy hospital care, not enough money to buy drugs. She was in and out of the hospital for about a month before she died. I believe to this day that my mother was murdered. The doctors said she died of cancer of the breast, but I know that City Hospital in Newark is just as much a butcher shop as Harlem Hospital, and that people die at those institutions each day because of neglect or just plain mistakes. And the hospital administrations go right along with what the doctors say, so there is never any way for the survivors of the victims to prove their cases.

RICHARD HARRIS; born April 21, 1940, East Orange, New Jersey: I was raised by grandparents on my mother's side and aunts and uncles in the East Orange, New Jersey, ghetto—the part that's now the New Jersey Parkway—and by my father's mother in Newark during a few summers. I recall nothing that influenced me more than the confrontations between the two branches of the family. I was the only substantial link—loved by all of them; by some more than others, but loved by all. I didn't live with my mother and stepfather as a family until those

confrontations finally broke up the large home in East
Orange. Aunts and uncles got married and moved out,
and so we got ourselves moving about to one place then
another in Newark.

My real father drove nothing but Cadillacs, smoked El
Producto cigars, and was part-owner and later owner of
a poolroom. He had a well-established name in the
Third Ward and as his son I didn't have to fight my way
into cliques—all I had to do was mention that Hogan
was my father. But then wanting to prove I was worthy of
the friendship granted made me perform outlandish and
foolhardy and unnecessary deeds. On a couple of occasions my father was called to save me from the law, because he was down with everything, and merchants in the
area knew him.

**LUMUMBA SHAKUR; born January 9, 1943, Atlan-
tic City, New Jersey:** My mother, my brothers Zayd and
Michael, my sister Lorraine and I lived in a two-room
apartment. My mother, Aremeda Coston, worked as a
waitress in a large hotel, at a base pay of 35¢ an hour;
her actual income depended on the tips she made. She
and my father, James Coston, were divorced ever since
I could remember it. I did not understand that that is a
ghetto phenomenon until I was about twenty years old,
because 90 per cent of the parents of all the ghetto
brothers and sisters I knew from Atlantic City to New
York to Philly were separated.

I lived in Portsmouth, Virginia, with my aunt and
uncle for about a year, until the navy transferred my uncle
to Puerto Rico, then lived in Atlantic City again. After
that I moved to North Philadelphia to live with my Aunt
Ethel, Uncle Handy, and Cousin Russell. When Aunt

Ethel found out I was hookying school and into gang fights, she called my mother and it was decided that I should go to live with my father. So that next school year was spent in Queens, New York City, and after school was over and I went back to Atlantic City, I told my mother that I did not want to go to New York again because my father did not understand me or communicate with me. Every problem there had been, he'd just solved with a horsewhip. Then one day in Atlantic City—I was with Aunt Rita, my father's sister—my father came in from New York unexpectedly. The first he said to me was, "I heard you got in some trouble with the police about gang fighting, and I'm going to whip your ass." I was about thirteen years old and was thinking that if he weren't an ex-professional boxer he would sure get a hell-fired fight out of me, when Aunt Rita came to my rescue with some cold historical facts. She told my father he should stop whipping on me because the only reason he whipped me was that I was the mirror of his youth. She told my father that I looked like he did, talked like he did, and acted rebellious like he did. She also told him that I inherited the rebelliousness from him and he had inherited his rebelliousness from my grandfather. She told him that he could not whip the rebelliousness and the bad nigger out of me because I was just like my grandfather and my father and all of the men of the Coston family. The rap my Aunt Rita put on my father sure cooled him out. I never realized the historical significance in what my Aunt Rita told my father until I read the book *Black Rage*, which deals with how black parents suppressed the bad-nigger and rebellious-nigger qualities in black children in America, otherwise their children would die young. I always wonder if Aunt Rita realized that she had just built the bridge of communication between my father and me, because he really tried to understand me after that rap with my aunt. Aunt Rita is a very grass-root woman.

DHARUBA (Richard Moore); **born June 30, 1944, New York City:** My grandfather and my father migrated to the North in the late '20s, I believe, and my father being a little older than my mother was hanging out then in the streets of Harlem. He picked up the nickname "Cokey" in the streets.

Harlem in the late '20s and early '30s was somewhat of a gay place, somewhat of a lively place. It was the epitome of the finger-popping nightmare. My father hung out. He used to deal a little light reefer and he used to hang out with a whole lot of fellows who are today either dead or in jail or strung out on narcotics. They had a little gang called the Slicksters, just an ordinary street gang, and it was here that my father acquired his super-slick, super-nigger façade where he would have his hair fried and dyed and tossed aside, and he was wearing good suits and pistol pockets. I remember some descriptions that I heard very young of how he was when he came into the house to see my mother. They were separated on an on-and-off basis in the early stages of their marriage, but they were separated for the most part since I was born. My aunt used to get very uptight when he came into the house because she was figuring that he was a dope fiend and hanging out with a whole bunch of hoodlums and trash.

My father used to have a hell of a talent for dancing. He was a very good dancer, so good that people from all over the neighborhood and people that knew him and that knew of him wondered why Cokey never really went into dancing. Cokey could really dance. He was telling me about a time that Sammy Davis, Jr., was down into this spot, I think it was the Cotton Club, in Harlem, and the niggers that he was with and some niggers that Cokey was with got off into a thing of dancing. That led Cokey to the conclusion that motherfucker Sammy Davis, Jr., couldn't dance.

Anyway, I remember he used to come into the house and it seemed like my mother was happy at the same time she was kind of sad. But my mother was a very dominant personality and Cokey was just a good-time nigger, you know, he would just like to have a good time, and I think that's what was part of the trouble: he always wanted to have a good time, regardless of the import of any responsibility. But I would say that Cokey did accept responsibility because he had a very heavy burden to deal with, which I'll talk about later. But my mother used to respond to him in somewhat of a positive-negative manner, you know, in a joking or jovial manner. And Cokey used to always put on this side, "Tell Me How Long the Train's Been Gone." You remember that? He had it on 78. He had this old big funny-looking record player. The record player was real big to me, I was so small, it used to come up past my chin. My head would be up there, you know, the top of my head. And he would play this side, "Tell Me How Long the Train's Been Gone," and he would go off into his thing. He used to get a hell of a kick out of beating on my mama's legs, you know, with his hands, staccato-type fashion, because he could play the drums too. He was very talented.

I was mainly in the household with my mother, my grandfather, and my aunt, and only saw my father from time to time. Whenever I didn't see him for a long period of time, if he was mentioned at all by Mother, it was in a derogatory manner. She felt that he was totally irresponsible because he didn't help support me, and that he totally couldn't be forgiven for that. But I think that the main reason he was irresponsible toward his obligations was that he had that very heavy street influence. My mother couldn't seem to reconcile this. My mother, though, could take care of herself on the streets. There were very few niggers in the neighborhood that could beat her. I bet half of the niggers that hung out with my father couldn't beat her. In fact, my father couldn't beat her. So it was really a funny situation. But the main contradiction was the family—my aunt and my grandfather, who made him feel that he was not a part of the house, he was not a part of anything that had to do with me or with my mother. So having to subject himself to the type of conflict that grew out of him trying to relate to my mother, he just withdrew instead, and he would only try to see her every now and then.

I know, for what it's worth, that my father for a very long time felt very strongly toward my mother. Talking to him in later years, when I had grown up and I had experienced quite a few things, and talking to him when we were in jail together, I found out that he had a very strong affection for my mother. He could never express that affection the way he wanted too—it was stifled, and I think a whole lot of forces played a part. In the early '40s, when Cokey was in the army, he went AWOL; my mother thought he was in the army and thought he was off serving his country, and Pops was on Prospect Avenue selling some reefer, you know. I think my aunt discovered him or my grandfather discovered him. He was out on the block selling some reefer and hustling. I got the idea that it was a very bad experience. It led to some conflict and physical confrontation between my mother and my father.

BABA ODINGA;   born **October 20, 1944, Antigua:**
I can remember one day when I was about two I was in
the yard playing when my mother called me and asked
who I was talking to. I told her that I was talking to a
man and he asked me to bring him some of my food. An
old woman who lived next door came out and told Mother
she'd been watching me and she didn't see anyone so I
must have been talking to a jumby, a ghost. She said my
mother must be careful for this jumby is very bad, he has
been giving her a lot of trouble since she had been trying
to catch him.

When I was about three, my mother took me to the pier
and showed me a boat and told me that we were going
to go on it. After a while a small boat with an engine
came up to the pier and a man got out; Mother told me
that he was my uncle and I was going to live with him
for a while. Well, I thought I was going to live with him
on the boat, but he told me that he was taking me on
another island to live with him and his wife, who later
became my second mother. All I can remember of the first
time I saw my second mother is that she was very nice
to me for she gave me a music box. I guess the music box
was to pacify any case of nostalgia that might develop.
Finally I came to the realization that I was not going
back to Antigua in a long time. I guess that my uncle and
my mother had already made plans for me to stay but I
was too young to understand what was happening.

My earliest memory of my childhood on the island
named Nevis is of a woman by the name of Miss Elsie,
who lived next door and who danced every time I played
my music box. To think of it now makes me laugh. I
would be in the yard playing and she would pick me up
and put me on the step. She'd wind up the music box and
give it to me, then she would dance; and that would be
when I began to crack up. She was kind of heavy, not fat

but heavy. I can remember hollering so loud one day that my second mother came out and asked me what was the matter—when she saw what was happening, she also began to laugh.

At this time, my second mother began to take me to the beach every Sunday and from the beach she'd take me with her to the hot spring that was the women's bath. She took me there and I played in the water until one Sunday—I and this other boy were playing a game where you try to keep your head underwater as long as possible. We'd walk upstream bent down with our heads under the water till we came to a certain rock and then we'd go back down. This is something that we did every time we came to the spring until this Sunday. On this particular day when we got up from under the water, we came up between a woman's legs, it was right there in front of us so we began to howl and scream, and all the women, when they found out, they all began to laugh. My second mother was at the other end; I ran to her and she asked me why I was crying. I pointed in the direction that I came from so she left and when she came back she was laughing. The following Sunday she took me to the beach and from the beach she took me to the spring, but nothing in this world was going to make me go back in there. After trying to get me to go with her, she gave me to this little girl about eight years old and told her to take me where the other kids were bathing.

My second mother was a small business woman. Her business consisted of buying and selling coal, goats, sheep, and pigs, and later on she sold eggs. The money she made from selling the animals was kept in the house and when she was not home I would go in the drawer where she kept the money and take it out. My friends and I would then proceed to play cards with the money. I almost got caught one time. We were in the house playing when we heard my mother in the yard. Pandemonium was about to break out when a woman came to buy some coal. That gave us sufficient time. I threw the money in the bag and put it back where she kept it. After that I never played cards with the money again. Sometimes I don't know what I would have done if we'd played for real, for every time we played I was the loser.

At the age of about seven, my ambition was to become the world's greatest swimmer. Uncle George promised to teach me. His method was not too encouraging. I would agree that it was functional, but man, it was not encouraging. His modus operandi was to take me on the pier, and ask me if I was ready. After looking over the pier at the water, which was very blue and also very deep, I came to a very hasty conclusion that under no circumstance would I venture into what seemed to be an abyss. I then turned to him and said, "Uncle George, what's that?" pointing to the water. "Is that a shark?" He said, "Yes, would you like to catch it?"—but before I could give an answer he picked me up and threw me in the water. I remember hitting the water. I had to sink but I do not remember staying under the usual time that one stays under. I was almost drowned the week before and the memory was still in my mind. So there I was on top of the water doing a quasi dog swim, along with a now-you-see-me-now-you-don't, and each time you see me I am doing my quasi dog swim on top of the water. As for my uncle, he stands up there and tells me to throw my hands. I finally made it to the pier. He pulled me up and told me to watch him, watch the way he swam. Now my uncle is an old sea shark, you should see my uncle swim: all he does is throw a lot of water up in the air and if there are any fish nearby they go in the air too. Man, my uncle does not have any style whatsoever, but when he dives—that's when he has style. He looks like a fish. When my second mother swims she has style, but she doesn't dive too well. There are a lot of women who can swim but they don't dive too well, which has always puzzled me. Anyway Uncle George threw me back in the water a few more times, then he took me home. We went a lot of times after that—he didn't always have to throw me in—and after a while I learned to swim properly.

KWANDO M'BIASSI KINSHASA (William King); born September 21, 1939, New York City: I grew up in that highly controlled environment known to the world as Harlem. Harlem was then, as today, a city all by itself, and in many respects very like another country—an under-developed, overexploited country, a country that lacks the ability to provide its own food, transportation, or basic necessities for life; most of all, a country unable to defend itself. I spent part of my childhood near one of Harlem's southern borders and part near the northern, and I became quite aware that Harlem was our area, our turf. The rest of the city, the surrounding nonblack area, wasn't really important, mainly because we never went there. For all practical purposes, it was enemy territory.

One of my first memories is of my uncle going off to war. I was about four years old, and I remember a lot of people saying "Be careful," "Take care of yourself," and "Come back safely." I don't really know why I remember it so well; the concept of war meant nothing to me then. Maybe it was the accumulation of other activities in Harlem centered around World War Two. Like the blackouts. I really dug the blackouts: there was mystery and excitement in them. Little did I realize that in other parts of the world children my age were not finding the blackouts so exciting. And then there were the coupons. It seemed the most natural thing in the world, having to buy all our food with coupons—coupons that bought us some rolls, milk, and the ever-present soup. Mom must have made that soup taste fifty different ways, all the time using the same kind of tomato soup. Those were hard times.

Another thing I remember is a toy airplane that Mom was somehow able to buy for me. It was a huge thing— it seemed to me about the size of a chair. Mostly I remember the airplane because one day when I was playing with it in the living room, I heard my parents talking with some neighbors in the kitchen, and they sounded very excited and loud. So I went to see what was up and there they were, holding the newspapers and pointing at it. I grabbed the news section and went back to the living room with it. I don't know what I expected to find—I was only six and you can imagine what my reading was like —but it turned out that I didn't need to read to find out what was bothering my parents. The centerfold had a picture of an atomic bomb explosion, the Bikini Island test, and I was frightened. My father had told me about the bomb a few days before that, after I heard a radio broadcast of the news of the explosion, what it was and what it could do to people, but the words didn't get to me the way that picture did. I still remember that photograph.

My parents were very concerned that I should get a wide understanding of life. Once my father took me to a riot, but they also did things like see that I took piano lessons! My father and I went on a lot of trips to different cities. In Boston, I remember distinctly seeing Bunker Hill and some Revolutionary War sites. In Washington we walked for what seemed hours, looking at large, empty, cold-white buildings. We also saw the Constitution and a lot of other fictitious documents from America's history. In Washington one time my old man took me into a restaurant to get something to eat, and we were told that blacks weren't served there. For the first time I saw on my father's face a look of complete anger and hatred. I'll never forget it. I think I had a dim realization at the time that I had met a real enemy.

My father never got tired of talking about the military tactics of the Americans and the Nazis, or about the Japanese raid on Pearl Harbor and the subsequent war in the Pacific. I can remember days when hour after hour we would talk about World War Two and the Korean War. I didn't realize it at the time, but he was giving me a basic understanding and knowledge of man's oldest profession and constant occupation. My father's personality and way of dealing with life was based on a solid, deeply rooted personal strength. When he was thirteen he hitched a ride on a boat from Charleston, South Carolina, to New York so he could start seeing the country. He is still that sort of adventurer. He has traveled all over America several times, and has spent time in Canada and Mexico.

My father always had a rocklike quality about him, a kind of steadfastness, but my mother was very different: she was ultraquick, restless. Her basic theme in our conversations was that one should always project himself into firsthand contact with a subject in order to understand it. I can remember her saying, "Negroes always talk, talk, talk, but we never do nothing about anything, that's our whole problem." As for her, she put her thoughts into practice. When I was a kid, it seemed to me she never stopped going. If she wasn't planning some way to save money on our next meal, she was designing and sewing clothes for the family. She was always busy.

And she was unpredictable: years later, when I was in

the marines down in Guatemala—and right in the middle of an attempt at revolutionary takeover—she decided she would surprise me by flying down to see me. To say I was surprised is an understatement. It was while I was in the service I found out my mother was dying of an incurable disease. No one could have guessed from the way she acted that she knew she was going to die: her strength of character was really shown those last years. She never showed self-pity or weakness. And those two personalities, mother and father, made me understand the things that I still dig in people—strength, ability, and courage.

KUWASI BALAGOON (Donald Weems);   born December 22, 1946, Lakeland, Maryland: My father and mother were very law-abiding people, who paid taxes and got up early to go to work, ate miniature breakfasts and made sandwiches out of lunch meat or leftovers and made separate dashes five times a week to work, and kept a close eye on every paycheck and expenditure, slaving and saving. My oldest sister, Mary, joined them when she became of age, making three mad dashes five times a week. My father worked for the U.S. Printing Office, and my mom and Mary Day worked at Fort Meade, Maryland. Their love for my other sister Diane and for me, the only boy and the baby of the family—and the concept that you've got to work somewhere, and all-suffering determination—enabled them to rush to the job, and getting there, work and teach white folks how to do the type of work encountered, and then watch them climb the governmental ladder quickly, while they themselves rose slowly and painfully step by slow step. They did that for twenty-five years, so we could have food and clothes and goodies.

My youngest sister and I were left during the day under

the supreme guidance of "Mama," our grandmother, Aka Mama Shine, Ann Shine, Mama Hattie, Mrs. Williams, and different combinations thereof. We lived very clannishly, and our family transcended blood lines. People I've called "cousin" all my life—I've yet to see the hook-up.

As I arrived, my father announced to all within range of his voice that I would be a doctor and a professional football player, boxer, or baseball player, but that is not the case, as you see. Nobody knows my first words, because it took me four years to be understood. Mama (my grandmother), the spiritual leader of the family, hipped us to some highlights of her past. Wasn't none of that three-pigs bullshit around the house. We heard no Humpty Dumpty poetry; instead she said, "If a man is what he isn't, if he isn't what he am, then as sure as I'm atalking then he isn't worth a damn." Right on, Mama!

Before even learning how to talk kids look for their cues. Black kids like all kids are subject to having TV invade their consciousnesses, and indeed TV reflects all situations as bad and black people's worst. Of course I remember Tarzan movies and Jungle Jim flicks, and I watched them closely and often. I suppose I related to it but of course after a while I nixed both of them off. My main TV hero was Superman. After the TV pictured him coming out of a phone booth and taking to the sky I began to picture myself faster than a speeding bullet and able to leap tall buildings in a single bound. It went to my head. Until one day I tied a towel around my neck fashioned like a cape and after finding out I couldn't take off the ground, climbed on top of a swing and jumped off. It's a bird, it's a plane, it's that nutty Weems kid—crunch! I rolled around holding my ankle with both hands and hollering for Mama. It was broken, I knew it was, because anything that hurt that bad had to be broken.

Mama came to my aid, checked it out, and became the first person in history to heal a broken bone with rubbing alcohol. After that I started using more conventional means of transportation, like walking, bicycles, things like that.

I was a wild kid, but my folks took very good care of me. When I was a child I never went hungry, and everything I asked for within reason I had—if not immediately, then as surely as the coming of running water and indoor toilets. I ate until I was full and fed the rest to Nippy, my sneaky, vicious, obedient friend and family watchdog. Nippy didn't bark or vacillate before attack. The immediate family loved Nippy and Nippy loved the immediate family; everyone else was subject to being chewed for the slightest provocation or for free. He attacked Uncle John every time he had a chance—as if Uncle John didn't have enough problems with a little old lady across the tracks burning roots on him and Aunt Teresa.

Once a new insurance man plodded his route to our house. Nippy watched and waited for the alien to get up on the front porch, then dogged along behind him in a good-natured manner showing no intentions to do harm, playing it to a bust, even wagging his tail—then snap-rip, snap! The alien was petrified, begging for "help!" Luckily for him Mama was home. I watched as long as it lasted, and if it would have lasted longer, then longer I would have watched. To my dismay, and the alien's prayer, Mama appeared and called Nip off. Making one last threatening grab, he left the scene as he came, and went back to his bone. Barking dogs don't bite. Strange how a lot of big-mouthed, long-winded, so-called revolutionaries possess less initiative than an apolitical dog.

Mary Day met Jimmy, and everybody dug him. My mother's only complaint was that he wouldn't keep a job.

He played guitar, talked cool, and was like a big

brother to me. And a beer partner of sorts. My father would let my sister and me sip out of a bottle or can he was drinking, and once or twice, while company was over, I managed to steal a whole can to myself—but was caught, obviously drunk. Jimmy was cooler than that. He'd just pick up a couple of bottles at the package store and we would ride around, you know, shooting the shit, until I was cool too.

The Christmas I was thirteen was a super Christmas for a materialistic youth. Jimmy had a job at a department store warehouse, as a truck driver. Whenever he could he liberated. Good God he liberated, we couldn't get everything under the tree. I had at least one of everything that Matell and all their competitors put out. Santa Claus drove a truck that year. The whole family had surprises.

The summer I was fourteen went on in the usual way— you know, baseball, the creek, shooting birds, standing on the corner. Then one day a friend told me that Jimmy was in jail. "Naw, man." He said it was in the papers. That Jimmy had raped a white girl. "Naw man." I shot home and my sister and Mom corrected me, "The cops got Jimmy, they say he raped a white girl."

He was being held in Marlboro County jail, which looked like one of those jails in the westerns. Mary Day started getting money together for bail but then there wasn't no bail. Jimmy knew of this Negro lawyer that was supposed to be all right and passed word out to obtain this guy. Soon conferences followed and sometimes on Sunday we would go out to that racist jail. His cell was at the corner of it and a small window, blocked by a large shade tree, was his only source of fresh air. Today I know I would climb a tree like that with a fistful of hacksaw blades.

Marlboro County jail was and probably still is a chamber of horrors where a black man could get whipped half or all the way to death for breaking the cold, concrete silence, replying to a question or statement with any sign of resentment, or for having the wrong tone in his voice. State storm troopers would drop by with super-large flashlights and sticks and check out the menu. Everybody I'd seen after a stay there came back with bad news, because Marlboro was bad news, even worse news than Hyattsville, and it's no secret that the cops would put a telephone book on a "nigger's" head, take out their "niggersticks" and try to kill that book. I've heard brothers say that the cops were so mean that they even used to break up white boys. Cowing down did no good.

The trial began. The family stood by him; I wasn't permitted to go to court, but this was how it was related to me later. The courthouse had segregated toilets, not that my folks wanted to sit down and shit beside crackers but with them came the signs: "white ladies"—"colored," and "white gentlemen"—"colored males." They gave doubtless support to the doctrine of white supremacy. The pigs lightened up on the water fountains, with just "white" and "colored" signs over them. Jimmy was escorted by ten police. The jury was all racist cracker local yokels. The white girl's clothes weren't torn and she didn't have any kind of cuts or unusual red spots. Virgin Mary's untorn dress and contradictory testimony didn't mean a thing. The jury went out for about fifteen minutes and came back with a guilty verdict, and Jimmy was sentenced to life.

Jimmy had been living off tea and bread and spent the last four days at Marlboro without anything to eat, and then was sent to Maryland State Pen in Baltimore. There's only one good that came out of the whole thing:

in November of '68 he busted out that motherfucker and to this day, it's my understanding that he's still at large.

JAMAL: My mother—Gladys—died, I was about seven, and I didn't really understand that. Noonie told me when I came in the door after school. I could see that it meant Gladys wouldn't be coming by any more, and I was sorry —she used to run up and hug and kiss me all over, which I thought was mushy by then; and she always had a package for me. Every time I'd hoped it would be a toy, and I was always disappointed, it was always clothes. But I had told my best friend I would meet him at four o'clock to play—and when Noonie said I couldn't, that the woman who brought me into the world had died and I must go into mourning, and Noonie was angry with me—then I sat down and I felt very alone and very hurt. I cried for a long time, and I didn't understand then what was making me cry.

From that point on, it seemed like the nature of that sometimes happy household changed. Anna had been home once more since the last time she entered the hospital, but she only stayed home for about a month, and she was so different, you really didn't know it was Anna. She was very sick physically; and she became delirious, and thought God was punishing her because she failed in raising the children. Walter, Johnny, and Dolores were all in reformatories or prisons then, though I didn't know it then. She put all the blame on herself. One night a month after she came home, she started screaming out and got up out of the bed and tried to walk around the house. She was too weak, and she collapsed to the floor. My foster father and Pop Baltimore picked her up and put her back on the bed, and Noonie held her down while my foster father called the hospital.

I was scared. I'd seen things like that on television, but this was real, I didn't know what was wrong. All I was told was that Mommy was tired and as soon as she got some rest in the hospital, she would come back home and be as good as new. But she didn't come home, and from eavesdropping on different conversations, I found out that she was getting sicker.

The following year, Anna Jackson passed from life to death. The causes of her death were cancer, respiratory disease, and the fact that she had lost the will to live because she felt that she had failed. On Christmas Eve, about eleven o'clock in the night, I was trying to go to sleep because I thought that if I was awake when Santa came, I would scare him away and blow whatever presents I had coming that year. It was then that the phone rang and the call was from the hospital, to inform my foster father that Anna Jackson had died. He began calling all his friends and telling them she had passed away, and I kept on trying to go to sleep as if I hadn't heard anything. He went to the store and bought some liquor and came back and drank all night and called people all night and cried all night.

Anna's funeral was about a week later. Her body had lain in state overnight at the Trinity Baptist Church the night before the funeral. At the end, when people were passing by to review the body, I stopped to kiss my foster mother goodbye for the last time. When my mouth touched hers, it was cold. This really sent a shock-wave of fear through my body. And I really understood what death was about. I began to cry and I wanted to stop because I wanted to show everybody that I was almost eight and I was grown-up enough to hold the hurting feeling inside of me, but I couldn't do it. I cried all the way, until we got to the wake. People got together at the house and began watching a baseball game and drinking, laughing, and talking, and that made me very angry.

My foster father changed then. He began drinking, ten quarts of liquor a week, stayed out late at night, and he started running around with all kinds of women. He took me with him sometimes, but I never really liked that. I didn't like just going downtown with him someplace, sitting down while he and all his friends got drunk and started talking crazy, coming home at night nearly dying every time my father was drunk behind the wheel. Finally Noonie put an end to this.

Pop Baltimore got sick too. A few years before he had bumped his head, riding in a taxi cab, and since then he'd had dizzy spells: he would shake and become semiconscious. The only way we knew of to deal with that was just to place ice on his head, or go over his face with a cold washrag. The spells became more frequent, and he got so sick he had to go to a nursing home.

Noonie had to go out and mind other people's children at various homes in order to get some more money into the household to pay the bills, which my foster father was neglecting, and also to help pay the bills at the nursing home. By this time my foster father had remarried, and his wife and I were on bad terms with each other, so when she and I were the only ones in the house in the afternoons and evenings, I liked it better outside. I joined the Cub Scouts, which wasn't very interesting. I joined the NAACP Youth Council, which was mostly teenagers; I had junior membership. On Saturdays we would go get donations of books and clothes from the community and then box them up to send them down South. But when the teenagers began graduating from high school and leaving the community, the Youth Council stopped existing.

On top of the drinking and all the chronic health problems my foster father had attained from thirty-six years working in the same dusty factory, he became acutely ill, too. First he had to limit his work week from six days to five, then it got so bad he had to go into the hospital. In about a month he came home, rested for about another month, and then went back to work on a part-time basis. The problems flared up again—he and his wife were battling, and his one real daughter, Dorothy, was telling him the house was hers, not his—and the pressure became more intense. Walter, the oldest of the foster children, got released from prison. This was the first time I'd met him —I was about eleven years old. He had just finished doing ten years in the penitentiary for rape and robbery. Whether he was guilty or not I can't judge; sometimes he acts in a manner that makes me believe that he was framed and other times I just don't know. One thing that I did know about Walter is that he had a thing for white women: every time he would come up to the house, he would be with a white girl. But I liked Walter, primarily because he used to buy me a lot of toys—football helmets and footballs and things, and he taught me how to play various sports. He was especially good in football and I think the reason is that he played with the prison team while he was upstate in the jailhouse.

When I started seventh grade, I was put in the special progress class—this meant that you would get three years of academic work compiled into two years and therefore skip one grade. By this time, though, I wasn't too interested in what was going on in school. I had more interest in the Cadet Corps, which I'd joined. And I had a lot of home distractions. Pop by this time was so ill he had to be transferred from the nursing home to the hospital, and my foster father also went into the hospital. On December 6, 1966, Pop Baltimore died. He was eighty-six years old. A month after that, my foster father passed away. He was about sixty-three.

The two deaths, one right behind the other, had a tremendous effect. My father's wife said ghosts were after her in the house, so she packed a suitcase and went to Virginia to live with her mother. Noonie went for solace to the church, so I didn't see too much of her any more.

part 2

LUMUMBA SHAKUR: In Virginia, there was a candy store by the school that I loved to go into. An old woman —white—ran it, and when any black came into the store this old woman would always ask, "What you want, nigg-ra?" When I went into the store, she asked as usual, "What you want, nigg-ra?" I said, "I want five cookies, cracker." She said, "Nigg-ra, don't call me cracker." I told her, "Cracker, don't call me nigger." She said, "But you are a nigger." I told her, "If I'm a nigger, then you are a cracker." She got so infuriated she said I must be a "crazy nigg-ra from up North," and she gave me my five cookies.

Zayd and myself stayed in Portsmouth for about a year, until Uncle Bates was transferred to Puerto Rico. We went back to Atlantic City, then, to live with our mother. I often wonder what my prospects for longevity would have been in the South.

KWANDO KINSHASA: A cat named Clayton, a neighbor's friend from Georgia, visited in New York in the summer of 1954. The racist crackers had this blood and the other people in the town he came from so spooked up, they automatically moved aside for white people.

They weren't even supposed to walk on the shady side of the street, in the summer—that side was for crackers. When I first heard these things, and a whole lot worse, I thought the stories were wild. I mean, I know some white boys thought pretty well of themselves, but I didn't know anything about the history of black people, about the 50 million blacks killed by those crackers, and their parents, and their grandparents. In any case, I started to educate the blood to the fact that he was just as good as any man, if not better. I told him that not only did you not have to get off the street when a white person came by, here you could bump right into him if you wanted to. In a few months he really started to get his head together. (In fact, he got it so together, he started to cut in on my time with some of the sisters, but I figured it was OK because he was a right-on brother.) When the summer was over, I tried to talk Clayton's aunt into keeping him here in the city. I wish I had succeeded, because two months after he went back to Georgia he was lynched and castrated by a mob of crackers. His crime was touching (maybe just looking at, it didn't matter) some cracker female in his home town. I won't forget Clayton Brooks. His death will be avenged. And those who should have been dealt with a long time ago will be dealt with.

KATARA: The summer we were visiting in North Carolina, the word got around that Martin Luther King was coming to Charleston to put on a big rally. The word also got around among the local racists that Sara McKeiver's "uppity grandsons from up North" were advance men for Reverend King and were going to start a riot when he came. When Grandma told us that, we almost died laughing, especially since I hated King at the time because it was his thing to tell the people not to fight the cops and I couldn't go down for that. It was funny to us, but the white people of that little town we were in were dead serious. About two days later, five carloads of whites drove into the little black section. They drove up and down the road for about two hours, not saying a word, and now and then they stopped in front of our house and just stared for a while. We didn't know what those fools might do, so we borrowed some guns and next day when they came back, we just went out on the porch with our shit and stared back at them.

We had three more weeks before school was going to start, and Pops had called to tell us to come on back, but at first we didn't know what those fools might do to Grandma if we left. Then some of the brothers said that the rednecks wouldn't roll if we left because it was us, and not Sara, they were after. That sounded OK, but then we had another problem: we didn't dig the idea of being caught alone on the road between that little town and Charleston. One of the neighbors offered to drive us in, but we wouldn't go if we couldn't have a shotgun with us, and he wouldn't take us if we did, so we laid low for three days, waiting for the bus to come through. When it did, I was never so glad to get out of a town as I was to get out of that one.

KWANDO KINSHASA: I took a trip to Norfolk, Virginia, with my aunt and uncle in the summer after sev-·enth grade. On the ferry going across Delaware Bay there was a sign saying "All Dogs and Negroes to the Rear," and that was just the first of my lessons that summer about what it was like to be black in America. That summer in Norfolk I actually saw my people move off the sidewalks to let white people by. My cousin and I went into a 5-and-10-cent store and sat at the counter for about a half hour before we realized that those pigs were not going to serve us. We went to a movie and had to sit upstairs—so far in the back that it was a waste of time. I learned a lot that summer. When I went back to school I dug that in New York it was the same kind of people telling me what to do, it was just disguised a little, and I began to pay more attention to the war between me and them.

Much later—in 1961—when I was in the marines and being sent to Central America, I remember my southbound train pulling out of the station at Washington, D.C., heading for Charleston. That train passed town after town filled with blacks—and they were standing and working outside accumulations of shacks, their homes. I used to stand between the cars, watching those "towns," those shacks that my people lived in, and it really started to hurt. The train stopped a lot along the route, and the children from the shacks would wave at the train. Many times I waved back, and I remember thinking that these were my people, and for some reason I had been kept away from them and they from me. I know now how true that feeling was. Black people are kept apart by political and cultural barriers so strong that blacks in one part of the country rarely have much understanding of blacks in other parts of the country. Racism keeps them apart, the racism America has built up and built into her system.

When the train arrived in Charleston, I decided to spend the free time I had—overnight—seeing as much as I could of Charleston. I even thought of trying to find my old man's house. I never found the house, but I did find the elementary school he went to, and walked down the street the house used to be on. I also walked through the so-called "old" section of Charleston, and saw the houses the slave owners had lived in, most of them so big they've been converted to rooming houses. I found the slave market, with its shackles, Confederate flags, and slave block, with Fort Sumter sitting there just offshore. That was too much for me, and I went back to the barracks to wait for my flight out.

AFENI SHAKUR: I've been what you might call "race conscious" for a long time, because I came from North Carolina, you know. I mean it would have to start from there. I used to be walking down the North Carolina street and white people would ride down the highway or the road and then we would become a bunch of motherfuckers, you know, a bunch of the filthiest names that you could say, and I was from five and six and seven years old, I guess. I was very young at that time and they didn't give a damn what they were doing. And there was my family; like my grandmother, she had married this dude who was half-Indian and half-white. When they got married his family disowned him, but not only did they disown him, they tied him to a wagon and just dragged him all the way through the town. It was all over you, it was all around you, this shit. So of course I had to be aware of it because it was stuff that existed in my life, it wasn't foreign to me. I never called it discrimination or prejudice. I called it hate and that's what it was. Like the Ku Klux Klan. While I was living down there, the Ku Klux Klan came out and decided that they were going to put a curfew on the whole black community. The niggers had to be in the house by ten o'clock.

It just so happened that in Lumberton, North Carolina, they have a fairly large Indian population and they weren't going for it. The Ku Klux Klan came around the Indian community and the Indians kicked their ass and that was the reason why the niggers could go out after ten. The niggers weren't going to do it, they were scared. But the Indians did it. Lumberton was famous for that one act. The fact that they delivered a resounding blow against the Ku Klux Klan, man, that was really right on.

They had three different bathrooms: bathrooms for the niggers, for the Indians, and for the white people. And they were all filthy. What was the point of it?

LUMUMBA SHAKUR: My mother and father always told us, don't let anyone disrespect us regardless of who it is, but if they are white, be extra hard on them, because white people have been repressing us for three hundred years; when whites abuse or disrespect us, give them pure hell. I lived in Atlantic City. I had an Uncle Bates who was in the navy, stationed in Portsmouth, Virginia. Uncle Bates and Aunt Rita asked my mother if I and my brother Zayd could come to live in Portsmouth with them. You can dig the attitude Zayd and myself went to Portsmouth, Virginia with. My Uncle Bates and Aunt Rita lived in an all-black public housing project that looked like old army barracks. White kids would love to come in the black community to beat up black kids and call us "niggers," "buckwheats," "black bastards." The black kids were conditioned by their parents to run in their houses when the cracker kids came. Zayd and I were shocked; in Atlantic City white kids in their wildest whims would not come into the black community and act like this. Zayd and I punched those cracker kids in the face next time they came with their name-calling. It was nothing to talk about; it was only about six crackers acting like the junior Ku Klux Klan, and they didn't stay to fight— they ran. After Zayd and I got home, Aunt Rita asked us if we knew what would have happened if those crackers had beaten us up or run us into the house. We said, "Yes, Aunt Rita, you would have beaten us until we could not sit down for days." Aunt Rita said, "That's right. In our family, when we are right, we make a firm stand on our principles."

KATARA: McCellonsville, South Carolina, where my grandma lived, is a small town about the size of five square city blocks. The black section is off a sort of alley-like dirt road, and it is so small we walked past it twice before we figured out it was the right place. The houses are all in a straight line on one side of the road, with fields behind them, and the other side of the road is a cornfield. My grandma had a three-room pad. It was so small that a couple of times I saw copperheads—copperheads would get in all the time—crawling over each other for lack of space.

There was no way to just walk through the white section like you could through the black part of town: first of all, it looked different—the sidewalks were paved and lined with trees, and the grass was a healthy green. I was walking my way somewhere looking at the sights when up ahead a bit was a chick talking and laughing with her father on their lawn. The scene was so peaceful I smiled when I went by; they stopped talking and stared at me like I was nude or something and split inside the house. Well I wasn't going to let some bigoted fools spoil my day so I just kept on strolling. A couple of houses

down, two little kids were playing, with their mother
watching through a screen door I guess. Man, as soon
as I got near on the sidewalk she came running out into
the yard, grabbed the kids. Locked the door and watched
me through a window. That was the first and last time
I walked in that part of town.

There was a beach outside of town that everybody
went to on weekends. The white section was separated
from the black section by a wall with barbed wire on
it that stretched all the way down the beach and about
one hundred yards into the water. It was a bad old place,
though we had some fine times in the open-air "dance
hall," which was really just a rickety roof held up by
some poles, with a jukebox in the middle.

I hadn't sent a letter home in a while so I went to the
post office to buy some envelopes. The dude that ran
the P.O. was the funniest looking dude I ever saw, he
had a huge head with little eyes, he reminded me of an
ant. That's what everybody called him, "Ant Man." Well
I asked him for three envelopes. The dude had a wide-
enough smile on his face but I didn't like the way he was
looking at me. Anyway, I tried to hand him a $5 bill for
the envelopes, but he turned his head like he was busy
and said, "Just lay it down on the counter." But I didn't
like to just put down a big bill like that, I like to give it
to people in their hand, so I kept holding it out and
saying "Here" to him, like we were just standing there,
me with the bill in my hand and him trying to act like
he was too busy to take it from me. Finally he grabbed
for the end of the bill, so I pushed forward and touched
his hand and that dude jerked his hand back like he'd
just touched a hot stove and turned red. That shit made
me so mad I felt like jumping over the counter and
hugging the fool and getting all of my "dirty black skin"

on him. But I just told him to get my fucking change. He got it and slammed it down and I picked it up and left a nickel tip.

SHABA OM: I went to an integrated school in North Carolina, and dig this, the same honkys we went to school with and played on the same team with, came by at night, just as Nature is about to set the Sun. They came by and tried to run us over with their cars and motorcycles—then we got into a good one. We would be sitting on a large yellow rail on the corner beside the Sweet Shack when the white monkey men would drive by shooting BBs, throwing rocks and bricks and bottles at us. There was a park right across the street from the rail and the Sweet Shack, so we got some old wine bottles, some rocks, bricks, and everything we could find; the older bloods and sisters told us younger ones to stand behind some trees along the boulevard, and some of us hid in the park; then the older ones would stay on the rail or go in and out of the Sweet Shack as if everything is everything. Then when the monkey men came back by, all they saw was the older people on the corner. Those whites would do the regular—throwing beer or wine bottles and rocks, shooting BBs at them—and then we would jump out from behind the trees and come out from the park with bottles and bricks in hand, and light their asses up—cars and all.

One Halloween night in 1963 we were coming from a together party. When we had a party in the center of the park, it was wow, out of sight, but so in sight—you dig that? Some of the bloods I hung out with would drink a little wine and beer—like that was the thing to prove your manhood, get your head mellow-yellow or downright drunk. I mean so drunk you would hold onto the grass to keep from falling off the planet Earth, see trees, cars, and the streets moving away from you. So we'd get our beer or wine and go into the dark park, get our heads nice, and eat potato chips and rap. That night, as we came out of the dark park we looked up and on the corner we saw little sisters and brothers doing their Halloween shopping. We also saw cops—so we all laid in the park a little longer, because the girls didn't want the cops to see them. We couldn't leave the girls in the park by themselves, so we all lay down and dug on the actions on the corner and in the park. The reason we went back into the park was because the cops were known to stop black people coming out of the parks at night, beat and kick the boys' asses and rape the girls in the cop car. They wouldn't come into the parks. As we watched the action on the corner, two cars full of white monkey men came by and they shot a man on the rail with a gas-pump BB rifle and they threw some wine bottles, the larger gallon ones. They cut a woman on the leg; a big gash was made, blood went all over everything, street and people, and the racist ass pigs never did anything. Not one move did the insane dogs make to help the hurt black woman or the hurt black man, not even try to catch the white monkey men who did it. The pigs didn't know we were watching in the park. We waited, and when the monkey men came back again we could hear their cars coming, sounded like a jet landing. We had our wine bottles, bricks, and sticks all ready. We jacked up their front and back. The two pigs jumped out of their car, ran across the street by the park and began shooting all wild and everything, calling: "You black bitches, you son of a bitch motherfucking crazy-ass niggers I'll kill you!" We were in the wind running fast,

fast, fast. Talk about some fast-running people, we were burning across the baseball, football, and basketball fields, moving out, lead was flying all over the park.

That night in 1963 I began to really see the true American policeman as a real insane, inhuman dog and enemy. After that, every time I saw a pig coming I would get out of the way, I would think to myself the policeman is crazy, not a real human being. They spook me all up after that. As I was running I could see my little life passing in front of my eyes.

KWANDO KINSHASA: In 1955 I drove from New York to California with my father. My father made sure I saw the conditions of the red men, who lived in the prisons that white people called reservations. Before that trip I thought the caveman was a thing of the past, but in Mexico, some of the Indians still live in cave dwellings in the sides of cliffs, and people pay admission to see other people struggling to live—all part of the tourist "see America" trip. I saw America all right. I saw a lot of hotels and motels we were not allowed to stay the night in. I saw racism in every state we passed through. I became painfully aware that somehow or other I had to learn more about what really goes down in this world.

CLARK SQUIRE; born January 14, 1937: I was raised in Vernon, Texas, a small town just below the Texas Panhandle. My stepfather was a railroad section hand and my mother was a domestic. Like most Texas towns, Vernon was laid out so that whites occupied the main downtown area and the outlying suburbs, Mexicans lived near the railroad tracks, and blacks lived literally on the other side of the tracks. Up until I was seven or eight we lived in the white section of town. My mother cleaned for one of the white residents, which entitled us to live rent-free in the small servants' quarters in the back yard. A number of other black families lived that way, and we formed a sort of black subculture in the white community.

One Sunday Moms and I and a neighbor were coming home from church. For some reason or other I had fallen behind and was trotting along to catch up. I took a shortcut across an open lot where four or five white kids were playing in one corner. They must have mistaken me for a moving practice target, because they started throwing rocks at me. I stopped and started scratching around in the sand for some rocks because one thing I could do as a kid was throw a mean rock.

I cut loose once, but they broke and ran to their back door, falling all over themselves telling their mom how they had been attacked. I decided to set the record straight and go on over and tell my side of the story. I rolled up to the back door to describe how I had only been cutting across the lot, and how *they* started throwing rocks at *me*, and how, furthermore, I didn't appreciate it at all. So I started out "Miss—" to this big redhead who looked to be about six feet six inches tall, but before I could get anything out she spat, "Nigger!"

So I thought, if that's the way she's going to be about it then forget it, and turned to walk away. By this time she had come down from the screened-in porch, and she said "Nigger, don't you ever throw at white kids!" Then she kicked me dead in the ass, whomp! That pissed me off, so I spun around, but decided she was a little too big for me and backed out of the yard.

I had no doubt that, when I told my moms, she could and would beat Big Red. I saw her rumble with Dad too often to think any different. But on the way home I began thinking. I knew that when I told Moms she would tackle Big Red, and she was going to beat her. But then, being in a white neighborhood, the neighbors were sure to join in and gang my moms, and when that happened I was definitely going to help. And then someone would call the pigs, and when the pigs arrived they would arrest my moms. Any investigation of injuries, or any other pre-liminaries, was out of the question. They would simply walk right up and drag my moms off to jail. So I quashed the idea of telling her about it.

I didn't relate this incident to point up a traumatic experience that had a profound effect on me for the rest of my life. I've seen far worse examples of racism. I just wanted to emphasize the fact that even when I was very young it was already perfectly clear to me that the laws for blacks were completely different from the laws for whites. It was clear to me that if my moms attacked the woman who hit me, it would set in motion a chain of events the outcome of which was as sure as the sunrise the next morning.

Somewhere I have read a black psychologist's assertion that it is the duty of the black mother (and parents) to interpret the outside world for their children, and espe-cially the son, so as to enable him to survive, but without stifling so much of his aggressiveness as to emasculate him, which is indeed a delicate balance.

I cannot remember my mother or stepfather sitting me down to explain these ABCs of survival, but by the time I was five or six I had my diploma. The message came across so strong and clear it could not be ignored.

Since almost all of the violence, hostility and hatred I saw was perpetrated by whites, I began to observe and study their actions. I think this is something that all black people do either consciously or unconsciously, for it's necessary to survival. It's also necessary for black people to conceal or blunt their true emotions, reactions to what they see, through an intricate system of subterfuges and smokescreens. That is why so many blacks really do have a deep understanding of whites, even though they seldom tell them, and conversely why whites have little real understanding or knowledge of blacks.

BABA ODINGA: Every afternoon after school I would go and find the biggest and most difficult trees with my friends Verna, Stump, and Spike. Of the four of us, Verna was the best climber. Man, that girl could climb any tree; not only could she climb, she could jump, swing, swim, dive, fish, run, shoot, use a slingshot, set traps for birds, traps for crabs, climb a coconut tree like any one of us—and to climb a coconut tree is not the same as to climb any other tree. You might find anything from a lizard to rats or a chicken hawk in the coconut trees, you need strength and nerves; and she was one of the best night climbers. Sometimes she would be going up a tree and there would be a chicken hawk, and she'd have to drive the chicken hawk away from the tree. That is very dangerous: if she slips, that's it for her. She might break her neck or fall in the swamp. The water in the swamp is not deep but the bottom is mud and it is like quicksand. All this and more this girl could do. And when it came to fighting, where we used to live there was no kid, male or female, who could kick her ass, except me, and she used to give me trouble. We would be fighting on Monday night till our parents called us to go to bed, and Tuesday after school we would take up where we'd left off. As for doing the things that other girls usually do,

she came out on top there too. If you'd seen her you'd
never have thought she could do all that and some more.
She was rough—so was she beautiful. She was the spitting
image of an African goddess. The word beautiful is inade-
quate—man, Cleopatra or Nefertiti had nothing on that
woman. And not only was she beautiful, but also intelligent. If not for her, many a time we would have been
caught raiding someone's fruit garden.

When we had just made a successful raid on someone's
fruit garden we'd go back to the cemetery to divide up
what we had. I was usually the one who did the dividing:
I did "one for Stump, one for me, one for Spike, one for
me, one for Verna, one for me"—like that. Whatever we had,
I always got the most. I got away with the shit because
of two things: one, we always had plenty, and two, they
could not kick my ass. One night we only got eight or-
anges, so when we got back to the cemetery I began to
divide them among us. I did the same old thing, one for
you and one for me. Verna got two, Stump got one, Spike
got one, and I got four. They were not happy, but Verna
came to my defense so I thought I had them fooled. Then
Verna called me over in the tall grass and told me to give
it to her, so I told her to take her panties down; she said,
"No, not that, the orange." "What orange?" I said, so she
said, "You have four and you must give me one." I gave
it to her, and from that time I never held out on her.

Fishing became one of my favorite hobbies when I
turned eight or nine or so. Every afternoon after school
I changed my clothes, picked up my fishing line and my
knife and headed for the pier. If you wanted to catch
anything worthwhile catching, the best thing would be to
dive under the pier. You could dive under or you could
climb under, but where it would be easy to climb under
sometimes would not be advantageous for it would be

close to shore. Diving under the pier was not something that you just got up and did because you felt like doing it. The pillars that kept the pier up had small, sharp sea shells attached to them. Then there were the ones that crossed the ones that went straight down—so you had something like a crossword puzzle. Each of the pillars that crossed was about four feet wide and all over the pillars were these shells. The pillars looked like a wall with bottle-glass stuck up all over. You also had to contend with the tide. If the tide was coming in and you got caught between the pillars, unless you were a good diver your chances of not getting out were very great. The best time to dive under the pier was when the tide was going out, for the tide goes out slowly, and it does not pull so much as when it comes in.

Going under the pier was not something I liked to do, but I had no alternative, for if a policeman caught you fishing he would run you off the pier, and if he found your fishing line he would take it away from you. The only time that you could fish without the police bothering you was when you were with your parents or when some fine women were on the pier.

At times the danger we had to contend with in order to fish under the pier was very bad. You not only had to contend with the shells on the pillars but you never knew what awaited you under the pier. Sometimes barracudas and sharks and other dangerous sea creatures were under the pier relaxing in the shade. To secure our safety, first we would drop stones into the water from on top of the pier to disturb any sharks or barracudas, then one boy would dive under the pier and get up on one of the lower pillars, then the rest of us would dive under to the block he was on. While sitting on the pillars under the pier sometimes the cry would go up, "Barracuda!" and we'd all take our lines out of the water and that damn barracuda would come strolling in with a nonchalant manner, pause, then go over in the shade, as arrogant as if to say this was his territory and whenever he was on the set, all and any fishing would most definitely not be tolerated. We would just sit there and holler for someone to drop something into the water so this fool would just go somewhere else.

When I was twenty years old, something happened that could be a large problem for me and my friend ——— if we did not leave Antigua in a hurry. I will not go into it because other parties are still in Antigua. ——— and I were at the park looking at a football game—or soccer—when a woman I knew who went with a policeman came up and asked me what trouble I was in. I didn't know what she was talking about, so she told me that she'd heard her boyfriend say that the police were going to get me and ——— for something that had happened last night—someone told them it was me. I told her that I was home all night that night and sick, so it could not have been me, and she said she believed me. The kind of relationship we had was like brother and sister. Her boyfriend had never liked me for he always thought something was going on, while in reality nothing was. I did some favors for her a few times and anything I wanted that she had, she would give to me. She was like a big sister to me, and for this that fool policeman hated me. When she told me what was happening, my friend and I started to walk the back streets of St. John's. A few days later the people that really had this problem came and told me they would help me if I ran, so I said, shit, man, you help and I will run. With the money I had and the money they gave me, I ended up in Harlem.

I'd always thought that Harlem was a place where

black people lived and that black people controlled and ran. Although I knew it was part of America, I never thought of it as such. In 1965, when I came to Harlem, the first impression I got was that something was wrong. What it was I did not know, but I knew that everywhere I went all I saw was a whole lot of white police—I didn't see any black police, yet all the people that lived in Harlem were black.

AFENI SHAKUR: When I came to New York, I thought I was coming to the land of milk and honey, right? I remember that first of all my mother told me, you know; she wrote a letter to say that I shouldn't expect too much because it's not like they say. But we always referred to New York as "going up the road." It was something that you always looked forward to because you figured that when you got to New York you would live in a house that was decent and have clothes that were pretty. Every time somebody came down there from New York, they looked so good. But the reason for that, I found out later because I did it myself, was that when you go down South you bring your whole wardrobe and you make people think that it's only a small part of it. You borrow a car, a flashy, snazzy car, and you go down there and you pretend. But because of that and because of ignorance, up the road was always what was happening. Everything in the world was better up the road. Food was better, everything was better. White people didn't call you a bunch of motherfuckers up the road. It was like heaven, it was the land of milk and honey up the road. And when I got up the road I was disgusted.

Up the road looked sick. It looked nasty and I wanted to go back down South. I couldn't stand the smells, New

York smelled terrible. And you couldn't see the stars. I mean I was ten or eleven years old and those are the things that I was really worried about. I couldn't see the stars, I couldn't run out at twelve o'clock at night and play hide and seek like I could down South—I was a tomboy first of all. In New York I had to be worried about somebody raping me and shit. I never thought that anybody would want to rape me when I was down South. Why in hell would somebody want to rape me? I never related to no sex, what are you talking about? I had to keep worrying about things like that. Then, the food was awful. My mother had a bill at the butcher, the Jewish butcher, and we couldn't eat anything but kosher bologna and hamburger meat that was full of fat. His way of putting it was that he wouldn't want her to overstep her means so he would only let her buy certain things on credit, and they were always scraps. It was never good food. She was doing the best she could. She wasn't making but about $40 a week. And we were renting a room in another lady's apartment; my sister and my mother and I all lived in one room. It was really bad.

KWANDO KINSHASA: The only consistent thing that plays on my mind is or rather was the intense reservation atmosphere of Harlem. I remember my old man, Moms, or my uncle would take me and my cousin for a bus ride down Seventh Avenue into the lower section of Manhattan. This bus ride always made me notice that we were leaving one area, a poor, dirty, but friendly area, and proceeding into a rich, sparkling clean, but hostile area of the city. My parents were always very particular to see that I was clean, you know, clean shoes, shirt, suit, face, teeth, hair combed—just to travel into an area where white people predominated and all of a sudden blacks acted differently. What was really funny is that we never seemed to visit any of these strange white people, but just rode a bus or drove in a car into an area of the city where these whites either lived or were in heavy numbers. As time went on I disliked these trips more and more. Even at an early age, I almost instinctively rebelled against anything unnatural, be it the environment, clothes, attitudes, or people I was around. To me then, as now, I am most comfortable and interested in people who are themselves and who are not afraid to challenge all unnatural things around them, be it bad housing conditions, reactionary blacks, racist whites, exploitive businessmen, an enemy American government, or genocide. If they are willing to challenge these inhuman things as I am, then I can relate to them. If not then I'm likely to attack them.

SHABA OM: I came back to the Big Apple in 1965 to live with my mother, Rachel. She and my brother and my two sisters, Justina and Diane, were all living in an apartment at 6 East 118th Street in Harlem. The apartment had two and a half rooms. Dig on who lived in the apartment: Rachel, David, Justina, Diane, myself, one dog, and one cat. I had wanted to come back to Harlem in the Big Apple and I did; in the first month or more I just dug on the city and people; but this was a mind blower. This took me some time to get used to. In the apartment it was madness because it was so small. I would get up in the morning and would have to let everyone in the house know I was getting up: I would call to everyone so I wouldn't step on or over anyone. I finally adjusted myself to it somewhat.

Schooltime came around. Here we go up to the pigs'

so-called welfare center, so I could get on Rachel's budget to receive money for school and other things one needs as a human being. The center put Rachel and me through all kinds of wild questions about my life, where I had been, why I came to New York City, all kinds of silly-ass stuff.

JAMAL: Now the area we lived in had three parts to it: blacks who lived in houses, blacks who lived in the housing project (tall apartment buildings), and whites in Hillside Homes, also a housing project. The blacks in the project brought with them that niggertown culture, and the blacks in houses discouraged contact. They were afraid we would get ripped off by a junkie or a wino, or by one of the jitterbugs that lived in the project. At that time gang wars were being waged between the black projects and Hillside Homes. The black teenagers and white teenagers, girls and guys, would get into fights. There were gang wars going on constantly. There had been a lot of kids hurt, over the years, and even a few deaths. One policeman got killed when I was still young. So I was really discouraged away from the projects.

But the majority of the black children who went to PS 21 came from the projects, so these were the people I associated with. Most of the younger black children from the projects fell into a clique. It wasn't really an organized gang, but they all lived in the projects and would rumble with anyone that didn't, saying you didn't have any hang-out card unless you came from the projects. I played stickball and basketball with them, so I didn't encounter too much difficulty, but I know other children in the school did—got their lunch money taken away, got beat up on the spur of the moment. It was a spontaneous thing: a cat from the projects would come up to you and hit you in your eye because he didn't like the shirt you had on. When I was about in the second grade, I began to run with them some, but I never liked the idea of participating when they were just jacking a cat up in the school for no apparent reason. So during school hours I primarily kept to myself. Then I'd come home and go upstairs and change, and come outside and play football or ride my bike or indulge in some other type of activity like that until it was time to go in and eat, do whatever little homework I had to do, watch some TV and go to bed. On Sundays Noonie would wake me up, dress me up in a suit and take me down to Trinity Baptist Church to Sunday school, and when I got a little older, I began singing with the junior choir. And I was pretty much content with the whole situation.

But it was the usual thing in that black community to cover up things that went wrong. One family on the block had come from the deep South. A block association was organized—not to improve the housing standards, not to try to keep dope out of the community, not to deal with police brutality, but just for the purpose of running those people out the block. They said that they were rowdy, they drank too much, their children always got in fights with other children in the community, and they were undesirable. And finally enough pressure was applied to them so they moved. Now I think they live in an apartment somewhere in Brownsville. They were forced out of a community where the housing was a little better, back into the ghettos, and back into the misery and poverty they were trying to escape, because a few petit-bourgeois blacks in the neighborhood felt disturbed and embarrassed that these people lived in the same community with them.

I started detecting the strange vibes, you know, the vibrations, I would get from people in the community.

Not from my peers, not the friends that I had in the community, but from the parents. They would tell their children not to get too deeply associated with me because of the background of my foster brothers and sisters and for other reasons. My friends told me this. I asked Noonie about it, and every time she just tried to say to go ahead and keep to myself and not bother with that. I wasn't satisfied, but there was no way to understand it, then.

My block increasingly reminded me of a television show named *Peyton Place.* People saying this about other people, cutting each other's throats, sneaking with each other's wives, and then trying to cover it up and make the community look happy, healthy, and wholesome. I didn't want to be involved.

BOB COLLIER: After fourteen, you start noticing things. The guys I had grown up with were splitting up, going off in different directions. Ethnic and racial divisions started to make a difference. Like the Italian girl down the block changed her attitude toward me. Her father didn't like her talking to me, and his looks told me I should keep away from her and their house. The Irish kids I'd grown up with were avoiding me too. But it was different with the Greenes and the Wards and the Andersons. We had grown up together too, but they were black. They didn't give me mean looks for coming around or talking to their daughters. It took me a while to realize I hadn't done anything wrong to that girl, or to the Irish kids, I was just born black.

ALI BEY HASSAN: When I was ten, living on 118th Street in Harlem, I began to notice lots of things—numbers writers, hustlers, pimps, whores, winos, addicts, street gangs. I joined a gang for a while, and later I got to know some of the prostitutes on 118th Street. My mother used to drink with them a lot, and they sometimes gave me some change to spend. I never saw anything wrong with them—they were just like any other women in the community. Often I would see the police take advantage of the women on the block or in the bars. I believe one thing that gave police the courage to mess with black women was that the police could see black pimps or hustlers beating on the women almost daily. So the cops moved in whenever they chose, they knew they would not get any resistance from black men.

Protection was what the average prostitute was looking for from her so-called man—looking for him to bail her out of jail when she was busted, or give out with a few sweet lies now and then. A lot of black women turned to prostitution for one basic reason: to make ends meet—especially if they had children.

And naturally every black community had its dope addicts, thanks to the government and the police department, which never did anything to stop it. My mother told me about the evils of dope while I was young, and I didn't try it for a long time. But even at age thirteen I smoked and drank a lot. On weekends I watched people go through their routine—cutting each other up, shooting, fighting. Business was always booming for the local cops and the government: niggers killed niggers, niggers hustled niggers. One day in the summer of 1949, a hustler at our door talked my mother into putting a $5 deposit down on saxophone lessons. Moms agreed and gave the dude a five. I was standing there all the while the game was being played, and I was suspicious, but I didn't say anything because he ran it down so slick I halfway believed it myself. Anyway the guy never showed again.

All in all it was one big family, where everyone had his own way of struggling to survive, and it was just the most visible aspect of the defeatism created among black people by the capitalist racist structure. But that's old news now.

I started growing up fast, I was street-wise. I was a runner in the block, putting numbers in for people, picking up cigarettes, liquor, beer. I was doing a lot of things men would do, even though I wasn't going with grown women or messing with dope yet.

DHARUBA: It was in the mid-'40s or early '40s that my father started shooting dope. Then, dope didn't have the stigma it has now. It was somewhat slick, somewhat of a cool thing to do. All the jazz musicians did it, all the fly niggers did it, you know, so I guess he thought it was something slick, so he did it. That's determined his life for almost thirty years now. He went to jail a lot of times, and all of his busts revolved around that dope. I think what he told me one time was true: that dope erased a whole generation of black people. We can see that's what it's doing now to the generation of youth, there's nothing more you can say. It's not one generation that dope has eradicated, it's two or three—in the black community, that is.

CETEWAYO*: When I was about eleven and a half, one Friday night I was walking the dog. I used to have to walk the dog every night. It was about two in the morn-

---

* Excerpted from Cetewayo's autobiography to be published by Bantam Books.

ing. I had just come into the house. I was high off of wine
and smoke. I had come from a party. My father had just
come in from work. He said, "Did you walk the dog?"
"No." "When the fuck are you going to walk the dog?"
I said, "That's cool. I'll walk the dog." Rusty was extremely well trained and I never had to put a leash on
him, I would just walk with him so he wouldn't attack
cats or get into a fight with other dogs. Some dogs had
a very combative attitude in that neighborhood. I rolled
up a joint before I went out. I went down on the stoop
and stood there smoking. The dog was running up and
down the street, doing what dogs do when they're running up and down the street.

A police car came by while I was smoking. I thought
he might hop out of his car and frisk me and I don't
need that. I eased off the stoop and called the dog. I
walked down to Lenox Avenue and stopped at the Silver
Rail Bar. Somebody bought me a drink or something. I
started walking up 138th Street. There's a little candy
store on the corner of Lenox Avenue. I went up to get
some cigarettes and the *Daily News* and some cigars. The
cigars and the *Daily News* were for my father and the
cigarettes were for me. While I was standing there, two
dudes I knew came up to the stand. One dude was nicknamed Cocaine, for obvious reasons. Cocaine and this
other dude came up to the stand. I said, "What's going
on?" "Nothing to it. The same ol' same ol'." He said,
"I got a little something, I don't know if you're down
with it." I said, "What is it?" He said, "You want some
blow?" I said, "That's cool." He said, "Come on in the
hallway." We went in the hallway and he busted out this
little glassine bag with a white, powdery substance in it.
He made what is called a snorting quill out of a piece of
matchbook. He crimped it like a scoop and dipped it in

the bag and sniffed. He and his friend went through this ritual of breaking the bag, handling it so delicately and fashioning it like an expert. He passed me the quill and—it was very important that I didn't display my ignorance that I didn't know what to do. I said, "You go first." He took it. He took a 2 & 2, two blows in each nostril. Now I had the idea. Yeah. I wasn't going to put my ignorance on display by asking what was in the bag because I'm supposed to know what's in the bag. He passed me the bag. I stuck the quill in the bag and put the substance up my nose like he did. Snorted it. I repeated that same operation three or four more times. Now the cat said, "Damn, man, you sure got a vacuum cleaner for a nose." I took that as a compliment so that inspired me to take two more. He looked at me and said, "Hold up, Jack. This guy don't know how to be sociable. He's going to snort it all up." They sniffed up the rest of it.

We were standing on the stoop rapping. I don't know how much time elapsed between my taking the blow and when I felt the effects of it, but one thing for certain, at one point while standing on that stoop, this strange unexpected wave of tranquillity and calmness just enveloped me. I was just rapping, talking about basketball. He asked me whose team I was going to play for this year. He was saying, man, you should come on and play for some community center he wanted me to play with. I said I don't play with no losers. He said, "Get down with the Seniors." I said then I won't get no games because they got a clique thing going. I said, "I'm going to play with Kennedy Community Center," which had one of the best community center teams in Harlem. All kinds of local stars played for Kennedy. Pablo Robinson, who now plays for the Harlem Globetrotters. Popcorn Ferguson, Ralph Dunbar, Bob McCullough—several current NBA stars and

Harlem Globetrotters at that time played with J.F. Kennedy C.Y.O. team. I said, "I'm going to play with Kennedy this year. I'll probably play with St. Joseph's also."

At that point, while rapping, this feeling of tranquillity engulfed me. I felt myself keeling over slowly or slowing over keelingly. I felt myself dipping down. My eyelids got very heavy, but I felt very good. Very good. The only drawback was that I felt itchy. My throat got very dry, and I had difficulty in swallowing. But aside from that, I was feeling some kind of good. Next thing I knew, I was nodding. I also noticed a change in my voice. It started to drag with a whining sound. Instead of saying, "Yeah, man, everything is cool," I was saying, "Y e a h, m a n, e v e r y t h i n g i s c o o l." It's known as a dope fiend's whine. I said, "Yeah, man, that's some hip shit." He said, "Yeah, man, I'm dealing. We got some pretty good smack. Any time you want to cop you know somebody. If you know anybody who wants to cop, shoot them on me." I said, "As a matter of fact, I'll see you tomorrow." "That's cool."

Then I started walking back toward my house at 137th Street. It took me about two hours to get there. I didn't get home until the bars closed. I talked to other dudes, stopped for a drink. I threw up before I got home. That happened a few times before the night was over. But everything felt beautiful. I had never felt so beautiful before in my life.

I went upstairs and gave my father the cigars and the newspaper and went into the bedroom and put some sides on the record player and stayed up the rest of the night nodding and listening to the sides. I was saying to myself, "Damn, I sure feel good. I don't feel sad or blue at all. I got to do this more often."

At some point or another, I went to sleep. I woke up that afternoon. My stomach was all messed up and I had a hell of a hangover. I had breakfast. At two o'clock I had a basketball game and I played ball.

Later on that night, I ran into the dudes on the block. They said, "You got a smoke?" I said, "Yeah, I got some upstairs. Why don't you get the wine?" They got the wine and we went to my house, drinking wine and smoking. We were rapping, trying to decide what to do. I said, "Why don't we get some dugee?" (Heroin.) They looked at me with sort of subdued shock. They didn't want me to know how shocked they were. They looked at each other. A few seconds elapsed and they said, "Man, you fucking with that shit?" I said, "I'm only snorting. I did it one time last night. It's really hip, you should try it. I'm not shooting. I'm just snorting." The original position on heroin was under no circumstances would you use heroin. That original position, however, in time was modified and came out that you wouldn't *shoot* any heroin. The modification, needless to say, did not take place until you required a rationalization for snorting. In other words, once we started snorting, we had to rationalize it and decree that snorting was all right as long as you didn't shoot it.

But that night they didn't dig snorting. I said, "I ain't going to get strung out. I know how to control it." This, of course, is what every drug addict says at first. They said, "Dig you later someplace," and cut on out. I sat up in the house for a while listening to some sides and then went downstairs to the corner by the Silver Rail Bar.

I ran into some dude and he put in $2.50 and I put in $2.50 and went and copped a bag of dugee. Somewhere along the line, we ran into a third party, a sister who snorted, also, so the three of us went up my house and snorted up the heroin. We got righteously fucked up. In

those days, on one $5 bag you could snort it between
three people and be fucked up for the rest of the night.
This was back in the days when heroin was of such quality that two drug addicts, like strung out, could wake up
in the morning sick and split a $5 bag between them;
not only would it alleviate their illness, but they would
also get high. This was back in the days when the quality
of heroin was such that it was commonplace to see an addict tap dancing up and down the street. This was during
the era when two dudes would get high off a bag of smack,
dugee, and stand up in the street boxing for four to five
hours. This was back during the days—I remember one
incident on 125th Street: a dope fiend, who was obviously
extremely high and feeling no pain whatsoever, in a
world of his own, locked up in his own world of sub-
jectivity—he was coming down 125th Street between
Seventh and Eighth Avenues rowing a boat. He was coming up the street backwards like he was rowing a boat.
This was how high he was. He stopped in front of the
Apollo Theater. There was a long line, I don't remember
who was at the Apollo, maybe Jackie Wilson. At any rate,
he stopped in front of the theater. He stopped rowing
his boat and started nodding. A cop walked up and said,
"Move along before I bust your ass." He tapped him on
the ass with his nightstick. The dope fiend just came out
of his nod and continued rowing up the block.

That was back in the era of good dope, you know.
In fact, that was back during the era when you could
buy a piece of heroin, an ounce of heroin, for $500 and
cut it three times for a 3-to-1 cut on it and the dope would
still be good. That's how it was then.

So after we got high, we just hung out all night. It
was at that point that I dug that I would be sniffing more

heroin than smoking marijuana and drinking wine, from that point on.

On my thirteenth birthday, December 13, 1959, I celebrated the day by declaring it a holiday, which meant I wasn't going to school, which meant I didn't go to school. A group of brothers and sisters drank wine and smoked reefer all that morning. Later on that night, I ran into some dudes; all these cats were older than me. They were seventeen, eighteen, nineteen. We had all been in the same gangs, the Sportsmen and the Cobras. They had been shooting dope for over a year. I was coming up the street, they ran into me. I wasn't hip to what was going down. I said, "Everything's cool. Today's my birthday. What are you going to do for me?" They said, "Damn, wish we would have known. We're broke. We're going to take off some devils." The Muslim influence was beginning to be felt then.

One of my claims to fame was that at that age I was sticking up, so I said, "Man, it don't make sense to mug somebody. You won't get more than $10, $20, or at the most, $50, and between the three of you—and you risk fifteen years in the pen. It don't make no sense." They said, "Yeah, but we don't have any money." I said, "I have some money, we can get high." They said, "You don't get high like we do. We were going to get some dugee." I said, "I can dig that." They said, "You fuck with that stuff?" I said, "You got to be cool." . . . This cat on 140th Street had a shooting gallery and used to rent the gimmicks out for 50¢, so we all went up there.

[*Cetewayo tried skin-popping then, injecting the heroin under the skin (not into a vein). It had no effect at all—then a day later he discovered that the others*

*with him had used all the heroin and duped him by
injecting plain water under his skin. So he went with
a man named Spike that night for some "real stuff."]*

. . . He took the belt, looked at my arms. He said, "You
got some hellified veins. They just bulge out. I used to
have veins like that when I was younger. I'd give my
whole right arm for just one of those veins." I said, "Go
on, man." He stuck the spike in, the blood came up in
the spike. He squeezed the eyedropper. I watched the
liquid disappear out of the dropper and into my arm.
Like a few seconds later, that same wave of tranquillity
and peacefulness, just totally hip feeling, enveloped me.
It was like ten times as heavy as the feeling I got when
I first snorted heroin. I immediately went off into a nod.
Immediately.

The next thing I knew, he was shaking my arm. "Are
you all right?" I said, "Yeah," but I had to throw up. I
threw up four or five times. Aside from that and the
itching and scratching, everything was mellow.

I came back in the street and just walked around for
the next five or six hours, feeling beautiful. Feeling beautiful. There was nothing in that environment that affected
me adversely. I just paid no attention to everything. Garbage? That didn't mean nothing. Everything was just cool
—mellow. From that point, there was no looking back.
Every night after that I would have my get-down money.
My $2.50 get-down money. I'd find a partner and just get
down.

. . . After I don't know how much time elapsed—it
couldn't have been more than a few weeks—some of the
older hustlers in the neighborhood found out I was shooting heroin. I came in my building one night, and went
up to the second floor, where I lived. About seven dudes

were standing there waiting for me. The older hustlers in the block. I immediately got apprehensive. What are all these motherfuckers doing in front of my door? They didn't live there. They didn't look friendly.

They said, "Come on upstairs. We want to talk." I said, "Wait a minute, let me go in a minute and I'll be right out." I was going to get my gun and then find out what they wanted to talk about. One was a boxer, and he just stood in front of the door, eliminating the possibility of my getting in. They dragged me up to the roof, and went into this whole thing about shooting dope. I said, "No, man, I don't mess with that." They said, "That's what we thought, but we seen you ease off with some dope fiends. You ain't selling dope?" I said, "No, just smoke." They said, "Those cats don't use reefer, just dope." Then they started debating over whether or not the issue was just to kick my ass or throw me off the roof.

After that, they went through this whole thing about what heroin would do to you. One of the dudes started crying. Then I really dug the seriousness of this whole scene. I was his protégé. He taught me how to play ball. He would say, "You're NBA material. You're going to play in the pros." That was my ambition. He started to cry, about how I was fucking up my career and he would rather see me dead than a dope fiend. He was the main advocate of the throw-me-off-the-roof thing, which got no endorsement from me whatsoever. I was totally opposed to it! When it became clear I was going to get an ass-whipping, I aligned myself with the ass-whipping faction. They kicked my ass, then took me downstairs to the apartment, knocked on the door, my father answered and they threw me in and ran down to my father about why they did it. He thanked them.

Now, realizing how seriously older hustlers in the

neighborhood, how strongly opposed they were to my shooting dope and remembering their promise that if they ever saw me shooting dope, they would kill me—I had to make a choice: stop shooting dope or go someplace else, because I couldn't do it in the neighborhood. So I started hanging out downtown and just kept on.

I think I was still going to St. Aloysius at that time. One night about two months later, I was coming in the house. Three dudes from the block were waiting for me again. I said, "What's happening?" I wasn't about to get no more ass-licking, so I just pulled my switchblade. They said, "We just want to talk to you." I said I didn't want no repeat performance here. They said, "No, man, we ain't seen you around. What you been doing?" "Nothing, going to school and playing ball." "You're not hanging out in the neighborhood." "I'm just too busy with basketball and school." "You're not shooting shit no more?" I said, "No, man. I dug it and cut that thing loose." Popcorn gave me a real serious rap and had me doing a lot of thinking. When I went in the house, I thought they might be right.

I had noticed that getting high was having an adverse effect on my ballplaying. I wasn't getting down court as fast as before in the fast breaks. I decided I was going to stop.

The next morning I got up and went to school. In all probability, I played some ball that night. The morning after, when I woke up I had cold chills, I was sweating, my nose was running and I was yawning uncontrollably. I couldn't figure it out. I said, "Damn, I'm not going to school. I'm sick." I took some medicine, some cough medicine or something. Around twelve o'clock I felt extremely bad. I thought, maybe if I get some fresh air, I'll feel better. I walked down the street and ran into one of the local fiends and we started rapping. He said, "You want to get high?" I said, "No, I cut it loose." "Yeah?" "Yeah. It might not be too good for me." He said, "How long you been fucking around?" I said, "A few months. Every night. Sometimes twice on Saturday." He said, "Yeah, man, you might have a Jones. What you shaking for?" I said, "No, I ain't got no Jones." His suggestion I might be addicted to heroin filled me with such fright, what I was previously experiencing—the running nose, chills, sweating, and yawning—became amplified a hundred times. He said, "You're sick." I said, "I do feel sick. I'm going back to bed." He said, "That's not going to do any good. You need a shot." I said, "I don't have a habit." He said, "You might be hooked." I refused to even consider the possibility that I was strung out to heroin. I turned, walked away and went upstairs to bed.

At six o'clock that night, there was no getting around it. I was throwing up and going from bad to worse. I went down to the corner and ran into this man. We were rapping. He said he was going to cop and asked "What's wrong with you?" I said, "I might have a habit." "When did you get high last?" "Not since night before last. I used to shoot every day." "Man, you're strung out." I said, "Yeah, man. Fuck it. Let's get a bag." I gave him $5 to get another bag. We went up to my house, me, him and another dude and drew two bags into the cooker. I was shivering. They said, "You get your sickness off, go first." By this time I was hitting myself, taking off on my own. I was shaking so uncontrollably now that they had to give me the shot.

Just moments after that shot, the skag in my veins, the sickness was totally gone. I was high. Just feeling good. At that point I knew I was strung out. I was strung out on heroin. Every morning after that, before I went to school, every night around ten o'clock or so, I would get high. Take off on skag.

[*Cetewayo rented a room and kitchenette for himself and lived there while he was starting high school. He mainlined heroin on a schedule, once every morning and once every evening. He attended Rice Catholic High School—90 per cent white—on a basketball scholarship, and supported himself and his habit with his gun.*

In March, 1961, there was a sudden shortage of heroin. Cetewayo spent all one day—and with increasing desperation, and increasing physical pain, most of that night—searching from streetcorner to streetcorner for a dealer with some heroin to sell. About five o'clock in the morning he went back to his room.]

. . . I just lay there on the bed. At this point my mind wasn't even focused upon or preoccupied with getting a fix. That whole need and that whole craving for a shot of heroin to alleviate my physical pain was soon superseded by feelings of utter shame, loneliness, isolation, depression and self-pity. I had money. I had money to cop with. That wasn't no problem, but I just didn't have the strength to go back out in the streets and start to search again.

After a while I started to cry. I just lay there on the bed crying. In my mind, on the stage of my mind, all kinds of weird dramas were being enacted. A whole lot of memories that had been buried in the vault of my mind suddenly became very vivid. A lot of old memories. Memories about my childhood and my mother pushing me in a baby carriage. Memories about my little sister Lorraine, and how she used to wear braces on her feet because she was born with club feet, and how we used to have to sleep in the same bed—me, her, and her braces. And how she used to kick me. My legs used to be all scarred up by the braces banging me on the leg. Memories about my grandmother and how mysterious and mystical she seemed during my childhood. Memories about my mother taking me from bar to bar and me collecting quarters and half-dollars and dollars from all of her friends. Memories about my dog Butch, who was now dead. Memories about my most glorious days on the basketball court. Whole scenes, whole chapters and episodes from my past were re-enacted upon the stage of my mind. In Technicolor. In Panavision.

I just lay there going through those changes. Crying, and all this shit going on in my mind. Memories about the times that I used to—when I didn't have anything to do, no place to go, I just felt isolated from the rest of humanity, and I would get on the subway and just ride. Just ride. Memories about old gang fights, back in the days when I was a Sportsman. We would fight against other black street gangs, the Assassins, Enchanters, or the Englishmen, or the Imperial Knights, or anybody who we could get a fight out of. Memories about the cold winter nights when me and three or four other brothers would be standing up in the tenement hallway with a quart of apple wine, do-woppin. Singing. Memories about school and how much I despised it.

All of these different scenes and different experiences from my past were just flashing back and forth, across the screen of my mind. Turning back and forth and up and down upon the stage of my soul. There is an emotional experience that I would go through. I didn't come to label it or put a term on it but several years later, I would slip off into an emotional state, sink into it, I would call it my sack of woe. I took the name from a jazz tune by Cannonball Adderley, "Sack of Woe." I would righteously be in a big sack of woe. That is how I would perceive of myself—as being trapped in a huge burlap sack, with a lot of decaying garbage in the sack with me. It was foul in that sack. I would just call it my sack of woe.

... At some point or another, I summoned up enough will power and enough strength to lift myself up off the bed. It was a rather perverted kind of victory. It was a victory in that I was on my feet again. I was in my coat, going out the door. That was a victory. But it was a perverted victory and a negative victory in that I was going out the door to resume my quest for death. I was going out the door to search for a fix.

So I hit the streets—and it was cold. March. It was cold. And the winter air, the hawk, seemed as though it was just slicing through my body like giant razor blades. Gillette, double-edge blades. My fingers were numb. I was frozen with cold, and at the same time I was sweating profusely. Yawning and sniffling. Walking almost at a 45 degree angle, because of the cramps in my stomach.

I stood out on the corner of 131st Street and Madison Avenue, one of the major dope centers in Harlem. I stood out there in the midst of what seemed like tens of thousands of other addicts who were in a similar plight.

[Eventually he got some heroin.]

... That's when the metamorphosis went down.

... Up until that point I maintained a sizable degree of control over how much dope I shot. Up until that point, it was rare for me to just shoot dope to shoot dope.

I had a schedule. I would get high at certain times. I only felt the need to get high at certain times. Now I had a need to be high all the time. I started sticking up more, pulling more robberies. It really wasn't a thing of more robberies in a quantitative sense. It was more robberies in a qualitative sense. I started going after bigger money. Instead of liquor stores and grocery stores, I started moving on jewelry stores and supermarkets and payroll stickups. I hooked up with three other dudes, three other bloods from down 117th Street off Lenox. These dudes were cold-blooded professional stick-up artists. Now instead of pulling off stings that resulted in $200, $300, $400 profit, I was pulling off stings where we would get two and three grand.

One night after a supermarket job in Brooklyn, Reggie, one of my stick-up partners, asked me if I ever speed-balled. I said no. Speedball was a combination of heroin and cocaine. What did he turn me on to that for! Good God Almighty! We bought about ten $5 caps of cocaine and about three half-loads of heroin. There were three of us. He threw four $3 bags of skag into the cooker and then on top of that, he put two $5 caps of cocaine into the cooker. They got off first, Reggie and the other brother. They were going through some hellified changes. I didn't know what the fuck was going down. He just sat up and he's booting the dope, booting the heroin and cocaine back and forth in his veins, twelve, thirteen times. I said, "Man, you're going to clog up the works and I ain't got no wires." He said, "No, man, this is the way you shoot a speedball. Real slow, and boot it back and forth." I said, "I wish you would hurry up so I could find out what it's all about."

Finally, I got the works and drew up a shot. He said, "Man, you better let me hit you. You might shoot it too fast and freeze your heart up." He hit me and shot the substance in real slow. Real slow. Not all of it, about half of it. Like wow, I don't know what the fuck happened but this real hellified sensation overcame me. It wasn't the lethargic drowsiness of a heroin high. Rather it was genuinely soul-stirring, uplifting—it felt like a shot of life—a shot of super life. It just felt extremely good and extremely alive and extremely powerful.

I'm sitting there with my arm out. He's shooting it in and out, real slow, and the feeling is just building, just becoming greater. I started sweating and got a dry taste in my mouth. I felt real cool inside. Real cool. Real good. He just booted it about four or five times, real slow, and shot it all. I followed his instructions to a tee because I didn't want to do anything that would result in the loss of this blissful feeling. After the fifth boot, I pulled the spike out. I couldn't sit still. Just walked up and down. The three of us. Slipping each other five. Telling jokes and shit. That high faded away. It was replaced by the heroin high. That's what a speedball is all about. The cocaine takes you way, way up and makes you almost feel like a god. You feel damn immune to death. That fades away and the calmness and tranquillity of the heroin takes over. It was beyond a doubt the most ecstatic feeling I ever experienced until that point.

I didn't realize it at the time but I had adopted a brand-new Jones.

AFENI SHAKUR: My girlfriend Sandra died when we were eighteen. And it was caused by heroin and by her being pregnant and her body being all fucked up. Earlier that year she had had a tube removed. She was supposed to have had a complete hysterectomy, but they didn't do that, they just removed one tube and didn't tell her that they had only removed one tube. So as soon as she felt like screwing, she did, and she got pregnant. And her body wasn't well. She didn't even know she was pregnant till she was about five months pregnant, because she was the kind of woman that had her period when she was pregnant and shit, so she didn't think to go to a doctor to check it out. We don't go to doctors often, we don't go to doctors till we're dead. So she hadn't gone to the doctor. And when she finally went, she found out she was pregnant. She was snorting dope too—I think I found out later, you know, after she died, that she was also skin popping. Well one morning she got up in the middle of the night, like about five o'clock in the morning and she was on her way to the bathroom and she just collapsed. She had water on the brain or hemorrhage on the brain or something like that. When she got to the hospital, they operated and the child was alive but they killed the baby. They wouldn't put the baby in an incubator or something. You know, like the nurses told us that they just killed the baby. They just let the child die.

My friend died, she never recovered. Her brain or something was all fucked up. I can't understand this stuff, but I know she died, and that really turned me off the drugs, off pot and coke and horse. It didn't make me not like drugs, it just made me so that drugs made me puke at the sight of them. Because it was the only friend that I ever had. And I was very close to her. I remember that night I found out she was dead, I got a phone call from my mother saying come uptown and I walked in my mother's house and my mother and my sister were sitting around looking all fucked up and sad and shit. I didn't know what was wrong with them. And they said it's Sandra. I thought that she had the baby or had a miscarriage. And then my mother bust out crying and I found out she was dead. I walked out of the house and I didn't go back for about twenty-four hours. I just walked the street. I was really fucked up. It was the first time in my life I'd ever felt somebody's death, you know, because she was all I had.

After that I couldn't relate to drugs. I guess that's why I don't feel any bitterness toward addicts. I feel bad because we haven't done enough to help them, we haven't come up with any solutions and we have to have one, man. I know that they're fucking us around and conniving us and shit like that, but I can't look at it like that. I look at all of those talents that people say are so fucked up, but I think they're talents and those talents should be used in a positive way. If they can use up all of that energy to connive, there's nothing wrong with them except that we haven't done enough.

ALI BEY HASSAN: After my mother died I used to lie back in my room and think about things I'd done and seen—things my mother told me and things she had to do in order to survive. I remember some things more vividly than others. My mother told me about once when I was a baby in her arms, and she had had an argument with a policeman and the pig hit her in the head while she was holding me in her arms. After he hit her, she laid me down in the snow and whipped his ass, and then took his badge, his gun, and his nightstick, and picked me up out of the snow and left. A lot of people in the Third Ward knew my mother from that incident. I guess it was true, because I've heard other people speak of my mother as a fighter—in self-defense, that is.

I also remember minor run-ins with the cops. Once the

police caught me hitching a ride on the back of a bus, took my name and address and let me go. I never heard any more about it. Another time, when I was eleven, a Puerto Rican friend and I opened up a fire hydrant with a clothes hanger and a piece of wood. After we got it turned on and got into the water the cops showed, so we ran, each a different way. He ran up the street and got caught right away. I ran down into the back yards, which I knew very well—got away for a few minutes— and got caught coming out on Park Avenue and 118th Street, a block from where we started running. Both of us were in a precinct somewhere up on 126th Street. Anyway, one cop slapped my friend on his face, hard, with the back of his hand, because the cop claimed that he was looking over his shoulder while he was writing out cards on us. We were picked up about 10:30 A.M. and not cut loose until about six that evening.

KWANDO KINSHASA: I saw my first riot when I was about five. A cop had shot a black serviceman for nobody really knew what. My father took me over to where the people were rioting—near 145th Street and Seventh Avenue—and I remember a lot of people screaming and blood all over the streetcorner. I didn't really think much about it. I guess I figured it was something that big people just did—a regular event in their lives. But it is a vivid memory.

KUWASI BALAGOON: I missed the March on Washington—by going to football practice—but later I read Malcolm's comments on it and heard him rap twice on TV and his logic and stance took root in my mind. I had also heard Dr. King, but wasn't particularly impressed. Pictures of Bull Connor, beating demonstrators, turned my stomach. And the events that took place at the rebellion in Cambridge, Maryland, showed a far better action for black people to take even then. A sure-enough riot jumped off at the then-new D.C. stadium on Thanksgiving Day. With a predominantly white high school football team playing Eastern, the brothers lost the game but didn't lose the fight. The reports of the multiplicity of ass-whippings administered by black folks to white folks, for a change, turned me on. That to me was a moment for rejoicing. Many nights while walking home on the side of Route 1 or through the white community, College Park, a carload of crackers would ride past and throw bottles out of the windows and shout, "Nigger!"

ALI BEY HASSAN: In the summer of 1967 the Newark rebellion broke out. The press called it a riot, but the people saw it as a true rebellion, the people's answer to intolerable ghetto conditions and police brutality and murder. And all those murders of black people by police were labeled "justifiable homicide," and that was the end of it. I saw a lot during the so-called "riots." One time I was standing in a doorway on Sixteenth Avenue at the corner of Littleton and I saw about twenty cops chasing one black guy, with the crazy pig captain shouting, "Shoot the black bastards! Shoot them!" And I saw a pregnant woman shot down, armed just in the dress she wore. And black people falling to the ground—sometimes from buckshot and sometimes from pistol fire and sometimes from vicious clubbing. Some people tried to claim the Newark rebellion was started by "outside agitators," which is a convenient way of ignoring the realities in a community—but the people know better. Human beings can live under subhuman conditions for only so long and then there is bound to be an explosion.

One of the things that struck me about the 1967 rebellion was that my people had no arms to defend themselves; that was why they could be shot down in cold blood. I and some other bloods tried to form a self-defense organization to protect the people in our community. But the cops found out about it before we could really begin to move on our ideas.

LUMUMBA SHAKUR: My grandfather was arch anti-white repression. He would sit down and talk about white repression for days. My grandfather was a cop for three days until a white man told him no nigger was going to arrest *him*, and Grandpa whipped that cracker half to death.

KATARA: In the ghetto you learn at an early age who the enemy is—the cops. And you don't have to go searching for that knowledge. One group we called the "King Kole Trio." The K.K.T. were three "Knee-grow" uniformed patrolmen that rode around in an unmarked car with a white sergeant driving. It might sound strange to have such service for three nigger patrolmen but the K.K.T. earned every bit of it. The K.K.T., with their niggerknockers and .38s, shed as much black blood on the streets of Harlem as the worst racist plantation overseer during the times of legal slavery.

One time the K.K.T. came into a bar on my block,

and a brother who had the misfortune to be a little drunk was playing around with a pocketknife, mouthing off about he was going to cut the cat he was talking to. I wasn't there, I heard about it later. Everybody in the bar knew he was kidding, you couldn't even cut your finger with that little thing he had, and everybody was laughing. He had his back to the door and only knew who had come in from the cold silence and looks of fear that came over the bar. When he turned around there were two nightsticks and the butt of a gun sailing down on his head. When they got finished, you couldn't tell if you were looking at a man or a piece of raw liver. Following their usual, they walked around the bar then, asking the brothers and sisters what they were looking at, trying to get another victim; walked up to the cash register, grabbed some money, and walked out.

The 32nd Precinct seemed to have more than its share of pathological nigger fools like the K.K.T. One of them we called Paladin—the fastest .38 service revolver in Harlem, if he didn't pull that gun or shoot a black dude for some jive-time shit each day he'd go home mad. Like the K.K.T. and some other fuzz from the 32nd, he had almost worn out the stock of his gun with notches, and his nightstick looked like it had been through a buzzsaw.

One night my family was sitting in the living room and I heard what sounded like firecrackers. I looked out the window and saw a black man running down the street with what looked to be an army of cops running after him (I found out later he had tried to hold up a store and a rookie cop had fired on him.) There were people all over the street, but the cops didn't even tell them to get down, they just kept on firing. When the brother got to 135th Street he stopped on the corner and held his hands up, but the cops just kept coming and shooting. People were shouting out of the windows at the cops, telling them to stop, couldn't they see the brother was trying to give up, and so the cops started pointing their guns at the windows, telling everybody to keep inside and mind their own business. And about then a bullet chipped a piece of brick between the window I was hanging out of and the apartment next to ours. We never did figure out whether that bullet ricocheted or whether one of those cops just wanted to see a lot of black blood, but it was sure hard to see where it could have ricocheted *from*. They finally caught up with the brother in the schoolyard, and you could hear him screaming all the way down the street as they dragged him to a patrol car.

CLARK SQUIRE: In New York, where I'd come to apply for a job (but hadn't got it), I was given money for return airfare to my home in Texas. I went back to my Harlem hotel and noticed a huge sign at the check-in desk—"Not responsible for cash or valuables unless left at desk." I peeled off $250 and gave it to the clerk. Turning to walk away, I noticed he had scrawled a receipt not for $250, but $2.50. For a second I said nothing, thinking the old man was simply uneducated and that was his way of writing $250. But I decided against it and gave him a short course in elementary arithmetic.

The word must have got out that I had some money, because each time I entered or left my room the door opposite mine opened and a dynamite sister stood there in a negligee. She would say hello and continue talking to someone inside her room. Later that afternoon, when I came back to my room, there was no one else with her, and she started up a conversation (negligee again) and asked me to meet her at the Chock Full o' Nuts on 125th and Seventh. There was a little too much fox in her to turn down, so I agreed. That started a round of the kind of drinking and bar-hopping which I'd only seen in the movies. At every bar she knew other bloods, other foxes, barmaids and bartenders, which triggered a fresh round of greetings, drink buying and partying. I bought drinks, they bought drinks—everybody was buying drinks and having a ball—and the band played on. Luckily I was from a dry county in Texas, so I was used to drinking bootleg whisky straight out of the bottle; I figured to last even longer with shotglasses and mix. As the day wore on into the night, I was getting a little weak in the knees, and still no closer to my objective. The fox was still going strong, and now suggested buying a bottle and going to a house party. That was too much for me. I bought her the bottle and put her in a cab, and drug myself back up to the hotel room. I fell across the bed and counted my money—I was out about $25.00.

I decided New York was fast and I would just have to get fast at learning.

Harlem in the summer of '56 was something else. Be-bopping youth gangs, teenage groups harmonizing on every stoop, junkies on the corners nodding at 45-degree angles, flagrant faggots in passionate pink jumpsuits swishing out of the Apollo Bar, prostitutes strolling down 125th between Seventh and Eighth Avenues, young girls from the Bronx and Brooklyn lonely and looking to be picked up, three-for-a-dollar shirts on sidewalk carts, Panama Red at 50¢ a stick, Murphy men soliciting for phantom houses stocked with black, Spanish, white and Chinese girls $5 and $2 a throw, stuff players selling "hot" cut-glass rings, numbers runners everywhere, and the Apollo 65¢ day show . . .

DHARUBA: The Harlem community was completely different when I was growing up from what it is now, because then my mother could leave me on the street or parents could leave their kids on the block and the block would look out for the kids. Nothing would happen to that child. He would have the whole run of the neighborhood, the whole run of the block. Just going around the corner was a major experience, it meant you were going off into a completely new block, and a completely new set of personalities and characters in a whole new set of things. When I was young my mother used to leave me outside while she'd sit on a stoop down the block, and I would play loadies and games like "hot peas and butter" and "kick the can," funny games like that. No one would let a child do anything that was harmful to himself or harmful to other kids. It was a community spirit of rapport that we all had with each other then. Of course we had our contradictions, but the spirit was so strong then that it could be truly called a socialist community. Impressive; but because it was an oppressed community, that strong tendency toward individualism existed, and that strong self-hatred existed.

The kids I started growing up with were as diverse as anyone could get. We had everything from a bookworm to an arch hood, niggers destined to be engineers, niggers destined to O.D. in greasy, slimy, urine-ridden hallways. The neighborhood was teeming with life, though, overflowing with life. It is amazing to me now that those people even survived. But the neighborhood used to look out for all the kids, from the corner grocery store to the corner candy store.

JOAN BIRD; born March 9, 1949, New York City:
During elementary school time, my mother had extra-curricular activities for me—dancing school, tap and ballet. You know she worked real hard for all of this stuff. She was still working as a maid. You know black people find it very hard to survive and she was definitely working very hard, know what I mean, to provide this. I guess I started attending dancing school around the age of nine or so. I chose dancing because I found that dancing gave me great pleasure, it was an exciting thing, and I enjoyed it. Some of the things that we did were tap, ballet, acrobatics, and twirling. We had groups set up, teams of children, and our group was one of the youngest. The name of the group was the Cracker-jacks. We came in to do some warm-up practices and we all used to dress in leotards and tap shoes just like big people used to do, like we'd seen the big grown-up people do on TV or whatever, and it gave us this feeling that we were growing and that we were capable of dancing just as well as they could, if not better than they could. We were practicing for a yearly concert that was given at Carnegie Hall. We always wanted to be the best group in our performance because we really enjoyed entertaining people and on top of that, it gave us pleasure out of doing it. We used to dress in all types of sparkly sequined costumes, and very often we used to get a chance to put on a whole lot of makeup and lipstick. So when we got up on stage, we were really ready to get off into our own little thing. This went on for quite a few years, I'd say at least maybe four or five,

and when I stopped going, I know that I was very sad about the matter, but due to the fact that my family couldn't afford it any more, especially my mother, there was nothing that I could do. I just had to put that aside in my mind, and then I began to—actually, I learned it wasn't even necessary for me to go to any type of dancing school to learn how to dance because black people have rhythm just naturally. You're born with it. At the time I was attending, I guess I really thought about making a career out of it, but that part is all over.

KWANDO KINSHASA: Around the age of ten I was really dealing on the piano. My parents had me taking lessons every week, and every fall, spring, and summer there would be a concert at Carnegie Hall. Needless to say, Carnegie Hall was in "enemy" territory. And needless to say the "enemy" was always out in force at these concerts which I played at. I remember one time I caused some confusion and anger at one of these concerts, which eventually made everyone understand completely how I felt about the entire music scene.

I had just finished playing a tune by Beethoven (who to this day I still dig) and I approached the edge of the stage and bowed. After doing this I walked off the stage. Well the people (enemy) still clapped their hands, so I was told by the head music director to go out for some more bowing. This I did, and returned behind the curtains—where I was told the people (enemy) still clapped as loud as before. Now, after doing this for a few years and twice already that night, it occurred to me to somehow let these people (enemy) know how I felt about all of this bullshit. So this time when I went out, now for the third time, I bopped out, just as if I were on the block, and it wasn't a slight bop, it was a bop and a half. Well these people, these clowns who came to Carnegie Hall to see some "musical Negroes" didn't think too much of my attitude. I remember hearing some wise remarks, some hissing and such. If I remember correctly, this time I don't even think I bothered to bow, it was sort of a slight nudge.

Well when I returned behind the curtains this time, Moms was there, and as you guess it, she didn't waste any time in letting me know how she felt about my little act at who I considered to be my enemy. In fact the music director, my music teacher, and all the other members of the enemy class henceforth treated me as some pain-in-the-ass brat. But I'll tell you one thing: I did learn the pleasant satisfaction of letting your enemy or potential enemy know that you already consider him to be your enemy and are therefore at war with him even at the age of ten. For they considered me an enemy upon day of conception. So right on to a righteous war.

My street life consisted of stickball, fighting with 53rd Street brothers, messing around with the little sisters on Bradhurst, stealing candy from Mr. Peters' candy store, and playing more stickball and football. These two sports took up most of my time during the years between say elementary school and junior high school. Of course there was the constant vamping on the local Catholic school children. But as for other outstanding events or sights in Harlem while growing up, nothing except watching cops chase numbers men around, watching young sisters become prostitutes, watching your best friends getting involved in dope, watching another friend being shot (killed) in cold blood by a cop in front of you, having Moms trying to put me in a home for "uncontrollable children," learning how to play pool by sneaking into a pool hall, busting "square brothers" for nickels and dimes or lunch money, relating sexually to a sister older than you for the first time, watching my people, my parents and others, try to put some meaning into their exploited and abused lives, yes, nothing unusual, just living and growing up in the ghetto experience. An experience which has different lessons to teach if you want to learn—some being survival, others being dying, but the most valuable one being the ways and means by which a people are kept down. For once a revolutionary learns how his people are being kept down then he can move to deal with his enemy's basic motivations, by destroying the enemy—totally.

part 3

LUMUMBA SHAKUR: I started school in Atlantic City when I was six. The school was called Indiana Avenue School and was a half a block from where we lived. The school was 100 per cent black.

I attended Indiana Avenue School until the third grade. My teacher in the third grade was Miss Bush. At this time I was very ambitious about school. Then one day, when Miss Bush asked the class to answer some questions and I raised my hand to answer, as I began to answer the question I stuttered. Miss Bush told me to sit down and write the answer on paper because, she said, she did not have time for stuttering students. Miss Bush and the whole class began laughing. I was sitting by the window, feeling humiliated. I knew I had a speech defect which I did not have control over. I was infuriated, too, while Miss Bush and the class were still laughing. I picked up a flowerpot and threw it at Miss Bush. The flowerpot just missed her head. I was expelled from school. The whole incident had a hell of a psychological effect on me for years. My ambitions for education were destroyed and I began to dislike teachers, because I knew their duty was to educate, not to ridicule.

KWANDO KINSHASA: The grade school I went to in Harlem was for all practical purposes an extension of the street. It was down the street from Stitt, which was, and still is, one of the toughest junior high schools in Harlem. Every day at lunch time, these older bloods from Stitt would come on down to the grade school to get some lunch money. And when they came down on you, if you didn't fight you lost your money—your 25 cents or whatever. If you ran, you immediately became a punk, so you fought, and if you were lucky you fought long enough for some teacher to come along and break the whole thing up. Many a wise cat picked a fighting spot near some adults or teachers, thereby saving his money plus perfecting his ability to take on two or more older dudes. By the time three o'clock came, you'd had all afternoon to think about those clowns from Stitt, and revenge was on your mind. We knew it was futile to try and bust one of the Stitt cats, but *somebody* had to pay. So after school we piled on down to Resurrection Parochial School. Resurrection was one of those freaks that existed at about that time in Harlem, like Rice High School—it had about one-third white and two-thirds black. Whatever money we'd lost during the day we got back from those Catholic white boys—or, as we used to say, "Resurrection pays!" That's the way it was. It was only that if you lost something—if somebody took something away from you—you should get it back by taking something from another person, it didn't matter who.

JOAN BIRD: When I was five my mother enrolled me in Resurrection, the Catholic school. It was two blocks away from where I lived. I'm an only child. I've lived in Harlem all my life—that's the black colony, you know, the ghetto. I was born here March 9, 1949. I guess her reasons for putting me in Catholic school instead of public school was that she just felt I'll grow up able to achieve more, I'll be able to become more in the American system, able to gain the same goals black people have been working for so long but haven't been able to reach. She respected a Catholic education more than public school education—it was more refined, more respectable. My parents worked very hard: my mother worked as a housemaid for white folks, my father was a self-employed carpenter.

AFENI SHAKUR: The school I went to when I moved to New York was very different for me. I was used to a school that was all black kids, and there were only about three or maybe five black kids at the most in the school, and I was fighting all the time. It was the white kids I was fighting with. One time we were going out for recess and a kid named Myron Cohen said that I looked like something from outer space and I kicked his ass. The teacher came and tried to stop it and I tried to kick her ass. Because I was just ferocious. I wasn't bad, I was just ferocious because I didn't know any better. I was trying to protect myself and I felt like I just didn't belong there, you know. And I was very scared, I was really scared of all those white people all around me. I wasn't used to that. When I got back in the class the teacher, Miss Beck, had both of us up and she was trying to figure it, she wanted to know why we were fighting. And this dude Myron Cohen said that I was fighting, he was just standing up there just lying; he was just telling unmitigated lies. And I just went up to him and I was prejudiced, and I just punched him. One of the white boys, this kid named Paul Gold who drew a lot—he didn't do anything in class but sit and draw—he told the teacher that Myron Cohen had said that I looked like something from outer space. And everybody in the class just bust out laughing, they thought it was funny, and I tried to attack them again. Because I was very fucked up, I didn't understand, I didn't like it. But I got through that year anyway. I think I did.

KUWASI BALAGOON: My grandma taught me how to write my name and count and I started the first grade at five, fell in love with Miss Sheppard, kissed her every day, but simply could not stand being cooped up in one room all day, and failed, and barely squeezed through by the jagged edges of my teeth on the retake.

The third year in grade school found me at least looking at the blackboard and books. Miss Carson was a good enough teacher, but waiting for lunch still consumed most of the morning. Mama believed in heavy breakfasts and lunches and it was absolute law that it all be eaten. "Don't you know that there are people in the world that wished they had what you're throwing away?" For some time, too, because of speech difficulties I attended speech classes. I never passed a spelling test; the reasoning was that I couldn't spell a damn because I couldn't talk a damn. But somehow I passed, maybe because Miss Carson'd had enough.

The third grade was a very memorable year. The teacher was one of the most beautiful women on the face of the planet. Memory brings her right into focus: she was thin down to her hips, which flowered and tapered down to ample legs. And although at school I waded into my dreams, my attention came to her and daydreams

included her. I remember her saying, "Donald, stop looking at my—feet." I sang songs to her in my dreams. She,
being concerned, kept me from going to recess and kept
me after school, drilling the lessons to me—but I wasn't
very receptive, too stunned by her beauty to understand
anything else. My mother, concerned as ever, pressured
me to my studies after going to parent-teacher meetings
but—zonk.

I remember one day she wore a red dress to school
with no bra. I came out of a daydream just long enough
to see one of her small but ample, succulent breasts fall
from the dress. Good God Almighty—it sprang up and
stared out into my eyes. Embarrassed, she was caught off
guard. She whipped it right back behind the bright red
barrier, then followed my straight line of vision until our
eyes met, then nixed it and me off. One could tell that
she didn't feel like working that day, but in time it
passed. Let it be understood, the value of the whole
experience, especially at such a young age. I hope she
is not embarrassed by this but flattered.

Miss Reed taught sixth grade, and when I entered that
grade I entered petrified. Miss Reed didn't dig horse
playing, clowning, or daydreaming. My sister had been
an excellent student, which was one problem for me;
and Miss Reed was legend, a smoke-bringer. She wasn't
a big woman but obviously a healthy one. I must admit
that she was a good teacher, and that means she held
the interest of the students, and tried to make what she
was teaching relevant. She rapped about the issues of the
day, civil rights, the missile race, and so forth, and made
a rule that we had to bring in current events. Failing
that or any homework was trouble. My folks dug her.
Any means she used to teach me was all right with them.
To me, then, she was a monster, with my very own

mother giving her the green light. Miss Reed dug that I needed help on reading, like a few other students, and started a special reading class on Saturdays, and continued the class into the summer. She never ran out of gas. Before that I only tugged and pulled at the few things that interested me, but after that I could really read. And I began wanting to be a veterinarian.

KATARA: My mother placed a high emphasis on education and making good grades, so by the time I reached six and entered the first grade, I had most of the stuff they taught down pat. I got along well with most of my teachers and friends, except for one teacher, Mrs. H. Seeing that I'm what my brother calls "mellow yellow," she tried to make me her pet. If there was any talking in the class she would ask everyone who it was. Naturally they'd say it was me because it always *was* me, at which time she'd tell them they were lying. One day we were learning to tell time with a toy clock, some of the bloods didn't know it too good so I was helping them out. She caught me and told me to stop, when I didn't she came over to my desk and hit me upside the head and said something like, "If they didn't know it, don't help them, you shouldn't stay around them anyway because you're different and they are troublemakers." At six it was kind of hard to dig where she was coming from because everybody in the classroom were my friends and hung out around the block, so I let it slide as her being a nut. It wasn't until much later that I dug the "divide and conquer" system, which her treatment of me and the other light-skinned boys and girls was just an example of. This teacher used to have all the light-skinned kids sit up in the front of the class. And she would play up to them and tease them, even though most of us looked on light skin as a handicap. I remember once one of the girls asked me if I liked her. I said "No." Then she asked if it was because she was the lightest one in the class; jokingly I said "Yes." We were both the same age, nine, but sometimes I think back and remember the look of pain and hurt she had in her eyes.

LUMUMBA SHAKUR: When I first started at the North Philly school it was very hip because I was really enthusiastic about speech classes, which we had every day. The speech teacher was a beautiful black named Mrs. Johnson, and she was dedicated to her students. Eventually those classes got me more interested in school programs again. But then this cracker principal came into the speech class and told Mrs. Johnson that her speech classes were nonsense and a waste of the Board of Education's money. Mrs. Johnson told that cracker principal that stuttering and minor speech defects are a phenomenon of some children of the all-black communities, rooted in three hundred years of white repression. I was ready to swear to what Mrs. Johnson said because I personally had seen the problem in black communities in Virginia and Atlantic City and Philly. The cracker principal said Mrs. Johnson was confusing the race issue with laziness, and he expelled Mrs. Johnson from her duties as a teacher.

BOB COLLIER: A lot of times when I went to school, I would just sit outside on the curb, not wanting to go in because I knew there would be name-calling and the other kids making fun of me because of my patched-up clothes. I was little and skinny and couldn't win the fights I kept getting into with the kids who picked on me. So I started winning the only way I could—I started using a pipe or a stick as a weapon. I used surprise as a weapon, too: I tried not to let them know I was coming.

BABA ODINGA: School was not a pleasant place for me. I never liked the teachers and I also never liked the school. Home and school were a gigantic contradiction. It has been said that a mother's duty at home is to instill a sense of discipline and respect for other people, and teachers in the school are supposed to prepare you for the outside world. When I attended school I found most of the teachers to be a bunch of sadistic, pusillanimous, misunderstanding, unsympathetic, unprincipled jive motherfuckers toward children whose parents they considered to be from a totally different class. Man, if your parents were entrepreneurs, in the medical profession, education profession, a civil service employee up in the hierarchy, a bank clerk, a store clerk, shirt-and-necktie-wearing—if your parents were all that you wouldn't have any problem learning: for you, the teachers will act like teachers. Brothers who went to school in America tell me it's no different, just as bad.

LUMUMBA SHAKUR: When school started in Portsmouth, Virginia, we had to walk past an all-white school four stories high and a half-block wide to get to the black school. The black school was just a two-story house converted into a school, with about three hundred students. In the black schoolhouse you really knew what a can of sardines felt like. There was a lack of books, chairs, desks, pencils, paper—you name it and that school lacked it. Students were sitting on the floor—but everybody was enthusiastic about learning. The teachers were very concerned about all the students; also there was a strong feeling of togetherness in the little schoolhouse, something that the northern black teachers and schools lack.

Every day going to and from school we had to pass the white school. Our teachers told us to always walk on the other side of the street from the white school. Every day some cracker kids would be waiting by their school, calling us and our mothers every derogatory name under the sun. Our teachers and the black students called Zayd and me "crazy niggers from up North" because every morning and after school, Zayd and myself were fighting those crackers. All the students said that their mothers and fathers told them to never fight crackers, because white people were always right. Most blacks in our community stood firm on that myth, too, though they would fight other blacks at the drop of a hat.

The ironic fact was that even though those crackers knew how to call us all kinds of niggers, none of them could fight. When you punched one cracker in the face, four of them would run. One morning about twenty crackers jumped on Zayd and me and kicked our asses. The black students came to our aid righteously, and after that, other black students began to join with us. When winter came, and we had to bring wood to school for the wood stove so we could heat up our classrooms, carrying the wood to school had an extra survival purpose for Zayd and me, because along with the wood we brought broomsticks to defend ourselves from the crackers. We could not relate to getting an ass-kicking. After a couple of times beating the crackers in the head with broomsticks, the crackers began to act very civilized.

CLARK SQUIRE: During my pre-school years Moms would frequently bring home slightly used clothes, linen, left-over food and other items given her by her employers. Once, she brought home a discarded ABC reader, and at night she taught my sister, who was two years older, to say her ABCs and count. When Moms was working, my sister taught me what she had learned, so by the time we started school we were saying our ABCs forward, backward, and crossways, and counting up to 20 or 30. This was sort of unique in our schools, and we had a big jump on other kids. Both my sister and I did very well in school.

The school system in my hometown in rural Texas was like thousands of others, a monument to the way of keeping blacks, Mexicans or any oppressed minority ignorant, uneducated, unskilled and, in fact, miseducated. In our town this was a deliberate process to ensure availability of a large labor pool which could supply cheap labor for pulling cotton. As a rule only blacks and Mexicans pulled cotton. Most Mexicans were migrant workers who started in Texas, Oklahoma, and Arkansas at the beginning of the cotton season, worked their way west as the crops opened up in New Mexico and Arizona, and finally moved on to California. There were no schools for the Mexicans who stayed in town for the winter, and many did not speak English.

Cotton-pulling season began in September and ran through November. This meant not only that black youths attended inferior segregated schools, but that they attended these schools for much shorter periods than whites—about six months of the year. It is no wonder there was an educational gap. What is more amazing is that the gap wasn't greater. It might have been, were it not for the fact that much of the "better education" the whites got really meant a bigger dose of brainwashing in studies that are irrelevant to blacks anyway.

The schoolteachers in my hometown belonged to that respected class of blacks which also included the undertakers and the preachers. The undertaker was respected simply because he made a decent living, which wasn't hard, considering how often blacks killed each other. The preachers were respected for peddling Jesus and salvation. The teachers had college degrees and were respected for their education, but even then it seemed the most ridiculous thing in the world, to hear black teachers educating black children to the beauty of American democracy—"justice is blind," proportional representation, constitutional guarantees, universal suffrage, due process of the law, "every boy can grow up to be President"—free enterprise!—"highest standard of living in the world," "land of the free," "all men are born equal," "savage Indians," "happy slaves," etc., ad nauseam. All of this in the face of poverty, disease, fighting, killing, and exploitation running amok in the black community. We never heard one word from "respected" blacks about those evil conditions—either their cause or their cure.

Nobody could have expected direct action by them; teachers were under the complete domination of the Board of Education. But to continue like a robot to teach the "American Dream" in the very teeth of the hellish Nightmare was more than ludicrous: it was downright suicidal.

So I never cultivated much respect for the black bourgeoisie, teachers, preachers, intelligentsia and so-called leaders. I had a lot more respect for the bloods off the block because they were much less hypocritical, less brainwashed, more courageous, more volatile, had more fun, and were more willing to fight. Those were the bloods I hung out with as I grew up, much to the distress of my parents and some "respected" blacks, who predicted I would never finish high school. But, as I said, I had a big jump on school. I even got double promoted a couple of times, and I finished high school at fifteen.

BABA ODINGA: My first day at school was not very pleasing due to the fact that the teachers were beating the kids left and right. What saved me that day was that it was my first day. It would not have bothered me so much but when I got home and I told my second mother what school was like, she said, "That's what will happen to you if you don't follow the school rules, you will be beaten." Well, she'd always told me not to let anyone hit me—that if anyone hit me and I did not defend myself, she was going to beat me, and if it wasn't possible for me to defend myself, if the individual was too much for me, come to her and both of us would go beat whoever interfered with her son. If I got beat up by some other kid, as long as I did not refuse to fight, that's cool. In the event that I did refuse to defend myself then anything the kids could do to me would never come near the ass-licking I would receive from her.

When I had to fight, man, I would fight like hell. I used to get my ass kicked and I used to kick ass every day. My mother used to tell me that she was going to make all my clothes from canvas and if I did not want my clothes made from canvas, I would have to learn to mend my torn clothes. Mending my torn clothes was a job; if you ever tried to mend dungarees you know what I mean. She told me she understood that it is the most natural way for kids to act—she told me that when she was a child her mother beat her for getting her clothes all torn up but she was not going to do the same thing to me. She explained the value and the reason why I must try and take care of my material possessions. She had me divide my clothes into three parts: the clothes to wear to church, those to wear to school, and then the rest for me to play in.

The school I attended while living in Nevis was an all-boys public school. All of the teachers were black. Most of the teachers were women; the headmaster was a man. It was on the outskirts of the city, the ground floor of a huge Methodist church. There was a huge playground with sufficient room to hold two cricket games; a school garden, large enough for every student to have an 8-by-4 plot of land; also a church lawn that was available, plus trees at the back of all this.

A school week ran like this: on Monday at nine o'clock the school bell will ring. You line up in your classes, then the classes line up in order by grade. Each teacher takes her position in front of her class and roll is called, one grade at a time. Then we will all be put together for "exercise time." After the exercise you will be told to go back where you were before. Then you will be made to sing a song.

I guess if we'd had to sing a calypso we would not have minded, but instead we were made to sing a song about God—somebody we'd never seen. The obeah man made more sense to me than God, for at the age of eight, the obeah man is all around you. You'd be going up the street and the obeah man would be coming down the street. The only time God made any sense to me was in church and after church, that would be it as far as God was concerned. For example, a lady had a very big plum tree on the outskirts of the city. Every day after school the kids would raid the tree, until one day they stopped. What stopped them? Let me say that at the closing of school each day was a prayer to God promising to uphold his commandments but no sooner than we got in the street everything was the opposite until one day when we got to the plum tree. Under the plum tree stood Miss Elsie. In her hand she held a funny-looking bottle; in the bottle was a dead green lizard, some dirt, and some cooking oil. Tied to the neck of the bottle was a piece of red and black string. She told the kids that the obeah man was there and he blessed the tree and gave her the bottle to put in the tree. She tied it to the tree. Then she turned to us and said that whoever touched one plum of this tree or any other tree in her garden would receive a swollen belly. After that she had no problem with the kids. There would be plums on the ground and no kids would ever think of touching one. At the same time some of these kids would be given church boxes to collect money for the church. We took the boxes and collected money from the people but instead of taking it to the church we went to this place on the waterfront that sells ice cream and sandwiches and just spent the church's money, thinking nothing of it.

Anyway, when we got in school after roll call we all go to our classes, the headmaster rings the bell and everyone sits down. The headmaster will call on a teacher and the teacher in turn calls on a student in her class and tells him to read a verse from the Testament. Then this stupid motherfucker will take up his strap and put it on his shoulder. Now whoever is reading, the minute he sees this fool with the strap he begins to get scared. Whatever self-confidence the boy did have, he begins to lose it. He realizes that if he utters an incorrect sound, a mispronounced word, or if his modulation is not pleasant, the headmaster, his mind shorted-out in the face of reason, sees only a target, something for him to beat some sense into. But it doesn't stop there. The boys' teacher also wants her pound of flesh. Why should she not have her pound? Was not the boy from her class? Did he not make it appear that she was derelict in her duty?

After the morning reading lesson we have class. Mondays usually are the time when you get new lessons for the rest of the week ending on Friday. From Monday to Thursday not much happens except that you will be trying to learn the irrelevant bullshit lesson that the teacher is ramming down your throat. For instance, the teacher will be standing in front of the class and reading you a story about Br'er Rabbit and the Tar Baby, or Don Quixote along with his boy Sancho, or Robinson Crusoe along with his slave Friday. Some of the kids will be listening, at least the ones in the front, while the ones in the back including me are playing marbles in the desk. The only time we paid attention was when the teacher spoke about slavery and how the slaves would rebel and the cruelty of the white slave masters. We would be even more attentive when she got to the part where some of the slaves escaped and went to join the pirates. Man, there were not sufficient marbles in the world to keep me when she was telling us about the rebelliousness of the slaves. I would daydream that I was a slave: when the other slaves and I broke our chains then we attacked the master's house and fed him to the sharks.

On Friday you will be given a different place to sit, not next to any of your friends. You will then be given

a test on reading, writing, and arithmetic. The test will
go on until twelve o'clock. Then, lunch. When you get
back from lunch, the teacher will give you your book—
and that's when all hell breaks loose inside you. The
minute you get your book the first thing you do is look
to see how many lashes you are going to get. You are
allowed a certain number of words wrong, maybe three
or four, and if you have any more it is your ass. In
arithmetic you are allowed two wrong. Sometimes you
will have so many wrong that when the headmaster gets
to your class he'll give you some of your lashes. Then he
will write a note to your parents in your book. The note
usually says one thing: the reason for your many mistakes is that you do not pay attention to your teacher
even though your teacher has repeatedly beaten you.
The kids did not even read what the headmaster wrote,
it was sufficient to know that he wrote something in
your book. You couldn't tear the page out because there
would be no way to explain the missing page. So there
is only one thing left for you to do. You get your friends
and go in the woods. There you will take off your clothes
so your friends can rub your body with leaves from
certain trees so your body will become immune from the
lashes that will be given you by your parents.

   I did not have a typical situation in this. One of the
things I always loved and respected my second mother
for was that when I had to take home something written
in by the headmaster, which was often, she would sit
down with me and show me my mistakes. She did not
beat me for mistakes. Then she would give me a test of
the same nature; if I got it right she let me go to play
and if I got it wrong she still let me go but when I got
through playing we would go over my mistakes until I
properly understood them. Then she would tell me jokes

and little things, tricky things; we would be in the house and she'd say to me, "Can you jump higher than the table?" and I'd say no. Then she'd say, "Of course you can, just jump." So I'd jump, then she'd say, "See? You can jump but the table can't." Now my second mother did beat me but you can bet that when she did I merited beating. There is an old saying that if you are an only child, you will become disrespectful. That saying did not apply to me, for my second mother did not stand for any kind of disrespectfulness toward anyone older than me. The only one older than me I was allowed and even encouraged to disrespect was the Queen of England, whom she always referred to as the Slut of England. In school one day we were practicing for Empire Day, so when I came home from school I was singing "God Save the Queen." Well, my second mother took me inside the house and told me what she would do to me if she ever heard me singing that song again—so I told her that I have to sing it in school and she told me that I didn't. I told her that if I didn't the teachers would beat me. She said, "Stand up on that chair." Then she said that if any teacher ever hit me for not singing that song, man or woman, she would bust them; and that the only queen I had was my mother. When I was old enough to get married my wife would become my queen, and if I have a daughter she would be my queen too. Then and only then should I refer to another woman as being a queen.

SHABA OM: Grandma wanted me to go to an all-white school because of the jive Civil Rights Bill that passed, the big integration thing was jumping off in the South.

About one hundred black kids from Walltown, North Carolina, including me, went to the integrated school by the name of Brogden Junior High School in 1961–62. This is where I really began to dig and understand racism and what it's all about, because I was faced with it every day I went to school. After school all of the blacks would walk the ten blocks up the hill to the bus stop; fights would break out almost every day going to and from the bus stop and school. I remember one afternoon: we were fighting after school because a white boy hit and spit on a black boy's sister and—wow, that was a good fight—sticks, racks, and dogs, everyone and everything was getting down. It lasted for an hour. But the teachers of Brogden Junior High School were not bad, I was used to all of their madness by then. I couldn't get myself interested in what they called heroes—the great white founding fathers of white America—I was putting up with it because I wanted to make my grandma as happy as I could.

The first year I was there I went out for the football team and made second string. I and one of my so-called teammates, a white boy, were both after the same positions: guard and tackle. We would fight in practice like madmen if a game was going up. I dug football from the time I was seven—I played a lot in the afternoons with the big dudes from the community. We played until the sun went down, in the park or on the school grounds across the street from Grandma's house. If one of us little kids got hurt we couldn't cry, because that would blow it for hanging out or playing with the big ones, so by the time I went to junior high I was ready for football. That white boy had a very hard fight on his hands. I had been playing without any equipment at all—none of the pads or helmets that the junior high had—and against big, rough and wild bloods from Walltown, you know. So there was no doubt in my mind about being ready. Being on the football team at Brogden Junior High could get a black kid so-called respect from the teachers and students. You know, a little limelight would bounce on and off of you because of the move you made in the game to help the team win. Going to that school corrupted my little mind somewhat. I began trying to relate to the white chicks on the cheering team. In fact I did relate, but it was on a very small scale. See, I could cop my homework and answers from her and talk, but that was it. She would let my black ass know I was still a nigger. After school was out, when I went home, it would really be all over.

KWANDO KINSHASA: When I was thirteen my parents moved to the North Bronx. That move entailed a change of environment so great that we might as well have moved to Woodstock. I hated being away from the brothers I had known all my life, but the junior high school was half black—mostly brothers from Harlem or the South Bronx. Picture a school with about five hundred black students—right in the middle of a white neighborhood. PS 113 was really something else. I was there for almost three years, and during that time I must have been suspended ten times. Every day was a battle. The teachers had their shit and we had ours. They could fail us in any subject they wanted to—including study hall— and we, the blacks and "outside" whites—could make each one of their days a living hell. Now that may seem like a lousy way to run a school, but then I don't think those teachers ever had any intention of teaching anything to anybody, except maybe the SP students. These SPs, or

"special students," had separate homeroom classes—the
SPs were white, of course—and they received special attention in everything.

The first month I was in this school, in seventh grade,
I remember taking a French test, a "placement" test or
some such jive, which was supposed to be our big jumping-off point into the international scene, I guess. Well,
I really studied hard for that test, it was like the first
real thing I had to do in the new school, and I got a 98.
It turned out that we had been given the test by mistake;
it was really for the eighth graders, not us, and that piss-
ant teacher told me I must have cheated to do so well.
So I told her that she was crazy, full of shit, and a whole
lot of other stuff. She listened patiently and then told
me I shouldn't be taking French anyway because it
couldn't possibly do me any good. Well, on that point
I could agree with her. Right on the spot I became one
of the "forces of distribution" in PS 113. The teachers
called us "niggers" and we called them "guinea lovers."

BABA ODINGA: At the age of twelve I was sent to
live with my mother in Antigua. My father had died by
then. The same boat that took me to Nevis took me back
to Antigua, and my mother was at the pier to meet me.
When I lived in Nevis, I came to Antigua for five weeks'
vacation once every year, and every time Antigua fascinated me. But where I lived with my mother in
Antigua had nothing fascinating about it. As I stated at
the opening, it is a slum, and there is nothing pleasant
about a slum, for rats and roaches tend to hold title in
perpetuity.

I tried my best to prevent my mother from taking me
to school,but after two weeks she succeeded. It was no

surprise to me to find the teachers in Antigua behaving the same way as in Nevis, but I was no longer ready to submit to that shit. But I was fortunate: my teacher was more than just "a teacher"—he was a humanistic teacher, a black man who was concerned with the education of black children, a teacher in the fullest sense of the word. His name was Mr. Lindsay. His method of teaching was definitely encouraging. At first I thought he was acting, that he was talking this way because he had new students in his class, but after being in that class for a while I found out it was no acting, that the things he said were what he meant to say. Sometimes when we were reading something as a class he told us that some of the things in the books were not meant to educate us to the true value of our selves—that they were meant to give us a sense of inferiority.

One of the things that was so unique with Mr. Lindsay was that you always felt free to make a mistake, for when he corrected you it was with words, not lashes. He took time to explain whatever you did not understand. One day he went to this boy who was sleeping in the back of the class and brought him to the front of the room to tell the class why he was sleeping. That boy felt so bad—for in Mr. Lindsay's class was the only time, as far as I know, that anyone paid attention. The rest of the class came down on this boy for sleeping, but Mr. Lindsay began to explain that it could have been any one of us, and before we passed judgment on anyone, we must first understand why the individual did what he did. With any other teacher, the only thing that would have happened was the sleeping boy would have got his ass kicked. Mr. Lindsay never had a belt or a ruler in his hand; the only thing he kept in his hand was a piece of chalk.

LUMUMBA SHAKUR: When I first arrived in Jamaica, Queens (part of New York City), I went to a junior high that was about 80 per cent black. My first day there I was invited to be stomped by twenty kids, because I was new. On your first day in a new ghetto school you expect a fight, but not twenty-to-one. One of the two bloods who insisted I get a fair fight, one-to-one, was a brother called Beany—now Sekou Odinga.

JAMAL: According to standards laid down by Noonie and by other people's parents, we were supposed to go to school and get a good education so we could get a good job. Yet the subjects were so boring and the teachers seemed to be more wooden than the desk you had to sit behind. All this began to turn you off. In junior high I began playing regular hooky, and I spent quite a bit of time crashed on some Gypsy Rose from the liquor store. I was still popping that racist, Five-Percenter ideology in school, and the teachers were saying that I was a problem and I would never make it anywhere. More out of spite than anything else, I took the test* for one of the best high schools in New York, and I passed—which stunned my teachers. But then I dropped out of the summer program I was supposed to go to, and blew it.

That was the year that one might call the beginning of the big drift. It was a time of gang fights, of running the streets, of finding out what the street life was about, of drinking wine, smoking reefer, and just checking out

---

* New York City has a variety of specialized high schools, for admission to which students must pass special tests. Students who are not admitted to specialized high schools attend either neighborhood or vocational schools.

cold life. In the fall I made an attempt to give up on that and to attend Evander Childs High School. But Evander Childs was pretty bad. It was a drugstore: drugs were sold in every corridor and every corner of the school. Nobody related to classes, it was simply a matter of making contact and getting high and going to whatever hooky party was going on.

The veil over certain facts in my life had been slashed off by then—I had found out that I am of Puerto Rican and possibly black descent, and the reason certain people in the block looked on me with a certain amount of taboo is that I was born out of wedlock. I also found out at that time all the facts of the different arrests of my foster brothers and sister, and I had come to the end of my idealistic rope. I didn't see anything that I could do except follow other examples, just say, "Later for everybody else. I just got to get out here on the street and see what I can do for myself and try to put together a little bit of bread and possibly get my claim to fame by becoming a pimp, hustler, or a Murphy man, whatever type of game I can get off into." I'd begun sniffing heroin around the age of thirteen, and it wasn't too long before I went to skin-popping, then to shooting it. The high never really intrigued me, it wasn't that beautiful, but it gave me an effect that my problems were cooled out. I had a little chippy—chippy is slang that means you have a light habit, not to the point that you're strung out. But I knew I never wanted to attain a reputation as a dope fiend. I found myself losing weight and getting off into a bag that I never wanted—asking people in school for nickels and dimes and quarters to put it together so I could go buy myself a bag of smack. Some of the cats in the group that I hung with would snatch pocketbooks and sometimes I even got down with that. Or we would do little jive things like stealing soda bottles from the supermarket or taking them off the trucks and then selling that. So I just began to decline the amount of stuff I was messing with till finally I cut it loose.

What I was doing was committing what I now recognize as reactionary suicide. The conditions had become so intense in the neighborhood in terms of what was happening to other people, what was happening to friends: they were getting busted, and getting killed, in this life-and death struggle that niggers get in with one another. Instead of trying to combat this, instead of trying to do something to stop this, I just submitted to the conditions. If certain things hadn't happened to me a little later on, I would have died at the hands of these conditions. Died a reactionary death, you know. Died by being submissive, not trying to change any of this.

CURTIS POWELL: I went through the South Orange-Maplewood school system—the same one Mark Rudd went through later. It was about 90 per cent white. I hated the schools and everything they taught.

When I was in eighth grade, our school—which was supposed to be one of the better ones—was part of an experiment connected with the University of Chicago. The top three scorers on a special IQ test were supposed to go to the University of Chicago after the eighth grade, and graduate at the time most people graduate from high school. I got the highest score in the school. That messed up their plans; so they told my mother and her preacher that it wouldn't be good for me to leave home so early—that I wasn't emotionally ready for college. My mother and her preacher didn't really dig what was coming down —they didn't think anybody would go to those lengths in *New Jersey* to keep black people down—so they believed it. Only two went from the school, two white boys. For me, the shit hit the fan. I started getting into fights with my teachers and skipping school, I even tried to join the army. I quit school when I was in tenth grade, but Reverend Edgar Thomas persuaded me to go back after a year. I made up two years in one and then went into the marines.

ALI BEY HASSAN: Everything I was taught was about what the white man had done. Like social studies—when they talked about the struggles in Asia they only talked about white heroes. I knew that black people had been in those wars right along with white soldiers, but they were always left out of the story. Like dig the picture of George Washington crossing the Delaware—him standing up in front, with other faceless people in the background. I found out later in the streets that there was a black man in that boat. But this was never taught in any of the schools I attended. And I know for a fact he didn't do anything for the black man or woman but help keep them in bondage and misery. But still teachers tell black and white students alike he was a great man, and that is just one expression of the big lie, what the United States is all about.

AFENI SHAKUR: I went to a lot of high schools because I was constantly moving, I was such a fuck-up around there. I was constantly moving.

Like I didn't really mean to go to Performing Arts. I didn't mean to go to anything like that, but I was in a journalism class, you see, in junior high, and I was kind of majoring in journalism, if you can do that in junior high, because I was very interested in writing. At the end of junior high in New York you start taking tests to see which high school you'll be in. I wanted to take the test for Hunter College High School, and my English teacher suggested that I take it for Bronx High School of Science and for the High School of Performing Arts. I didn't really know what Performing Arts was or why I should take it.

I couldn't take the test for Hunter because my IQ was two points below the level for you to take it or some other nonsense like that. I took the Bronx Science test and I passed that but I didn't want to go to Bronx Science because I didn't think I could relate to all of those brilliant white rich kids, you know? I took the one for Performing Arts and I went there; I'd always thought that actors and actresses were uninhibited and it was easier to relate to them. I found out that that wasn't correct. That's why I left. I forced myself to be forced to leave. I mean, I would go, you know, and I would just walk up to white children and just hit them, and then I would get angry because they didn't want to hit me back. Like these were rich kids. Performing Arts is the only high school that majors in dramatics. And these kids were just coming out of private schools all their lives, and they were being picked up by chauffeurs and all that nonsense, and you know I hated them. I hated them with a passion. First of all, every day I would come to school high off of some Thunderbird. I would get fucked-up with my friends behind some Thunderbird and then I would go to Performing Arts. I would go for part of the day—like I would go to acting classes. I refused to go to any other classes. And then I'd get down there and I would get uptight because I saw this white child who had all of these beautiful clothes and who was showing off. And I couldn't stand this so I'd walk up to her and just call her a bitch and smack her, you know, and she would look at me like I was some kind of other life form. And I was.

I don't know how old I was, I can't get all those ages together. Tenth grade, maybe. You know Angie Dickinson? You know her daughter Charlotte? Well we were there together. I couldn't remember where I'd seen her and that's where it was, we went to Performing Arts together.

When I was at Performing Arts I had Eartha Kitt's acting teacher. She used to take me aside and try and talk to me, and she knew that I was just rejecting everything—it must've been awful for her. She used to take me aside and try and talk to me. Her story was that Eartha Kitt was just like me and she had many problems, but together they solved them, you know. But I wasn't going for it because I didn't want to talk to that woman. I didn't want to tell her shit, because as far as I was concerned I didn't have any problems except that I didn't have money, and she wasn't going to give me money; all I needed was some clothes and some lunch money. I couldn't even eat lunch there. That was one reason why I went to school just part of the day, because I didn't have the money to go to the Automat and buy food to eat. My mother just didn't have it. And to go to Performing Arts costs money: you have to have leotards and all kinds of shit. You have to go to all kinds of little plays and they don't have any cafeteria so you have to go to restaurants to eat. For a high school kid, are you crazy? From 169th

Street and Washington Avenue, are you kidding? It was enough to get to school—to buy bus or train passes, that was enough.

I couldn't even relate to the kids in the school who were black. Most of the kids were white, and they were just totally other. I tried to relate to a black kid named Glenn—he's the dude that plays the son on *Peyton Place* now—but I couldn't because he had been in drama, I think he had been in *Raisin in the Sun,* the original play, so I couldn't relate to him but so much. And then like hell, he didn't understand anything about me because he lived in Greenwich Village. So I had problems. I remember I had a fight with him because he slapped me and the next day I brought every knife that I had and a zip gun to school and put them in my locker and I was going to kill him. But I was like that—I couldn't relate to talking about anything. When somebody hit me or somebody hurt my feelings, all I wanted to do was kill them. I just wanted to hurt them. I wanted to hurt them physically because it was all I could do. I couldn't sit down and be sophisticated or any of those things, you know, I couldn't look pretty, you know, outslick them or outtalk them or anything. The only thing I had, the only defense I had was the things that I did in the street. I was in a gang called the Disciples, in my neighborhood, at the same time I was going to Performing Arts.

ALI BEY HASSAN: My relatives and my mother always told me that I should finish high school because without a diploma I wouldn't be able to secure a good job. But my mother *had* a diploma, and after working eighteen years as a nurse's aide she was making $1.25 an hour.

I quit school to help my mother with the bills. I began by making cheap jewelry at $1 an hour. And here is where I dug that the piece of paper—that diploma—didn't mean much as far as employment was concerned. My mother was just making 25¢ an hour more than I, and she had that piece of paper plus an eighteen-year headstart.

KATARA: In 1967 I was going to high school—and that's what half the school was, high! You could buy a nickel bag of smoke faster than you could a notebook; students, teachers, everybody was fucked up.

My first year at Franklin they were using teachers fresh out of Columbia Teachers College, and half of them looked as young as we were. My first science teacher got pregnant and the second got married. But they had some fly young mamas. One of my math teachers was sent home because her micro-mini was showing too much, and we didn't dig that too tough because we thought it was just right, and she acted like she was down, and so somebody slashed the principal's tires for revenge. One other math teacher had a game it took us a while to get hip to. She wore minis and would sit on the desk and swing her legs. She must have been down on some kind of Pavlov theory of conditioned reflex because when we were ready and dug what was going down in class her legs would part a little, when we didn't do our homework and jived around, she would sit behind the desk. When things were really right, you could see her pink lace panties. By the time the term was over, we were figuring equations at top speed and getting 80 on every test she gave. I had her for the last class of the day, and a lot of us used to stay and rap a while. Her tactics might not have been by the rules, but she was a good teacher—at anything she taught!

LUMUMBA SHAKUR: When it was time for me to go to high school—I was living in Jamaica, Queens— I picked Andrew Jackson because everyone said that was where all the fine sisters were at. One day I took one of J. A. Rogers's books, *From "Superman" to Man*, to school with me. (My father had a very hip black history library. Those books really blew my mind.) The white history teacher at Jackson told me that A. J. Rogers's books are fiction, pornography, and contraband, and if I brought any book like that to school again he would see to it that I got expelled from school. I thought the teacher's remarks were typical of the experience I'd had with teachers.

KATARA: At the start of the term one year in high school I found I was being given a course called African History. I didn't want to learn about some damn savages in the jungle so I and about half the class asked for transfers the first day. The teacher was Mr. John Hunter. He asked us to wait a week and then if we wanted out we could get it. There wasn't anything that hip to take anyway, so we stayed. At the end of that week, nobody felt like leaving. The main textbooks we used were *The Negro in American History* and *Before the Mayflower*. In one week we learned more about our history than we had through all the years of school we had behind us. The myth of naked savages being eaten by wild animals and each other was replaced with the reality of a people with a highly sophisticated culture. The distortions and lies about happy-go-lucky slaves broke to the truth of over one hundred slave rebellions, and the truth of an ex-slave named Toussaint L'Ouverture who stopped the armies of Napoleon. The Dark Continent was not only not dark but had been the birthplace of the dawn of man.

JOAN BIRD: In that type of Catholic high school I was going to, the talk of all the corridors was status, to be able to go on up there and go to college and grab this righteous education. We thought about that, in high school we always did that collectively. We were what you might call "good" students. So I took a test, along with the rest of the people I hung with. I wanted to be a nurse, so at first I thought I'd go to nursing school, but the test for getting into college was there for taking, so I took it, and I was accepted in Bronx Community College. I had thought about going to college. My mother had *definitely* thought about it. The parents of the other kids, of my friends, had basically the same ideas, outlook on life for children, as my parents, I guess.

CLARK SQUIRE: Moms was convinced that education was the way for blacks to raise themselves "by their bootstraps," and her main desire in life was to see my sister and me go to college. No one from my home had ever gone to college. A short time before we graduated, the necessary money was raised.

CURTIS POWELL: Things were groovy for me at the University of Stockholm, where I went for a Ph.D.— being sure I couldn't get one in America. Since I had left Seton Hall in 1959 I had thought about a theory that I felt would bring us closer to discerning the actual mechanism of cancer. I had brought part of it before some top people in biochemistry, who seemed to think it had merit. But because of their racism and my "attitude"—or their attitude and my race—I had never had a chance to work on this theory. In Stockholm I finally had that chance.

I really want to publicly thank those cats—they gave

me the latitude to work on the theory, and the first work on my thesis worked out beautifully. In fact, they didn't want me to leave, and still want me to come back. It was a gas! To work on your own thing, your own way, in your own time! I would like to continue in this work—I think it would aid, in the end, in saving millions of lives—but I am in jail, awaiting a kangaroo court that is going to give us 175 years apiece, for nothing. But I will never forget doing my own research, and getting paid $6,000 a year besides!

In the beginning of 1968, something happened to me. A feeling came over me. I was ready—it was time. It was just a feeling. I don't think I was the only one who felt it. I talked to the brothers in Stockholm. There are bloods there from Africa, the Caribbean, South America, and Babylon—we used to rap a lot. A number of brother expatriates had come to the conclusion that it was time, time to go home, time to begin the struggle.

I told the heads at the lab. They said that whenever I finished my thesis I would have my degree. I began working night and day.

I stopped heavy drinking, without thinking much about it—just naturally stopped. I spent more and more time thinking of what had to be done.

The work on the thesis was quite successful. It took me until some time in August, 1968, to finish writing it up. That's a funny thing: according to this bizarre, ridiculous fantasy indictment, I was supposed to be in New York "conspiring" during this period while I was in Stockholm finishing the thesis—conspiring with some bloods whom I did not even meet until around January of 1969, and in fact some of whom I met for the first time when we got busted. There are even a few cats on this indictment I have not met to this day! A weird conspiracy.

But one must remember—since 1663, whenever black people have got together to deal with the problem of slavery they have been busted for "conspiracy." It's nothing new.

ALI BEY HASSAN: By 1958, after the navy, I was really bored. I'd finished high school in the navy. I began to ask around about going to school under the G.I. bill, and discovered I could be paid while studying. I decided to try to get into dentistry school because I was told I could work there as an assistant at the same time. I called them on the phone, answered some questions, and was told to call back the next day. Next day when I called I was asked if I had called before, and when I said yes, he told me there weren't any openings for assistants. The next day I called again, and the same guy told me there *was* an opening for an assistant, and I told him I would be right down. I told a few friends I was going to school, and I headed on down to sign up. When I got to the office the white secretary asked me who I wanted to see, and I said I had an appointment with Mr. B. to see about entering school. She then told me that all the assistant positions were filled and that Mr. B. wasn't in. As I was turning to leave, she answered the phone, said "One moment," into the phone, got up and went to a side door in the office and told Mr. B. he was wanted on the phone. I was pretty mad and so I waited for him to finish and insisted on seeing him. I told him who I was and he repeated what his secretary had told me. After he saw me I could tell he had thought I was white when he'd told me on the phone there was an opening. I left disgusted and angry and didn't try to find out who I could have reported him to, whatever good that might have done.

I finally found a job—as a machine operator, at $1.10 an hour. So I made flower stands and picnic boxes for about a year and a half until I got laid off. I was nineteen then. I started hanging out, drinking, and partying again, but after six months on unemployment I was called back to work.

BOB COLLIER: One day in 1959 I heard Malcolm X speak, and I started doing some thinking about the things he was saying. Some of this thinking, and talking with an old friend of mine from the service, convinced me I should go back to school. I still had to hustle, but I made it part-time, and in 1961 I got my high school diploma and I did well on college entrance exams. I was married now, and a baby was due in a few months. I entered Lowell Institute of Technology as a night student to get a degree in Electronics. After just half a semester I switched to Northeastern University night school—Engineering Division. But I was hungry for a different kind of knowledge and so I started auditing day courses in social and political science at Harvard and Boston University. I couldn't even consider registering for credit because I didn't have the money. It was getting harder and harder to keep up my studies and still make enough money for rent and food.

I managed to find work mopping floors, and I gave my wife—and daughter—whatever money I could, and I kept up with my studies, although a few times I came close to getting kicked out because they "couldn't find my records." Even though I couldn't take the finals, I usually managed to find out what my letter grade would have been, and I felt the important thing was comprehension of the subject matter. It seemed to me a crucial time; I needed to study. I was determined to be a useful man. I was attending seminars and lectures and reading voraciously.

I worked with some students from CORE, organizing in the ghettos and negotiating with businessmen to institute increased hiring programs for the "disadvantaged." One thing I learned from this was that white students, well-meaning as they were, thought they could tell the people from the ghetto what was right or wrong, and never seemed to think of asking the people what they *wanted*, what their problems were. I kept learning, but couldn't fit what I was learning together.

AFENI SHAKUR: I was president or some old shit of the Disciple Debs, which means the female Disciples, you know, and we used to just run around beating up people, shooting people with zip guns and nonsense like that. Or taking antennas off parked cars and whipping people. I remember they had a pool in Cretona Park and every summer that pool used to just be red, the water is blue but the pool would be red with blood because it was right in the middle of the borderline. On the other side there was a Puerto Rican gang called the Horsemen, La Cabeza, or whatever the Spanish word is for horsemen. We used to all go to the pool, and we would go there for no other reason at all except to knife each other. We fought each other furiously. It was just really something. It wasn't even funny, it was really very serious; a very serious situation. I didn't like the Puerto Ricans because I couldn't understand what they were saying, and because I didn't like the smell of garlic. That's all I had against Puerto Rican people. I didn't understand what they said so I always thought they were talking about me and I didn't like the smell of garlic so I thought that they were foreign. I didn't know why they didn't like us, but I'm sure there was something as simple as that. It wasn't based on anything at all except some simpleness, you know, and it just had us fighting each other constantly and we were righteously fighting. We were killing each other. I mean every week there was a body in Cretona Pool. Every week. It wasn't funny. We were playing, but we were playing for keeps. I was going to Performing Arts High School—the school that's supposed to be such a big deal to get into—and at the same time that I was going to Performing Arts and my mother was bragging about me for that, I was running around shooting and cutting people.

RICHARD HARRIS: When I was growing up, gangs were coming in strong in Newark. Needless to say, all of my summers had been spent in neighborhoods where it was necessary to be part of a gang, and I was. By my being so mobile in earlier times, I had got into two separate gangs. The first was the Junior Outlaws—I knew most of them from my summers in Newark. We hung out together and fought other gangs, thereby establishing ourselves a rep. A few years later I became a member of the Junior Mohawks. Between these two gangs it was possible for me to travel at will over and through most of Newark, and in the process acquire and maintain a rep from both gangs, independent of each other. I soon became a dude that knew a lot of bad mothers and who was far from being a pushover himself.

In the summer I was fifteen I was living in a neighborhood that was predominantly white, ruled by three Italian gangs. The largest was the Romans—at that time the largest white gang in Jersey. Their rival gang was the Barbarians. The Juniors of both allied with each other to fight us, calling themselves the Morticians. We battled with them constantly all winter in small groups—and we allied with anybody that wanted to stomp one of them.

But with the coming of summer, those gangs that we relied on for help began their own gang wars. The Morticians didn't invade their territories, so were not their problem.

We then formed a loose gang, called ourselves the Counts, branded each other with "C" and went to war. We took as much as we got, and got a lot. That summer of 1955 found me as the war counselor for the Counts. I and others in our clique (there were never more than one hundred all told) got hip to zip guns. I always carried two. Nightsticks, daggers, pipes—weapons of war in general were accumulated and stashed. Whenever we put something heavy on them, they would come back with older cats who had real guns. We got hip to that and stole .22s from the shooting gallery. We also stole cars. I became one of the quickest at stealing them and loved to drive. My first sure-enough stickup was done that same summer during a running fight with the Morticians. We used the money to buy two messed-up .32 automatics. That summer of gang wars in Newark saw as many deaths and serious injuries as any major battle in a conventional war. Dudes were shotgunned, stabbed, stomped, and run over. The Outlaws and Mohawks went to war, bringing almost every teenager and young adult in the city under one or the other. I was too busy with the Morticians to participate fully, but I did take part against individuals who crossed my path at one time or another. I was told later that this was when I was recognized as a crazy wild-assed nigger who wouldn't see twenty-one. The police, my friends, and family constantly told me this, and I believed it.

Late that summer two of our fellows got busted, and we helped them escape from Parental Home. They met a few dudes while inside who I knew had been doing

B and E (breaking and entering). We listened, learned, and started doing B and E too. As the summer was ending, gang-fighting became a matter of not getting caught while outnumbered or outgunned. Four out of five Counts were locked up. Two had gone South after a killing. The Romans and Barbarians began fighting each other again and this left the Morticians with little or no back-up, and no initiative to start fights.

I was wild when winter started. I had a real pistol, money from B and Es, and was one of the best car thieves in the city. When a fight broke out in Jersey City between the Outlaws and another gang, I was among those chosen to drive a load of dudes over and back. That fight lasted two weeks, we raiding them nightly and being raided back and when it ended, I was hanging with older cats. After Jersey City came Potters Crossing. Then Elizabeth and East Orange—we were riding high. At the celebrations afterward, I would get drunk and do tricks with the cars, usually wrecking them. I told my family I was spending the nights over at friends' houses.

When hanging out you are liable to find yourself doing almost anything imaginable, and I did. These new cliques I was with were older by three or four years, and they did most things for profit—whereas in the Counts, we had done them for fun or dares or to impress. I got hip to boosting, mugging, picking pockets—I was jostler, not pickpocket, my hands were too fat. The money was mostly used on clothes, flashy, hip, gangster-looking clothes. This was me at fifteen and a half.

KATARA: When I was growing up the fratricidal gang wars were coming to an end, but young bloods from the Thirties—129th to 138th Streets—and the Forties—140th to 148th—still rumbled in St. Nicholas Park. One time the Forties cats caught a brother that lived in my building and hung him upside down from a tree and started a fire under him, then encircled him. It took three wild-assed attacks to get to him and cut him down. But the main thing I learned from these insane black-against-black fights was where the cops were at. Whenever a heavy rumble started, some older people around the block would call the police and you could see the patrol cars circling the park but they didn't stop, they'd just turn on their flashers and keep going. The only time they got out of the cars was when the badly beaten or bleeding came staggering out of the park and then the police would beat them.

DHARUBA: All the kids that start school together get to know each other in a few years, if not by sight, by name, and you start to hang out with various kids. When they send you to junior high school, it may or may not be in the same area that your elementary school was, and in my case I went to Junior High School 40. Now 40 is a peculiar school. It had kids from both sides of Prospect Avenue. At that time, Prospect Avenue was a dividing line for various gangs: on the east side of Prospect the predominating gang was the Crowns and the predominating gang on the west was the Sportsmen. The majority of the kids on the east side of Prospect were Puerto Rican; on the west side of Prospect Avenue, black. There was a tradition in the school then, or a tradition in all schools, that the new kids coming in were subject at any time during that whole year to get vamped on, to get their ass kicked. And it was really such that in certain classes that got out the east doorway of the school, if you were in the Sportsmen, you would try your best to be in the middle of the line so you could sneak around and come out of the west side, and all that.

It was very dangerous just going to school because I wasn't a Crown or a Sportsman at the time and therefore it was open season on me for anybody. The first day I went, there were some treacherous-looking niggers hanging around there. They were only like thirteen or fourteen years old, but they were treacherous-looking. They were just hanging out there and their old ladies were hanging out there with them. They lived across the street, down the block, and all around the school. In that school then, you could get jacked up just for going to the bathroom and bumping into a Crown or bumping into a Sportsman, they'd jack you up right there. They were so crazy they were just shooting each other. The street I lived on was all Sportsmen, or all Disciples, and I grew up with quite a few of the young bloods that were in that club. One day after school, in the candy store that was the local hangout on the corner, I had got some static with some of the members and out of this static I wound up being very tight with some dudes in the club and I wound up joining the club. Later on I became vice-president of the club.

Let it suffice to say that my joining a gang or a club or whatever was a turning point in me because before then I wasn't really involved in hanging out too tough. I used to hang out, but I didn't hang out to the point, you know, where it was a fetish. From the time I joined on I did a lot of things I didn't particularly care to do, more so than before. The unique thing about living in a colony is that you have to seek recognition among your peers, yet still remain anonymous to your oppressor. And the more recognition you seek among your peers, quite naturally the more you become a focus of some police attention. You become a standout and a target for the fuzz.

In the black community, young people were in gangs not so much for what the average sociologist tells you—to belong to something—although I wouldn't doubt that's part of it. I think the main reason that you hook up in a gang is in order to ensure your social status, whatever little social position the colonizers left you. The life that I led at that time was very wild and carefree. My mother tried to impose some type of shackles on me, some type of discipline, but I would just totally rebel because I thought I was the only one who had to undergo these type of changes. Everybody else was hanging out and I had to wage struggle with Moms, you know, so I just said like later for that and did what I wanted.

BOB COLLIER: I started hanging out with the fellows on "the Hill." The Blackhawks ruled the Hill and the Rams ran things downtown. Our "rumbles" were more like small wars—reconnaissance to check out the area picked out for the fight, sizing up our strength and the enemy's strength, planning tactics and strategy. We used weapons, too: bats, steel crowbars, bayonets, or even pistols. The fights sometimes lasted for hours, and a lot of kids were scarred or maimed for life. To the victor belonged the glory—at least until the next rumble. In the eyes of the chicks, we were men—heroes.

Once I went to a dance in "enemy" territory because I dug the chick who was giving the party. We started out about 7:00 P.M. and picked up a pint of wine and a half-pint of rot-gut bourbon. By the time we got to the subway we were high. We were threaded down like something out of a juvenile *Esquire*, and we intimidated the people on the train with our bravado and our pimp stance, as we flashed our push-button stilettos. We knew we were bad and sharp—talking game like it was our own invention. We got to the dance very high, almost drunk.

About an hour after we got there we were up against the wall with several chicks. One of the girls I was laying out the love rap to was thought of as the finest sister downtown, and I knew if I could make it with her, it would raise my standing a lot. All of a sudden an argument broke out, and the shit was on: the place erupted.

The gang concept is a basic and fundamental historical development. It is a feeling of security after being isolated from society because of group origin. Psychologists are stupid. Instead of them realizing or admitting that historical patterns of development mold the conscious attitudes of survival, they ignorantly attribute such behavior to dogmatic definitions which apply—most probably—to their own consciousness of white historical development. Black people actually believe in justice and democracy whereas whites do not fully understand its qualitative application. Why? It is impossible for a racist group to define values and concepts which must in their very definition discriminate only because the group cannot think but in a prejudice frame of reference. This infectious disease influences the recipients of such culture so that even in their assimilation they display the same tendencies. Hence, the straightening of hair to conform to the white standard of beauty. Hence, the criteria for black value judgment is or was actually defined in terms of white concepts unconsciously. This thinking process was the direct result of the educational and social destruction (genocide) of a black relevancy among its ethnic members. Man is still basically an animal with herd or pack tendencies. We band together to survive—physically, emotionally, and naturally.

KWANDO KINSHASA: My eighth-grade year I started to resent anything a nonblack person said or tried to tell me, and consequently I was completely anti-school, and street life was spent trying to bust "crackers." At that time an Italian gang called the Golden Guineas controlled the area around PS 113. I joined some of the bloods in a rival gang—the Crusaders—and we not only jugged with the Golden Guineas but with a lot of gangs from the lower Bronx.

LUMUMBA SHAKUR: In the summer after the sixth grade, in Atlantic City, we would always go swimming in the daytime, and at night we went to dances or parties. Before we went to a party, we drank wine and smoked reefers. All the dances always ended in a mass gang fight, because Philly was only an hour's drive from Atlantic City and the gangs from Philly loved to come to Atlantic City to crash our dances and parties. In Atlantic City, later, we organized a gang called the Syndicate, allied with the Syndicate in North Philly. We had some get-down brothers.

Later on, each of us took a "street name"—street names are typical in all street gangs from Philly to New York to Atlantic City. Dig some of the street names these cats had: Benny Blood, Tombstone, Graveyard, China, Lash, Chan, Ghost, Kino, Cherokee, Apache, Piece, Snake, Killer, Sinbad, Zorro, Chink, Crip, Torch, Ace, Batman, Jap, Spider, Beaver, Dino, Chico, Tico, Spade, Big Hands Chips, Tee, and Bop. My name was Shotgun. Some souls had personalities that fit their street names to a tee, which built up ghetto reputations; and some died trying to live up to their reputations.

When I was living in Philly, I would hang with a cat named Baba. We rode trolley cars all over Philly. In Philly I got my baptism into a street gang, the Syndicate. Belonging to a street gang was almost a necessity: if you didn't, all gangs would have open season on you. And you couldn't get a girlfriend without belonging to a gang.

Gangs were the only symbols of masculinity in the ghettos of America. I experienced gang fighting in Philly, New York City, and Atlantic City. In all three states the phenomenon was the same: the animosity and hostility of the blacks, created by hundreds of years of white repression, and created by the conditions in the white-created ghetto, were directed against each other instead of against the system that created the repression and hostilities. It was a bad-nigger-kill-bad-nigger process and it was encouraged by the police and the power structure. The gangs were organized in a paramilitary manner with a president, vice-president, and warlord. I had a knack for being the warlord. In the mid-1950s gangs like the Syndicate and the Tyogo Tees in Philly and the Bishops and the Chaplains in Brooklyn, New York City, had memberships of ten thousand each. The gangs were actually apolitical small armies, which had strong discipline and togetherness. Some of these gangs were better equipped militarily than some African and Latin American states were when they first got so-called independence. For instance, all the gangs in New York knew where to go to rip off guns.

The most notorious gangs that I think existed were in Brooklyn, called the Bishops and the Chaplains. These two gangs had divisions all through Brooklyn and Queens. The Bishops and Chaplains were so cold that when they were fighting each other, the pigs would not come until the fighting was over. One day R of the Chaplains shot-gunned A of the Bishops to death. The Bishops retaliated by shotgunning R to death. At R's funeral the sisters, or what we called Bishop Debs, had the audacity to go to the Chaplain's, R's, funeral, and straight-razor R in his coffin and drag the body out of the coffin out into the streets. The Bishops Debs' rationalization was that they loved their brother A because he had a whole lot of heart and the motherfucker who killed him must die the death of a rag doll—a thousand deaths. In Fort Greene Project the Mau Mau Chaplains would rip off the navy yard for guns at will: any kind of gun you can name, Bishops and Chaplains had them.

Years after, when I was in prison, I knew about 100 ex-Bishops and ex-Chaplains who were in prison for murder during the gang fighting of the 1950s. Today, instead of nourishing street gangs, the American government constantly saturates the black communities with heroin. I guess America calls heroin the automated way to kill black people.

For a year, while I was living in Jamaica (a city in the Queens section of New York City), the only time I hung out in Jamaica was after school. I would be with brothers in the Sinners gang. After school we would go over to what we called "crosstown" Jamaica and fight other gangs called the Cheyennes and the Chaplains. On the weekends I would always go to Brooklyn because Brooklyn reminded me of Philly. South Jamaica is a rural ghetto and Brooklyn and Philly are urban ghettos —which I dug better because there were more blacks living there. This brother I met named Danny who moved from Brooklyn was a Bishop and would always take me to Brooklyn to party and to gang fight with the Bishops. I met these two get-down brothers named Lash and Beaver, who would later become some very good friends of mine in prison. Gang fighting in Brooklyn took on a tremendously deadly form.

Danny and a brother named Bone began organizing the Bishops in South Jamaica. I told them that I would be down with them as long as they didn't fight the Sinners, because I was still fighting with the Sinners against the Cheyennes and the Chaplains. Danny and the Bishops agreed with my position with the Sinners, because everybody in Jamaica knew that the Sinners were the baddest gang in Jamaica. Personally, some of my best friends were in the Sinners—like Sam, and Beany (Sekou Odinga). We would hang out together sometimes, but they lived a mile from me. Another brother named Chink was organizing the Bishops in St. Albans and Hollis, which is walking distance from Jamaica.

In New York City on May 30 all the gangs had an annual mass gang fight. This was some ritual—all the gangs from Brooklyn and Queens would go to Coney Island and have a shootout. On the same day the gangs from Manhattan and the Bronx would go to Pelham Bay to have a shootout. The brothers and sisters in the gangs had an attitude that they would kill a ghost, stick a stone, strangle a stick or drown a drop of water. If the street-gang brothers and sisters were ever politicized to the point where they knew who their real enemy was, the American system would be in danger of collapse.

part 5

ALI BEY HASSAN: In 1948 or '49 we were living on 118th Street in Harlem, on the top floor in a single room. I was going to Cooper High School, and my mother worked as a nurse's aide. She had a high school diploma, whatever that was good for, and I later discovered that had she put in two more years at school (she had been working in hospitals for eighteen years altogether) and taken a test, she might have become a registered nurse. But hardships and racism kept her from that. About this time I started noticing that my mother was doing a lot of drinking when she wasn't working. She also gave me a little drop every now and then, and sometimes I would take a little when she wasn't around.

I started having problems with my job. I was working at Major Car Corporation, spraying freight cars. I had worked there for two years and seven months and had just joined the union when we went on strike. I'd been told that all members could collect $10 to $20 per week during the strike, but unfortunately this didn't include me. So in order to keep some food in our apartment and pay the rent, I went on welfare.

DHARUBA: I came back to New York in the winter of '61, a few days before Christmas. I really didn't want to go home because I didn't want to confront my mother with the fact that I had an undesirable discharge from the army, you know. Not wanting to confront her with this, I figured I should try to make it on my own, try to go it alone. And I got involved with one of the capitalist con games that they have going, as a door-to-door salesman. If I remember correctly, I was on 43rd Street, it was very cold and I was only out of the army one day. I wasn't staying anywhere in particular and I didn't want to go back around the neighborhood because I was very much uptight about what I would do and which way I would go, what people would think about me getting out the army the way I did.

I was approached by this cat who started rapping to me about did I need a gig and would I want to work as a door-to-door salesman selling magazine subscriptions. I took him up on that. This magazine subscription company had a whole three floors in this hotel in the West Forties. Some of the rooms were the living quarters for the people who worked for the subscription company and a few other rooms were used as office space for the executive personnel of the company. It was a mobile operation, the whole company moved from city to city selling subscriptions. I was very young—I was about seventeen getting ready to go on eighteen—and I got involved with a woman who was working there who was from Boise, Idaho. We had a very torrid love affair, you know. She was much older than I was. I think she was about twenty-two. She was teaching me how to deal with my sales and I upped my sales and she told me a whole lot about the dude that owned the company.

This was a white dude. He hired mainly women—black women—and I could see that it was nothing but a form of modified slavery because he terrorized everybody that worked for him. He was a gangster. In order to curry his favor, various women had to go to bed with him and so forth and so on. And this particular woman had done that and she was very regretful that she had, and because of where the authority in that particular organization was placed, pressure was brought to bear on her to do this again. It was a very uptight situation. The pig that controlled the little subscription company sent me to Hartford to work up there. At that particular point I had cultivated the idea that I would stick with the subscription company as long as it would take for us to make a tour across the country so I could get to the West Coast, and when I got there, I was going to quit. But that seemed the dream of everybody that was working in the company, getting to the West Coast and then quitting. The median age of these people was about twenty, and the majority were black and Puerto Rican. It was hard to feel any allegiance to that bastard's company. I doubt that many of the people made it to the West Coast.

I got some static in Bridgeport or Hartford, wherever the hell it was, and I left and went uptown to check out this man who I used to work for before as an orthodontist's assistant, and I got another job with him. He asked me if my family knew I was out of the army and I told him no. And one day I came in to do some work and they were sitting there. It was a very emotional reunion, to say the least. My mother hadn't known whether I was alive or dead. The army didn't give her that information. In fact, when the army discharged me, they didn't even give me discharge papers. I had to borrow five dollars from the sergeant who discharged me to get on the bus, and when I got to New York I had a dollar to my name. The army processed me out in approximately three hours, and normally it takes a week to get processed out. The army was very anxious to get rid of me, you know.

Back in New York, I started hanging out again, but this time I was more refined. I wasn't a jitterbug or a bebop any more, I was wheeling and dealing some smoke, and hanging out and sticking up, you know.

SHABA OM: Around the age of fourteen I began to dig on the other black kids, their parents too. We were all in the same old bag, inferior to the man, the all-mighty white man. As I began to understand this I wanted to help myself and Grandma. So I got a newspaper route and became the community paperboy. Then I began to make a little money, $10 or $11 a week, to try and help myself and Grandma, because she was still slaving. I felt bad, because I was getting near to a man's age now and in very good health. (My health was good because my grandma can really cook, I mean cook for days. I can remember and wish for some of the mouth-watering food she would cook right now: cornbread, buttered beans, collard greens, and fried or baked chicken; sweet potato pie; and my main dish would be the three-layer chocolate cake. She could make a cake like ABC cake and it would melt in your mouth, the best in the world in my opinion.)

KUWASI BALAGOON: The summer after ninth grade I began to work at Berwyn Fuel and Feed, loading trucks with bags of cement, kegs of nails, and wallboard. It was a time of growth mentally and physically. I ate breakfasts of six eggs and six slices of bacon and two lunches, plus with the extra money I could buy more wine. Working around older cats I turned into a wizard at cutting down people's mothers.

RICHARD HARRIS: When I was out of the marines, one thing stuck more on my mind from that experience than all the traveling and the women, and that was how unscrupulous you had to be to really succeed. I made up my mind to succeed. I fooled around with one of my teenage friends for a while, stealing cars and selling parts, did some muggings, B and Es (breaking and entering)— just run-of-the-mill hustling. I met this fox and we started living together. I never had enough money, so I'd pick up the gun and go in on some stickups with others that I knew to be as good at it as I, or better. I spent two years sticking up any and every thing that had money. Our first clique of three broke up with the death of one; I immediately hooked up with others, and changed the hiding places and things to people who always had money and wouldn't call the police—supposedly. We stuck up numbers men—runners, writers, and bankers—crap games, and parties. This made us extremely hot to everybody, because at that time in Jersey black men just didn't stick up the Mafia. But we did, and we did it with the intention of living to spend the money we took. Eventually the word came around that we had contracts on us, so we lightened up a little. We took off bank messengers and company payrolls. It sounds as if we should have had quite a piece of money, but in reality we were sticking up with little or no plans for the money we got. At least every week, no matter how big the amount taken previously, we would be broke or carrying borrowed money while we took off the next joint. We were living high: clothes, silks, mohairs, custom-made suits, shirts, topcoats, liquor, reefer, and the new thing then was dugee (heroin) for snorting. You could spend $100 or $200 at a whop at any crap game. We were doing our thing, playing it to the bust.

SHABA OM: In high school, in Harlem, I began to dig on the dudes in the streets doing their thing and going to school too. The bloods were doing what they called hustling, selling drugs and gambling in the streets of Harlem. I was thinking about the words Grandma said, how she didn't want me to slave and be saying Yes sir, No sir, to some insane honky. But also, how she wanted me to get a good education. I began to check out the bloods who were hustlers and gamblers in the streets of Harlem. They dug where I was coming from in my rap, because from being around older dudes at a young age in the South, I was what the bloods on the block called slick, cool, and a very sharp mind. I began to learn the streets of Harlem and how to survive in them. I stopped hookying and started part-time hustling a little drugs and gambling up the money. After I learned the art of shooting dice I would down my skag and go hustle with the dicers, win a little money. Meantime, I was not doing my homework or studying in school. School became a place to go and meet the foxes and dudes to make plans for what we were going to do after school. I was a nigger thinking big and wild about life. I didn't care about anyone but me, that was it. The more I learned about the streets the cooler I tried to be in doing my thing. After a few months I began to buy myself the kind of clothes that the niggers on the blocks who were making big hustling money bought—like tailor-made pants in silk and mohair, alligator and lizard shoes. I was on a wild, mad trip about clothes and my looks. Selling skag is very fast and big money— also blood and death money—but at the time all I could see was myself, foxes, and my wild little world, a hustler in the Big Apple, you dig. I didn't care about school or homework because I was making money. My mind was very unstable at the time—still I saw that the so-called education the schools gave was not relevant to my life. Music and black history were the only things that made me want to go to school at all—I dug those two subjects and the teachers I had were really teaching me well in those subjects—today all power to them. But my mind was really in the streets and making money.

Now I was also what the dudes in the streets call a pimp. I was relating to about two foxes on an exploitative basis at the time. That's all a pimp is—one who's mastered the art of finding a woman's weakness and exploiting it for his own benefit. This art I dug I could master, because I had a cool and sharp mind when I wanted it to be used. The more I became involved the more I dug it. I wanted money; I would hustle skag, gamble, and the foxes were giving me a little money. Then after a while I got into what I now call "conservative pimping." I was still going to school and doing my thing in the streets of the Big Apple, and keeping out of the hands of the police and junkies.

When I was about seventeen I said to myself, if school is going to put me in a low tracking system and give me all of this irrelevant miseducation, why not make myself some money. By now I had mastered the art of survival in the streets of Harlem. I always tried to justify my hustling by remembering what Grandma said about slaving for some honky. I developed a thing with older women. I would go to bars or house parties in Harlem. Dig, I would like slide in the place in my flyest clothes, dance or buy myself a drink, and just lay and dig on the action. If I was at a bar, I would sit at the bar, spot a fox about twenty or older, then sit and just move on her actions. She would catch my eye and she'd either begin to dig on me, or she'd round on me—ignore me. Her eyes and facial expression would tell me yes or no, then I'd know how to move and when. I have mastered all of the baser skills and perfected them to an art.

If she really dug on me, she would come over or call me over to where she is at. Then I knew I was working on pretty safe ground. We would rap, dance, or whatever was happening at the place. By rapping to her, I could tell more or less what she was into. This is one of the times I would use my sharp mind, to try and judge where she was coming from—try to look at her soul and mine—and I would win most of the time. Most of the foxes I was relating to were nineteen to thirty-five, because most women at this age dig themselves a young, together man. I was living at my cousin's by then, and conservative pimping was part of my survival. On weekends I would go over to one of my foxes' apartments and stay there till Monday, or as long as I wished.

When one of my foxes was over twenty, I would call her Ma-ee. Because over twenty they would treat me as if I was their baby. I can remember very well the nights in one of my Ma-ee's pads. Dig on the setting in the pad. She works, she's about twenty-five years old. The lights are blue or red; there's warm, loving jazz playing in the background. We begin to rap about her day at her slave and about herself, my day at school and all of the mis-education I was receiving, what's happening in the news and the world of niggers, little things like that. Ma-ees are very cool and together women. I dug it, that kind of pimping, because it kept me out of fights—also in the shade, with my clothes clean, money in my pocket.

A Ma-ee always had something interesting to rap about—I dug this because it kept my mind open, wondering about people and what life is all about, you know? In the summertime I would go to Mount Morris Park by myself with two or three sticks of old-age smoke and a large can of Colt 45. Burn the smoke and down my Colt 45, my mind is mellow and clear after I down all of my smoke and 45. I am like nice and now I would begin to think, about myself and my role in life. Sometimes I'd be in the park for two hours, just wondering and thinking, digging on Nature. Mother Nature and her lover Father Time rolling along together as one.

I dropped out of school in the tenth grade, and got myself a full-time slave as a delivery man at a film-editing house, doing my conservative pimping and things, also, on the side. The foxes and Ma-ees didn't want me to work at all. I began to save my money because I wanted to get my own pad and I wanted to get into my thing in the streets on a higher level. So in August, I moved into my own pad, at the age of eighteen, and this was where I really began to go into my conservative bag of tricks. Because now I was slaving I could stretch out, see, I could take it or leave it with the women—I didn't care, you dig? The slave I had was very cool, not hard at all. In fact it was somewhat educational because I spent most of the time reading the *New York Times* and listening to conversations about politics. I developed my "arts" in a somewhat different style at this time, like keeping the skag at my pad, and I began to relate to foxes more my age. My pad was laid out cool, blue lights and all.

CLARK SQUIRE: After college I forced myself to look for a job. One thing I was absolutely sure of—I was not going to be a schoolteacher. I had already decided I would rather pull cotton than submit to the domination, dehumanization, and emasculation that a black Texas schoolteacher had to face. Needless to say this attitude enraged my Moms, especially since there were almost no other jobs for blacks with degrees in Texas.

As the summer wore on, I rejected one teaching job after another.

A few weeks before leaving school, I had filled out a general job-application form in a college scientific publication. These applications were reproduced and circulated nationwide to major companies for a fee of $5. I had also filed applications for every federal job requiring a math background that appeared in the periodic post office listings. The result was that I received offers of employment as a sheet-metal molding instructor, aircraft mechanic, arc welder—and other peculiar jobs at various air bases, weather bureaus, and government installations around Texas. I received offers for almost every kind of job not relating to mathematics. I accepted all the jobs anyway, but I never heard from any of the places again. About this time my sister married her college boyfriend and left for Ohio. I was now the only one left at home, and Mom's disposition grew harsher accordingly.

Then out of the blue came a call from New York. Western Electric Corporation was asking me to come up for an expense-paid interview. After four and a half days—on the back of the bus through Arkansas, Louisiana, Alabama, and Mississippi—eating bread, bologna and candy bars, and studying differential equations all the way, I arrived in New York. At the Port Authority I asked a red cap where I could find a "colored" hotel. He told me to take the A train uptown two stops, exit, and walk two blocks east. I followed directions, came up at 125th Street and dragged my suitcase up to the Theresa Hotel in the heart of Harlem. The hotel clerk told me he had only one suite left, for $25. I asked him if it was for a week, and he indignantly said, no, for a day!

I had a total of $16 in my pockets and so I moved on. I found a room in the St. Marie a few blocks down on Seventh Avenue, for $4.20. I called up and made an appointment for my interview the next day, had my blue serge suit pressed, and went out to look over the town.

I arrived the next morning at the stroke of nine, introduced myself, and waited in a booth while someone went to search for my interviewer. His first question was "What is a superhetrodyne receiver?" My mind spun like slick tires on an ice bed, but I couldn't grab onto anything. I thought, "Hell, that's an electronics question!" Finally, I said, "I don't know." He then fired question after question dealing with problems of decreasing difficulty in electronics. To each question I answered, "I don't know." After about fifteen successive don't know's he worked himself down to Ohm's law, which I was familiar with from my first-year physics course. I answered that one and he immediately switched to math and asked the equation of a circle. I also got that one and figured finally we were getting someplace, but he suddenly ended the interview saying I was very good in math but weak in electronics. I stuttered, stammered, and tried to explain that the job concerned computer programming and anyway he had a copy of my transcript and knew in advance I was a math major and had only an elementary basic course in physics—but he just kept on going, instructing me to take a couple more electronic courses and come back in about six months. He pointed to the cashier, who he said would reimburse me for my ticket and hotel.

I stammered a few more words but by now, my voice seemed very heavy and crude compared to the slick, suave roll of this New Yorker. I turned and went to the cashier's office. I figured my total expenses up from Texas had been about $45, and doubling that for expenses back

I expected to receive about $90. But the cashier must have taken one look at me and known I was a hick, because he began dictating my expenses. He told me I was flying back, for $150; hotel, $20 a day; meals, $10 a day; etc., etc., and totaled up a bill of $276.00. I thanked him and left. I had known beforehand that win, lose, or draw, I was not going back to Texas, and now I had enough to maneuver on, yet I couldn't get the taste out of my mouth that I had been tricked.

I found a permanent room on Lenox Avenue and 123rd Street, five-by-eight for $7 a week, and began looking around for a job requiring a math background. It didn't take long to find there was no such job in New York for a nineteen-year-old black, no experience, draft-classification 1A, with a heavy Texas accent. So I worked at this factory and that one. Most of the jobs I bought from cheap employment agencies around Chambers Street. You have to pay the agency a $10 minimum down for a job, and then work a few weeks, paying on the balance as slow as possible, because often after paying off the agency you were laid off. Or, after working a few weeks, the union would demand you join, at an astronomical initial fee, and I would have to quit and repeat the process. In between factory jobs I canvassed various city firms for a job in my field, and filed application after application for various federal jobs listed across the country.

After about six months I got a job with NASA in California. I said goodbye to all my friends and took the bus trip West.

CURTIS POWELL: In San Francisco, in the summer of 1960, I stopped reading other people's philosophy; I decided that none of it answered all the questions I had.

I had read Marx and Lenin and thought—as I think now—that they offer a lot, but not all, of the answers I was searching for. I was still drinking and smoking and occasionally shooting up, and doing a lot of hanging out. But I was cool. That is, I wasn't strung out on anything.

I started doing research at the medical center in the fall—at the same time I was doing all those other things. I was working on my master's degree then. It was beautiful, but as I look back I can see that with all that and my social life, I probably couldn't have stood it too long. I wasn't getting much sleep, and I felt tired all the time. My mother got sick in February and I had to give it all up anyway and come back to the East Coast—back to South Orange, New Jersey.

The same old harassment started as soon as I returned. I got a gig at the NYU Medical Center, blew it, got another one, and finally moved to the Lower East Side, in Manhattan. It was not so much that I wanted to live in New York City, but South Orange—and the New Jersey brand of racism—was getting to be too much. One night when a friend and I were driving home through Newark we saw a white cop who had a black man up against the wall, shouting things at him like "nigger" and "black bastard." So I leaned out of the car and asked the pig if all that bullshit was really necessary and he came on over to the car and put his pistol to my head and told me I was under arrest. At the station house, some of the pigs got together and kicked my ass. The next day in court the judge threw the case out, but I saw that New Jersey and I weren't going to make it. I rapped with all of my black friends about how bad things were and how there was a need for black unity to stop all the racism, but they were afraid to do anything. So I moved to New York City, hoping it would at least be better than New Jersey.

Anyway I had a gig at NYU, working under a maniac. This dude had everybody at the lab petrified of him. He came on like Hitler. He had a thing about colds, he couldn't stand to be around anybody with a cold. One chick who worked there came in one day with a cold, and he made her wear a surgical mask when she talked to him. Once a big, big experiment was coming up, and this dude wanted to discuss it with me. Unfortunately, I had the flu and I sniffled at him or something during the meeting, so he kicked me out of the office. I told him I was going to kick his ass, and I got fired. Next week he cooled off and apologized, but the university wouldn't take me back in that gig; they said our tempers were too fiery for us to work together. They wouldn't take me in any other lab work, either, so my next gig was at a hospital in Newark that was trying to start a research center, but it soon proved to be too costly a proposition, and that was that. Then I found that Seton Hall had opened a medical school in New Jersey, and in September I applied to the biochemistry department, but I was told they hadn't yet opened for applications. In October I got a job in the biochemistry department there, and found they *had* accepted one graduate student. A black woman who worked with me said the new chairman of the biochemistry department was from Missouri and he felt that if he let "one" in, "they" would storm the doors.

New Year's Eve, 1962: I went to the lab to inject some animals for an experiment. That place was so cheap, they cut off the water on weekends and holidays. While I was working I heard some water rushing somewhere. I looked in one of the labs and saw water pouring from the ceiling—the pipes had frozen and burst. I saw this white graduate student and told him what was happening. He knew where a master key was (I was only allowed a key to the lab that I worked in) so we went through all the labs, moving expensive equipment out of the way of a possible flood. We had called the fire department, and they arrived just in time to keep the water from flooding the emergency room at the hospital in the basement. I had called the department chairman on the phone. He arrived, and thanked the white graduate student—and ignored me. The following Monday the faculty met—so I heard—and worried over how I had "got hold of a master key."

The cat I was gigging for moved soon, to Albert Einstein College of Medicine in New York, and I went with him. But he was a nut too. He was Italian—married to a South African white woman—and they had a black foster baby for a while. But she got pregnant and they gave the baby away and got a puppy dog. I said, this isn't it.

KUWASI BALAGOON: I came back from the army, and Lakeland was exactly the same as I left it. Entering by cab was like being in a time machine, the same dogs barking and every tree and rock in place. The family was surprised. After the initial shock they ran down all about who got married and who died and me and Daddy drank rum until late and then retired. The next day I went out to see if things were the same. They were. School chums had hatted up for D.C. or college, and after a couple of days I was beat. So I started going into D.C., running down old friends and partners.

Meanwhile, after some test, I started working as a clerk and messenger at the U.S. Department of the Interior—which was an immediate drag. I went to parties all over the area and to New York every once in a while—later, every other weekend—but the escape wasn't enough, even with smoke and speed, so I quit the job and moved to New York. During this time also I read the *Autobiography of Malcolm X*, and thought about what was on my mind to do, and what I in fact was doing—walking around with eyeballs looking like they were cut with a razor, doing nonsense at work, helping somebody else's world go round, and falling to sleep coming home on the bus from work.

CLARK SQUIRE: Coming back into New York's JFK Airport—after working for years in the computer field, then taking a trip—I was the only black person on the plane, and I was the only one customs called into a side room. They stripped and searched me, and I was busted for packing a .38 strapped under my arm.

I sold my car, and with the money left over from my trip, put enough together to retain a good but very expensive lawyer. I got three years' probation for the gun charge. This is the same "blind justice" that sends other brothers, without the financial resources for bail and a good lawyer, to prison for five or seven years on exactly the same charge. In waiting for bail I had come face to face with the stark reality of the American system of "justice." I saw with my own eyes that overcrowded, inhuman, sadistic environment where, in New York City, 90 per cent of the inmates are black or Puerto Rican. I saw depraved, sadistic guards club brothers into unconsciousness; I saw sick addicts or just plain mentally disturbed prisoners slash their wrists, hang themselves with sheets, or burn themselves in a pile of blankets and newspapers. I saw prisoners try to turn every new inmate into a homosexual—and often succeed. And I saw what may be the most horrible of all: prisoners from upstate, often people who had been railroaded into jail, come down to New York City for appeal court with a starry, glassy look in their eyes—the look that comes from a long time in an isolation hole, plus electric shock treatments, which turn a man into a vegetable.

It is said that "The degree of civilization in a society can be judged by visiting its prisons." By that criterion, America is without a doubt the most barbaric nation in the world today, bar none.

RICHARD HARRIS: Going to a party one night in North Newark, the police chased a bunch of us who were in stolen cars. My car was singled out and chased until I ran out of gas—directly in front of a police station. My first real bust: I got beat for two days before my family missed me, and got me released in their custody to await trial. One week later I split open a dude's head for his $50 and left Newark with some friends. We went stickup-crazy on liquor stores, drugstores, and insurance men. Since I was the youngest—I was about fifteen and a half—I mostly drove and played chicky. When we reached North Carolina I had over a thousand dollars cash.

The older of the two guys I was with got busted in a fight one night, and I woke up to see police and state troopers coming to our cabin with shotguns and pistols drawn. Our friend had flipped out on us. The cabins were set in a square facing the highway and that is why I am not in North Carolina today doing time. We grabbed one pistol, our pants, three shoes, one desert-boot, two sweaters, and climbed out the back window into some woods. If the joint had had air conditioning we wouldn't have made it. We stayed hidden in the woods, scared to death, for the rest of that night, and beat up two

school kids the next day for a pair of shoes. Then we
split up. I went to a nearby town and called some friends.
They thought I was in jail. After a two- or three-dollar
conversation, they gave me some relatives' addresses in
Fayetteville and I caught the bus there. I was driven
back to Newark and got the worst beating of my life from
my stepfather. I had hidden my pistol and $500 in the
hollow inside of my closet door or I would have killed
him sure.

I was taken to court. The judge thought I was some
kind of nut, dressed up in a blue pin-striped double-
breasted suit, red shirt, and a big white velour hat, which
I refused to take off at first. I thought that the stolen-car
charges and the head-splitting charges were separate and
not that serious, and it was my first time in court, so I
figured I could get probation. My mother, father, stepfather, and the lame I had beaten up were there. The
judge read the stolen-car report, the assault charge, and
that I was a runaway. Then some punk from the juvenile
squad said I had been head of a bunch of gangs and told
about the fights I had been part of. This judge asked me
if I had anything to say. What could I say? Being slicker
than Vaseline I related that I wasn't driving the car, only
riding in it, and I didn't know the driver's name—that
the assault stemmed from the lame's attacking me, and that
I ran away because I was scared. He asked my mother
and father why they couldn't handle me. They said they
could, if only they could catch me. Whenever I stayed
away I would tell one I was with the other. They weren't
on very good terms, so it mostly worked.

My stepfather was still mad at almost getting whipped
by me, and he told the judge I was a threat to his life
and I wouldn't listen to, much less obey, anyone. The

judge sent me to Menlo Park Diagnostic Center to see if I was indeed a nut. There I fought the attendants, cursed out the psychiatrist and psychologist, and bullied all the inmates I could. Needless to say, on my return to court their report said that I resented authority. The judge sentenced me to Annandale Reformatory.

I went to Annandale as if it were the most natural thing in the world to do. I knew almost everyone there, black and white. I fit right in, what with the fights over TV seats and places in line, roughing off of store orders and canteen goodies. I learned how to fight with my hands, how to walk cool, and how to commit every crime you can think of. I was sixteen when I entered Annandale. Usually, you are sentenced to an indefinite term at the joint. After four months, the board tells you how long you'll be there, and after you're out, you're on probation until you're twenty-one. I was sentenced by the board to 9 months—that meant I should have had to do only 5, but between refusing to work and all the fighting, I spent over 4 months in the hole, and that time had to be done over—all told, I was away 19 months.

DHARUBA: The first time that I became a political prisoner, of course at that time I didn't call myself that, was when I was fourteen or fifteen. I was sent to Youth House for, I believe it was, a burglary. And I wasn't caught burglarizing anything, you know. I was next door to a place that had been burglarized. The fuzz didn't bust me in a correct manner according to their law, but I came to find out that that didn't make any difference in the court, that didn't make any difference to anyone. That the cops lie, and they seem paid to lie.

Seems that the police are the only people in the world who go to school just to learn how to lie.

The time I spent in Youth House wasn't extraordinary, except that it seemed like I would always be there. I felt that I'd been through this before, you know what I mean? There were various degrading searches and various degrading bureaucratic procedures. Then when the door shut, I felt like it was no big thing, like these doors are shut on me before, you know. Later on in my life I was in jail quite often.

ALI BEY HASSAN: One time a relative and I had been out together drinking in a hole-in-the-wall neighborhood bar with another friend, and when we left, I was high and my relative was just plain wiped out. He started beating up on some woman who had come out with us, and after a three-block chase (him chasing the woman, and me and the other guy chasing him), we finally persuaded him to leave off and we all got in his car to go home. We were about a block and a half from my house when about six pig cars surrounded us and told us to get out. But as we were getting out, the friend threw a switchblade on the floor, and unfortunately the cops saw it, so we were handcuffed, taken down to headquarters, and booked on felonious assault and battery with a deadly weapon.

I couldn't make bail and I stayed in jail about three weeks before our case came up. My relative got one year for assault and the other fellow got six months for having the knife. I asked the judge what I was being charged with, and he told me I had only been held as a material witness and that the charges against me had been dropped. Dig it. Three weeks in jail as a material witness! The judge told me the charges wouldn't go on the record and I was released.

But some time in 1958 I was pulled over on one of those "stop and frisk" things that go on continuously in the black community, and two Negro cops put me into their car—after taking my ID—and asked me if I had a record and if I was a Muslim. Subtle. Records and Muslims go together. I said no I didn't have a record and is that why you have me here in the car—to talk about religion? Meanwhile one of the cops had called downtown to run a check on me and when he came back he said, "You lying son-of-a-bitch, you have a felonious assault and battery on the books." I finally got out of it —after what seemed like a thousand phone calls and infinite harassment—and I later learned that the judge who had lied to me about my record was notorious. Back in the fifties, most young black people at least knew about him, even if they hadn't personally come up before him. His daughter had been messing around with a black man, who was supposed to have raped her, and so he was extra hard on black people—he gave them big time regardless of the charges.

In 1960 I went back to Newark and started to work for a company called Precisionware, where I sprayed film cabinets and other office furniture. After I got fired from that place, I went to New York one weekend and ended up staying for a year—with my mother. Her drinking was worse than ever. It seemed she just didn't care any more, about anything. The long years of oppression seemed finally to have defeated her. I tried to fight the frustration—hers and mine—but I didn't know what to fight or how. I kept moving back and forth from place to place, because deep inside I knew something wasn't right, but I didn't know what to do about whatever it was that was wrong.

BOB COLLIER: After the air force I returned to Boston, and I had to make a living, of course. But every time I managed to get a job, I lost it because of the air force discharge. It wasn't exactly dishonorable, but it had a jive wording of "discharged under other than honorable conditions." If I told the truth I wasn't hired in the first place, and if I didn't then the people who hired me found out about it and I was automatically fired. So I took to the streets—gambling, hustling, using my wits to make a living. I hung out at night with some old-timers, and they taught me enough finesse so my swindles usually worked—I stayed clean. I started smoking pot, then, and sniffing cocaine. Sticking a needle into my arm didn't appeal to me, and I stuck to "soft" stuff. My appeal to older women was an asset as well as a headache. For a couple of years I was part kept man, part con man, but I started getting leery after a few close calls—stabbings, and being shot at by jealous boyfriends and pimps.

JOAN BIRD: Some of us in La Group—you know, this little group of girlfriends that we had in high school—would work after school or take part-time jobs, or work during the summer, because we were very choice in the selection of our clothes. La Group had to be A-1, top class, first flight. In other words, we really had to be looking fly all the time. There was just no excuse for us not being able to look fly.

One of the jobs I had was being a counselor, a junior counselor, in around 1966 or 1965 or so. It was in a day-care center. I really enjoyed that. It gave me a chance to have some bread in my pocket, as the word goes. And it also gave me an opportunity to work with children, I really enjoyed doing that very much. I was counseling girls from the ages of—I'll say around five to maybe seven years old. And there were times when I found it very frustrating and even aggravating, with the confusion of young kids all around you all day long. But I also found it very rewarding. I can remember like taking them to the pool and then jumping in, and not really recognizing that they can't swim yet, you know, just diving on in, not into the maybe two feet of water or whatever, but into deep water, and just going all crazy.

LUMUMBA SHAKUR: About December, 1959, one of the most decisive events in my life occurred. It was in Jamaica, New York. About fifteen brothers and sisters and I were coming from a party. We got on the bus, and I sat next to this cracker in a United States Navy uniform. At this time I was about 5 feet 6 inches, 140 pounds. The cracker was about 6 feet 2 inches and 200 pounds. The cracker told me that where he came from niggers didn't sit next to white people on buses. I told the cracker that he wasn't in the South now. The cracker punched me in the face and we started fighting: all pandemonium broke out in the bus, and that cracker was whipped mercilessly. Later I found out that cracker was cut every place except on the soles of his feet.

I got off the bus, and on the way home, Spot and I were arrested by the cops. They took us to the hospital where this cracker was. The cracker said Spot and I

were the ones who assaulted him. The pigs beat us mercilessly in Jamaica Hospital in front of the doctors and
nurses.

We had a so-called hearing in front of Judge Piccolo
of Queens Criminal Court. The cracker came to court
on crutches; he looked like a mummy in his navy uniform,
with his face and hands almost completely bandaged up.
When the cracker saw the American toilet paper (flag),
he tried to salute the shitpaper. The cracker took the
stand to testify and said that he punched and attacked
me first because niggers aren't supposed to sit next to
white people on buses. Judge Piccolo said, "Take that
testimony off the record because that's not the issue in
this court." Then Judge Piccolo called a recess. When
we came back into court, we had our hearing in Judge
Piccolo's chamber, and the cracker just testified about me
and Spot attacking him with our fists. He said Spot and
I did not have any weapons. Judge Piccolo gave us each
$10,000 bail and waived the case to the grand jury. Spot
and I stayed in jail—about seven months. My lawyer,
Louis S. Flagg, told me and Spot to plead guilty to
"attempted assault two" and we'd probably get "time
served"; it sounded to me like he had it all fixed up,
we'd get out of jail right after sentencing. We pled
guilty. About a month later, we came back to court for
sentencing. Judge Edward Thompson (who later became
Fire Commissioner of New York City) sentenced us to
an "indefinite" sentence. Flagg is a judge today.

In 1960, then, I was sent to Woodbourne Correctional
Institution. I was finally told what an indefinite sentence
meant: one day to five years. They also told me I could
make parole in eighteen months.

Woodbourne was at this time the gang-fighting haven.
I thought I stopped gang fighting in 1959, but Wood-

bourne changed all my thoughts about gang fighting again. During my first ten minutes in Woodbourne the shit began. I walked into this huge basement where all the other inmates were at, and the first faces I saw were Dutch and Gopher, two Chaplains I used to always gang fight against in Jamaica. They started murder-mouthing about something that happened in 1958, and Gopher began pointing in my chest and saying, "Shotgun, I should kick your ass for what happened in 1958." But I told Gopher, "Don't point in my chest any more." Gopher told me to get a pass and meet him in the alley. By this time Bone, David, Vice, and other Bishops came over and asked what was happening. I told them about what Dutch and Gopher said and I asked them how do I get a pass and where was the alley at because it seemed like Gopher wanted to fight. Bone and David said they would talk to Gopher and cool everything out because new brothers didn't go to the alley and fight and Gopher was good with his hands. I told Bone and David to show me where the alley was at and how to get a pass because fighting Gopher was not any big thing. They said all right. Gopher was good with his hands and he did win the fight. But he was not enthusiastic about provoking or fighting me again. The fight had a psychological benefit for me—since new brothers don't fight in the alley after being in prison for twenty minutes, everybody started saying the new brother, name of "Shotgun," had a whole lot of heart.

The reason why Woodbourne was a haven for gang fighting was because the institutional officials set up the alley and places in the institution where inmates could fight for hours. This way all the hostilities of the inmates would be directed at other inmates instead of toward the prison and correction officers.

Later on, I found out the reason why Bone and David didn't want me to fight Gopher on my first day in Woodbourne was because the rules of the jail were if you get knocked out in the alley you get—literally—fucked.

Woodbourne's administration was racist from the warden on down. In a population of 800 inmates, of whom 600 were black and Puerto Rican, the minority whites were systematically the majority in the institutional schools and professional shops where you can learn a skilled trade. If you got caught fighting a black inmate, you got 5 days in the hole. If you got caught fighting a white inmate, you got 30 days in the hole. Whites made parole in six and nine months.

After you're in Woodbourne about two months, you're told when you will go before the New York State Parole Board. Most brothers had an eighteen-month date set for parole-board hearing; a few who had murder charges got a twenty-four-month date. I made institutional history: I was told I had a thirty-six-month date. While I was sitting before the board who set the dates—a board comprised of Woodbourne correctional officials—the deputy warden, William Corntop, told me that where he came from they would have hung me on the spot for what I did. Corntop told me he would guarantee that I would do every day of my five-year sentence. I didn't have any institutional infraction on my record. The brothers and the correctional officer in my dormitory didn't believe I was classified three years until I showed them the classification notice.

I was put in dormitory No. 6—the only Bishop in a dorm full of Chaplains, Corsair Lords, and Puerto Rican Dragons, but we got along fine: they gave me the same respect that I gave them. Most of the Chaplains and Corsair Lords were some beautiful get-down brothers.

One day a conflict in the yard began, and the conclusion was that the shit was all on. The Bishops were fighting Chaplains and the Corsair Lords. Everything was cool during the day because we were fighting in the alley, in the gym, and in the back of the school—plus everybody wanted to get off their latest techniques they had learned about boxing. When I think about it now it seemed like fun—all the brothers walking around with black, skin-tight gloves on, telling each other to get a pass to the alley or other place for a fair fight. The correctional officials would know what was happening. They encouraged nigger fighting nigger. At times the officers would be in the alley watching the fight like they were in Madison Square Garden.

In the dormitory the pressure really came down on me, the only Bishop in there. The shit started in the morning: as soon as I woke up I was told, "Shotgun, you got one in the shower room." After that fight, another brother would tell me I got another fight scheduled in the recreation room on the way to breakfast. After we left the mess hall, we would go to the yard, then to our jobs or school. When you went to your job, you would tear your pants or shirt and ask for a pass to the state shop where you got your clothes sewed and shoes repaired. To get to the state shop you had to go through the alley. Then at 4:00 P.M. you would line up to go back to the dormitories. While I was standing on line waiting to go to the dormitory, someone would tell me to get on the back of the line because I got a fight scheduled in the recreation room on the way to the dormitory. Dinner was at 5:00 P.M., so another brother would tell me I had fights in the recreation room going and coming from the mess hall. At 6:30, when everybody went to the recreation room, a blood told me I got a fight in the shower room. The Chaplains and Corsair Lords were some beautiful brothers because they always gave me a fair fight. The brothers knew this was the rule of the game for gang fighting in prison. I got what my hands called for and whoever I fought got what his hands called for. The factor I really dug was that at any time five of them could have jumped on me and kicked my ass mercilessly, but they always gave me a fair fight. Most of the times after the fights I would play cards with the same brothers, knowing I would fight two or three of them the next day. The other Bishops stopped asking me to get out of dormitory 6 because I told them to keep the pressure on Chaplains and Corsair Lords in their own dormitories. Everybody knew that dormitory 6 was a smoking hell-fire dormitory.

After about a month of fighting in dormitory 6, the Chaplains and Corsair Lords came over to me and said they were going to stop gang fighting in dormitory 6, but any other place they saw me in the institution we were going to fight. I said that's cool with me. Actually, I felt glad about what the brothers said, but I would have never initiated the idea. About a month later the gang fighting was called off all over Woodbourne for a while.

I was in Woodbourne about a year. The average brother in Woodbourne was between seventeen and nineteen years old. Most of the brothers did not belong in prison. Some brothers did not have lawyers when they were in court. The average brother in Woodbourne had a 3- or 5-year sentence. The brothers had contempt against the society because they knew they were railroaded to prison. Rehabilitation is a myth and a lie in Woodbourne. Woodbourne bred crime and hostilities.

Institutional officials were always trying to create hostilities between blacks and Puerto Ricans. Everybody knew it. The reason was that the gang fighting was stopping between the blacks. The blacks were coming together beautifully. One day some Puerto Rican from the gang called the Dragons cut this Bishop up real bad. The Bishops, Chaplains, and Corsair Lords united and vamped on the Dragons. The next day I was walking on the ballfield by myself and five Puerto Ricans from the Dragons stabbed me in the chest and shoulder. I was put in the hospital. A riot started the same day.

I was in the hospital with wounds in my chest and shoulder. The brothers who worked in the hospital told me that the brothers in population were vamping on the Puerto Ricans and whites mercilessly because the whites came to the Puerto Ricans' aid—and caught pure hell from the blacks. They told me that the whole institution was at a standstill because all shops, schools, and yards were closed. I heard the blacks were kicking ass in all the dormitories and cellblocks. The hole and the box were filled up completely with blacks.

The next day I way lying in bed in the hospital when racist pig Deputy Warden William Corntop came to talk to me. Pig Corntop told me I was one of the leaders of one of the gangs and I had influence with black inmates, and Pig Corntop told me that he wanted me to go to the yard and tell the black inmates that I was doing fine, and tell the blacks to stop fighting the Puerto Ricans and whites and go back to work to be progressive inmates. I laughed in Pig Corntop's face because this was really funny to me. I told Pig Corntop that his racist administration always encouraged gang fighting between blacks. Also, his racist administration encouraged Puerto Ricans to think they were superior to blacks by always telling

them that they were better than blacks and by allowing
Puerto Ricans to learn skilled trades with whites while
blacks were barred from those skilled trades. I told
Corntop that I hoped the blacks turned Woodburn inside
out and kicked some of his white racist officers' asses,
because we were only responding to his racism. I asked
Pig Corntop, did he remember when he told me that he
was going to guarantee that I do every day of my five
years? This is when I put my foot in my mouth. I told
Pig Corntop that every day I was in Woodbourne I would
guarantee that Woodbourne would have no tranquillity.
Pig Corntop stood by my bed and got very red in the
face. He ran from my bed calling the doctor. Ten minutes later the doctor told me that Pig Corntop pleaded
with him to call the goon squad to beat me up, but the
doctor told Pig Corntop that he would not permit that
or be responsible for what happened to me after being
beaten up in the hospital, because of my condition.

A week after, I was leaving the hospital. In the hospital
all you wear is a robe. When I got to the hospital door
I was told to take off my robe. I asked where my clothes
were, and this officer said I would get my clothes at the
end of the hall. I was walking down this hall naked
with my arm in a sling. I felt the flim-flam coming because everything seemed too cool. As I went through
the door, I saw the goon squad waiting for me with
rubber hoses. I punched one racist pig in the face, but
after one punch it was all over for me. Somebody kicked
me in the testicles. I fell to the floor in extreme pain.
While I was on the floor the last thing I heard before I
was beaten into unconsciousness was Pig Deputy Warden
Corntop saying hysterically, "Kill the nigger, kill the
nigger!"

I woke up in the box, with pain all over my body.

Chain and Bull were in the cell next to me. Chain said that the events of the last couple of weeks had really united all the blacks, and they were not relating to gangs any more. All the brothers were just relating to being black and sticking together, because Corntop was educating the brothers about the essentials of unity. This sounded beautiful coming from Chain because he was a Bishop, from Brooklyn, since he was ten years old.

In the fall of 1961, I was shackled, handcuffed, and transferred to Comstock, another prison. In New York State there is no iota of difference between a prison, correctional institution or reformatory.

Racism in Comstock was naked. Comstock had an inmate population of 1,800, 1,300 of them black. Black inmates were not allowed to touch or serve food in the mess hall. Black inmates were not allowed to work in the bakery. Black inmates were not allowed to have clerk jobs. There was only one black in the radio and television school. Only two blacks in machine school. Three blacks in the auto-mechanic school. It was hard for blacks to get in school for an education. Most blacks worked as porters on labor gangs, the laundry, the barber shop, the tailor shop. The blacks in the kitchen just washed pots and pans. Comstock had a thing called "idle"; in this all you did was sit in your cell all day until 3:00 P.M. Then you went to the yard. Ninety per cent of the inmates in idle were black.

In Comstock the most popular sport was handball. The big yard in Comstock had sixteen handball courts. Twelve handball courts were for white inmates only. Two handball courts for the blacks and two for the Puerto Ricans. If a black or a Puerto Rican stepped on a white handball court, the correctional officer would hit you in the head with a small baseball bat. Then you would get thirty days in the hole or the bing. There was a dual set of rules for everything in Comstock—one black and one white.

While I was in prison I saw some of the most devious activities in my life—that's why I'm shockproof today. Comstock prison's administration encourages and promotes hideousness, hostilities, racism, hopelessness, uselessness and deviation. The prison officials' attitude was that inmates were commodities, subhuman—a means of employment. Officials enjoyed seeing new inmates come in prison and loved to see old inmates come back. Rehabilitation in prison is a farce, a fallacy, a sham. The correctional officers consider rehabilitation as a genuine joke among themselves. The correctional officials would always tell black inmates that we were better off in prisons. They would always tell blacks, where else could we get three meals a day and the good hospitality of the prisons?

Homosexuality is out in the open in prisons. In prison you're only a faggot or a homosexual if you play the role of the woman. Some faggots actually thought they were women, and walked, talked, and acted just like women. Most faggots in prisons have women's names. After five years in prisons, I came to the conclusion that faggots became faggots out of psychological reasons rather than physical reasons. Most men who came to prison and became faggots did so because they would not fight for their manhood. The manly response in prison if somebody says he wants to fuck you—you must fight the person who said he wanted to fuck you immediately. If you fight and lose and the person who wanted to fuck you asks you again, you better get a pipe and beat that person in the head. The institutional official will tell you that you were right for fighting for your manhood, and discipline the person who tried to fuck you (that is, if you don't kill him). Sometimes the person who was fighting for his manhood got knocked out fighting. Then while he was knocked out, the other person would fuck him. When he woke up and dug he got fucked, if he went and piped the person in the head who fucked him, in this way he could restore his manhood and win the respect of the other inmates. Here's the other situation: if a person went over to another inmate and told him he wanted to fuck him and the other person said no and didn't want to fight for his manhood and said something like, "If you ask me again I'll tell the officers," the person who asked the other inmate to fuck, or as we called these persons, asshole bandits, the asshole bandit would put some mass psychological pressure on the punk who refused to fight for his manhood. The asshole bandit would tell about four hundred inmates constantly to ask the punk to fuck. Word was already out that the punk would not fight for his manhood. Within three months, he would be a faggot because he could not stand the psychological pressures. Most faggots became faggots like that. Some punks became faggots for protection. In Comstock the faggots got married in the yard, with a wedding, rice-throwing, a big picnic in the yard, and a so-called honeymoon. In the prisons I've been in, many correctional officers were faggots.

While I was in prison, I read everything relevant that I could get my hands on. I read every moment I could. The prison library was a sham. Some brothers had black history books but if they let another brother read them, the institutional official confiscated the books, and said that those black history books could not leave the owner's cells.

In February, 1964, while I was in solitary in Attica

Prison, I was reading a law book and found out that the law said attempted assault in the second degree had a maximum sentence of two-and-one-half years—and I was serving five years for attempted assault in the second degree. Aki Williams, and a white inmate named Richard, who spent a year in solitary confinement for helping other inmates write legal writs to fight their convictions, helped me to write a writ of habeas corpus because I was being illegally detained. New York State's so-called legal argument was that since I was under twenty-one when I got arrested, I could get five years for a crime that a twenty-one-year-old would get a maximum of two-and-a-half years for. The basic part of my writ of habeas corpus was that I was being held illegally and unconstitutionally in that I did not receive equal protection of the law, as guaranteed by the 14th Amendment of the United States Constitution: my young age was used to give me more years in prison. I had a sham hearing by a circuit judge who came to the prison. The judge said that my writ raised some very valid constitutional questions. And then he said that if he granted my writ, thousands of inmates would be released within weeks on the same grounds, so, "This Court will deny this writ of habeas corpus." I was expecting the motion to be denied because my attitude was to expect the worst from the racist devils. In 1967 the New York State Legislature revamped the laws of criminal procedures because New York State had so many unconstitutional laws on the books, but they still use a person's youth to keep him in prison longer.

After fourteen months in solitary confinement, I was put into the general population in Attica, and it was no surprise that Attica was just as racist as other New York State prisons. In the barber shop, black inmates were not allowed to cut white inmates' hair or shave whites and vice versa. Black inmates were not allowed in some shops. In the summertime when the officer gave out ice in the yard, he would say "white ice" and "nigger ice." Attica has a prison population of 2,500, of which two-thirds is black. Rehabilitation is a myth in Attica, too. The most enthusiastic event in Attica is football.

part 6

DHARUBA: It wasn't till I was sixteen going on seventeen that I realized a few things. I had a lot of enemies in the Bronx, in Manhattan, and in other areas of the city because of my gang affiliation. And the illusions that I had of grandeur, of becoming an aerodynamics engineer, just didn't correspond with the objective conditions. So I figured my best bet must be somehow, some way, to get away from the neighborhood for a while, and maybe come back when I had my shit more together, when my hand was a little more tight. I decided to join the army. I don't think this was out of patriotic obligation, I think it was more out of social necessity that I did that. Although I did feel somewhat gung-ho at the time of my enlistment, this was quickly obliterated.

Let it suffice to say that I had numerous confrontations in the army. The position I had acquired in the army when I was in basic training as a squad leader was cold-bloodedly and premeditatedly usurped by a racist who was undergoing basic with me who would do anything in his power to discredit my squad whenever they would show or exhibit any military prowess. He succeeded. From that point on it was a running battle between me and the military authorities until finally I was given an undesirable discharge. I was given this undesirable discharge by a sergeant, and a speech by a colonel who said he realized it was very unfair, what had gone down, and if I ever needed a job I could use him as a reference.

RICHARD HARRIS: On my release from reform school, my father was to be my guardian. I lived with him for almost a year, driving and helping him with his trucks, hauling sugar, steel, lead, moving people—you name it, we did it. It was cool until we fought one night and when the police came, he told them to lock me up, that I was on probation. They didn't, because he was drunk, but I left that same night. I began alternating between stickups and warehouse B and Es until a friend got shotgunned by the police one night. Then I went into exclusive B and Es and stealing and selling cars. In both my fields, the Mafia and the police were good customers and partners. Two narrow escapes with stool-pigeons, plus a good piece of money I and another cat picked up in a liquor-store job, made me stop everything in the beginning of '58. I got a job—a good job, long money, hard dirty work, and at night. I moved in with my aunt and was cool about reporting monthly to my probation officer. But I got a new P.O.—and that dude would come to my job during the day asking corny questions, and then come wake me up to rap about nothing. He made me come see him weekly plus all kinds of corny shit. The excuse he gave was that those were the rules and he had to follow them. I lost the job.

Well, I was well-dressed, but I hadn't saved any money. I tried stickups again. The money was good—but the more you made the bigger the chance you took. A shoot-out in front of a bank, a mad chase on the highway, brought visions of judges giving out time for armed robbery like it was rain and they were clouds. A fat wardrobe and about five grand told me that I could stop if I used my head: open a business, sell drugs, start a numbers bank. While I was making up my mind, I went with three other cats to watch a fourth join the service. We were drinking and took the test with him as a joke. I passed, and no one else did. At first I was going to forget it, but after talking to my mother and my girlfriend, I was persuaded that this would keep me out of trouble, at least, and I might like it. What decided me was that there were only two more years until I was twenty-one, and I'd be through with probation. I wanted to make it. So in June, 1959, I became a marine.

Parris Island, drill instructors with Smokey-the-Bear hats, the corny bullshit that makes a marine—I went through it. And then on my first pass I got drunk, mugged a whitey, and went AWOL. Nothing had changed. The marine corps was rotten with prejudice and had me wilder than ever when I got loose. They taught me an awful lot of useful things, though, such as all about guns, judo, how to build self-confidence. I met some bad cats there that were in my bag. We broke into lockers on the base, the PX, the pawnshop in town, and an appliance store. The ring was broken up when I got caught stealing some .45s. Before going to court for that, I went AWOL again. I was arrested in Newark by the FBI, served six months in the naval prison in New Hampshire, was given a bad-conduct discharge and sent home.

SHABA OM: When I was a child, about five of the dudes I hung out with were my age and the rest were two to ten years older. We all dug the older ones because we all wanted to be like them. Some were in the army, navy, and marines, and they would tell us big lies about what it's like and show us pictures of the guns, airplanes, and missiles, which we dug, being young, active, and curious about life.

KWANDO KINSHASA: My first two years in the marines were filled with month after month of indoctrination on the glories and justice of the country's military enterprises throughout the world. At the time, the attitude of the black marines was not so much one of dislike for their function as marines, but disgust at having to take orders from racist sergeants and officers. But I think, now, that I and a lot of other black marines were at the threshold of realizing that there was more to why we felt uneasy then than just the racism of the officers.

During those first two years, I took some side courses in military history and tactics. And out of all the military courses I took on tactics and strategy, not one of them covered in depth the tactics used by the Japanese in the Pacific in World War Two, or those used by the North Koreans. That is, in 1962 this country still refused to officially admit the fact that Third World forces had twice delivered defeats to American troops! Now of course it doesn't matter any more what they admit officially—the facts speak for themselves.

BOB COLLIER: In April, 1954, I joined the air force. When I was given a mop five minutes after walking into the reception center and told to clean the floors, I knew this life wasn't going to be like life on the streets. But I soldiered hard and got high scores on all the tests, and I was made color bearer. That meant I marched out in front of the rest of the platoon. Our unit won an award for drill excellence that year.

When the time came for assignment, I requested radio and radar school, and my first orders assigned me to a base in Biloxi, Mississippi, where I would receive the proper training. Just before I was supposed to leave, however, my orders were changed: now I was going to Montgomery, Alabama, to join the medical corps. I went to the company commander to protest, but he told me in no uncertain terms that I had to follow orders—or face court martial and dishonorable discharge. Needless to say, I went to Montgomery.

The minute I stepped off that plane in Alabama, I learned some more about racism. Of that crowd of American servicemen standing together waiting for the same transportation to the base, six of us were black. As I was waiting, a hand grabbed the back of my neck and a voice said, "All you niggers get next door where you belong." We spun around, ready to swing, but the major managed to get us out and aboard the bus heading to the base. At that time I was still proud of the U.S. Air Force, the motto, "Always Loyal," still rang in my ears, and I remember I had some idiotic notion of protesting in order to protect the good name of our outfit.

We got to the barracks and set up our footlockers and unpacked our gear, and then four white guys came over and told me to pack my gear. They said they weren't going to have a nigger sleeping in the same room with them. Two were from the South and two were from the North. I was stunned. This was the unit that was supposed to fight together to protect America? Anyway, I told them I wasn't moving. Some black G.I.s came in and asked what was happening, and as I started to explain, one of the white guys swung at me. The fight was on. The

room was in bad shape when we finished, but I still refused to leave. They went away, swearing they would
come back and finish the job, but they never did. After
I cleaned up, myself and two brothers and a white boy
from Detroit moved in. We got along fine—for a while.
The fellows dug me and elected me platoon leader. My
duties were to see that their dress was proper, their drill
was sharp, and their morale was high. We stood tall and
sharp.

A little two-bit day-room center for blacks was segregated from the big brick center for the white boys. The
dances were segregated, the mess halls—everything was
segregated. Feelings of hate ran high between blacks and
whites. The whites who associated with us caught hell
from the white men and officers. Bloods caught hell all
the time. There were a lot of fights. Brothers protested
about conditions on the base a few times, but to no avail.

I found some beautiful people in town—at the bars,
nightclubs, and black campuses—I will never forget their
hospitality and kindness.

One time a few of us brothers got on a bus that runs
from town to the base, and when I sat down the bus driver
stopped and told me to sit in back. I refused and he got
off to find a policeman. The rest of the servicemen on the
bus said it was time to move, so we piled out and hitched
a ride back.

After graduation I was sent to a base in California,
where I was assigned to the hospital unit. I couldn't
help seeing that many of the brothers were in the medical
corps, and I couldn't help realizing that was because the
armed forces didn't like giving technical training to
blacks.

I was eighteen when I heard they were accepting volunteers to ship out overseas. I was still trying to find my-

self and learn new experiences, so I went over to the office to sign up. The only slot left was for Germany and I took it.

On leave before I left for Europe I went back home to Roxbury, Massachusetts; the bloods were hanging out on the avenue and hustling. We drank together, spent much time with our women, and gambled.

In Germany, I was assigned to a hospital unit. The building seemed pretty lavish for a hospital, and it turned out that it had once been local headquarters for the Luftwaffe. The floors were marble, the ceilings were supported by fluted marble columns, and the walls were a stucco-type material, painted in pastel shades. Everything was immaculate. The floors were so clean that the reflection of sunlight off the marble on a bright day hurt your eyes.

My work was boring. I drove a jeep around, running errands and making deliveries, and I typed out subsistence reports and recorded the number of cases treated daily. I used to argue with the unit captain about promotion, since it seemed to me that whites were consistently moved up faster than blacks, but that only made it harder for me to get anywhere. We found out that in order to cover up the discrimination that was regularly practiced, the unit heads used to put memorandums criticizing a man's behavior in his folder, supposedly as record that a warning had been given—in fact, the men never saw these "warnings," the memorandums were used when the people in charge didn't want to promote somebody. If you found out and complained, you were asked if you were "implying that an officer was a liar" or if you were "questioning the credibility of an officer."

Germany was a strange place. Ruins were still in evidence, and building was going on everywhere. The new architecture—austere, square lines—looked strange next to the rustic and homey-looking cottages that filled much of the countryside. Once I attended an Oktoberfest and the children stared at me and rubbed my skin and smiled. I didn't quite know how to react to that kind of greeting. It didn't seem like the racism I was used to, but they obviously felt I was different.

After six or seven months in Germany I was transferred to England, where I was office clerk. I had trouble there. A new second lieutenant—from Mississippi—checked in one Saturday when I was on duty at the office. He and the major (the major was a Georgia boy) talked some, and then the lieutenant came out and looked at me. "Boy," he said. "Get my bags." I paid him no mind. He put his hands on his hips and looked around some, and then looked at me again and asked where I had put his bags. I said, "What bags?—SIR!" Then he started chewing me out, saying I should stay awake and listen when an officer was speaking to me, and finally he told me one more time to go and get his bags. I told him I wasn't a porter and since he did not address me the way I felt an officer should address his men I just did not feel I could perform that service for him. Then he blew his cool and started yelling and calling me nigger, and so I left the office. The next day the major told me I was restricted to base for two weeks.

A lot of guys used to stay around at different times to keep me company while I was restricted, and we tried to figure out what would happen if we tried to make a complaint. We pretty much figured it was hopeless, so we never did anything. One of the guys I talked to a lot was a white cat from Tennessee—Jerry.

When my restriction was lifted, Jerry decided we should go out to celebrate, and he took me to a dance on the outskirts of London. We got there early, and only a few people were there, but by eight o'clock the large hall had begun to fill up. We talked some and danced a lot (although it wasn't easy at first because the style was so different). Around eleven o'clock I noticed that Jerry was talking pretty loud with a group of guys across the hall, and I watched to see if they were arguing or just having a good time. About the time I figured they sure as hell weren't having a good time, all hell broke loose. Through the now-screaming crowd I caught a glimpse of Jerry being piled on by what I figured to be Teddy Boys, London's version of U.S. street gangs. As he went down he screamed something about being stabbed. I pushed my way through the crowd, but as I reached Jerry I slipped on something and grabbed at his jacket. My hand came away wet and sticky—covered with blood. The Teddies moved back for a minute when they saw my hand, and I took the opportunity to grab Jerry and head for the door. A lot of cats tried to stop us, but I grabbed a mug and dented a few noses and heads. Finally I picked up a metal chair and started swinging, trying to clear a path to the door. When we finally got there, some sympathetic observers had opened the door and when I pushed Jerry through they rushed him to a cab. By then our attackers had caught up, and I had to knock a few more heads before I could get through the door myself. I took a bus to the hospital where they'd taken Jerry and we both got patched up.

When we got back to the base, Scotland Yard was waiting to question us about the incident. They took us to the Yard. Some of the people who had been at the dance were already there, and we asked the detectives to be sure and get their names as witnesses. They must not have done this, however, because none of those people came to the trial to appear in our behalf.

The trial was a racist jive. The air force had given us no help, and we had hired our own lawyer, who turned out to be a shyster sell-out. The first thing they tried to do was separate Jerry from my case, but he refused. He said that any crime I was charged with he should be charged with too, and when he protested in court he was carried out—bodily. The trial only lasted a few hours. They denied me the right to try to get friendly witnesses, and tried to deny me the right to speak in my own defense. They even tried to say *I* had stabbed Jerry. In all this they were aided and abetted by the shyster lawyer, who obviously had no intention of working to get me off. When the trial was over I was fined court costs, damages, and hospital fees for the punks Jerry and I had banged up.

When I got back to the base, some colonel told me I had created an international incident. I told him that I had understood from basic training that G.I.s were supposed to maintain loyalty to each other at all times, that Jerry had been badly hurt by those punks, and what was I supposed to have done—leave him there to bleed to death? The colonel just muttered something about my being in the hospital unit and I had our reputation to keep up, etc., etc. The upshot was that I was cited for administrative punishment—Article 15—and busted. A few weeks later I was discharged as "undesirable for military service." This after three full years of service!

KUWASI BALAGOON: In the army, basic training, there was one sergeant who was the terror of the camp. After picking up cigarette butts in the rain—which I loathed, number one because I didn't smoke—we were called into a formation, whereupon this sergeant would call out names, to which we were to answer, "Here, Ser-

geant." Then when several dudes didn't answer loud
enough—I saw it, I swear—he said, "Come here." They
came and stood at attention. "Grab your balls." They
grabbed their balls. Then he demanded, "Squeeze!" And,
"Does it hurt?" "Yes, Sergeant." "Squeeze harder! Does
it hurt?" "Yes, Sergeant!" "Squeeze!" From the ranks I
could hardly control myself from laughing, but somehow
covered it. Fools were turning red and crying, and
squeezing.

I took so much bullshit that I got headaches from suppressing my anger, in order not to get a 208.*

I was sent to Germany. As time went on I got an Article 15** for "impersonating a Pfc." When I argued about
it, noting that wearing other people's field jackets was a
common occurrence, the punk-ass company commander
said that he had only seen *me* doing that, and the first
sergeant said, "Article 34, conduct unbecoming a soldier,
would hold up just as well."***

I hit it off all right later in the third platoon, being a
field soldier in the field, and being in good understandings
with the brothers. But there was a lot of shit that had been
bugging me for a long time. Besides the ridiculous changes
that all enlisted men went through, there was an added
factor: rampant racism on all levels. A captain who was
black was demoted to sergeant E-6 before our very eyes
and shipped out. Brothers would spend 34 or 35 months
of a 36-month enlistment and then get dishonorable dis-
charges—white soldiers had to make successive super-
duper fuck-ups before the same would happen to them

---

* A "208" is discharge as an "undesirable."

** Article 15 is a rule under which one is reprimanded but usually
not subject to court martial.

*** Article 34 is a rule under which one is subject to court martial.

(like throw a German citizen off a bridge into the river in the month of January). If a brother whipped a white boy, under just about any circumstances, then disciplinary action was on the way—but not vice versa. And mother-fuckers were still rapping that A-Company–C-Company shit. I rapped anti-American.

We blacks who felt we were marked men, on whom designs had been made to take care of 208-style, looked at the injustices on the post, had a secret meeting, and formed an organization based on fucking up racists. We called ourselves De Legislators, because we were going to make and enforce new laws that were fair. We were De Judge, De Prosecutor, De Executioner, Hannibal, and De Prophet. We said we would go to jail for a reason and not the season. We would get 208, but would make the brass go gray and bawl and stay up a whole lot of nights giving it to us.

From then on, every time a racial situation appeared, we did. Every time white G.I.s ganged a black G.I., we moved to more than even the score. One at a time we would catch up with them and beat and stomp them so bad that helicopters would have to be used to take them to better hospitals than the ones in the area. We were not playing. We would plan things so that we could kick something off inside a club that would instantly turn into a riotous condition—once everything was in chaos it was impossible to pick us out. We then broke faces and bodies of whoever we planned to get, and made our escape. Afterward we would have critiques, just like in the end of war games; get our alibis together; and keep the whole thing under our hats.

The CID* began investigating us, and the Provost Mar-

---

* Criminal Investigation Division of the armed services.

shal. We began to want 208s but were beating mother-fuckers up so bad they wouldn't name us. One of my part-ners, Huff, had a very high moral character, and broke me out of the habit of talking about people's mothers. He was an earnest social student and passed on worthy literature. He and Rhodes were the best of company. Rhodes was serious-minded about the struggle; and he ofttimes related that he grew up with the four sisters who were murdered by the racists in Birmingham in the explo-sion of the church.

We avenged an attack made on a brother and a Latin brother, by attacking and thoroughly whipping eight crazy geeks on another post, in their own company area. Our thing was stomping "chucks," as we called them: quickly knocking them off their feet, and kicking, stomp-ing, and jumping with both feet in their faces. I began keeping a close count of one-punch knockouts: 8 in Sep-tember, 10 in October, 14 in November. The CID kept on me and we kept on. One Legislator was soon court-martialed—actually on a frame-up—and I was getting an Article 15 for fighting in a riot-torn club.

The company commander at that time was a complete dodo. I mean, lost in space. Once, in the field, while pointing out a route from one tactical position to another on a map, he placed his entire palm on the map and said, "We're here." I mean where—Germany? Then he slid it straight across the map and stopped and said, "We're going there." Nobody could believe what they heard and saw, then dug who was talking. What the fool was saying was that there was a road on the map going across rivers and straight through or up and down mountains. Of course, there was no such road. But that was the end of his map orientation: "We are here and we're going there." This fool was sent to Vietnam, this babbling idiot, with maybe a hundred and sixty men at his disposal, and he showed he could dispose of every one of them.

When Westmoreland needed more pawns, he got some from our company. And a lot of men went home—two Legislators, and friends—and we got a new company commander, a new first sergeant, a new platoon leader, and I made Pfc. (after being in the army 18 months—it usually takes 6).

During this time other cats began to fight when we fought. The Latins, the Hawaiians, the Indians, and the sure-enough outlaw whites fought with us. Which made a really painful confusion for our enemies in these "race riots." We even made scared motherfuckers useful—by knocking out a creep in the doorway of a building with only one exit, everybody trying to leave the scene had to step on him. And if the MPs came in, the more the merrier.

There were some hip dudes in De Legislators. Hannibal had earned his name by kicking ass. I had earned the name De Prophet by prophesying that so-and-so was going to get fucked up in a predetermined amount of time, and then going on and fucking the chump up. Brothers had asked how come I had never got busted. First, we were careful; and second, we were decisive, never saying, "One more ass to kick and then I'm going to stop"—always five more asses to kick. I wish that I'd kept in touch with the Legislators, and a few other brothers from that time, because sincere comrades are hard to come by.

KWANDO KINSHASA: In the marines, after being in Guatemala, I returned to the United States via Jacksonville, Florida. I was there for almost a month, and several things happened that are worth noting. During the first week I was there I found myself right in the middle of a race war—not in Jacksonville, but on the base. It seems that at one of the regular base dances, one of the brothers was dancing with the wife of one of the crackers, and this cracker went up to the blood and asked him what he thought he was doing dancing with a white woman. The blood told him to mind his own business and the cracker turned to his wife and said, "What are you doing dancing with this nig——" He got only part of the word out when the brother moved in on him, and then it was on for everybody else. This incident was no simple barroom brawl. The entire base became a battleground. Chains, rifle stocks, knives—anything went. The local city cops were put on alert because the authorities were afraid that Jacksonville itself would explode, and it almost did. When things cooled down, the hospital was filled with men—mostly crackers and a few blacks. The base CO tried to minimize the importance of what had happened, probably not so much because of the race issue but because the wrong side won.

After the "war," the CO issued private orders to bust bloods for the slightest infraction. At that time I was a sergeant. My CO was a racist hog if there ever was one. I got word from a white marine that the CO was hot on me; he knew I was due for a discharge and he wanted to bust me so I would leave with the lowest possible rating. By this time I didn't give a good God damn what he wanted to do, but I kept my eye on him anyway because by then I had learned never to trust a pig. The only problem with pigs is spotting them in the first place—they use a lot of disguises.

While I was in Jacksonville I got an order to transfer a white prisoner to the air force base at Tampa. This cat was facing a maximum of five years for going AWOL. There was a shortage of manpower on the base, so I was assigned to transfer the prisoner alone. It was 1964; there were no blacks on the police forces of either Jacksonville or Tampa; and I know that no one in these towns had ever seen a black man walking down the street with a gun and a white prisoner. I marched that cat through Union Station in Jacksonville, and those black redcaps nearly died. The station guards stopped me three times to check my orders. Every time I was stopped, I made the prisoner get on his knees so I could watch him and those slimy bulls at the same time. I've always hoped that the black men watching understood a little that "an eye for an eye" is still a valid weapon in the hands of the oppressed.

ALI BEY HASSAN: When I was in my early teens I knew something was wrong but I did not have the answers or know what to do about it. I made many mistakes myself, day to day, but my thinking was becoming more clear.

My mother's heavy drinking started to worry me a lot. Sometimes she drank so much she couldn't stand upright. She would fall a lot, banging her head on the concrete street, and sometimes cutting herself up. This happened over and over again but she wouldn't stop. Of course I couldn't say too much, since I was drinking whenever I wanted to myself. Just about everybody I hung out with drank—cheap wine, beer, whiskey—anything, for that matter, that would get us high.

I stayed out late a lot and Moms hated it. She used to demand that I be home by midnight, which I rarely was. Once she even took me over to the 4th Precinct, trying to have me put away. I really didn't care one way or the other. We had no communication with each other, and she never showed me any affection, so there was no "love" shown by either of us—although there was a love hidden deep inside. The police told me to mind my mother and stay out of trouble. That was hard to do because if you're black you're in trouble if you do nothing and you're in trouble if you do something—either way.

So when the police wouldn't put me away, one night when I came home late she asked me for my door key, and told me to go back with whoever I was with and stay. She wouldn't listen to what I had to say, and I left, went over to a friend's mother's apartment, and spent the night. The next day Moms sent my cousin Gene out to find me, so I went home, but she didn't give me my key right away. She said if I wanted to get back in at night I'd have to be in front of the door when she got off from work at 11:15 P.M. Things were pretty intolerable. Finally, on my sixteenth birthday, she took me downtown to volunteer for the U.S. Navy. So nineteen days later, on January 17, 1955, I got sworn in with a couple of hundred other dudes.

My first hitch was at a base in Norfolk, Virginia, where I was assigned to the U.S.S. *Macon*, which was a heavy cruiser. Upon arriving on the quarterdeck I had to salute some white marine captain, and then got assigned to sleeping quarters for the night. The next morning I and three other sailors—two black and one white—reported to the lieutenant JG to be assigned to "divisions." This JG—white of course—asked one of the black sailors and then the other what division he wanted to be assigned to, and since none of us knew that much about which divisions were which, they didn't answer right away, and the lieutenant assigned them to Steward Division. When he asked me what division I wanted, I told him Gunnery.

He tried to persuade me to go into the Steward Division,
saying I could make my rating faster there, but I stuck
to my decision, so he had to go along. Then he asked the
white sailor where he wanted to go, and he said Steward.
Right away the officer said, "No, we have a better division
for you." All three of us black sailors were standing right
there while he was putting this racist game out. I don't
believe the other three sailors even knew what was going
on at first, though I imagine they found out later. I knew
that there were only blacks and Filipinos in Steward
Division. I found out later that the Filipinos were in a
special subdivision that served the top brass on the ship;
the black stewards served the lower brass. Stewards wait
on tables, wash dishes, keep sleeping quarters cleaned,
shine certain officers' shoes, and wash their clothes.

After I had been aboard awhile, I took the test for sea-
man's rating. They told me I'd failed, so I took it again.
Someone told me I had passed this one, but it was posted
on one bulletin board that I had failed and on another
that I had passed. The red tape was too much, I gave up.

The ship was in dry dock at this time, being repaired,
and the navy shipyard was our base until we pulled out
into Cuban waters for a shakedown cruise. My liberties
in Norfolk and Portsmouth, Virginia, gave me my first
taste of racism southern-style. I'd leave the ship to go into
town, and I learned pretty fast where black sailors could
and could not go. I remember in the summer of 1955,
I went to a dance in a nightclub in the black community,
and B. B. King, the blues singer, was there. A bunch of us
got a table, with some women, and it looked like everyone was having a good time with liquor and food and
music. I went over to the other side of the ballroom and
there I saw a seven-foot chickenwire fence dividing the
hall in two! The blacks had most of the room on one side

where the band was playing, and the white southerners had the other small portion of the room. Then I dug that while the band was playing, the black people were jamming—having a good time—and the whites were just sitting there. All of a sudden about three or four white women tried to climb over the fence, but of course none of them made it before the police stopped them. One white woman was dragged off the fence, hit the floor with a Boom! and got up and started fighting the pigs. They hit her with a nightstick and carried her out.

Our shakedown cruises—drills—were in Cuban waters. I remember one morning we were up topside working on the quarterdeck area, and I was up on a scaffold painting, and a white sailor who was living in the same division as I called me a nigger because I wouldn't come down off the scaffold to hand him a rag he had dropped. So I came down mad with a marlin spike in my hand, ready to use it on him. But when I got down to it I changed my mind, and reported it instead to my division officer, a white southerner who said, "Yeah, what you telling me for? Go see the master-at-arms." So I went to the master-at-arms shack. He was another southerner, who told me to go and see a different officer. So I did. He was a white northerner and he said that he would look into it, and I never heard about it again.

There were a lot of fights aboard ship between white and black sailors, and a lot of this stemmed from the way the ship was run by the racist officers. They tried to hide it sometimes, but many still called to black sailors, "Come here, boy." I couldn't stand them and they couldn't stand me. I guess that's why I did so much extra duty.

After about three months in Cuban waters, with liberty in Guantanamo Bay, we returned to the States and docked in Portsmouth. I had liberty there whenever I didn't have the watch on the quarterdeck. After some months in Portsmouth I began to know my way around, and I met a lot of people in the black community. I started hanging in the bars with other black sailors in civilian clothes, and began to identify with the people more. I remembered my earlier years of moving around from place to place, mostly in New York, and it became obvious that the same things went on here as everywhere I had lived. In the South there are the same slum areas, with run-down houses and the usual five or six bars in each block. It seemed to me that if the owners of those bars didn't live in the community they should get the fuck out.

For almost a year I did about the same things every time I had liberty—hung out in different bars, after-hours houses, the USO, drank on the street and in back yards, went to dances and the movies. But a few days before the ship was to pull out for another cruise to Cuba, a friend and I were going to a dance in Norfolk, and caught a bus from Portsmouth—the fare was only 10 cents then. We were in uniform. I sat down in a front seat and my friend went on to the back. After a few minutes I noticed that the white passengers—and a few black people who were sitting in the rear—were looking at me as if I was crazy. My friend asked me to come back and sit with him, but I said no, I wanted to stay where I was. Now the bus driver had not yet started the bus, so he says to me, "You have to sit in the back, boy." So I said, "What do you mean I have to sit in the back? I paid my fare just like everybody else and I will sit where I want to." He kept arguing and ended up telling me that it was the law, but I told him I didn't care what law it is, that I was in the U.S. Navy to keep this country secure and he wasn't telling me where to sit. I said I wasn't moving and if he wanted me to move he should give me back my fare. He didn't, and the bus pulled out and we arrived in Norfolk and bought a fifth of wine and drank the whole bottle.

Another time six of us were going on liberty—three white and three black sailors—and tried to board the ferry from Norfolk to Portsmouth together. But we found that one side of the boat was marked "Whites Only" and the other side "Negroes Only." The picture was getting clearer all the time. All this was in 1956, but I now know you can change all the signs and all the laws, and that doesn't change the racist mind.

I was released from the navy almost two years early with an honorable discharge. (One day in May one of the petty officers came around and asked who wanted out. Needless to say, I did.)

ALI BEY HASSAN: In Havana one time, on liberty, I saw how the Cuban poor people were living: in shacks, most of them no bigger than a one-room flat in any black ghetto—the only difference was there was plenty of land. This was 1956 or 1957. Batista was still running Cuba, but I didn't know who he was then. In the city itself I saw nothing but bars and whorehouses. The women kept a small cut of the money they made off U.S. servicemen and the Cuban pimps kept the rest. I was eighteen or nineteen then, and I saw that system operating just the same as in the black ghettos in the States. Oppressed people sold their bodies to survive, and the rich endorsed that way of life to avoid taking any responsibility for the society.

CLARK SQUIRE: While I was working for NASA in the Mojave Desert, I bought a convertible, and my weekend excursions ranged as far away as old Mexico. For the first time I began to understand the full meaning of the term "ugly American" in the form of the drunken, boisterous, arrogant American tourists and soldiers, with their habit of looking at all Mexican women as prostitutes, all the men as peons, and all Mexican children as dirty little waifs who were useful only if they had a teenage

sister. The Mexicans are completely aware of these attitudes of most "gringos," and they maintain a bitter hatred
for them. In all my excursions into Mexico, including border towns and as far south as Mexico City and Acapulco,
I found the Mexican people to be warm, friendly, un-
selfish, and fun-loving. In my most recent tour—1968—
I also found them moving toward another revolution.

Several years later, knowing that Malcolm had said,
"Travel broadens one's scope," I decided to satisfy my
urge to travel—to check out other countries and other
governments. In 1965 I took off a year and went to the
Caribbean, to Europe and to Africa. In the Caribbean I
moved among and talked to the masses of poor people
and found that many of them were oppressed, exploited,
and discriminated against, by their own black bourgeois
leaders. But, as in Mexico, I found they had had enough.
They too were moving in the direction of revolution. The
recent upheavals in the Caribbean are only the first overt
signs of a natural development in the inevitable process.

I also visited Geneva; Amsterdam—where a "hippie
type" group called the Provos are getting it together;
Stockholm; Copenhagen; and other places. In Paris I
moved around the Left Bank among the students, who at
that time were more advanced in revolutionary theory and
practice than their American counterparts. I went to
Madrid, where the contradictions between ruler and oppressed are much higher than in France, and the army
is visible everywhere; then back up through Marseilles,
where I rapped revolution in the African Quarter over
some dynamite "black gunjee."

KWANDO KINSHASA: In 1961, in the marines, I
took an examination for so-called "special" duty, which
would involve working with the American embassy in

some foreign country. The countries I applied for duty in were, in order, Cambodia, Israel, and the Sudan. Cambodia was out because, as I found out later, it was reserved for white marines. Israel was out because I had put down as my reason for wanting to go there that I was interested in studying the kibbutzim land system. I was too naive to realize that the last thing this country wanted was for blacks to study a paramilitary system based on the socialization of land. And I had told the board that I wanted to go to the Sudan because I thought anywhere on the African continent would be educational for me; that nationalism must have made them nervous, because they refused to let me go there, too. A few days later, they told me I was being sent to Guatemala. At the time I didn't even know what continent it was on.

The next two-and-a-half years were filled with revolution, intrigue, and personal political education.

The Canal Zone was the first stop on the way to Guatemala. There I went to what was known as "Marine House," which was reserved for the five marines who worked with the U.S. Embassy personnel. I was going to be in the Canal Zone for about a week. I met a black man who was one of the marine guards in Panama, and he told me to get my airline ticket straightened out before I did anything else, and then I would have time to look around. On the way to get the tickets, we passed a crowd of people marching down the main street. It turned out to be a march organized by Panamanian nationalists who were demanding the return of Panama to its people. The brother explained the situation, and it really blew my mind. The way he told it, we, the Americans, were exploiting the Panamanians and, in fact, treating Panama as a colony. As we walked around the city, the fact that for the first time in my life I was in a country where blacks were the majority race started to sink in. As the brother blew the facts down to me, I realized that the Panamanian bloods, whom I automatically identified with, were not only anti-U.S., but anti the *tools* of U.S. oppression, namely the marines who guarded the Canal and the U.S. Embassy. I realized that if I'd had my uniform on the people in the streets would have automatically regarded me as their enemy. In fact, considering what I represented at the time, I *was* their enemy.

That night the Panamanian government declared martial law in Panama City and Balboa because of the nationalist agitation. I decided I would walk around the city and check out what was really going down. Everything seemed cool in the center of the city, so I made a few excursions down side streets. On one of them I walked into a local bar, and I saw two brothers with their heads all bloody and people all around them, trying to stop the bleeding. Now, you got to dig this scene—everyone was speaking Spanish and there I was, not knowing any words except *si* and *no*, trying to figure out what was happening. All of a sudden some Panamanian soldiers came busting into the bar, swinging clubs at everybody in sight. I grabbed the quart of beer I'd bought and headed straight for the door. Outside, I saw what seemed like a thousand yelling and screaming people running in my direction. Behind them were Panamanian mounted soldiers, swinging their clubs and charging. So here I am, right in the middle of an unlawful demonstration against the Panamanian pigs! Me, my quart of beer, and my two words of Spanish. I headed as fast as I could for Marine House, which was near the U.S. Embassy. I was about two blocks away when I ran into a jeep full of Panamanian soldiers who were patrolling the area near the embassy. We spotted each other at the same time, but they moved faster than I did. They leveled their rifles at my head and started jabbering Spanish at me. They kept yelling "Cubano! Cubano!" which didn't mean a thing to me. Next thing I knew they had me spreadeagled on the street with a rifle to my head. They yelled "Cubano! Cubano!" and I yelled "American! American!" and we weren't getting anyplace. Finally they took me to the embassy, where the guard on duty explained that I was a new man who didn't understand Spanish. Everyone but me thought the whole thing was pretty funny. Later the guard told me that I'd been about to get shot because they thought the beer I was holding was a Molotov cocktail! And the "Cubano" bit was because all the reactionary governments of Latin America were, and are, spooked up about the Cuban revolutionaries. Right on, Cuba!

A few days later I arrived in Guatemala City, and the Guatemalans were in the middle of a revolutionary war, a war that is still going on. Right on to the Guatemalan revolutionaries! My political education progressed so far while I was in Guatemala that by the time I left two-and-one-half years later I was on the verge of being kicked out by the reactionary government in power, not to mention the Americans there who didn't like my friendships with known revolutionaries. I entered a country a very apolitical Negro marine, and came out a dedicated black revolutionary. I made it a point to learn all I could about our Latin American and black brothers in Central America; and these brothers whose friendship I gained made it a point to educate this black marine from America. At the time, there were only ten blacks from the U.S. in Guatemala, but the population itself is about 80 per cent Mayan, 10 per cent black, and 10 per cent a mixture of European and Mayan and black.

Many of the tactics one would or could use in an urban guerrilla situation were already thoroughly planned in

Guatemala, but some priority action was also planned: my Guatemalan friends explained to me that the only way the revolution could succeed would be to educate the masses first, in a period of two, five, ten years or so, to the necessity of an armed revolution throughout all of the country. Then and only then would it be desirable to move on the main city. At that time, support from the people would be of such a nature that the government would be overwhelmed by the people, whereas now the guerrillas might find themselves isolated in the fight.

It was in 1965 that many of the guerrilla units of F.A.R. and M.R.-13* began to organize and receive supplies in order to continue the struggle until today, in an area known as Escuintla. The people of Escuintla are truly a people unto themselves. They live in one of the richest areas of the country as far as natural food and climate are concerned, plus they have the naturalness about themselves that seems typical of guerrilla fighters. We found out that no matter how much the government sent its spies and its U.S. propaganda teams, its Peace Corps, even Mormon missionaries, the people in that area still related to the concept of the revolutionary guerrilla: "Freedom is where I put my foot and carry my rifle." When the revolutionary walks proudly into Guatemala City in the near future, it will not surprise me if among the first are the men from Escuintla.

---

* M.R.-13, Movimiento Revolucionario-13 (November 13) was headed by the Guatemalan revolutionary Yon Sosa. This revolutionary was killed recently, last year, by Mexican counter-revolutionary forces, near the Mexican-Guatemalan border. But his movement, M.R.-13, has grown to such an extent that today it coordinates its rural revolutionary activities with F.A.R. (Fuerzas Armadas Rebeldes), which is based in the Guatemalan capital, Guatemala City.

In Guatemala I learned how much this country is hated. Not disliked, but hated. I also learned that Cuba is respected and loved by almost all the people in Central America. The only ones who liked the United States were members of the ruling class of these countries—a powerful, but small, minority. (Like the average ruling class in the average Central American or South American country, they exploit the majority of the population cruelly, mercilessly—these ruling classes are the allies of the United States.) And, finally, the most enlightening thing I learned was the respect those millions of Latin brothers have for blacks in this country fighting for their freedom. To say that America does its best to keep this fact away from the Third World people in this country is to understate the fact.

I remember I began in 1962 to read different articles by Fidel Castro, Ernesto Che Guevara, Jacobo Arbenz—all Latins striving for the liberation of their people from oppression and exploitation of any type. And I came to realize that the oppressed Latin in Latin America and the oppressed black in the United States were not really different. In fact, the only thing that was different was the geographical address. Slowly, I came to realize that oppression and exploitation can be fought effectively only by individuals who are totally committed to a course of action known as revolution. I then finally was able to nourish the seed of revolt that was always inside of me with the practical experience of working and living with people who, despite my role as an American marine, were determined to relate to me as one oppressed person to another—for I was oppressed, and I was becoming very much aware of the depth and magnitude of my oppression.

When I was discharged from the marines, I decided to do some traveling, using the money I had saved in the marines. I visited Jamaica, Mexico, and all the countries of Central America. I returned to New York by way of the South. I worked at different jobs here and there, and I saw the similarity of the political and economic situation of exploited Third World people and some whites to what I had seen for the last three years below the Rio Grande. I began to see that the solving of these problems would have to be similar to the way other exploited people were moving on their situations: the developing of a revolutionary cadre.

KUWASI BALAGOON: One spring, in the army in Europe, I took leave in Spain and came back AWOL, broke, jet-black, and bony, with balls like BBs. I not only went to Spain, but out of my mind. Got hip to good reefer, and stayed at a pension in a small seaside village, ate octopus, played the sets, came from out of the lime pits and into a little Spanish castle magic. Even the long trip back was hip: I ran into brothers from Africa and we rapped all across the French frontier.

Then on the very last lap of the trip, I found myself eighty pfennigs short, and couldn't pay for a ticket back to post. One hundred pfennigs equal one mark, and a German mark is about one American quarter. Looking around the train station wondering what to do, I noticed a cracker Spec 5 standing around and approached the fellow American soldier. I explained my situation: since one Yankee dollar equals three marks and eighty pfennigs, I asked the dude to give me a dollar and I'd give him three marks, to which he replied, "Boy, that's like giving you a quarter." Now, this cracker really knew how to say "boy." There were too many people around to kill this motherfucker. He couldn't have known he was talking to De Prophet.

I got so angry I had to walk that shit off, and for a long time I walked, hardly seeing anything but straight in front of me. I thought about actually going to Vietnam to protect the shit this cracker represented to me. "God damn right I'd shoot him." I walked about two hours trying to get my stuff together, until I found a military post where a brother I did not know gladly gave me a dollar and said, "Ah, fuck it," when I attempted to hand three marks to him.

In Spain people had asked me if it was all right if they called me mister. I felt compelled to be respectful. It was as if I had actually become a part of the community, during that short time that I was there. I knew all the little kids, had nicknames for them, and people actually cried when I left.

Back at the post all the brothers were glad to see me and gleamed as I reported to them—but even as I told them I wondered why Spain had seemed so hip. Now Barcelona is fast. In fact I ran into a brother who seemed to be on the verge of a nervous breakdown because the hookers and con men had got over on him so tough, and I had to round on the dude immediately, because I figured that he might be running down a game himself. I mean that Playa del Toro was Spain's 42nd Street, and the neighborhood behind it was a Spanish ghetto, full of players. It came to me that the little resort town I'd stayed in was hip because most everybody there had bread, including myself, nobody seemed to be in need. The police were idle, they just stood on their favorite corner and smoked all day in this town, and people came there to spend money. I was unaware of the political climate, and until

I got back to Germany I was unaware of the lesser degree of racism.

At Barcelona station, I sat with a Spanish lady until four o'clock in the morning and we rapped in broken English and Spanish and sign language. The station was empty except for us, there was time on our hands, and we were hip to each other. She was waiting for a train bringing her children in and I for a train going out. There was no Queen-Virgin-Mary-about-to-be-"better-death-than-this"-raped by a gorilla, who grew a long tail at midnight, who would rip her pussy open. It wasn't on the scene on either mind, nor any fucked-up vibrations. A very un-American experience, un-German experience, a pleasant experience, which should be everyday people action.

Another time, I had waited and saved and I took off for London. Which was home. I vowed to stop processing my hair after seeing the nappy brothers and sisters there. And also there I felt and became more committed to black liberation. While standing on a corner one morning, rapping to some West Indian, African, Asian, and South American brothers, it occurred to me, like through the flow and substance of the conversation and their mannerisms, that we were really brothers. Among them and the beautiful black sisters, I was home. A brother got over on me for some gunjee and the rest of the bloods I had just run into gave him a choice to either give up the gunjee or the rest of the bread, and I ascended into the brotherhood. After hearing German music and that cowboy shit-kicking shit so often for so long, and then hearing nothing but Otis Redding and James Brown and sure-enough soul bands, and doing some honest-to-goodness jamming, my soul revived.

Relaxing, partying, learning and teaching and talking about what was happening with black people all over the world, was a natural tonic. Yeah baby, Revolutionary Cultural Exchange.

CURTIS POWELL: In the fall of 1963 I was writing to schools to apply for graduate study. University of California Medical Center was filled, but I got good replies from a few universities, including one in Japan and one in Paris. I chose Paris. The only catch was that I had to support myself. But I didn't care; I wanted to get out of this country—this racist, bigoted, jive Babylon. I borrowed some scratch and, about the time John Kennedy got iced, I went to Paris.

Paris—wow. Not because it was Paris, City of Light, but in Paris I met bloods from all over the world. When you go anywhere out of this country, it feels as if a weight is lifted off you—and it drops right back on you when you come back in. I had noticed it before, going to Canada and Mexico—small travels—but in Paris, man, I met bloods from all over the world. I cannot describe how I felt the first time I met a blood from Senegal and he showed me money with black faces on it. I was awed, I was speechless. I was elated.

All of the blacks from America who met in Paris had faced the same problems: racist oppression and exploitation. From Paris I traveled all over Europe, and everywhere I went I met bloods from this Babylon, all expatriates who had left because of racism. Although I would say that in Europe a black man is not free, still he has more freedom than here, and so he can find a better perspective, some concept of what freedom might be—a perspective and a concept denied to bloods who've never been outside. There are exceptions, but I believe this is basically true.

Part of it is the experience of meeting bloods from other countries. Comparing our experiences gave me a broader perspective, and helped me toward some solutions to our common problems. We who cannot even learn about *ourselves* here in this Babylon, can certainly never learn about our brothers in other oppressed lands, nor about black men who do somewhat control their own lives.

Anyway, I was doing research in the day, and after my money ran out I played a little piano at night for a while. (I had studied piano and violin, and could play a little jazz—at least enough to get by.) And I hustled. Of course there was a wild social life—drinking, smoking, hanging out. I had an apartment and at one time as many as three roommates—a hustler, a thief, and an M.D. This made it difficult for some social activities with the women, but we made out all right while it lasted—we had a schedule. All three of these bloods were out of sight, good at what they were doing, and had a common history as victims of oppression and racism. Each had a different way of reacting to it.

I was traveling a bit, meeting a lot of people, hearing and reading a lot of things that impressed me—music like Sam Cooke's "A Change Is Gonna Come," for one. And I kept searching for answers, toward an ideology, toward solving the problems of the black man.

Then I met Malcolm.

I had rapped with Jimmy Baldwin, and with Martin Luther King, but Malcolm was coming back from Mecca. Now I had met Malcolm before, but I hadn't been quite as ready as I was now. I had become somewhat involved with different black liberation struggles, now—and he was also changed: he had dropped a lot of the spookism. Dig —like when one becomes committed there comes a sense of direction and purpose. This is no Shazam, Captain Marvel type thing; you keep on keeping on, and one day it's there. I was there and Malcolm was there except he was farther there. Like he knew he was going to die— and soon—and he knew who was going to kill him: the American Government. I was getting near the stage of no alternatives, Victory or Death—he was already there. I was only at the beginning of having those moments when, as Che said, "Death is a concept a thousand times more real, a victory, a myth that only a revolutionary can dream of"—he was already there.

Change. Metamorphosis. Change. A general can tell when a battle has turned. A farmer or a forester can see signs of spring before anyone else. A professional can detect subtle, or sudden, changes. But for most of us, especially when we are deeply involved, significant changes become significant only in retrospect. My growth was a slow process, and not all voluntary. I was new at it. But looking back, I can see the changes in the shape of my thinking after I rapped with Malcolm. There is no doubt that Malcolm changed my thinking, or at least showed me that I was on the right track, accelerated the process and gave me new self-assuredness. Everything that had happened up to that time was influencing me, but nothing so greatly as Malcolm did.

The change didn't happen all at once. I continued to lead about the same life in Paris. Then in early 1965, the authorities would not let Malcolm re-enter Paris. Then he was assassinated. Both these things shook me up—but on top of these, a personal experience really finished the alternatives for me.

Just as I had paid six months' advance rent on my Paris apartment, the landlady kicked me out. There was no stated reason. She had been groovy up to that moment, then all of a sudden she was acting as if she was afraid of something.

And at the same time, equally suddenly, there was "no more room" at the lab. Again no reason.

I had to leave Paris. I went to the Middle East to a few friends' places to get my shit together, and then in April, 1965, came back to Babylon.

On a subsequent trip to Paris, about two years later, I learned what had happened. C.I.A. members of the U.S. government had visited the lab just before this mysterious bullshit. Right after I had split, the French pigs went to all my friends trying to locate me; they told some of my friends that they were checking up on my whereabout for the U.S. government. It seems that everybody who'd rapped to Malcolm got into some kind of static. But when it was happening, I wasn't able to figure it out. There was a vacuum in Babylon after Malcolm's murder. When I came back I talked to bloods I grew up with, murder-mouthing, talking about the pigs like dogs, but although they could dig where I was coming from, they weren't really ready. They just weren't ready.

BOB COLLIER: Some students asked me, in 1964, if I was interested in going on a student trip to Cuba. "Sure," I said, "if you're not kidding." In the bars and restaurants where the students hung out, talking about foreign affairs, civil rights, philosophy, etc., I had heard a lot of different opinions about Cuba, and I wanted to see for myself. We spent many hours, then, discussing the legal aspects. Constitutionally we were in the right, but the system had issued an *administrative* order not to go. We had to test the freedom of the people: we went.

We were greeted at José Marti Airport by a crowd of jubilant people. We went to our hotel to clean up and there discovered one of the minor problems of the revolution—poor plumbing. The upkeep of the hotel wasn't the most elegant, but it was explained that the revolutionary government had set up a system of economic priorities and keeping up pre-revolution luxury hotels was low on the list.

We were generally free to walk around and meet the Cuban people, although we were warned about possible counterrevolutionary activity. One day I went to a local park and talked to some teenagers. They said that things were hard, but they understood what the American blockade meant to them economically. Fidel had told them that they would have hard work, but things would get progressively better if they all stuck together and worked in a revolutionary spirit. One young girl said that Fidel told them to study hard, be good in heart and not selfish, and help each other whenever possible—that working together in this way was the key to success.

We joined another student group, in Santa Clara, and we were taken to visit state farms and factories. The coordination of mechanized and manual labor was remarkable, considering what was available. The factories had many training programs for young people in welding, mechanics, and machine operation. Many of the young workers said they were working, going to school, and learning a trade at the same time. I found this to be the rule all over the country. The high school was right there at the plant. Decisions about how to improve plant production or to make the work run more smoothly were made only after collective discussion. Women worked right next to the men. During the afternoon "heat break," I noticed that many of the workers seemed to be studying or discussing the alphabet. I was told that most of the workers attended school, as part of Castro's crash literacy program.

One evening in the park I heard a group of Cubans arguing about the revolution. A man was saying that things had run better in the plants when the Americans had been there. People answered in various ways: one man said that the Cuban people knew they could learn from the Americans, but they would rather do it themselves. A young girl asked him why he had so little confidence in the Cuban people. After all, she said, we are all the same. She asked him if he was ashamed to be Cuban and if he would rather be in America. She also reminded him that not many people had been able to get jobs before the revolution.

I left Cuba with very strong impressions. For example, one of the major economic goals of the country is rent-free housing, and much of their planning is done with this in mind. Yet the United States, with the greatest productive capacity in the world, has only one major city that even has *controls* on rent. It became obvious to me in Cuba that the elimination of the profit motive is absolutely essential for a sane society. The great personal and corporate fortunes in the United States will not be put to proper social use until the people take things into their own hands—until it is impossible to amass such fortunes for private use.

There are also vast differences between the United States and Cuba in the general purposes of education. Aside from the immediate goal of literacy, education in Cuba is a process that seeks to expand social consciousness at the same time it teaches people history, mathematics, and so on—and a trade. In the United States, where uncontrolled superindustrialization has caused ever-increasing intra-class competition for jobs, the colleges and universities have become tools of the corporate consciousness that pervades this country: culturally, they maintain the status quo.

Racism still exists in Cuba. Castro does not pretend to have finally defeated this vicious enemy of any people, but nationalism—in the sense that all Cubans are brothers together and that color or shade has nothing to do with citizenship—is continually stressed in the schools, in Castro's speeches, in the factories. It is assumed that the achievement of a socialist economy, with full employment and equal opportunity, will end at least the *class* reasons for racism.

I thought a lot about Cuba when I returned to the United States, and what the revolution had done for the people. I felt I had to help my people in a positive and constructive way.

I also had to eat. I went to New York City, got a job at the public library, and used the books there to study more in the social sciences and history. I had been back for about three months when I was approached by two FBI agents, who had inquired about me at the library, approached me and started asking questions about Cuba. Their attitude and approach turned me off, and I said I had nothing to discuss. (I told them to stop bothering people like me and do something to help black people, do something about enforcing the law against southern racists and people who practiced discrimination throughout the nation.) A few weeks later, a cat named Ray Woodall came out of nowhere. He came on strong and radical and visited me a lot, talking about politics and about helping the people in the ghetto. Pretty soon this

"Woodall" character started talking funny and acting crazy. I felt that something wasn't right, but I ignored it. Sure enough, the set-up was revealed on February 16, 1965, when I found out I was being charged with conspiracy to blow up the Statue of Liberty, the Washington Monument, and the Liberty Bell. It was the sweetest frame in the world. The "evidence" was pictures from the police file. No physical evidence of anything, and no witnesses but pigs. The courtroom was full of agents sitting around looking like Lucifer's henchmen. When I look back on the trial I remember there was more talk about my trip to Cuba than anything else. The district attorney used that trip to whip that white, middle-class jury to a frenzy of hatred for us—those middle-class whites who had been molded by bigoted, racist institutions. The jury didn't waste any time bringing in a verdict of guilty, so they could hurry up and go to their cocktail parties, back to their suburban homes, back to whatever place they came from so they could talk about how they sent three black men away to prison. As long as it wasn't them who were getting sent away, they could talk about how important it is to be strong, sure, and honest, how important it is to see justice done, to protect the nation from the black anarchists. And so we were given ten years for something that they not only couldn't prove we had done, but couldn't even prove we had *talked* about.

During the two years I was fighting the case, I studied law. I got to the Supreme Court and was denied a hearing. My appeal for a re-hearing was denied. After two years in prison I was paroled.

I was in New York again, looking for work again, and when I mentioned my name it was like the plague. Finally some friends of mine introduced me to a man named Alex Munsell, a brilliant scientist who spent much of his time campaigning against the war, and he was able to give me a job. It was quite an education, that job: we discussed science, philosophy, and social problems endlessly.

CURTIS POWELL: Early in 1966, as early as I could, I went to Africa—to Mother Africa. By late 1966 I was almost broke, in Egypt. I borrowed some money and went to Stockholm, where I began working again on my Ph.D.—this time, successfully.

I think Africa was very good for me, to go on my own, to see what was happening, and to continue my political and psychological education. Africa taught me a lot. In Babylon one learns a nature, an American nature, a European nature—a Negro nature. This is hard to explain. But there *is* an African nature, and we've all got it, down under the layers of the Negro nature we've learned. There are facets of our African nature, our black nature, that have been treated in such a way that most Negroes who begin to "make it" in Babylon become ashamed of themselves, of aspects of their real selves. One of the saddest facts of our oppression here is that most of these Negroes don't even know anything about their true African natures—they think the European or the American nature is the only thing going.

The most relevant thing I learned from the real mother country, Africa, was the importance of revolution—of a people's struggle like the ones going on in Mozambique, Angola, Portuguese Guinea, and South West Africa. That struggle is the hope of the future for Africa—that struggle is the hope of the world. I came away from Africa knowing that blacks in America will not be free until South Africans are free, Latin Americans are free, Asians are free, Palestinians are free—it's all together. The whole thing is about people who are oppressed worldwide, a worldwide people's struggle against the worldwide racist, fascist, capitalistic, greed-filled pigs.

The pork-chop cultural nationalists in America take an external slice of culture from one small segment of Africa, and become a distorted parody of African culture. That doesn't get us to our African nature. Then there are blacks from Babylon who really try to go back to the mother continent: many end up like the "Americo-Liberians," looking down on Africans, with—again—a European set of values; and still others march backwards into total tribalism. That doesn't get us to our African nature either. The only way to get to our real, free, black, African nature is to get our Third World free.

Africa taught me a lot.

part 8

CURTIS POWELL: Back in New York, no group seemed to be moving in the direction I wanted. I dug the Muslims some, but except for Malcolm they were too spooky. I couldn't relate at all to the thing about Yacub. I also couldn't accept the six-thousand-year bit—like in six thousand years, by will of some Black Allah, we would be ruling the world. I knew we would have to relate to that saying that can be found in all religions: God helps those who help themselves.

AFENI SHAKUR: In Harlem every day at about seven o'clock, Sandra and I would put on our clothes, comb our wigs and zanzy up our eyes with black eyeliner, eyebrow pencil and multicolor eye shadow. When we were satisfied that we looked fly we would prance around the corner to the bar. First we'd go over to the jukebox and play a record (Nina Simone's record, "Four Women," was out at the time), then we'd sit at the bar and drink Hennesseys or 151 all night. Brothers would come by and we'd talk the nicest to the ones who we knew had the most cash.

One night in the middle of our gaming, a brother came in who Sandra knew. His name was Omar. I remember that I kept calling him Cheyenne, instead, and he kept calling me "All I See." Omar was hustling roogie and coke and of course he was fly! That night I didn't talk to anyone else—Omar and I rapped and got high until well after all the bars were closed. After that we found every after-hours spot in the Bronx. In less than ten days, we were living together. He bought me everything I looked at! I used to be walking down the street and he'd walk up to me and put everything from rings to $80 knits in my hand. At night he'd tell me about his life and I would snort cocaine, smoke reefer, and play the part of his queen.

He had been a Muslim under Elijah Muhammad for about five years. When Malcolm left, he went with him. He would tell me about those first weeks when most of Malcolm's followers had to hole up in basements with guns in hand, not quite sure what the reprisals would be. The break was a bitter one, not so much with Malcolm and Elijah themselves, but with certain people whose loyalty to either of the men was so fierce that quite a few wounds and deaths resulted.

It was through Omar that I learned about both Malcolm and Elijah Muhammad. This dude was the first person who started teaching me about any kind of politics. The politics he was talking were apolitical, but it was the beginning of my having any knowledge at all of the teachings of Elijah Muhammad. Well that shit just blew my mind. The dude was saying that it's a whole thing that you have to learn, that black is the best color on the planet Earth. It was really a good feeling for somebody who has gone through all of that. It's a very good thing— it's an ego trip, you know. I wasn't doing anything else except snorting dope and talking about how great Malcolm was and this drag about the misunderstanding he and Elijah had. I was very naïve.

RICHARD HARRIS: Quite a few friends of mine were Muslims. With a little encouragement and prompting from them, and from my woman at the time, I went to the mosque in Newark to hear and observe. At first sight, it seemed just one more storefront church, with the emphasis on youth. I was not thinking in any definite terms one way or the other until I heard this visiting minister speak—that minister completely took me out of my indecisiveness at that meeting, and made me take the steps required to become a Muslim. He made me see and understand things I had not even thought about previously. Not only did he make me see and understand, but he also gave me the answer. He explained how black people had been brainwashed by slavery, past and present, and how black people had lived before slavery—all of this he made clear to me in the period of an hour and a half. Before this I could not and would not consider myself as anything other than a fast-living super-slick, big-money-making nigger—both this incident and what happened later, I consider my life.

His answer to the problems facing black people was his and my religion, Islam. But the most important thing, I think, was the man himself. Minister Malcolm X.

After Malcolm said that he would not think of traveling or of even passing the day without doing some informative reading, I became a fanatic. All the public libraries in and around Newark became my stomping grounds. I did and still do read with a dictionary at my side. I read on almost every subject possible. This thirst for reading, and the thirst to understand what I've read, are my most treasured possessions. And when I began to read like that, it helped me to understand even more about Malcolm—the so-called contradictions in his life and mine were almost the same: his escape from a life of crime into Islam as taught by Elijah Muhammad, from the free-and-easy existence of a hustler to one of the strictest religions there is, from indifference toward black people to the service of black people! There is no doubt that whether or not he intended to, Malcolm, by his constant investigation, his almost fanatical love of religious and moral obligations, which took him to Africa and Asia and changed so much of his thinking, was clearly showing and explaining the evolution of a revolutionary.

There were many brothers who loved Malcolm. His assassination, and the implications behind it, led to killing and dying. I stopped attending the mosque regularly, but with others who'd loved Malcolm and followed him closely, I read and discussed everything he'd suggested, and read almost all of the daily papers and all of the weekly news magazines—in other words, we were pretty well aware of the world situation.

LUMUMBA SHAKUR: In 1962, the black inmates became aware of the so-called civil rights movement. We appreciated what Martin Luther King was doing, but we did not agree with his nonviolent approach toward the American system. Some blacks actually thought Martin Luther King was setting up our people for genocide: niggers would be singing "We shall overcome" on the march to the gas chamber. Malcolm X won the black inmates' respect immediately. Malcolm X rehabilitated thousands of black inmates by just standing up to racist

America and telling it like it is, educating his people about our reality—self-defense—and our destiny. We all knew Malcolm X was one of the greatest men on this earth. A Puerto Rican brother in the cell next to mine would get the *New York Times* mailed to him every day. When the *Times* had something on Malcolm X, I would cut out the article and take it to the yard and show the article to other brothers. The brothers became very nationalistic in Comstock. When a brother in prison goes up to another brother and says, "The white man is a devil," no young brother would dispute or argue that issue, because in prison we felt and saw racism raw and buck-naked daily. In Comstock the ages were from sixteen to forty; only a black inmate in his late thirties would dispute or argue with the statement that "the white man is a devil." We would call the older brothers Uncle Toms and tell them that only uncivilized people and devils would run Comstock the way it was being administered. In the final analysis, when it was time to redress and change the racial conditions of Comstock, the older brothers who we called Uncle Toms told us we could not change the racial situation in Comstock. When the riot started, these older so-called brothers ran to their cells and locked themselves in.

In the summer of 1962, my father came to see me. He was telling me about the family, but he seemed reluctant about something. Then my father dropped it on me and it blew my mind, because I was thinking about how I was going to say the same thing to him. He asked me my opinion of Brother Malcolm X. I told my father that, "Malcolm X is a very beautiful brother and all the brothers in prison love Brother Malcolm X." I also told my father that I was a black nationalist and a Muslim but I could not relate to praying. I never before saw anything that affected my father like what I had just said. His facial expression became one of complete satisfaction. From that moment on, my father and I have kept an excellent communication that includes subjects both political and military in nature. My father told me he converted to Islam in 1960. He said he knew Malcolm X and that he went to hear Malcolm X educate blacks all of the time. Also, he said when Malcolm X was educating the people, Malcolm said that "most of our young warriors are in prisons." My father said then that Malcolm X was a genius. We must have talked for about four hours. He mostly was telling me what was happening in the streets concerning the repression upon the black communities. He must have said about twenty times that it was beautiful to see that the devil didn't have my mind and it was good to see my spirits so high.

He left me a box with underwear, food, and a Muslim bean pie. When I was in the cell block, because everybody is locked in by 5:00 P.M., I was talking from my cell to the brothers about how my father had just blew my mind. First I said my father was down with the Muslims. The brothers responded with a typical, "Oh spare us, Shotgun." Then I said my father knows the good brother Malcolm X. The brothers said again, "Oh spare us, Shotgun." Then I said my father is going to change his slave name to Shakur (the Thankful) and I got to find a bad African first name. The brothers said, "Oh spare us, Shotgun, because you are always going to be Shotgun to us." I told the brothers I'm going to spare all of them from this big Muslim bean pie I got. One said, "You jiving, Shotgun." Another said, "Shotgun, you wouldn't do that to your brothers." Everybody had heard about the Nation of Islam's bean pie, but very few had tasted one. About ten brothers ate that one bean pie like it was some

kind of ritual. I related to the brothers just about everything my father had related to me. It blew the brothers'
minds just like it had blown my mind to hear what was
happening with black people and Malcolm X in New
York City.

The Muslims and the nationalists began talking about
formulating some kind of action to redress and change
the racial conditions of Comstock. I must confess that we
talked about action for a year, because somebody would
always disagree with any method of action. Esaw, Beany
(Sekou Odinga), and Cheese were all in Comstock too by
then. The four of us finally told everybody we were sick
of talking, so when anybody wanted to get down with
some action, call us.

I had been in prison three years and four months. I was
twenty years old. I went before the New York State Parole Board. The first thing those racists asked me was I
sorry for assaulting that white man. I was not sorry, I said,
because the white man had assaulted me first and I only
acted in self-defense, and that was all stated in my records. The parole board said I should not have defended
myself. I told them, "I do not believe in passive resistance." The racists told me that I talked like I was not
ready for parole. Then they told me to disavow and denounce the Black Muslims and black nationalism. I said
no, and asked them would they disavow and denounce
Christianity? The racists said they saw that I was still
arrogant and told me to leave the room, and I would be
receiving a notice of their decision. That evening at 6:00
P.M., April 2, 1963, I got my notice: "Hold ten months
until February 1964." I was expecting to get held every
day until my five years expired.

After a massive riot in Comstock, the correction officials
made their decision on who the riot leaders were, and we

were all transferred to Attica State Prison. This was illegal in itself because New York State has a law that says
you must be twenty-one years old to go to an official
state prison. At the time we were transferred to Attica
Prison some of us were only nineteen and twenty years
old. We were all immediately placed in solitary confinement. Solitary confinement in Attica is designed to crash
you psychologically. There was only one white inmate in
solitary confinement. The rest of the white inmates would
come to solitary confinement and scream, try to hang
themselves or try to cut themselves to death or go crazy.
Usually the white inmates would not stay in solitary confinement over a week.

Deputy Warden Mason of Attica put all the brothers
from Comstock on the same gallery with two older Muslims, Aki Williams and Aki Nelson, who had a profound
influence on us. These righteous brothers would give us
political and Islamic classes twelve hours non-stop.

Of the brothers in solitary confinement, 99 per cent were
in there for teaching Islam or nationalism to other inmates. Aki Williams was in solitary confinement for three
years. Aki Williams and Aki Nelson submitted a writ of
show-cause to a Buffalo, New York, court, because Muslims were denied their freedom of religion in New York
State prisons. Aki Nelson and Aki Williams were taken to
a racist court in Buffalo to have a hearing on their writ
of show-cause. When they came back, they really blew
everybody's minds: they said Malcolm X testified at the
hearing to prove that Islam is an authentic religion. They
said Malcolm X talked for about a half-hour and electri-
fied the courtroom. After Malcolm X testified, the D.A.
was crushed and just shook his head. And the racist judge
just said that Islam is not a religion and denied the motion of show-cause. In 1966, when I was home, I read in

the *New York Times* that the court of appeals ruled that Islam is a religion, and ministers from the Nation of Islam are allowed to go inside New York prisons to teach Islam.

When I was out, finally, I went to court and so-called-legally changed my slave name. All my family had done it already except Zayd, and he changed his slave name so-called-legally while he was in the navy—and when he did he immediately got interviews from the C.I.D. We all used religious, cultural, and ancestral reasons. I knew I would be making some babies soon and I felt that giving my child a racist, cracker's name would be like cussing the child. And I felt when my son got about eighteen years old, he would try to kick my ass for giving him a racist, cracker name. Today I have two sons and a daughter—two of them are twins. The boys are named Dingiswayo Mbiassi Abdul Shakur and Mtetwa Kieta Shakur. My daughter's name is Sekyiwa Jamilla Shakur. I have never heard of a white person naming their children African, Asian, or American Indian names. Every white person I ever heard of, including socialists, radicals, revolutionaries, communists and all progressives, have given their children European names. I wonder why?

In October, 1966, I got married to a nationalist sister named Sayeeda Samad. Sayeeda and I were Muslim, so we got married by Islamic laws, which guarantee that I can have more than one wife. Sayeeda was not enthusiastic about my polygamist opinions, but I told her eventually I would be a polygamist. Every man I knew ever since I was about 8 years old was an underground polygamist, and I never believed in concealing. On February 3, 1967, I took Sayeeda to Harlem Hospital to have a baby. The doctor said the baby would not come out for about five hours. I went home and called Sekou to wait with me. Sayeeda had twins, and this blew our minds. We went to see Sayeeda, then went to my house. We smoked some reefer (we called reefer the Good Brother Roogie) and picked some bad African names from this list I had. I was joking with Sekou about giving him the formula for making two babies in one shot. I was telling Sekou, you got to fuck a special way. Sekou said, "Spare me, Lumumba, because I'm going to make some twins." On Malcolm X's birthday, May 19, 1970, Sekou's wife, Awode, gave birth to twin boys. That really blew my mind.

In the fall of 1968, I got married again. My second wife, Afeni Shakur, possesses some qualities that I never saw in other women. Her political consciousness combined with pure candidness, directness and lots of fire. Afeni was in tune with my opinions in depth on political, military and matrimonial issues. Afeni never hesitated to give me constructive criticism on some of my actions. This I consider an asset to any revolutionary. Polygamy was no problem in my home because revolutionary principles and Islamic law govern my home. In November, 1968, Sayeeda gave birth to my second son, Mtetwa Kieta Shakur.

SHABA OM: At the same time as I was hustling skag, doing my "conservative pimping," and still going to high school, a Muslim brother was always coming by selling *Muhammad Speaks*. I always bought one. I dug what *Muhammad Speaks* was saying, too. I had read *The Autobiography of Malcolm X* and other works of Malcolm's, and how at one point in his life he was a Black Muslim. This brother would stop and rap to me for hours. One Saturday afternoon he convinced me to go with him to a meeting at Mosque 7-A in the Bronx, and I began to dig on what was being said up at the mosque and what the minister was teaching. It was the knowledge of self. When

I say self, I mean the essence of the black man, who the black man is, self-respect and dignity; how and what to eat that is best for a healthy body. I began to dig and understand the difference between a so-called Negro and a black man; I dug I was living the life of a jive nigger and this is the worst life one could live in North America. I went to the meetings for about five weeks, and then stopped, but every week I bought *Muhammad Speaks*. When I was in the Muslim movement I went and got myself a slave, because I didn't want to be a jive nigger or "Negro," as the Black Muslim movement called black people who are gamblers, hustlers, and pimps. I moved out of my mother Rachel's hut, too, because we would get into some very hot arguments about the food she was cooking, pork and other things. I was about seventeen or so. I wouldn't eat pork at all—I still won't—because I dug the pig to be a very nasty beast. Rachel told me if I didn't dig what she was cooking, don't eat it, in fact I could get out of her house. And this I did.

JAMAL: When I was around thirteen it was the era of the birth of cries for black power. I was wearing dashikis and an Afro, and I was running around saying "black power" one minute and getting off into a nigger-kill-nigger bag the next. I joined the Five Percenters. We spouted a lot of abstract rhetoric, but it was just murder-mouthing; it wasn't a black liberation group, it was a gang. We would be involved in all types of things: picking fights, snatching wine bottles and vodka bottles from people coming out of the liquor store. They would stash pocketbooks and steal cars. I tried to stay off on the sidelines on this as much as I could, but I would always get caught up and chase after these crazy people. I left the Five Percenters after about a month and a half. Every day, then, they would come around the neighborhood and stay for about an hour and get their rocks off by telling me that I was the devil and had betrayed the Nation of Islam. I would simply ignore them—I wasn't too much into the rhetoric—and they would go away. After a while, most or all the members fell victim to the plague, heroin —skag, smack. Now, most of the Five Percenters I knew are notorious dope fiends, and can be found any time nodding up on Bronxwood Avenue. If you ask them, "Are you still a brother? Are you still part of the Five Percenter movement?" they respond almost with a reflex action by saying, "Peace."

ALI BEY HASSAN: I began to really hate white people when I was in my early twenties, and also got more and more angry with my own people, especially the men, who never seemed to do anything about their oppression. About this time, my cousin, Abdul Hakim, who was a Muslim, started teaching me about Islam. I learned pretty quick. In 1966 I had married an eighteen-year-old girl named Mary Ann (Maryum to me), and she and I and two cousins started attending Temple 25 in Newark regularly, to pick up on the teachings of the Honorable Elijah Muhammad. I also read the newspaper *Muhammad Speaks* just about every week. Since then Maryum and I separated—even though we still loved each other, various problems became too much to cope with—but I have always been glad that we were able to hear the teachings of Islam together.

After a while I stopped going to the temple, since it didn't seem to be able to provide the kind of things I felt I and my people needed. The Muslims helped me to try and sort out my feelings about myself and my people, but I couldn't see how they were benefiting the masses. They talked a lot, but conditions didn't change. Like most black people, I knew about Malcolm X, and I learned from his writings and speeches about the possibility of revolution for black people. But I still couldn't put it together to really take action.

part 9

CLARK SQUIRE: One morning in 1964 I opened the paper and learned that three brothers had been murdered registering voters in Mississippi. I became angry, and that summer I went down to Parola County in the Mississippi Delta to register voters. Even then, though, I didn't believe the vote was any kind of real solution because blacks had had the vote in the North for years, and their oppressive conditions had hardly changed.

Ever since I was a kid in Texas I had always had a gun, and always knew how to handle it, so I took it along just in case. If one of those racist crackers tried to kill me, he was going to get the surprise of his life! Later it proved unnecessary because the old sister who put me up related heavily to self-defense. She gave me the front bedroom and introduced me to a 12-gauge pump shotgun kept behind the dresser. We got along very well during my stay there. Contrary to popular belief, this mentality of defending the home, I found, is prevalent among even older people in the deep South.

When Malcolm X began his OAAU, it looked good, but I, like a number of other brothers, thought and acted as if Malcolm would always be among us and was slow about checking his organization out. Soon, much too soon, Malcolm was assassinated. His organization floundered and faded, and there was nothing to take its place. Reading Malcolm's autobiography and his works, I noted that he related heavily to self-defense, to human rights, and to elevating black people's struggle here to the international arena and the Third World. But Malcolm also related to reading and to checking things out for oneself. So, for the first time, I began to read everything that was available. Malcolm X, James Baldwin, Richard Wright, John O. Killens, LeRoi Jones, Calvin Hernton, W. E. B. Du Bois, and others.

BOB COLLIER: I was living in New York City's Lower East Side, an integrated slum. A community group had been formed by a VISTA worker, Richard X, to set up recreational facilities on the Lower East Side, and a committee found that there was a building in the neighborhood that had a swimming pool, a gym, and a theater, which hadn't been used for twenty-five years. We put on a series of demonstrations and negotiations, kept fighting, and finally the city agency that had been using some floors of the building moved out and we took over the whole building to develop a community-controlled unit. Needless to say the politicians were already behind the scenes, pitting one group against the other. I also found out that certain police officials were doing their best to provoke an incident that would get my parole revoked and discredit our whole attempt at setting up the community center.

I applied for a job in the Parks Department, and political hacks from Queens and from other agencies forced the mayor to deny me employment because I was Bob Collier—ex-convict and refugee from a political trial. They also disliked my repeated attempts to get the degree requirement for the position of Recreation Leader waived. Now the test for Parks Department Recreation Leader is simple bullshit, and any fool with an IQ of 85 can pass it, but you also have to have that little piece of paper. So many, many people with real ability and knowledge of kids and the communities they live in are denied these positions, while out-of-town hacks with B.A.s in their pockets sit around and read their newspapers on the job, and generally do nothing for the kids or the community.

In spite of all the harassment, Tompkins Square Community Center had built good rapport with the community by the end of 1967. From the very beginning, our center was different from other so-called community centers. There was no professional staff as such, there were not a lot of paid social workers telling the kids what and how to do things. The people made it; there were no outside agencies involved—either the people or the street kids did it themselves or it didn't get done. Those people ran the center, *really* ran it. They organized everything—dances, basketball, karate, security, office, bus trips—and helped to improve the center physically—painting, cleaning, rewiring, carpentering. We didn't need Ph.D.s or studies or observers to see what needed to be done.

But in 1968 things started happening—equipment was stolen, things were broken mysteriously. We knew the city must be behind it, but we didn't know exactly which agency. Later that year a fire started in the gymnasium, and we had to order the Fire Department. We saw them destroy equipment, food, and clothing while pretending to put out the fire. Later, evidence showed that the fire had only been in a small spot near the door, yet the firemen had broken out windows and frames and smashed up boxes of food all over the gym.

Not long after the fire, we started a community store—

free food and clothing for the people. We also cooperated with the people in making space available for meetings and English classes. Attempts were made to sabotage this by breaking into the rooms and destroying books, blackboards, and other equipment. The police regularly tried to intimidate some of the families of the kids who used to come to the center. They said that drugs were used and sold at the center. When they were confronted with this at a precinct-community council meeting, the pigs denied it.

In October, 1968, I was attacked and beaten, then arrested. There was feverish activity on the part of the police to get my parole revoked. The judge set a $10,-000 bail on me for a misdemeanor, but the grand jury refused to return an indictment. The D.A. had to go ahead on his own. (The case is still pending.)

In February, 1969, the police raided the community center at 1:30 A.M. to serve an eviction notice. After the raid a lot of material was destroyed and missing and we could only conclude that the pigs did it. Hundreds of gallons of paint disappeared, as well as electronic equipment given to us by Western Electric, to name just a few examples. The treasurer's records had also disappeared. The police tried to say that the workers at the center had stolen the equipment, but since only three of us were allowed in after the raid, and we had to sign for what we took, it hardly seems possible.

During the time I spent developing the community center, I had come to regard the theory of democracy and the practice of democracy as a contradiction. Dealing with different city agencies made me aware of the hypocrisy of elected officials and the dirty schemes they pulled on each other. People who tried to be honest within the corrupt system were crushed, and their faith and belief in the system was shattered. I felt that there must be some way for the people to control their own lives and have power to enforce whatever laws were just. An administration should be responsive to the needs of the people, and should be run by the direct participation of the members of society.

KUWASI BALAGOON: In New York, staying at my sister's place, I got on down with the tenants in the rent strike, joined the community council on housing, and started helping to organize other buildings, while doing volunteer work at Project Rescue. I soon found myself with a real purpose, doing things unselfishly and seeing direct results of it. That summer I continued to work under Mrs. Sims, until I got more experience and could teach and explain to others by having them follow me through by routine. When anti-poverty funds came in I got an apartment to myself. Spare time caught me at the Aruba Temple, the bookstores, and out in the neighborhood, or trying to hook up something with other community organizations. And then I met Devil Food. Wow! And fell in love and everything seemed OK. A blessing, new life, new love. And what I was doing with nothing before, I was doing now with a salary, was growing and felt complete.

I involved myself after a while with mostly one aspect of housing in our community: rats. Spent a lot of time as an understudy to Mr. Ratray at the Rescue Office in Brownsville, and on joint projects with Tony Sanchez in El Barrio.

Rats falling out of the ceilings giving old people heart attacks and biting children is common indeed. It's amazing how many babies are bitten by rats each year in Harlem alone—and you can't imagine the long-range physical and mental effect these bites have, how many young black and Puerto Rican children and adults are victims, and how many people stand guard all night, fearful that a rat will attack their children—and buy chicken and beef to place by the rat holes so the rats will be satisfied with that instead of human flesh.

Knowledge of this burned inside my head. The community council on housing and Jesse Gray's youth program mobilized around rats. We made posters, handed out leaflets, presented a play on it, organized tenants, and made and bought traps to combat the situation. We also demonstrated at the city's so-called Department of Housing—Housing Department creeps sabotaged Project Rescue, whose function was to get emergency repairs to tenants in slumlord apartments. We also demonstrated at OEO, the federal government's jive Office for Economic Opportunity.

Lyndon Baines Johnson sent a bill into Congress that was designed to eliminate the rat problem. That's the only hip thing I remember him doing, and that was laughed off the floor. Even L.B.J. himself said that the action of the congressmen was shameful. We thought they were slimy motherfuckers; we were smoking mad. We took our signs, posters, and a rat, jumped on a bus and went down to Washington to demonstrate at the Capitol. They didn't know we were coming and we didn't feel like walking around in circles in the hot sun when we got there so we walked right into the gallery of the House of Representatives, unrolled our posters and banners, brought our rat cage out from under cover, and started shouting about what was on our minds. The pigs came in to quiet us down and we nixed them off, then they systematically ushered the scared tyrant congressmen and the Boy and

Girl Scouts out, and then came back to us. They were openly shook up and stood around pulling their guns out on us and putting them back in their holsters. Then they picked Jesse Gray out as the spokesman and told him he was under arrest and began dragging him into the hallway—at which time we shouted, "If you arrest one of us, arrest us all," and moved on into the hallway. That was full of cops, and of us—mostly young adults and teenagers.

As they came at us we went to work with little ado, like the butcher, baker, and candlestick maker. I myself ramshacked six beering, baseball-watching fat farts, and most of us rumbled for a half hour, sending fifteen pigs to the hospital. I had a pile of pigs laying out on the floor when one grabbed me; I wrestled him down and began pounding the pig when four or five others grabbed me by my hands and feet and dragged me into an adjacent hallway. As the battle raged on, we were overpowered. Since I couldn't defend myself at that time, I played possum, but one pig hit me about four or five extra times anyway, and then stopped.

While I was lying in the hallway pretending to be knocked out, my sister fought through the barricade. Two pigs brought Bob in, trying to hold him while a detective tried to hit him with a blackjack, but as the pig got ready to swing, Bob kicked a field goal—as the pig grabbed his balls, the pig that had beat me the most and was standing over me waiting for me to move so he could beat me some more, turned around to help the others get Bob, and when he did I came to, jumped up, and body-slammed him, just crunched him in a corner. And the shit was on again.

After they handcuffed us and took us to the wagon, we looked out to see the shit was still going on. The brothers and sisters were fighting the pigs down the steps and all over the lawn. One man-and-wife team were battling at

least thirty of them. Pig Speaker of the House Mc-
Cormack yelled, "Get those niggers out of here!" and
turned and ran back into the building before anybody
could get to his old ass.

We stayed in the station house for about a half hour,
were charged as "disorderly persons," and were bailed
out. Feeling cleansed and sharp I went home to Lakeland
for a couple of days and shot back to New York and work.

Shortly after what the papers termed a mini-riot our
programs' funds were cut off, but since we had already
started a rent strike and couldn't leave people unprotected
and out on the limb, we continued. Also at that time I
joined the Central Harlem Committee for Self-Defense,
joined in educating the people of Harlem about the monster on the hill, Columbia University. We demonstrated
at Columbia and mobilized the community. My hands
were full. Those were days for stopping city marshals
from evicting tenants, notifying tenants of meetings, taking
complaints, and trying for and sometimes getting emergency repairs. The community council on housing's pockets were empty. Jesse Gray promised that we would get
some bread, but the promise never materialized, so we
pulled away from his leadership and continued on. All
that fall and winter Mrs. Jackson, Mr. Harold, Mrs. Sims,
Zontini Robinson and I drove on. And like the beautiful
thing was the way the people in the community accepted
us into their homes and heart.

LUMUMBA SHAKUR: Racial tension in Comstock
was intensified by the racial situations across America. In
the latter part of September, 1963, the bombing in Birmingham, Alabama that killed four black girls had a tremendous effect on the blacks in prisons. The Muslims and

the nationalists got together to formulate some means of action. We agreed that some brothers would ask to be assigned to shops and jobs that blacks were barred from, to confirm the fact that blacks always wanted to be in every professional shop or job in Comstock.

I asked for assignment to the bakery shop, and I was called for an interview by Deputy Warden Blow. Racist Blow said I knew the bakery shop is for white inmates only, so why did I ask to be put in the bake shop? I told Racist Blow, I've been in prisons for over three and a half years and never had an opportunity to learn a profession or trade so that I could get stable employment when I was released. Deputy Warden Blow told me that no black inmate would be allowed in any white-only shops or jobs. He said the racist traditional policies of Comstock would never change, and that was the best way for Comstock to function. All the brothers who had interviews with Deputy Warden Blow concerning reassignment to shops and jobs were told the same answer.

A couple of days later, the brothers got together. We said, white people don't respect anything but violence. The only way we are going to redress or change Comstock's racial situation is by violence—so let the shit hit the fan. On the last Friday in September in 1963, one of the most violent race riots that ever occurred in any New York State prison exploded.

The next day, everybody was locked in their cell all day and the correctional officers began beating brothers in their cells systematically. I was taken to Pig Blow's office. Warden Conboy was there and Pig McGinnis, the Commissioner of Correction, came from Albany to investigate the riot. Blow said that he saw me on the roof when his officer got thrown off. I told him he was lying —that if he had any evidence to prove what he said, take me to a court of law so I could stand trial for the charges. Then Racist Warden Conboy asked me what was my grievance against Comstock. I talked about the racism in Comstock for twenty minutes. I talked about how black inmates were treated as subhuman, how blacks were forbidden from attending professional shops, schools and trades, how blacks were forbidden from handling and serving food in the mess hall. Racist Blow said that blacks didn't ask for those jobs. I smiled. Racist Blow is a racist liar, I said, because I had an interview with Racist Blow last week about the bake shop. Racist Blow told his goon squad to get me. There were about fifteen correctional officers with baseball bats moving toward me. I grabbed a chair. Commissioner McGinnis told the goon squad to leave me alone, and I put down the chair. Commissioner McGinnis tried to pretend that he did not know that racism existed in Comstock. He said, "We will change the racial situation of Comstock." I told Commissioner McGinnis that he was a racist liar: I had been in Elmira, Woodbourne, and Comstock, all of which he was supposed to be the commissioner of, and all of them are racist institutions. Commissioner McGinnis told some officers to take me back to my cell but not beat on me. I was very surprised that I did not get beaten up. One cracker officer had tears in his eyes because he wanted to beat me so bad when he told me, "Walk first, nigger," and I told him, "Fuck you, cracker."

The next morning at 6:00 A.M. fourteen of us were shackled and handcuffed, while the pig deputy warden was telling us that we were being transferred to Attica Prison for organizing a riot in Comstock. I told Pig Blow that he knew that was a lie—if it wasn't, he would send us to a court outside to get some more years on our sentences —and that the prison conditions, the administration run by him and Conboy, organized the riot.

We found out later that the riot in Comstock was very successful. Many black inmates were assigned to every professional school, shop, trade and job in Comstock.

KWANDO KINSHASA: Now if I remember correctly, around the years 1965 to 1968 the word "revolution" was becoming very popular among many so-called political organizations that professed to be working for the interest of the black and oppressed people in this country. But as Malcolm X once stated, "If you knew anything about revolution, you'd jump back in the alley," and as the cops began to react from the verbal callers for revolution, many brothers did just that, they jumped back into the alley, and in fact they became non-existent. I remember clearly checking out several organizations who professed to be dealing with the man, and to my growing sadness, they all seemed to be involved in the bad situation of murder-mouthing. Their programs, if they had any, were based on the financial support—believe it or not—of the American government. Some of these organizations went so far as to ask for funds from private capitalistic enterprises such as the Ford Foundation. To me this was not only the height of hypocrisy, but the very essence and seed of treason. Government funds do not strengthen the people's forces or will; instead, they foster dependency, and stagnation of thought and action leading to a more entrenched, reactionary society, instead of a dynamic, socialistic, revolutionary society.

RICHARD HARRIS: In Newark, the brothers and I stuck to the Black Man's Liberation Army—we were unorganized, so we straggled, but we kept in touch. We met frequently, to take care of certain things, legal and illegal.

At the time of the Newark Rebellion there were, I think, six different loosely organized sections of the Black Man's Liberation Army.

Directly after the rebellion, brothers were getting busted right and left, and none left the courts and returned to the streets. We didn't see what was happening until it was critical—the pigs were getting rid of all that seemed any serious threat to them.

LUMUMBA SHAKUR: In December 1964—after five years in prisons and about three weeks before my twenty-second birthday—I was released from prison with $22. I had already plotted my course of direction. I had read that Malcolm X had split from the Nation of Islam and organized the OAAU, which would emphasize black nationalism instead of religion. I could relate to black nationalism instantly because I had a problem relating to religion. I always related to Islam culturally. So I knew I would join the Organization for Afro-American Unity.

The first thing I wanted to do was make love to a woman, and then I wanted to go talk to the brothers on the block and find out what was happening. But the brothers and sisters on the block scared me, because they were talking about the same things they'd been talking about when I left them five years ago, and because now there was more dope in the community. Brothers in prison were more politically conscious than brothers and sisters on the block. I was talking to brothers and sisters about nationalism and they would look at me like I went crazy in prison. This was December, 1964, and January, 1965.

My father took me to join the OAAU. You could see that the OAAU was just trying to get off the ground. The concrete programs of OAAU were never manifested in the black communities. Malcolm X was murdered because the pig power structure didn't want Malcolm X to develop and manifest the OAAU in the black communities.

When Malcolm X was assassinated, two so-called brothers of the leadership of OAAU ran like punks, namely, James Shabazz and Benjamin X. A brother who was an OAAU official in Detroit was murdered a few days after Malcolm X. In my opinion, Malcolm X's sister, Ella Collins, assumed the leadership of the OAAU because the so-called men among the leadership ran like punks.

I finally got in touch with Sekou again in about April, 1965. We got together and smoked some reefer. He joined the OAAU too, and we both agreed that we will always be activists in the struggle for liberation of black people. Then around this time, male chauvinism began to manifest itself in the OAAU. Brothers began to get hang-ups about following a woman, Sister Ella Collins. This way of thinking stopped the OAAU programs from getting into the black communities.

In 1966-67, Sekou and I investigated every black nationalist group in New York City. We found out that nobody was moving in the direction that Malcolm X was.

We got together with some nationalists in Jamaica, Queens, and organized the Grass Root Front. Our aim was to take the anti-poverty programs from the hands of the religious pimps and preachers and guarantee the grass-root people control of the anti-poverty programs. When the community people began to get more control of the anti-poverty programs, the religious pimp-preachers called OEO and the pigs. It was a split within the Grass Root Front because Sekou, Larry Mack, and I wanted to inflict a political consequence. The other brothers did not agree with us. So we quit and told them that they were jiving. Next the pork-chop-religious-pimp-preachers used the OEO and the pigs to get control of the anti-poverty programs in Jamaica again.

part 10

KWANDO KINSHASA: Becoming a revolutionary is not a matter of theory or words, but action; and it is not a decision made in one quick jump, but the result of a long, slow, process of growth. The nine years that led up to my entrance into the Black Panther Party were years of constant involvement and education in the struggle of the oppressed against the oppressor—this, of course, does not mean that I knew nine years ago that my commitment to the revolutionary struggle in this country would be total.

KUWASI BALAGOON: It had long occurred to me that the American government had the resources to reconstruct all the slums within its confines, if it had the will, and that working as I did as paid opposition was only a sham, making black people believe that things were getting better. Proof of that was the community council on housing funds' being cut off when we were doing all we could. I had seen that the judges in Slumlords and Tenants Court* were on the side of the

---

* Landlords and Tenants Court, part of New York City's civil court.

slumlords from the jump; and I found out early that a black man in criminal court was doomed. I saw firsthand that the Brooklyn House of Detention was full of nothing but brothers and Latin brothers. The Queens 17 frame-up made my stomach turn. So I knew that all court bullshit was out.

I also dug how the city government and the creep teachers' union tried to put a school in Brownsville, Brooklyn, out of action, taking control of the school away from the people in the area. I knew regardless of American propaganda that the Korean people had run across the 58th parallel, and that the Vietnamese people were putting something on the real Charlie's ass. A lot of things totalled in my mind, mostly that this society puts property before people, some sick motherfuckers are at the controls, and the very fate of humanity is at stake.

Now just this knowledge and no knowledge of how to deal with this shit has driven a lot of people crazy.

Rap Brown influenced me more than anybody except for Malcolm. And by that time I'd read Robert Williams' book, *Negroes with Guns*, and *The Crusaders*, which I studied, along with Mao's Red Book.

I decided that I wasn't doing enough. And I decided what I would be doing for the rest of my life.

When I heard that Huey Newton had been involved in a shootout with two pigs and one had died, I thought I'd check this brother out, as he seemed to be a sure-enough leader. And when the Panthers came to New York, I checked them out, and found the ten-point program unquestionable, and the fact that it was community-based a good thing. Digging that the cadre believed that political power stems from the barrel of a gun made me feel instant kinship. So I joined, and extended my energies and skills to the black community and mankind through the Party.

Since then I've been captured by the pigs, but have studied and acted to become a better man and a better revolutionary. I long to be on the streets with my people, and elevate the struggle to a higher level, and do whatever is necessary to bring this disgraceful period to an end.

ALI BEY HASSAN: It didn't take me long to discover that conditions in Harlem were worse, if that is possible, than conditions in Newark. There was nowhere to run and nowhere to live. Then one day in June, 1968, when I was down and out on 125th Street—a day like every other day—I heard Chairman Bobby Seale speak. And everything the brother was saying was what I was feeling, not just for myself but for the people.

I said to myself, Ali, your running days are over. And so I joined the Party, and began to learn about its programs, and about the revolutionary movements in different countries. About the constant struggle for self-determination that is being waged by Third World people not just here but all over the world. About imperialism—the U.S. and its lackeys—which serves the needs only of the ruling class. But the Party was not just talk. I attended community meetings about welfare, school conditions, housing, hospitals, found out from the people what their needs were, and brought the information back to the Party. We would study the information, and then bring our answers back to the people, attempting to help them in their struggles against such things as the welfare cuts and the racist United Federation of Teachers. And the people were moving with us, in the right direction. Naturally the people, and especially organizers like the Black Panther Party, had to be stopped.

My joining the Black Panther Party was a natural result of my past experiences. It is impossible for a black man not to notice that black people still live under the rotten conditions they have always lived under. Modern technology has improved certain people's lives, but this technology is still only for the few. Black people are the constant victims of racism—in the schools, the streets, on the job, in the service. Living in the ghetto, it is impossible *not* to notice the conditions and the racism; what is difficult is to find a way of resolving the contradictions that black people are faced with daily.

KATARA: It was while I was a junior in high school that due to economic difficulties I was prompted to seek employment (my Pops told me to get a fucking job or get out). Which came in the form of an anti-poverty program run by Haryou, I think. We were to have tutoring classes after the school day, and get taught how to fix computers. Well, the change was good so I stayed on that. I had been going to a lot of rallies around this time, and one day I heard on WWRL radio that Sonny Carson was renovating a church to turn it into a black-studies school. The announcement was a call for help from the community, for workers. I was out the door as soon as the address was given. We were knocking out the wall with sledge hammers for the rest of the day. At around the time we broke for lunch, about four or five brothers and sisters rolled in. That was my first encounter with the Black Panther Party.

I rapped on the bloods for a while, then we had to get

back to work. When we finished, they had left. I tried to find out where the Party office was, but had no luck.

One day at the tutoring session a brother told me there was a Party chapter in Harlem, and gave me an address of where it was supposed to be at. I arrived and no one was there, so I hung around until somebody came to the house. About an hour later, a brother in African clothes and a conk rolled up and read a note on the door and walked away. I guess he fitted my idea of a Panther, so I walked up to him and asked if he was going to the meeting. He said yeah, so I tagged along.

We finally got to the apartment. Inside were about five men and three women. We were late for the meeting, and they were already rapping about business. It seems everybody was giving reports about a rent strike that was going on. I sat and dug on everything that was going down, and it was hip, but they kept on using one word I didn't understand: "pig." The meeting was going beautifully, somebody even asked me what I thought about improving the rent strike. When I gave my opinion, it was written down.

At about 9:00 P.M. the meeting broke up and everybody started to file out. I hung around and a brother noticed me. We started rapping, and he asked me what section I was in. I told him I wasn't even in the Party, so he asked me if I wanted to join and I said, hell yes. After I signed up, I asked the brother if he knew what a pig was. Man, he looked at me as if I asked him what earth was. After he finished running it down, I was souped up for a motherfucker. I left the house saying "pig" over and over again. I got on a bus and everybody must have thought I was bugged out, because all the way home I just kept on saying "pig," because the way the brother ran it down, it fit perfectly.

We had meetings every week, twice a week. The third meeting I went to, we had to look for an office. All the next week everybody was looking all over Harlem for an office big enough for us. While we were looking for it, we were still organizing.

One day we had a rally on 117th Street to tell the rest of the people about the rent strike. There we were, seven of us in all-black, but we only had about seventy-five leaflets, so we spread out and started giving them out. After about half an hour, we went downstairs and stood in the middle of the street with a bullhorn and started rapping. It was a summer day, the heat was dry and almost oppressing. Bloods were hanging on the street playing cards, rapping with sisters, or just bullshitting the day away. So we jumped into the middle of the street and started rapping.

After about ten seconds, it was apparent that nobody was listening to us, so we started speaking louder. When nobody moved, we got the idea and started going about the stoops rapping to the people. At about this time, a loud crash came from up the street. Everybody came running up to see what had happened. Now if you live in Harlem you know about those Trailways buses that come zooming by, and you can dig what happened: a bus full of white-middle-class, blue-collar, God-and-country "citizens" had come speeding through trying to get out of "native" turf to the comfort of their suburban duplexes, and had crashed into a black, lumpen, dirty-collared, gypsy cab, and almost crushed it. As if on cue, the windows on the bus closed and the windows on the block opened. The people were mad as a motherfucker. Nobody had come out of the bus to see if the cabdriver was alive or dead, and the bus driver was looking like he was disgusted to have to be there.

A couple of young bloods started shouting about turning the mother over and burning it, and some bloods split as if they were going to put it into action. So we started telling the people that that wouldn't do anything because there would be more buses, that the way to fight that shit was we had to organize and get control of our communities so we could stop shit like this from happening.

Most of the people stopped and started digging on what we were saying. When most of the people were digging on us, we moved down the block and ran the rent strike down. That was the first rally, or anything organized, that I had participated in with the Party, and it came off "right on."

We had got an office by that time, a used-to-be beauty shop, and it had about seven linoleum rugs on the floor, so we dug in and started ripping them up, which took up most of our time. I'd come in every day after school and start working. Sometimes a strange brother or sister would stop in the office and start rapping and in a couple of minutes we'd both be on our knees ripping up the linoleum and painting the office. Even though the office was still a shambles, we still had to organize the people, so we'd be ripping rugs and painting when people would start coming in for the political education class we had twice a week. So we'd stop and pick up books and start rapping. When the class was over, we'd finish up and lock up the office and sell papers and rap to the people in the bars.

The cops had escalated their attacks on the Party and had busted the then-captain of the New York chapter, Joudon Ford, and there was to be a rally for his support at the courthouse, in Brooklyn. When we got there the place was surrounded by pigs. About fifteen of us were in uniform and went upstairs to the courtroom. When we got upstairs there were about 250 civilian-clothes cops up there, wall-to-wall pork chops. Later we found out they belonged to LEG (Law Enforcement Group), the local right-wing fascists. When we were able to get to the courtroom, it was packed pig to the left, right, front, and back. The cops in back of us were trying to start something by poking us in the back with their nightsticks. We weren't fools, and were completely outnumbered, so when the hearing was over, we started to move out. When we got out in the hall, the cops started like they were going to roll on us but stopped short and settled for cursing us out for a while. "White tigers eat black panthers" was the chant of the day.

We were about to get on the elevator to cut out when the eager God-and-country pigs that were in the back started shouting, "They're getting away, get them fucking bastards," and they got us—I must admit, we got a thorough ass wiping, but four or five pigs paid for it. Funny thing, while the plainclothes pigs were vamping, the ones in uniform were dropping their nightsticks so they could use them against us. The pigs came up to this one cop, black, to grab his club, and he wouldn't let go and in fact started swinging out. The last time I saw him he was going down, with about five plainclothesmen on his ass, but he was still swinging out.

We were finally able to get into the elevator, but there were pigs upstairs pushing the elevator buttons, so we went up instead of down, but we pushed the button fast, fast, fast when we saw that the pigs were up there too. The then-chairman of the New York chapter decided to call the mayor's office. It seemed that everyone had picked that time to be out to lunch—Human Rights Commission, borough presidents, city councilmen, everybody was out to lunch. So we hopped into this courtroom and asked this old pig judge to give a helping hand.

He didn't dig having ten bloody Panthers in his court and told us to leave. We told him we were staying until he did something about those wild, foaming-at-the-mouth boars downstairs. Eventually the dude got up a court guard to take us downstairs in a back elevator.

When we got outside, the pigs had beaten us to it and were waiting for us, so we had to split up and the chase was on. The pigs had stationed themselves at the subway and bus stops and were laying for us. Me and another brother who had got hit kind of bad split four stops downtown to go uptown, and had taken off our shirts and berets. It was lucky we did, because two stops later, about twenty pigs that had been up at the courthouse came bopping through the car looking for us, so we went into our nodding-boy.

When we got to Harlem, the brother went to the office to report what had happened and I went to WLIB and the *Amsterdam News*. I spent a whole hour rapping at the Dam* on what happened, and when the paper came out they had about four lines on the "alleged attack." WLIB gave good coverage.

I was still going to Franklin High School and had become the president of the Afro-American history club. We would meet after school and show films and have rap sessions. We put a poster up in the main lobby of three different stages of the struggle. The principal told us we'd have to take it down because it didn't show both sides of the story. The poster showed a sister being beaten by a

---

* The Dam is short for the *Amsterdam News* because it's so damn fucked up.

cop, Bull Connor and his dogs. The second phase was pictures of SNCC, and the third was pictures of members of the Black Panther Party. One was a snap of Kathleen Cleaver with a shotgun in her hand. The dude said that was a violent scene and had to be taken out.

We pointed out that the news media shows nothing but the so-called other side, and that our history book had more violent scenes than a black woman with a gun in her hand. We got word that the UFT teachers were talking about walking back out unless the poster was taken down, and a few days later, Mr. Hunter's tires were slashed.

On February 22 at the Party office we had a tribute to Malcolm X. We had a mike hooked up to a record player and were playing records of his speeches and commenting on them and essays of Huey P. Newton, broadcasting to the street. I had just changed a record when this car pulled to a dead stop in the middle of the street out front and these two white dudes jumped out with guns in their hands. The shit fucked me up for a few seconds, then I called to everybody in the office. I was almost out the door when one brother told me to stay at the mike and blow down what was happening. About five brothers went outside to see what the fuck they were doing. The pigs had grabbed a brother and were about to jack him up when the bloods got there. They righteously told the pigs to round on the brother and asked the pigs what the fuck did they think they were doing. Now to get the picture of the pig courage, you have to picture the scene: high noon, on the corner of 121st Street, two pigs, one with a .357 magnum, the other with a .38, grabbing two black men, surrounded by five Black Panthers—and the pigs were scared shitless. The pigs started talking all that shit about they weren't going to hurt them, etc., so the brothers asked them why they had their guns out—and what was he doing with a .357, because .38 was the standard arm for New York City pigs. After a couple of minutes they decided the people were greater than their technology and split.

Brother Abdul decided that he and I should file a complaint at the precinct, so we bopped over there. When we started out of the office the people made it quite clear that they weren't going to let us walk into that pen and get our asses kicked; outside was what looked like an army of junkies, pushers, street sisters, everybody. It was mind-blowing to see strung-out brothers stop nodding and grab bottles, sticks, anything, just to have our back covered. It really fucked me up to see the same brothers that were a few seconds ago afraid to even speak to those pigs now readying up to roll on them suckers with their ragamuffin armory. Like it's one thing when you're rapping about the people moving as a body, but when you see it it's like a natural high. Abdul told the people we were just going to lodge a complaint, but they didn't want to hear it; the people gave us a ten-minute deadline and said if we weren't out by then they were going to storm the motherfuckers and free us—and they were serious as cancer, so we told them, right on. When we got to the precinct there were some pigs laying outside trying to block us from coming in, but we got in. At that time they had a nigger named Hill who was trying to mucho himself off on the people as a good pig and was in charge of the precinct.

It looked like every pig in the place came out of nowhere when we came in. I guess they thought we were a Kamikaze team or something, because they came out of nowhere and were about to vamp when this captain told them to get back to what they were doing. Some of those pigs got so mad it looked like somebody had turned on a red light in there.

Hill was somewhere so this captain took us into Hill's office and told us he'd call him. Just about every pig decided then that they had to go through Hill's office to get where they were going—so to counteract that shit we started walking around and checking out the books in the office, listening to his radio, acting like we were taking notes, etc. That shit really burned them up so that captain closed the door.

Hill came in a couple of minutes and we told him what happened and he gave us some jive shit about he'd look into it, so when we were leaving all the white pigs that wanted us so bad were outside in the hall, so we turned around and said, "All power to the people, Brother Hill." That fool was playing his game of being with the people for so long he forgot himself and raised his fist to give the power sign. He tried to catch himself, but it was too late. Boy that red light went on again and we just "right on, Brother Hill" and "keep on keeping on, Brother Hill" our way out of there.

When we came out the people started shouting and cheering and we told them what had happened and they said, right on.

At that time we were helping the Welfare Rights Organization brothers and sisters at the 125th Street office and a group of tenants that had taken over a building on 147th Street. One day a sister from PS 119 called and said they wanted us to come over and check out what was happening over there.

The parents and teachers were protesting the fact that they wanted the assistant vice principal to be named principal, and the Board of Education didn't want to go for it, so the parents and teachers were going to close the school and occupy it. They wanted Party members to guard against anything being stolen so the pigs couldn't blame it on them.

We helped the sisters secure the building and stayed to make sure if the pigs vamped, they wouldn't be alone. When the pigs came out they came in force, and were about to break in when I guess they got orders from up top not to. Lo and behold, who should show up to try and talk the sisters out but old Inspector Hill himself. There were about three white captains around him and I was sitting in a chair close to the window, so I slid up to the window and poked my head right in his mug, and yelled, "Power, Brother Hill! Why don't you get those other pigs out of here?" It took a lot to force myself to call that boot-licker "brother," but the way the cops around reacted to it was worth it. They looked like they were going to have a shootout right there, I mean pure, virgin, intense hate was on their mugs and all of it was aimed at Hill. He hurried up and split fast, fast, fast. While the pigs were busting in the front door we made it out the side door and stood there watching them. When the people in the community saw us they started to shout and stuff, and the pigs just stood there mad as hell.

Just before the April bust we received a call from a sister at this school on 114th Street, about the vice principal beating up kids, and a little "black Mafia" of older kids roughing up the younger ones and taking their money. We almost had to patrol the place for a while, but the sister got hold of the ringleaders and we put the fear of God on and told them how dumb that shit was and they cooled it out and in fact started coming around the office asking if they could sell papers. As for the vice principal, after a couple of hours of political education, he cooled that shit out.

Around the middle of March, 1969, we had the basic outline of the breakfast program and were collecting names and addresses of stores and groups to get down on it with us. Then on April 2, at 5:00 A.M., the gestapo tactics of D.A. Hogan's Special Services pigs—dig it, S.S.*— put a halt to it. But not for long—because those who were still on the street took up where we left off, as it shall always be. You can jail a revolutionary but you can't jail a revolution.

CURTIS POWELL: In August, 1968, I arrived in Babylon with my Ph.D. ready and eager to get into the struggle. The time was right, I felt, and our people were ready. I stayed with my mother in New Jersey until October, when I got a pad on the Lower East Side again. I got a gig at Columbia College of Physicians and Surgeons, Institute of Cancer Research, Francis Delafield Hospital. With a Ph.D., I had a wide latitude. I could work my own hours.

I started checking out the organizations. Around October I started working with SNCC; but they weren't going far: there was something missing.

At about this time, the pigs attacked the Panthers in a Brooklyn courthouse. I started checking the Panthers out, and they looked pretty cool. But I checked carefully; I did not join until January, 1969.

I joined the Party because I am a revolutionist—an active revolutionist. I am oriented toward that. My people call. The revolution calls—and its pulsebeat is my own. I know the theory, and I also know that theory that is not

---

* The official new title is Bureau of Special Services, abbreviated in the *New York Times* as BOSS.

put into practice becomes dreams. Look at the situation in racist America! The only answer is revolutionary action with the right revolutionary, political ideology. The Black Panther Party is the closest to that ideal. The spirit of the Black Panther Party is not new, but it was put into a modern, relevant perspective. Like Malcolm put it into words, Fanon put it on paper, and the Party put it into action.

Revolution is never just the idea or wishes of a few, but a remedy—a bitter remedy—to a situation that has no other solution. The American dream is a nightmare for the whole world. It is built on slavery and force and racism and legalized grand larceny and fascism. It cannot survive—and it cannot continue. We, as black people, have done everything we could short of revolution—yet the same plight continues still in 1971. I could go on for days, but it would only be patterns on the same theme. Given the present condition, if I were Chinese—I would have been with Mao; if I were Cuban—I would have been with Fidel; if I were Vietnamese—I would have been in the NLF; I am an African American—I am a Black Panther.

It was beautiful. We worked on problems like community control of schools and hospitals, and welfare problems. I did some work in security, too. I found one FBI pig who had infiltrated—a slimy cat. I took all the data on this pig and sent it to national headquarters so that we could expose him—now he will be a "witness" against us in our trial as a "co-conspirator." Dig that: an FBI pig infiltrator that hardly anybody knew, whom I met while investigating him, is a "co-conspirator" in a case against us! It's all completely insane.

The Party was beautiful. Our attitudes were the same. We were tired sick of racism, of exploitation, of slavery, of oppression, and we were getting together and getting our people together, to unite so that we could begin to change our situation. I was getting about three hours' sleep a night, but I had never been so happy. The dedication and commitment were tremendous. There was a swelling sense of coming accomplishment.

SHABA OM: It was just a little while ago that I started putting myself together. I've gone through a lot of changes; the big change that came out of all those little ones, that the little ones were leading me toward, is joining the Black Panther Party.

I had been into a very jive black nationalist bag. I'd dug on jive dudes like LeRoi Jones. Most of the foxes I'd begun to relate to wore their hair natural, I'd started wearing African clothing, the things that made up a jive black nationalist at that time. I say "jive" because I was still doing the same thing in the streets—the only difference was I looked and talked black, that was all. I went to my slave only if I wanted to, not if I didn't.

I became very interested in black nationalism and decided to break into a new world. I stopped hustling skag; I dug it was killing my sisters and brothers. I tried to stop pimping but it was very, very hard—still, over a period of time I stopped that too. I was trying to get myself together in the righteous way, stop jiving in the streets and begin to help my people. After my day at slave was over, I'd come into my pad, dig on some jazz like Charles Lloyd and the late Honorable John Coltrane, because something about their music makes you think heavy about life and yourself. I'd like come in and not answer the door for anyone at all, burn myself some smokes, get nice, and just think. I'd always think about what I was doing in the street. I knew what I was doing to my people was wrong as hell, to myself and my people alike.

One of the main things that really made me dig my true self in life was, one day at slave I was walking down the streets in midtown Manhattan and saw this magazine called *Ramparts*, and Black Panthers were on the cover of the magazine. I'd heard about the Blank Panther Party before, so I bought a copy of *Ramparts* and began reading it—and man these dudes are together and as crazy as hell. The more I learned about the Party the more it excited me. I read in *Ramparts* about the time Chairman Bobby Seale, Little Bobby Hutton, and other sisters and brothers went to the capital of fascist California to deliver a message written by the Minister of Defense of the Black Panther Party, Huey P. Newton: Executive Mandate #1, telling all black people to arm themselves against racist pigs. There are very important things in there—please read it sometime: Executive Mandate #1.

The day came when I met a man selling *The Black Panther*, the paper. I went wild in my pad reading that. The brother I bought the paper from told me to come to the meeting that night at 2026 Seventh Avenue, and I really dug it.

I began to go to political education classes—but I was still hung up in the bag of pimping. What really got me out of that madness was political education, me digging on my true self as a black man, and the Honorable John Coltrane's music. I dug what I was doing to my people and myself. In September, 1968, I had got myself together and stopped jiving. Began to go to political education classes every night after slave. After political education classes I would go to my pad to try and hide from the jive niggers I knew.

It was past time for the true me to come forward and

correct the wrong I'd done. I knew all the madness I was doing in the streets was wrong as two right shoes, dig, because I went through the Black Muslim movement, the black nationalist bag—the only thing left was to become a true helper and servant of my beautiful people. What also made me dig myself was my childhood in the South. And then this sister I was relating to as my main love died from skag. Man like this blew my mind, because she had quit skag once, and come to me for help because she dug me and my way of thinking—and I turned my back on her; this really blew my mind when she died. I was going to political education classes then, too, when she died. The first thing that came into my mind was, I helped the pigs kill one of my sisters.

This is when I really became a Black Panther, warrior of my people. I began to dig how the system uses us to brutalize and murder black, poor, oppressed people.

When the pigs saw I was not going to be a slave any longer, not going to exploit my people any longer—when they saw me become a warrior of my people, a Black Panther, the racist fascist pigs vamped on me and my Panther sisters and brothers for helping our people.

When I was an exploiter and slave my name was Lee Roper. After I dug where this fascist, imperialist nation is at—after I was spending my time working to help my people in the hospitals, schools, welfare centers, housing programs—I just couldn't relate at all to the name that the slave master put on me from birth. I dug to have a true name come into being along with my true self. The Muslim movement helped me gain knowledge of my true being as a black man, self-respect; that is where Shaba comes from, the Black Muslim part of my life. From the black nationalist part of life came Ogun, which means warlord. Also I dug music; my main thing is jazz; the late

Honorable John Coltrane made a record titled "Om." I would put it on after slave, after political education, everything, because it is the best recording I ever heard in my life. I played it and dug on what he was saying about the essence of the universe, the spirit that sets all things into being. I dug this: people are the spirits that will set the revolution into being.

AFENI SHAKUR: After Sandra died, I just wandered, you know. I graduated from smoke and cocaine to acid— used to trip about once every week or two. I went to some demonstrations and rallies, and I was reading some in the underground, black, and left magazines, and for a while, I went to peace demonstrations and be-ins with the hippies. I found dudes to take care of me, and I just wandered around.

It wasn't too long after that, early in 1967, when I saw Bobby. I was walking down 125th Street and got to Seventh Avenue and saw the same old crowd, a lot of people standing around listening to somebody on the box. Now 125th Street and Seventh Avenue is the corner where everybody and his brother has to make at least one speech in his lifetime. Marcus Garvey, Malcolm, Kenyatta, all of them have used that corner as a meeting hall. There is never a Saturday that doesn't find at least a small crowd gathered there.

But it was different. The people listening were a mixture of people, it wasn't just cultural nationalists, the people dressed in dashikis, but it was niggers with processes too, and hustlers—I mean everybody was standing listening.

Up on a wooden platform was this little cute nigger. There were other cats on the platform: each one of them, including the little nigger, was dressed in black from head to foot, and they stood on either side of the little dude like they were soldiers or something. I found out from the people near me that the little dude was Bobby Seale—Chairman of the Black Panther Party. I don't remember much of what Bobby said that day, but I do remember him saying that the Black Panther Party didn't care whether you wore your hair processed or nappy or wigged. He said there were Panthers with processes (can you imagine?), Panthers with wigs, and they were some of the baddest niggers in the world. I knew he was right, because even though I didn't know anything about the Black Panther Party, I knew I had more respect for them than I had for all the organizations in the world. I *knew* they had heart. According to Bobby's speech, a chapter of the Party had just been started in New York and in another month or so, an office was scheduled to open on Seventh Avenue. Membership would be open then.

And everybody standing there listening seemed to love Brother Bobby. I didn't know anything else about it, I didn't know who he was. But some time after that, I read an old newspaper about the Sacramento thing. I didn't read it when it happened; I found out about it after it happened. What impressed me at that time was a line that said a policeman had put his hand on one brother's gun and he said, "Am I under arrest?" "No." "Then take your hands off my motherfucking gun. I have a constitutional right to have this gun." I mean in 1967 that in itself was enough to blow anybody's mind.

All I did then was wait for the Black Panther Party to come to New York. Somebody told me they were coming; you know, I knew they just *had* to come, they just couldn't stay on the Coast, I just couldn't relate to that. Nothing that strong could stay in one area. I just knew from the beginning that it would branch out into something beautiful—it had to. I just knew there were niggers all over the place that felt like I did.

The Party got here around April. Bobby came to organize, to get some people to organize or something like that. I can't remember what it was, because I never knew, I guess. But I know that after Bobby left, these people were walking around and they were concerned as I was, but they knew what to do, because they'd been in other organizations before. They started getting people together. I found out later that it was Ali that was doing it, and some more brothers. Ali and Dharuba and some others —all those brothers were around then.

I think it was August when I found out that they were having a rally in Mount Morris Park in Harlem. Eldridge was there. Somebody told me that I should go hear him. I wouldn't have known about it if somebody hadn't told me to go, because just to know the man's name, Eldridge Cleaver, didn't tell me who the hell he was. But when I heard him it was the same thing—it was like that was the dope, man. I mean, on top of listening to all of this, I would still be confronted with these dudes that were walking around there taking care of the crowd, and they were *brothers*—they were concerned about the people that were in the audience. They were concerned about something happening to them. I couldn't understand all this danger—I couldn't imagine all that much danger, I couldn't see it, but they were concerned about it, and they were serious about what they were doing. And there were just so many people that said so many things that made so much sense, you know. They told you about love. It was just something different, it wasn't like that same old thing that I'd heard and dismissed. It was different, because they were talking about fighting at the same time that they were talking about things that were relevant to me right now. I just had to relate to it. Eldridge dared people, he just said I dare you to go to the political education class tomorrow, PE, and join the Black Panther Party. And I went. And I just never left. I just can't see leaving, because I know that this is what has done it for me.

It's like, all of the things that I used to do against my people or against people or against humanity, all of those traits that I had that I know are incorrect, they've been turned around and I just don't use them against the people any more. I could use them against the enemy.

I know that basically I'm a very fucked-up person. I'm not a very good person, I'm not pure and loving like a lot of people are that I know. A lot of revolutionaries that I know are. I'm not great, I'm none of those things. All I am is an ex-Disciple. But I'm able now to use the things that I had when I was a Disciple, the desire to survive, you know. I'm able to use that desire in a manner that has nothing to do with just having fun and cutting somebody. It has to do with something greater than that. It has so much to do with this that I know that when the Party tells me that I cannot, I shall not, I could not, it's not correct to do anything physically to anybody right now, then I won't do it. I mean that has to come from respect because I know that I've always been impetuous enough to feel nothing at smacking people. It's all I can do in court now to not smack Phillips—sometimes he says things and all I want to do is smack him. But I'll transform it: I won't smack him, I'll just look at him very hard. I still have that same desire to jump up and hit him in the face. I just don't like him. The shit he does is incorrect and I still want to do that same old gang-style shit of striking back, impetuously, with everything I have without thinking, but that's not what the Black Panther Party is about. Man, it's about stopping the source of that evil, that whole evil, not half of it or part of it, but the very root of the evil so that it never comes back any more. So it's never there again. It's all over. You can live now, you can walk down the street and you can run through some grass and you can eat apples off the ground. I mean that's beautiful. That's basically what it is. We're all here for different reasons, but that's why I'm here in the Black Panther Party. I just like the feeling of looking forward to something like that, knowing that I'm helping to make that possible. I don't understand things like Huey does, you know, I'm not a Huey P. Newton or an Erica or a Kathleen. I'm just a little pebble. I'm a shit, a nothing. But I want some things to happen. And I love them; it's just good; it's just very good.

When I walked into the door to that Panther class—it was really amazing how you got into the Party at that time. It was just so easy, all you had to do, you went to the PE, like I went there and Joudon Ford—the Deputy Minister of Defense in New York then—was chairing the meeting. In the middle of it he said, "How many people in here are Panthers or plan to become Panthers?" And I raised my hand and I was a Panther. It was really that simple, you know. All of a sudden I was a Panther. He introduced me to the person who'd be my section leader, Sekou, one of the 21 who's now terribly terribly free in Algeria. They told me to come to the office at eight o'clock that night and I went. When I got to the desk, the person that was on the desk didn't want to let me in the meeting. And Sekou looked back and Sekou told them that I was a Panther. That was really funny—curious—

but that's where our minds were at then. We really didn't know what we were protecting ourselves against too much.

When I met Sekou and Lumumba it was the first time in my life that I ever met men who didn't abuse women. As simple as that. It had nothing to do with anything about political movements. It was just that never in my life had I met men who didn't abuse women, and who loved women because they were women and because they were people. They used to help me a lot because I used to sit around and they knew that I had what I thought then were important problems, with my family and stuff like that. They shouldn't have been problems but they were to me because I was so totally fucked up. Sekou would help me to understand my mother. Things like that. Like he would sit down and tell me about how my mother was the people. It wasn't abstract; he told me it was impossible for me to mistreat my mother and say that I loved the people. I mean, he would do that for me when I did something, like I would come to him with all my problems, you know, and he would just sit down patiently in the middle of my giddiness and say something as simple as that. He was sincere about what he was saying. He was just such a beautiful person. He didn't talk much: when he said something to you, it was just good. Sekou wasn't a rhetorician or somebody who knew all the theories, all he knew about was the basic love, and what you do when you love somebody, which is really what all deep feelings are about, anyway. He said everything springs forth from that. He was the most pure person I ever met in my life. That's one of the things that put me so uptight when he started getting busted. He and Lumumba—when they got busted they were branded as arch criminals. I just couldn't understand why they were being called all those names because you remember, I don't have any politics, I'm not in the Party out of political awareness. I couldn't relate to why they would be called all those names or why they would have manhunts and all that nonsense. It's something else.

Anyway, at some point, Lumumba became my husband. He had a wife, and he was very deep into a cultural thing—he asked me to be his second wife and I didn't care because I don't think I ever cared about being an only woman. I never would give that much of my time to any one man anyway. It was a very welcome thing to me.

Lumumba and Sekou got busted in November, 1968. First Sekou got busted for some kind of robbery or some old nonsense and he was supposed to go to court the next day. Lumumba is a very loyal person. I mean there was just nothing you could say to him to convince him that he shouldn't go to that Connecticut court to see Sekou. He did go and he never got to court because when they got to a red light or something they put him in jail too—for the same robbery, I believe. Or for some old nonsense. A shotgun, that's what it was. A shotgun that they said was in the car. Anyhow, Lumumba and Sekou were in jail and Cet and Dharuba and I were left alone to try and carry on the leadership. I didn't have any leadership ability because I'm just not a brilliant person but they did, you know, and every time I'd tell them that I shouldn't be in any position like that, they would just look at me and tell me there's nobody else to do it. That's how they justified it. Really something. Anyway, they made me section leader or some old nonsense. Yeah, I was section leader. But I was very happy to tell my husband that I had made some progress in the Party. I was very glad to tell him that when I went to visit him in jail.

Lumumba got out the 30th of December, or the last day of December, he got out of jail. The next to the last day? One of those days he got out of jail. But he went back to jail on January 17th. He was never really out on the street a long time. I know what happened: Sekou got bailed out of jail on the 10th of January. I remember it because the 10th of January is my birthday. His wife had their baby that day—as soon as he walked into the house his wife went into labor pains. She named the baby after me. Now when Sekou had only been out of jail for seven days, on the 17th of January, he had to go into hiding because they wanted to put him in jail again. They put Lumumba in jail that day, you know, and they put Joan in jail. That's when they tortured her and beat her up. This is the beginning of the 21 thing; the very beginning What was really so fantastic about it is that that's when it really occurred to me that I didn't understand the pigs at all, because that's when they started calling us murderers and stuff like that. Joan Bird—of all people—they called a murderer. I just didn't understand it at all. But it was with that bust that I started to understand things, and I really think that it started to politicize me, that whole bust thing. Anyway, from January 17th up until now Sekou has never been able to walk the streets of Babylon without looking over his shoulder. And now he's not in Babylon. It's really a very cruel thing; his child now is almost two, and he's only seen her when she was very small, when she was just born. This is the beginning of the many broken families, broken hearts and broken dreams, you know, in the Party. It just was something else, something that I'll never be able to forgive this government for. I think that that's one of my biggest beefs, that Sekou is unable to walk the streets and talk to people like he's supposed to because he's so beautiful. I heard that in Algeria, the children come to the window and they're just screaming, "Sekou, Sekou, Sekou." They're always around the house because they love that man. I understand it. I could just see it. I know that it happens. I mean it's not hard for me to believe.

LUMUMBA SHAKUR: In April, 1968, Belal Sunni Ali asked Sekou and me to come meet Captain Ron Pennywell, who was sent from Oakland, California, to organize a Black Panther Party in New York City. Captain Pennywell was a very grass-root brother, who would always ask the cadre for suggestions. Captain Pennywell asked Belal, Sekou, and me to organize in Harlem and the Bronx. After we organized three functional sections, Captain Pennywell made Belal the Section Leader and Sekou Sub-Section Leader of the Bronx. I was made Section Leader of Harlem.

Belal had to go underground and Sekou became Section Leader of the Bronx. We were having section meetings in my house on 117th Street. The sections had some very get-down and enthusiastic brothers and sisters involved. The cadre came to the conclusion to implement point four of the Black Panther Party ten-point program and platform. We were implementing point four, and also worked on other points in the ten-point program. When the PTA asked for help, we worked to open up twenty-eight public schools while the racist teacher's union tried to keep them closed to show their power. We organized a section in Jamaica, Queens, and there like everywhere else we were working we kept on educating the people and educating ourselves in the Party. We were asked to help the Harlem community in their struggle to get a black principal in their black school—it has a black principal now, a true victory.

The Black Panther Party joined in a local coalition with the Welfare Rights Organization groups headed by Beulah Sanders. Panther cadre were assigned to welfare centers in Harlem, the Bronx, Queens, and Brooklyn, to guarantee the welfare recipients their rights, to educate welfare recipients about community control of the welfare centers, also to try to get welfare recipients jobs as case worker aides in the welfare centers.

The workers at Lincoln Hospital and community people asked the Black Panther Party to aid them in trying to get community control of Lincoln Hospital. The community, the workers, some doctors and the Black Panther Party were working beautifully together until the pig power structure created a conflict between Puerto Ricans and blacks. At the time of our capture, we were still working at Lincoln Hospital and Harlem Hospital for community control of community hospitals.

In March, 1969, Cetewayo, Dharuba and I heard a rumor that soon there would be a big arrest of some Panthers. Cetewayo, Dharuba, Curtis Powell and I talked about the rumor in depth. We came to the conclusion that we did not do or were not involved in any illegal activities, so we didn't have anything to worry about. At this time, we couldn't conceive of the Alfred Hitchcock and Ian Fleming indictment that fascist pig Frank Hogan had waiting for us. Then on the morning of April 2, Afeni and I were awakened by somebody banging on our door and hollering, "Fire! Fire!" As I was going to the door, I smelled smoke. I peeped through the peephole in the door and saw something burning. When I opened the door, a double-barrelled shotgun pushed me in the chest and a gun was at my head. Some more pigs came through the window by the fire escape and put guns to Afeni's head. I asked the pigs what were we arrested for and the pigs said murder and arson. Afeni and I laughed in the pig's face because we knew he was lying. After being in jail two years, finding out we are facing 175 years in prison, all the humor is out of me. Because now I realize the Panther 21 arrest is all part and parcel of a national conspiracy by the American government to destroy the Black Panther Party and all revolutionaries.

Since 1965, over twenty blacks who were members of Malcolm X's OAAU in New York City, and still adhered to Malcolm X's principle of revolutionary nationalism for liberation of oppressed people, have been arrested by the pigs for conspiracies and various other fallacious criminal charges. This has been a systematic plan by the fascist pigs to stifle the black liberation struggle in New York City.

BABA ODINGA: One day on Seventh Avenue, in 1968, a black man with some boxes asked my help. I took some boxes that he had and went with him. We took the boxes to the Black Panther Party office. He told me thanks and asked me where I was going. "To work," I said, and he said all right and thanks again. I generally worked for about three months, then took the money and lent it out for interest at crap games, then took a gamble, and if I lost, then I worked some more. I asked him, did he have any more boxes? He said no, and would I like to go feed some hungry children? So I said yes, for I was tired of work, and so I went with him. In the Party I did all sorts of things for the community—welfare, housing. On April 2, 1969, there was a loud rapping on my door. I went to open it and when I did the police came in and put a shot-gun to my head. They went all over the house, then they put a pair of handcuffs on me and took me to court where the judge gave me $100,000 bail.

CLARK SQUIRE: I was making "big bucks" at work, and I began to realize that by staying in the system and looking successful I was misleading a lot of other black people unwillingly. I was being used as a pawn in a game in which I did not care to participate. I was not free, but I possessed many of the symbols and appearances of freedom. I felt I was leading brothers to mistake Brooks Brothers suits for freedom—attaché cases, American Express cards, first-class flights, sports cars, and lunching at exclusive midtown restaurants, for freedom—and that was a lie!

All I had done was survive. But I couldn't be proud of survival under the system in America, because too many of my brothers hadn't survived. A lot of them were much more talented than I, but they just had never had a chance. I had seen too many of my brothers cut down along the way—smashed, broken and castrated, by racism, oppression, exploitation, poverty, ignorance, and disease—to be proud of my own survival. I was also becoming increasingly schizoid from maintaining two sets of friends, two vocabularies, and two methods of dressing—one at work and the other away from work. I was aware of subtle pressures working to force upon me the acceptance of white values, to give up more and more of being black. That was absurd. I didn't dig racism, oppression, and exploitation. I loved being black—the black mentality, black mores, habits and associations. I looked around for an organization that was dedicated to alleviating the suffering of black people.

JAMAL: I decided to join the Black Panther Party in October, 1968. I was fifteen years old and a tenth-grade student at Evander Childs. I had read Malcolm X's *Autobiography* and heard Rap Brown talk and tried Black Enlightenment—a high school group—and the dashiki trip, and I was talking revolution.

I had heard of the Black Panther Party before—the first thing I'd heard was that they were the extreme of the extremists and when you joined the Black Panther Party, they gave you a gun with a panther on it, a knife with a panther on it, some black sunglasses, and a beret, and you just went out to kill all the devils and savages that there were. So I thought it was a totally suicidal movement. The next thing I heard about the Black Panther Party was when Bobby and the rest went into the state legislature in Sacramento. I was watching the news one night and I saw these niggers come walking into the legislature with guns. I said wow, these niggers are crazy, you know. They were cool, really committed—but I wasn't ready to go that far, not then. It seemed like the only fate they had was death, because of the type of things they were doing. And I didn't know if they were too rational whatsoever. But a friend wanted to go check them out, so one Monday morning we got up early and got on the train to Brooklyn to the Black Panther office. The brother behind the desk told me about Eldridge and about Huey and about Bobby and the different things about the Party. And I became interested. I came back to the community meetings. And my friend and I got together to go over the Panther newspapers and I began talking to my friends about the Black Panther Party, getting their opinions. All I know is that I found the program interesting and I continued going to the community meetings that the Black Panther Party had.

After I joined I would come out to Brooklyn every day

after school and sit down and do a little work around the office. Then an office in Harlem was opened, and I was transferred to Harlem. I was to contact a brother by the name of Lumumba there. And I found that the Harlem office of the Black Panther Party hadn't really been established yet: the people were still bringing in desks and still painting, still trying to get the office together. I began to help fix up the office. We would bring in folding chairs and let community people come in and we would talk to them about the Party, and primarily we would talk to them about their problems in the community and try to figure out ways we could help them solve their problems.

In Harlem many nights we would be in the office and we would get a phone call to come around to somebody's house. We'd go down to their house, and for instance we'd find we had to take a four-year-old black child who had a roach caught in her ear to the hospital. We would have to watch the child in agony as the doctor put a delicate instrument in her ear, probing around nerves and other delicate parts of the inner ear, the child screaming in pain as the instrument brushed up against the nerves. Once we had to take a little black girl to the hospital who had been bitten by a rat, who had been infected with rabies. This was a rat that wasn't in a vacant lot, it wasn't downstairs in her basement, it was right in her apartment. She was three years old, sitting in the middle of the floor, and she was bitten by a rat.

Once we attended the funeral of a young brother, an infant, who had died from lead poisoning. He'd eaten a few pieces of chipped-off paint from the wall of his apartment. This paint was made with a lead base, and after eating this for a period of time, it developed into lead poisoning to the point of fatality for the child.

Now the night of April 1, 1969, I remember, we had

just finished attending a rally for Sam Butler and it was about three o'clock in the morning when I arrived in Noonie's house. I lay down to get a few hours of sleep so I can be up and to the office early the next morning. About five o'clock in the morning the doorbell rang and Noonie went downstairs to answer the doorbell and asked who it was. They said it was the police, that they came to check for a gas leak. I came downstairs and asked the question again and got the same reply. At that point the police broke down the door and came in and threw me up against the wall, handcuffed me behind my back, trained guns in on my head and guns in on my mother and told me that I was under arrest. I was never shown an arrest warrant. They brought me upstairs and began to tear up the room. When I asked to see a search warrant, I was never shown that—the only reply I got is that it would be shown to me downtown. On February 6, 1970, my bail was posted and I was released from jail. All I wanted to do was work to free the 21, to free all brothers and sisters who were in prison and to free my people.

The New York 21 had been arrested, framed up on a conspiracy. A Panther from New York had been kidnapped and murdered. Our National Chairman Bobby Seale was in prison with a charge of conspiracy to commit murder, kidnap and murder. Raids and attacks had gone down all across the country and twenty-eight members of the Black Panther Party were dead. But in the face of all this, the Party hadn't been wiped out. It hadn't even been weakened. Because all the attacks only served to show the community the necessity for them to move. There was no distinction drawn between Panthers and black people—they were oppressed people who were being attacked, who were being murdered, and the people had to band together in order to stop this. While I was in prison, a

National Committee to Combat Fascism was organized and called together thousands of people. Also, the free-breakfast program in New York had become a reality. The free medical clinic had become a reality. The free-clothing program had become a reality. And other community programs that we had wanted to establish—that the 21 had been working to establish—had become a reality. Panthers were now working full-time, drawing their subsistence from the money that was made from the Party newspaper. The primary focus, the primary thrust, was to work on helping people organize survival programs in the community and around political prisoners. We had rapport on an international level because our Minister of Information, Eldridge Cleaver, had been working in Algiers, Algeria, to establish an international relationship. The only thing I want to do is follow into the work. I have faith in the fact that if I am killed, others will come forth to do this work. I hope when you read this book you will get a little bit of an insight on what I'm about and why I joined the Party. And you're motivated to come down and help us help ourselves, help us secure freedom and our liberation. All power to the people, because that's where it all belongs. That's where it has to be.

BOB COLLIER: My first contact with Black Panther existence was during an investigation into a feud between two motorcycle gangs. One of the members was relating to me that he was a Panther. This was in October, 1968. My inquiries were answered by a visit from a couple of Panther representatives, who were directed to me at the center by community people. I told them of the unusual and antagonistic behavior of the individual who portrayed himself as a Panther. It was then revealed to me that there were no Panthers in the Lower East Side area. We then went to see the person who had called himself a Panther—after being confronted with two authentic members he stopped pretending. He moved away soon after. You get to realize that there are a lot of people who say they are Panthers who really aren't.

JOAN BIRD: The first time I thought about the Black Panther Party at all, I remember reading in the newspaper—*Daily News*, mass media paper—that Panthers at Brooklyn Criminal Court were viciously assaulted and attacked by off-duty members of the New York police force.

Right then I was too individualistic to recognize much of the things that were really happening to me, although they were happening. And basically that specific scene that happened to the Panthers was one thing that I did see that was happening around me. After reading about that—an experience that was happening—although I had definitely been familiar with police brutality in the black community, living there all my life, this incident that was happening to these brothers really caused me to want to investigate further and find out more about the Black Panther Party and why these black people were receiving so much more repression than other movement groups that were active during that time. I mean, I'd known my whole life about different policemen in the black community taking extortion from black shopkeepers, also collecting graft from the numbers game, collecting money for dope, from pushers there on the street, arresting brothers and sisters on the street and actually beating them with clubs, seeing them thrown into pig cars and carted away like animals. This is the type of thing you see in the black community, and you also come to recognize clearly that they are not there in any shape, form, or fashion in the attitude of being there to protect you or the people of your community. Their total purpose there is to be some sort of authoritarian, occupation armed force, controlling you, watching your every move, to see that you operate, move like robots to the command of the troops. Gestapo troops.

Well I had heard about the Black Panther Party before, it had been mentioned previously to me, I can't remember by who, where, or when. I can remember that there was talk of some bad niggers out from Oakland, California, and they were carrying some guns and they were going to defend their people. And I dug that whole idea, and you know I still do. Then I met some people one night at a friend's house who were members of the Black Panther Party; they told me about the Party's program that they had built in the community, and desired me to come down to the Harlem office. The next day I went down to the office and I met some more people who were members of the Party. I attended a community meeting. And I heard more about the program the Party had set up, which is the exact same program that all black people are looking for. The Party spoke in the name of the people, said what the people had been saying for so very long, saying what the people had wanted for so very long, getting down to actually basically meeting their immediate needs. Programs, you know, calling for freedom, power to determine our own destiny, the destiny of our own black community. It goes on to say in the final analysis that what we want is peace.

At that point the Party in New Haven and New York was just getting underway. A breakfast program was starting to be set up, and we were involved in the teachers' strike—community control of schools—at that period of time. We had tried to organize by having classes for the children. Although the schools were closed, we were going to continue to teach and give our children knowledge and understanding of the situation. This is what we were organizing on, high school and college students that would be willing to help the high school coalition.

I started attending college at night then, I was doing Party work in the daytime.

The first bust was on January 17, 1969. I had been in the Party since approximately September or October of 1968. That was the first bust that I had ever had in my lifetime. The pigs alleged that myself and two other people conspired together to commit attempted murder against them and to inflict heavy blows upon them, and they also charged us with felonious assault. On January 17, that night first started out when I was in this car with two brothers and we were approached by the pigs. This isn't unusual in the black community that pigs stop you just for the mere fact that you are black. And being Panthers we were quite naturally targets all the time, any time, but we are always targets of police brutality, and the next thing that happened was the pigs started shooting. Well, I was found in the car by the pigs and they dragged me out and began to beat and stomp on me and use heavy blackjacks and beat and kicked me in the stomach, lungs, back, and handcuffed me, and then took me up to a racist pig station and told me that I'm under arrest and that I have no rights they are bound to respect, telling me that I had better tell them the truth or else they were going to kill me or bomb up Panther offices. And what they attempted to do was to use me as a tool to place more repression on the Party. I think that from the moment they dragged me out of the car and began to pound on me and beat me and dug that I was a woman, they felt that because of that they could also use that to weaken my spirit and when I refused to weaken they began to threaten me and threaten my life or the life of my family. And they put on this masquerade: They put out to the public's eye through the mass media that I was going to be held as a material witness and turn evidence on the rest of the defendants. This is the type of tactic they tend to use—divide and conquer. We are not going to allow them to do that at all.

In the Panther Party what keeps your spirit up is the fact that you are willing to die for your freedom. You know that in a revolution, when you talk about armed struggle you are really going to the point of winning or dying. And that is a part of it. You know that all your faith lies in the masses of people in a party. We are all striving for humanity's sake, for dignity. Because of that, and because of being stomped and being put into the inhumane conditions at the same time, I knew that I had to strive even harder for humanity's sake, for universal salvation.

After being at the 34th Precinct for eighteen or nineteen hours, being constantly threatened, I was taken downtown to 100 Centre Street where the Manhattan criminal court is and at that point I was told that I was going into the courtroom and being held as a material witness. I hadn't had a chance to see a lawyer or anything. A lawyer previously went up to the precinct, together with Lumumba Abdul Shakur; Lumumba came up there to see me and he brought a lawyer with him, but I wasn't there, and Lumumba was automatically arrested. He walked into the precinct with the lawyer to see about me, and they arrested him. They also arrested Clark Squire, and charged both of them with conspiracy, attempted murder, and felonious assault.

When they took me to 100 Centre Street a lawyer did get down to see me. What they did then was take me into closed chambers. This was Saturday, January 18. A lawyer came in, right before we began to start the proceedings, and I got a chance to talk to him. We went into open court that night and I was charged with conspiracy, attempted murder, and felonious assault, and my bail was originally placed at $50,000, but was reduced to $20,000 that night in front of Archibald—the judge—and from there I was taken to the Women's House of Detention.

Finally, the bail was reduced to $5,000, and people got the money together and I got out February 4. And what happened is, on February 27 I went down for a hearing on the case and again I was re-arrested—on charges of attempted armed robbery, grand larceny. They say I robbed a subway token booth, or something, in the Bronx. So I was indicted in Manhattan and re-arrested in Manhattan by some Bronx pigs on these trumped-up charges, and placed on another $5,000 bail. I had been out altogether twenty-three days. So then after that I was taken back to the pig corruption center and I was held there, and the people were righteously indignant and were able to get up another $5,000 bail, so then I'm out on two $5,000 bails, you see. During this time that I was out I started working and I went back into night school to try and still get off on some nursing—that was still on my mind, the necessity of that. I was out for not quite a month, and then April 2nd of 1969 the pigs came again, at 5 A.M., not only to my parents' house to arrest me, but to many other homes of members of the Black Panther Party. With shotguns, you see, armed. Armed pigs, breaking down doors, holding shotguns to babies' heads. And the planned, vicious, terrorist act really of trying to mur-

der members of the Black Panther Party. I'm not even
going to use the word "arrest" because the first move
that we attempted to make would have given them the
opportunity of blowing our heads off. And that—that
whole case of the New York Panther 21—has been going
on for two years now. The charges that were placed
against us, I know that many people have heard about it,
conspiracy, attempted murder, conspiracy to commit
murder, conspiracy to commit arson in the first and second
degrees, conspiracy to bomb department stores and the
Brooklyn Botanical Gardens and railroad stations—all
these charges add up to about a thirty-count indictment,
and my bail was then raised to $100,000, and we were
all placed in detention centers throughout New York City,
throughout the seven different detention—I should say
corruption—centers. I was there for a year and a half, in
the Women's House of Detention. Finally, in July, 1970,
the people got the money up and I was out.

When I got out, that racist courtroom and that racist
jail, where black people were continually denied their
constitutional rights, had made me relate more and more
to the fact that our people are denied their constitutional
rights all the time. I was more aware of what was happening, then. What had happened also was that the pigs had
upped their tactics: there was more outright genocide
in their tactics with the people, with the murder of Mark
Clark and Fred Hampton in December of 1969, with the
arrest in New Haven of Chairman Bobby Seale in May
of 1969, and the other political prisoners there. And after
I got out of jail, when I first got out, everything was all
new to me because the Party had moved to a higher level
in the sense that there were really tighter communications
lines set up. Like when we were busted, a lot of us who

were busted had basically composed a lot of the leadership, so people from the Coast came here and started dealing with organizing the Party and making it one unified force. The set-up was absolutely beautiful. Panthers became unified. Panthers can go anywhere and know that there is another Panther, another comrade, another person that will watch your back the same as you would watch theirs.

What I did, what I got into was to head the medical cadre program and was the medical officer for one area. And what we really want to do with that field is not only organizing within on a higher medical level for the Party, but also organizing the people in the community and educating them to the diseases that exist and the reason why these diseases do exist, and to the fucked-up city hospital organization, which has now turned into a capitalistic industry of drugs and products. We recognize that basically the hospitals are not set up here in the community to meet the needs of the people in the community. We recognize that the mortality rate of people has gone up more than 90 per cent in the last few years, and people are actually dying in these hospitals for lack of proper care and malpractice on the part of the racist physicians who are in these hospitals and give less than a damn about the lives of black people. We want to move on this.

We've also moved on one of our socialistic programs, to set up free health clinics throughout the areas where the Black Panther Party exists. And we will continue to do this throughout all our communities with the help of the masses of people because we are all fighting to end our past of oppression and the racism that exists throughout America today and throughout the world as a whole. We know that we can only do this by setting up these different socialistic programs by which people can see that we, the Party, care for them, care for them and have an undying love for them and want to see them free.

Recently, like Nixon came out with a bill that says that from now on the pigs would have the right to use wiretapping and eavesdropping and all types of electronic equipment to find out who are the people who oppose them. I mean, I'm quite sure that by this time they know who it is who is opposing them. And even if you don't oppose them, especially if you are black, you are going to be considered part of the people who are opposing the pigs' laws. So therefore the beat is going to come down and light on your heads the same as it would come down on a Panther's head. We have to recognize that there are many people out here who are defending themselves but who are not Panthers. They recognize the need for freedom and peace, and the right to do what they want to do, and they are also going to receive a whole lot of repression.

The pigs have always used various pretexts to come into our homes and dust them down, but now they are not going to use any at all except the fact that we are black or we're white or we're brown and we don't like what they are doing to us. They are going to come in and just break down the door. Maybe this is not a bad thing, maybe we can look at it as a good thing because it's going to take some more repression to come down on people in order for them to actually realize what a serious war it is that we are into against these pigs.

That's what the game is all about—survival. And you've got the pigs, the enemy, on one side, and the people on the other side, and we've been just surviving for so long, and we're beginning to move, and we're not going to take that shit no more.

CURTIS POWELL: On April 2, 1969, I was at my mother's home. I'd spent the night there. I called Lumumba's brother Zayd and asked him what was happening. He said the pigs were vamping. Vamping for what? He said: "Conspiracy to commit murder and arson." That blew my mind. In fact, I sort of thought he might be joking. I asked, "Murder who—arson what?" He said he didn't know—but that the pigs were in my crib, answering my telephone. I hung up and called my crib. Some motherfucker answered my phone! I said, "Is Dr. Powell at home?" He said, "No." I hung up. That *really* blew my mind. I was righteously indignant—what the hell were these motherfucking pigs doing in my crib! My mother asked me what was happening. I told her I was probably going to be busted, but that since we hadn't done anything, it was probably going to be just a harassment bust, and we would be out in a couple of days. That was April 2, 1969; on April 2, 1971 we are still in prison. Twenty-four months now.

If I had really known what was in store for us, I would have split. I had $800 in my pocket. But I left the scratch at my mom's, and got in touch with the Newsreel people and the Swedish press. I wanted them with me when I went to my crib.

I wanted them there, because at that moment several suspicions were beginning to crawl into my mind. I had been shot at a few times by "unknown people." I still felt this was just a harassment bust because we had done nothing illegal, but it was possible that the pigs might be looking for an excuse to ice us. They had attacked bloods from the Party all over the country, including the attacks in the Brooklyn courthouse, had savagely beaten Joan Bird, had shot at a few of us a few times. We were aware the pigs did not mean us any good. I felt they might use any pretext to try to ice us, so I asked these press people to come with me. They photographed the whole thing—which got the pigs in my crib uptight.

From then on, until June or July when I started to get my bearings—I had never been in jail before—everything was an unreal, too-real nightmare. I was in jail for twenty-four hours before I even knew what the charges were about. Then a cat on the help snuck me a New York *News*, and wow. I didn't know what they were talking about, but there it was: a "Fellini indictment."

For two months I couldn't come out of my cell for anything, could not wash clothes or take a shower. The pigs were spooked up. It was a difficult time. But after I got my bearings—and learned how to jail—it got a little cooler. Not a lot. I was in isolation; I was at times denied sheets, towels, pillowcases, toilet paper, food, medicine, and soap. Once I found a rat's tail in my soup. In July they started letting me out one hour in the afternoon and one hour in the evening to shower and wash clothes. We were isolated from each other and from the other inmates, but during my two hours out I used to stop at some of the cells—the other inmates were all locked up when I was allowed out of my cell. I would rap with them about the Party and politics generally.

There's a lot to be learned from being in jail. I'm thinking of three quotations: one is from Dostoevsky, "The degree of civilization in a society can be judged by entering its prisons." I've seen some bad things before, but I have never seen such inhumanity and lack of basic understanding of people as in here. I have seen people go crazy, completely insane. Some try to commit suicide. Some succeed. I have seen people beaten nearly dead, and some beaten to death.

A second quotation is from Malcolm: "To be a black

revolutionary you are going to have to spend some time in jail." I didn't dig it when I first read it, but I can dig it while I'm here—because, as Trotsky said, "Jail is the university of a revolutionary."

These jails, filled with non-white, oppressed, innocent people, must be opened. The ghettos must be opened. This country must cease its oppression and genocide and exploitation and racism against poor people, against black people, against brown people, against red people. I dig my cancer research, and I think I have a lot to offer in that field, but the plight of my people—the plight of oppressed people generally—is more important, and more pressing.

We of the 21 know we are innocent, and we know what the pigs are going to try to do to us. We are madder than hell. We hadn't begun to really serve the people as we wanted to. We were just getting started. We don't ask for sympathy. We ask for vengeance.

part 11

JOAN BIRD: In February, 1971, I was thrown into the Women's House of Detention here in New York City again, at 10 Greenwich Avenue, in the middle of Greenwich Village, because two people had not appeared that day in court. I had been there two times before, once for a year and a half. The outer layers of this grotesque building are reddish-brown brick. Inside the prison, the walls are made of stone and the bars of steel and brass.

On April 2, 1971, after we had been in pig D.A. Hogan's office all afternoon and also in court, it was very late, and Sister Afeni and the two other sisters who had been arrested at that time had been asking me about the Women's House of Detention and how I had found it, because I had been there. And I was telling them that although they were very hungry and very tired, they need not have the thought in their minds that they would be able to get a decent meal or be able to rest their heads down and relax for one moment, because it was impossible. And I was telling them that conditions were so horrendous and terrible that the hideousness of it would make you vomit. And I was telling them about the rats that run around at night. I was also telling them that when I had been there before, I did not receive any type of medical attention whatsoever for the beatings. And all these things they found out for themselves. And Afeni and I saw them clearly as all being directly a part of the jail experience.

The sisters in there are actually very beautiful. Because they are all from the colony and they know about how rough it is and how hard it is to survive. And they know about how to use different methods to get around and survive. When you are in there you learn to do some time, you learn that you can't actually control what is happening out there in the street. So you have to deal with what you are confronted with, and that is basically the Women's House of Detention. So that's the complication that we have to deal with. The sisters in there have come in and out of the House for years now. We found them to be very beautiful. I mean, there wasn't a time that we would actually have to want or need for anything in terms of knowing how to jail—as far as linens or blankets or pillows or anything of that sort was concerned—because we always had a connection somewhere. You see, we knew that they would do the same for us, and we would also do the same for them. There are both "detention women" and "sentenced women" there. The ages run from sixteen on up, to maybe sixty-five.

Upon entrance the women are taken to a section in the prison called the receiving room, which is located on the main floor. We are told to sit down on long, hard wooden benches on one side of the room, at which time you sit or sleep for hours until a guard—called "female officer"—is available to process you. First you are stripped of all your possessions—jewelry, money, watch, cigarettes, wig, pocketbook, etc. If a sister happens to be an addict who is sick and is asking for medical attention, she is told to shut up or is totally ignored. The prison's outstanding character is complete disregard for humanity, human life.

There's a big sign in the receiving area: "You can write Legal Aid for a lawyer after you've been here two weeks."

The next act of degradation and humiliation comes as the women are told that we must take a shower. For those sisters who are addicts and are sick with chills and sweats, this is the perfect opportunity for them to die of pneumonia. After this shower we are given a dingy cloth robe to wrap around our bodies and a pair of rubber shower slippers to put on our feet. We are sent to the back of the receiving room to once again sit and wait. Then the prison doctor comes in to search our bodies, internally and externally. This part of the processing is a standard rule of the prison. Those who refuse to be "finger searched" are then placed in a locked cell until they change their minds. The prison doctor goes along with the entire prison program in that he comes along when he wants to do searching, disregarding the bare fact that the women have been up for hours (up to ten hours) going through the prison authorities' "procedures," and are tired and hungry and want most of all to sleep. The women are called into a dim and dirty office one by one and are told to lie down on an examining table with their legs spread wide apart, at which point the doctor jams his rubber-gloved index finger up the vaginal and rectal areas of the body. The authorities' attempted justification is that someone *might* be smuggling in drugs, weapons, chewing gum, cigarettes to take into population. Now the women are assigned to cells according to the alleged charge you are arrested for. Depending on what time of the day you are brought in, you might be fed possibly a slice of bologna on stale white bread and a cup of water or watery coffee or tea.

Onto the elevator and onto your respective floor, and then to a cold, stone-wall cell not big enough to hold a hyena. Now you are double-locked in a cell until the following day when you are again taken to the receiving room to undergo further physical pain and mental torture of more alleged "medical" examination. The women's height and weight are taken; rectal temperature and blood pressure are taken; and a series of unrelated questions are asked. For instance: "Are you a virgin?" "When is the last time you have had sexual intercourse?"

In the chaos of women sitting on benches and lying on the cold concrete floor—since there are never enough seats—each one is rushed into the doctor's office to face further maltreatment. Sisters are told to lie down on the examining table again and spread their legs wide apart so that this "healer of the sick" can jam a surgical clamp up into the vagina, whether the person is a virgin or not, frequently causing hemorrhaging and severe damage to internal female organs. The reason given for this morbid procedure is that a Pap smear must be taken of every woman who enters the building. The entire ordeal is suffered by all women who are arrested.

Up on the floors where the girls exist from day to day is found a world of maximum security in terms of its relationship to existence in the streets. On the street, which is a larger area, there are police precincts to patrol our communities; in prison there are two female guards assigned to each sixty or eighty women, patrolling every tier and corridor with keys which madly jingle, which communicate the thought imbedded in mind that only the guards can turn the key to unlock the gates.

The fourth floor is specified for women who come in on drug busts, women who are kicking drugs—at which time you can hear cries of pain which are in vain for there is no help given to those in need. Women vomit, urinate, and kick in a cold cell all alone; also, the fourth floor is set aside for "diagnostic" cases, women whom the authorities claim cannot cope with jailhouse living and are classified as crazy—when actually any woman has a right to fuss and raise hell under the existing, deplorable conditions. And last the fourth floor is also used as a disciplinary area, Corridor 4A, which blocks off from the rest of the corridor 4B, 4C, 4D. Women who talk after lights are out, who talk back to the guards in defense of true human rights are thrown into A as punishment for "offenses" against the established prison "rules and regulations." These "punishment" and "psychiatric" cells are without beds, mattresses, or toilets. They have wash basins and water. There is no hot water in the punishment cells, but there is hot water in the psychiatric cells. Women live in these cells for months. They have to ask the officers when they need to go to the bathroom.

The fifth floor is specified for drug addicts, robbers, and women who have been in jail before. Both adolescents and adults are on this floor.

The sixth floor is a placement floor for what the authorities call "first offenders" and women with very serious crimes who are classified as "extremely dangerous." An example: homicide, conspiracy, and of all things prostitution.

The seventh floor is used basically the same as the fifth floor.

Floors eight, nine, and ten are used for sentenced women who are doing up to a year. Eight is also used for detention women who are working, as a means of utilizing the time and the days and the months away until their court date. The eleventh floor is the hospital area and clinic area, which appear more as a morgue than an area to heal the sick. The atmosphere is not one which is exactly conducive to recovering and getting well. The twelfth floor is called the roof. Here there is an arts and crafts room where women can draw, two rooms where women can play cards and listen to records for an hour. Also on the twelfth floor there is a beauty parlor, which you only have access to after you have been in jail for two weeks.

Two floors that I must mention are the second and third floors. On the second floor there is a library which contains books that are irrelevant to our current-day situation. All books which relate to law and constitutional rights of human beings, and they are few in number, are kept locked up and are not to be taken out of the library. Afeni and I were without any type of literature over a period of nine or ten months. Only after major efforts by the attorneys and constant pressuring and going to different courts did they finally give us permission even to receive our legal papers, our writs of habeas corpus, or whatever legal matters that had to be attended to or that we should know about. So after nine or ten months, we were only able to get that little bit of information. But information about the Party, or the Party newspaper, or movement leaflets or such things, we were not permitted to receive.

Also on the second floor is an alleged learning school for the adolescents—which is actually a game which the adolescents play to get whatever candy, cigarettes, pencils, pens they can con out of the teacher. Also there is a chapel on the second floor, where on Sunday the women come from different floors to see one another and talk to their friends. Also on two is a priest and a nun who offer you the forgiveness of the Lord and offer the advice, "Sinner, repent, or to hell you will go," when actually you are living in hell—jail—called the Women's House of Detention. Basically, like the people who are in there have been through oppression all their lives so it's nothing new to them. But coming in and out of there can be a thing for some.

Then there is the diagnostic area, which a lot of sisters are in, where a quack doctor fills you up with thorazine and chloral-hydrate to keep you from shouting out how awful and horrible the place actually is, they just drug them up. Many women walk around like zombies from these drugs called medication. They just walk around all day in a daze and not relate to anything except being high.

On the third floor we find a slave work area, where women slave in the laundry and sewing room all day and receive no wages for their labor. Recently, after mass protest from the inmates, some of the sentenced women are receiving 10¢ an hour. The scale of payment now goes from 3¢ for janitor work to 10¢ for cooking. The maximum a woman is allowed to earn in jail is $120 in a year. You can't take it out with you or save it up, you're not allowed to, you have to spend it at the commissary. Detention women who're working receive nothing. As the authorities put it, "It is a privilege to be a detention and allowed to work the time away." Detention women are the ones the courts haven't declared guilty. They're there because they don't have enough money for bail. Most of the sisters in jail are detention women.

Also on the third floor is the commissary area where women can buy the following items: wool, grease, powder, paper, soap, candy, sugar (50 cents a box), milk, non-filtered cigarettes, cookies, crackers, cupcakes, and doughnuts. Three times a week detention women are permitted to go to commissary, spending three dollars on the first two days and four dollars on the last day. Sentenced women are permitted to go to commissary once a week, spending nothing exceeding ten dollars. The problem is, most women do not have money to spend on the items since the prices are exploitative—that is, sky-high! Some women receive one dollar from a voluntary group of women called the Friendly Visitors, who in turn take all the wool goods made by the women and profit off of them while the women receive nothing but three cigarettes wrapped in foil, deodorant, and candy—and this they expect you to be thankful for.

The day-to-day living is a rigid program set up by the prison authorities. At 6:30 A.M. the female guards switch on all the lights on the floors and open up the cell gates for the women to take a shower. The shower room is a dirty cubicle consisting of two showers and a wet concrete floor. In the shower room can be found rat holes, dead rats, dirty sanitary napkins, and roaches, yet the shower room is supposed to be used for women to keep themselves clean and healthy in terms of good physical hygiene. Breakfast is served at 6:45 A.M. to 7:15 A.M. which means each corridor of women, usually consisting of thirty totally, has fifteen minutes to shower. This procedure makes it impossible for all women to clean their bodies.

Breakfast consists of the most unhealthy and nonnutritious artificial food available, since 37 cents a day is spent on each inmate for meals. For breakfast the women are served a limited variety of foods, specifically: powdered milk, coffee, hard stale bread, dry cereal or oatmeal, one slab of margarine. Lunch, like all meals, consists of starch and powdered products. Powdered eggs, rice, potatoes are fixed into a sundry amount of concoctions and as a base for pork, pork fat, and grease. Only on rare occasions—for example, Christmas or Thanksgiving—is fresh fruit available for the women. Specifically, each sister receives *one* orange! (That is the vitamin C for the year.) Dinner is basically the same composition of food except once every two or three weeks the women are fed one chicken part or bologna, or "mystery balls" (the name given to jailhouse hamburger meat by the women prisoners). The meat is a definite mystery as to the bad-tasting components authorities call "good healthy meat."

The daily curriculum of activities for the women consists of cleaning out the cells, playing cards, or watching TV from 9:30 A.M. until 10:45 A.M. Then all women are locked into their cells for an afternoon-lunchtime count of the entire population. Lock-ins are forty-five minutes long. After the lunch count, the women are let out (like animals from cages) to eat. After eating, recreation begins at 1:00 P.M., at which time the activities are card playing and TV on the floors, or going up to the roof area to listen to records, until 3:00 P.M. At 3:00 P.M. all women are again locked into their cells for another count until 4:45 P.M. Then at 4:45 P.M. the gates are opened for the women to eat supper. After supper the women have recreation for thirty minutes, during which time detention women are called to go on their visits—for those who have visitors. The visits last thirty minutes (included in recreation time). Visits for detention women are on the main floor in a closed area with booths and a phone, through which each woman communicates with her visitor. Seeing your visitor is complicated and uncomfortable, because persons view each other through a glass window (approximately 12 by 18 inches). Before and after seeing any visitor, sisters are searched externally, then made to squat and jump up and down squatting so that anything that may be hidden in the vagina will fall out. This happens before and after visits to court too. When you're taken to court and back again policewomen are with you all the time. Sentenced women receive their visits on Saturday and Sunday only, and detention women Monday through Friday, holidays not included. Money orders may be left for the women, which they sometimes never get. Clothes (skirts, socks, underwear, etc.) can also be left for detention women only. For sentenced women the state supplies cloth to make dresses, and sneakers, underwear, socks, and loafers for them to wear.

They say that now they're closing the Women's House of Detention on Greenwich Avenue and they're going to have it in a new building. But don't you see it really isn't going to change things, it's not the building, it's the people, the cruel and corrupt people who can treat other human beings in a way they would never in the world think of treating their dogs.

This is actually the way or form of rehabilitation the system is offering. These conditions we do not need, want, or desire. Therefore we as human beings must move to eliminate all elements in society that are contrary to existence of freedom and humanity.

KUWASI BALAGOON: Brother Malcolm said once: "If you're black, you were born in jail." Jail—the buildings, the cells, the bars—means only a change in the *form* of our restrictions and confinement. It is only a matter of degree.

And the barless jails and the jails with bars will and certainly must be disrupted more and more. All who seek to put justice in the place of injustice, are moving in that direction, black people, Puerto Ricans, Mexican Americans, Indians, poor whites. The pigs have nothing going

for them but beastly repression and fancy murder machines. All power is truly in the hands of the people, and
in the end the people will win.

A certain sector of our confinement, referred to as
Branch Queens House of Detention, was out of order for
a while. It was no longer serving its established function.
We know that the conditions at these places are not
the result of accident. Most of the prisons inside the
United States are filled to the brim with poor people, and
90 per cent of the prisoners are non-white. The bail imposed on us is many times above our reach, and implicit in
the bail system is the madness that "freedom" in this country is determined by the amount of material wealth one
has. A poor person has started serving a sentence as soon as
he feels the snap of handcuffs. He is then taken to a police
station, and if not beaten, is at least degraded. He is inter-
rogated by members of an occupying army, beings who
live elsewhere, not his neighbors. He is then taken to the
local warehouse of souls, which is often a warehouse of
soul brothers, and there he is made to wait—most often
for months; sometimes for years.

While he is waiting he has no law books to begin work
on his case. He is also denied political literature. He
finds himself fighting mental suffocation and stagnation,
being unable to pursue most fields of knowledge to any
extensive degree. He is denied adequate medical attention and adequate recreation and space for exercise and
his woman. If he is allowed visits they are painfully
short, and female visitors are often the target of slimy
remarks by the incompetent administration and racist,
vicious guards who are like the police who arrested him.
And many times we feel free to curse the guards, keeping
in mind that if the prisoner returns the obscenities, the
officer can wait until the inmate is locked in his cell, at

which time a mob of pigs can charge in, outnumber and brutalize him. The inmate knows that and *lives* with it, either by taking the insults or standing his shaky ground.

The food in most jails averages around horrible. Unsanitary conditions, rats, mice, insects, and censorship, add up to genocide, and those responsible for it are the real criminals. Most jails are sweatboxes in the summer and iceboxes in the winter. Bail hearings are hard to come by, and constitutional rights such as a bail within reach, a jury of one's own peers—only hearsay. At trial the "arresting officer's" word is 99 times out of a 100 taken over the defendant's. It is amazing how many people are in jail solely by the say-so of a cop, or any one witness more to a judge's liking than the defendant. The police, judges, and prosecutors have a coalition. And the so-called legal aid given to defendants unable to meet the cost of hiring their own attorneys has long taken an attitude, "If you can't beat them, join them." A coalition of creeps. The prosecutor moves for a conviction, his job has nothing to with justice. His goal is to get the convict in question a sentence and nothing else, and the more convictions he has, the better his record. When defendants are charged in political cases, there results an even more obvious disdain for the judicial system, and the power structure and judges and the prosecutor move even closer together.

In the jails, an increase of outbursts and burst-outs is inevitable. The fact that the prisoners of war in the Tombs, the Brooklyn House of Detention, Rikers Island, Kew Gardens, and Queens House of Detention vomited up all the injustices that had been crammed down their throats is a people's indictment of the corrupt city and state government. Number one in the people's indictment is the American government, from Nixon and Wall Street and generals at the top on down to sly, slimy, crawly, creepy Lindsay, to wild boar McGrath, to all the poppy-ass flunkeys and overseers who help maintain their beastly order. The charge is first-degree genocide and conspiracy to commit genocide.

As might be anticipated by any rational human being with adequate knowledge of Branch Queens prison, it—like a large percentage of the prisoners entrapped in that torture chamber—exploded. Guards (some of whom get "guards" mixed up with "gods") were captured by the people, and put on the right side of the bars, for a change, along with a black civilian cook, and a pig captain. In total, seven were locked up. And every inmate's cell in the concentration camp was opened, with all keys in the hands of the prisoners of war. In fact, a few inmates could have escaped when the rebellion started because the pigs were caught completely off guard. The first day could rightly be called "turnabout day."

Before the new prisoners could get hip to the hunters getting captured by the game, they were secured. The doors to the building were barricaded tightly. In virtually one clean sweep, the entire part of the building in which the POWs were being held was taken, along with the church. There are some who say that at that time the warden's office could have been taken over also, along with the church. The mess hall was not considered worth-while, so was closed off and barricaded. The prisoners of war began arming, and defensive sectors were occupied, in case of immediate moves from the pigs.

Someone, perhaps a provocateur, set a fire. The smoke was so thick that we could hardly see our breath in one section of the building. A rumor started that the whole building was on fire, but the rumor and fire were quickly extinguished. I saw that as a test—a test that was passed.

Maintenance on the barricades was established. Look-outs watched over the area for an expected onrush of pigs. All telephones were smashed. Everything that helped the jail to operate, that we did not have any use for, was put out of order. In the excitement, mostly every window was smashed. Towels were dampened for the protection of each inmate against tear gas, and blankets were watered down and placed on the floor. The building was secured. What a beautiful feeling! Next to getting out of jail, turnabout day is where it's at.

It was a trip, a really hip experience. The only relief oppressed people can get is to strike out against the oppressor, and it is the only freedom we know of. The freedom of doing what you think is right and doing what you must do, of saying fuck the consequences. Embraced by a natural high, I looked into the faces and the eyes of my brothers; the vibrations were right on. I wish I could express the spiritual explorations that took place. It was a religious experience. 'Trane would have to play it, and Henderson and Villion would have to put it into colors. It was art and it was life.

The rest of that day was spent tightening up the defense, and the brotherhood. Everybody seemed to be flying. Messengers to carry out the word to and from every part of the building were appointed. All tiers had representatives, and guard posts and reliefs were set up. At least two security teams roamed the building at all times. The battle plan was mapped out.

The most vulnerable sector was the dorm, and the forces there were to fight and pull back, letting the pigs have it if they could take it, move to the top of the steps and set up another barricade. The fourth and fifth tiers would help them after receiving word from a messenger. The material for the barricade was prearranged, and ready for assembly.

The main entrance was the responsibility of the comrades on the flats, and the second and third tiers, who could see if anything was jumping off and quickly join the fight. The annex was secured, with guards in every room watching pig movements from the height advantage and listening through the roof for some idiot to try to cut through with a torch and prepared to put something on the idiot pig's ass. There was no way we could have been taken by surprise. Security was checked and rechecked constantly. The pigs couldn't take the flats if they had come with guns. If they'd come with armored suits, we would have put dents in them. The demands had long been printed and through democratic vote the negotiating team was picked.

A few things had already became a hassle, however. The brothers who took over the commissary began to help themselves. And most of the brothers who were aware of it were irritated, and rightly so. This was quickly ironed out, however, in a very just and socialist manner. Since the commissary was in fact a means of exploitation, it was taken over and distributed evenly among the POWs.

That night too many of us roamed the building, many false alarms and rumors were cried out. Another thing that also began to show was, not a few inmates were not sharing the guard duty. However, a far more than adequate number did and were vigilant. Sandwiches and coffee were passed through the front gate and that night complaints about not getting anything to eat were heard, noted, and moved upon. However, we were plagued by dishonesty the entire time of the siege. A few were not getting their share and a few chowhounds were getting

fat shares. Any inmates not receiving equal treatment was
real bad, in a jail run by inmates, and was crucial.

One of the guards, one who'd issued an extra amount
of harassment to inmates, tried to hang up. He either
couldn't take being locked up or he feared "payback."
Cause "payback is a motherfucker" and turnabout day
was an entirely different thing to him than it was to us.
The pig captain shook like a bowl full of clabber, although all captives were assured that no unprovoked
attacks would be made. We at no time slunk to the slimy
character of the pigs.

The next day two out of our seven captives were released as a sign of good faith so we could start negotiations, a black one and the white pig who'd tried to hang
up. Negotiations began. The team did a good job that
day, all demands were pressed, along with one demanding full TV coverage and the fascist press to come and
serve a just function. Among the demands was that a
judge from the so-called Supreme Court come to the jail
and immediately begin hearings on bail reductions. The
pigs tried to bypass the issues, saying that it was impossible to submit to anything so close to justice. So the
brothers cursed them out and danced on back home,
court was adjourned. Food was distributed and defense
maintained.

Also, we began organizing tighter, all committees met,
mapped out their plans of action and carried the word
to every POW, within the confines. The second day found
things in far better revolutionary order. The pigs were
massing outside the building and were carefully watched
from every corner. And as one comrade noted later, the
pigs could not cut off any part of the building, and
match an undetermined amount of pig power against a
determined amount of black, Puerto Rican, and white

power. Wasn't no cutting off one floor at a time, and couldn't but so many fit through a doorway or window at one time.

LeRoi Jones gave black people a poem, where he says that all you have to do is say the magic words.

> The magic words are: Up against the wall mother-fucker this is a stick up! Or: Smash the window at night . . . (from "Black People!" in LeRoi Jones' *Black Magic*, published by The Bobbs-Merrill Company)

Ain't that a rewarding sound. Kids love it. It can't be spelled. "   " ain't it. "   " ain't it. Some people can sound like cars. Hot rods even. Some can imitate a fire engine. But to hear the sound of glass breaking, glass must be broken. Some of us had to be restrained by the collective to cut down on the confusion at times. But it was good clean entertainment.

The next day, the Tombs exploded. And surprisingly enough three judges from the so-called State Supreme Court arrived on the scene. Progress was being made, a number of brothers had hearings and a few were cut loose. In all, over twenty hearings were held and a few bail reductions were the order of the day. A precedent was set; never before in the history of this racist empire had judges been summoned to a jail by inmates to hold court. It was only an act to obtain justice, although a few brothers' outcome was not pleasing. The judges didn't dig submitting to anything close to justice, but just did as much as they had to. It was good to see some of those brothers go to the streets.

Later that night we received bean pies from the Nation of Islam. On these a very weird development occurred. The thought was that it would be best to pass them out to those who were awake, since 90 per cent of those awake had been carrying the burden of most of the responsibilities; however, there were enough pies for everyone and the pies that were left over were devoured by a few people who had pies before, while a sizable amount of inmates did not receive any.

Over the radio, we heard about all the other uprisings in other jails and the support we were getting from the outside.

The next day, Sunday, there was no court held. But better yet: the people came out to support us in person, and demonstrations were held throughout the city by the Black Panther Party and the Young Lords Party. Again the negotiation team went out to rap and it is then that a split became evident.

McGrath, the state's man in charge of prisons, put out the word that we would release all of our prisoners. But in fact the agreement was if we see some signs of justice, then we would release two more, and all our prisoners would be released after all the bail hearings were held. The pigs had stated that they would have bail hearings on everyone's bail in the jail except the Panthers in the Panther 21 case. Out of 366 prisoners of war only 23 had had hearings. That is a token gesture, not a sign of justice.

In this writer's opinion, we should have not given up shit, after giving up those first two captives in some motherfucking "good faith." But some members of the team went out there and fucked up, talking about letting all captives go. A general consensus of all inmates, after learning about the fuck-up, was to let two go. I agreed, too. We had to keep a just image and keep the pigs in the light on going back on their word. When the team announced what had happened, how it had done in our collective instructions, many of us were smoking mad. But after hearing everyone who had anything to say on the matter, we voted to release two more. The fuck-up was taken out of the negotiating team, and we prepared for an attack.

Two of our prisoners were released, and they and the rest were interviewed by newsmen. The three we had left were taken to different cells for security reasons. During this time I began to note signs of fear—the realization that the pigs could possibly charge our confines and result in a life-or-death struggle on a mass scale. This feeling began to flow like lava in the faces of many. If the pigs came with gun and we fought, many of us would die and many of them would die, and we would have guns. If they teargassed us and came with clubs, then the battle would take the form of a medieval war, the Crusades, a gory, bloody, extremely down-to-earth old-fashioned real war, extremely real. With every weapon used up to the invention of the gun, how many inside the building would die? Maybe all of us before the shit was over. But surely the count was too high for anyone not to consider the possibility of himself departing life via Branch Queens. "Encirclement faces" began to flash, and some were panic-stricken, near a state of shock. So many of them that had been right on with the building of barricades, surely they asked themselves, "What the fuck done come over me?" They began to vent their fears. It was funny as hell, a super-duper trip. Somebody down for action started singing, "Everybody wants to go to heaven but nobody wants to die"— background music for niggers to punk out by—as a couple advanced cases shouted to "Let all the hostages go." It is not strange for a drowning man to grab for anything that may possibly save his life, and be found a day or weeks later—dead, with a "death lock" on a straw, a beer can or stick that couldn't have possibly saved him.

Now what would happen to our captives if such a battle took place? They would be *killed dead*, that's all. The frantic ones among us called for the release of all prisoners, as if to say, "In the name of reason, let's stop this thing, let's bring a halt to it." As the slaves began to return to their master and seek forgiveness, the warriors shouted, "Bullshit-punk motherfuckers, if we ain't got no captives we can't deal with nobody for nothing. That's the only thing that has stopped the pigs from coming in here already. We play it to a bust and if the pigs come we will fight, kill and die."

Do you—*you* who is reading this, here and now, know how it is to feel like nothing? Can you dig how it feels to be tired of feeling like nothing, a piece of shit? Can you dig how it feels to be a human being? A man? A man with a will and a purpose and a quest for justice? Can you relate to being a man for four days—and then stepping back into a cage, that houses a hollow shell, a bundle of blues, a being who receives whatever a treacherous society throws at him, who has been forgotten by so many people that he's forgotten his damn self, on your own accord? For the sake of an unjust peace? And a continuation of non-existence? Those of us who wanted to be a man for five days and until death said, in effect, we ain't giving in another inch. We're prepared—and we want to fight anyway!

In barless jails across Babylon this question will arise, and it is one that will have to be answered, in word and in deed. Many will die with it on their minds, in the act of hesitating. And some will say that the question has nothing to do with being a man and will accept the cage and the death as their fate, and as the "overpowering" will of who does it to them. And some will continue to die every day until their final death is rationed out to them.

There are only two sides, and two things to do, after all the jive changes are gone through and all is said.

By that time Brooklyn House of Detention, Kew Gardens and Rikers Island had exploded, but were suppressed, only us and the brothers in the Tombs were still holding out. As a gesture of solidarity, it was brought to the floor that instead of releasing two more captives and cutting down so much on our bargaining position, we would release one and ask them to release one, since they had mucho bargaining power. I dug the hell out of that idea, but it didn't go over too tough.

Sunday night a new tactic was developed. All the lights were cut off. The pigs would have to deal with "darkies in the darkness." That night the word was to make sure that, if possible, half of the guards in the jail would relax and get some sleep, while others stood and walked their post. It was getting very tense. The police were massed outside. It was explained that every night and every day would be an emergency situation, and we had to be prepared to hold out for as long as it took. I thought of six months and the periods that Japanese students had held universities. We had the upper hand, and we had it together. Many of the prisoners of war were almost to the point where we had to fight, as the pigs showed their racism by refusing a brother inmate emergency medical treatment that night. Early that day, we'd taken one of our hostages down the steps to get his shots, but after we did the doctor refused him, in fact the doctor placed the needle outside the barricade and rejoined the herd of pigs.

Because of the food shortage, we, after careful consideration, had torn part of a barricade down and raided the storage room, after which we had actually relocated it, without the pigs being aware. A small detachment got to work on the other storage room, but we decided to stop when the brother was asking for medical treatment, fearing that his case was one of life or death and that the pigs would hear the hammering and think that we were pulling another diversionary move and refuse the brother. We stopped but they did not consider not refusing the brother anyway.

The night passed into Monday morning, and as it did, people began to cluster in groups according to their feelings. Feelings had accelerated from an already supersonic speed. And the different undercurrents began to ascend to the sea of consciousness of all. Political consciousness varied in a fan of degrees; the tide of political consciousness had surely risen since the rebellion erupted. "Power to the people" and "off the pig" was shouted, and certainly understood and meant, by a large segment of prisoner population from the git-go. And cultural differences were brought to light at the start and not permitted to become barriers. Everything said in English at the meetings was also said in Spanish, from the onstart. And "brothers" became a thing of who thinks alike rather than a thing of who looks alike.

However, rumors were on the rampage, one that we, the Panthers, had taken over the rebellion and we were really running things and using the situation to project ourselves and to reap the political benefits from it. Other rumors came to the surface—that many of the members of the security teams on the flats and elsewhere were getting more than their rightful share of the food, and different other groups were also, like the Panthers and the tier captains.

To that we, the Panthers, stated flatly that we would step out of the whole thing, go back to our tiers and get some sleep; and also that there should be a general meeting excluding us and there everything should be brought to light, in order to determine just what's true and what's bullshit. We also stated that we would abide by the majority. We wanted all the whispering in little cliques to be brought into the open so it could be righteously dealt with. The news media had projected us and from the jumping-off and all through their coverage of the siege we were credited for organizing the rebellion. We felt that the brunt of the reprisals would fall on us, we pictured another indictment in the tradition of Jimmy Garrison and Frank Hogan and laughed about it—we didn't give a flying fuck about no pigs or pig reprisals anyway; we felt good about getting into the rebellion, because we feel good when something is being done about the pigs running planet Earth, and are ready, willing, and able to take the struggle higher! Since we can't get along with the pigs, we can get it *on* with them and dance to the death to soul music. In fact, "Engine Engine No. 9" by Wilson Pickett is as good a song as any to get down to some sure-enough, sure-enough battle to.

As events developed and contradictions developed, militancy and vigilance began to dissolve on one end of the scale, as readiness to go into battle rose on the other. It was easy to see that regardless of what anyone was saying, the issue was to get justice for all the population. And the choice was that either the prisoners of war would fight to keep the upper hand, and keep our hostages to help ensure getting justice done, or we would give up our bargaining power and accept whatever comes.

All of us had by that time been subjected to sophisticated Fun-City-style flim-flams; our very presence in that dungeon was proof of that. And all of us should have known that instead of New York being nicknamed Fun City it should be known as Flim-Flam City. There is no pity in Flim-Flam City. At that stage of the game, a lot of us had been beaten and deceived, and seemingly should have known that for us to receive amnesty would set a bigger precedent than making a judge come to a jail to have hearings. Slimy-snake Lindsay, mayor of Flim-Flam City, knew better than that when he said it. All the pigs, McGrath on down to the little pawn pigs waiting outside the building, knew the statement of "no reprisals" was bullshit.

All the committees had rapped, and a general meeting was called to ask one question: "If the pigs attack, are we gonna kill the hostages?" Here are some of the responses: "Yeah." "Motherfucking right." "No! No! No!" "Let's cut their throats, hang them, set them on fire and throw them out the eighth floor window." "We'll put them up to the window and tell the pigs to stop and if they keep coming, we'll throw them out one by one." A string of speakers one by one picked up the bullhorn and stated their case. One speaker—in essence: Let's do them in. Another—in part, in essence: This is revolution; if the pig come in here we'll off them! At that point an inmate approached me to rap, "You hear that, I've just been drafted into the army." Another, pointing to the floor, "You God-damn revolutionaries going to do all the time?" Another speaker, in essence and in quote, you read me, quote: "I think we have gone far enough. I think we should call a press conference and give the prisoners up." As he said that, I pictured the pig guard captain dying of a heart attack after hearing the earlier statements. During the people's arrest, he had flipped out, he was seeing things that no one else was: madmen at the back of his cell threatening to kill him. He was particularly hostile to the populace of Branch Queens before turn-about day, and like most racists, feared the people he victimized. He was looking to receive "payback." He "knew" it was coming. His mental disorders turned inward to destroy him. For every push there is a pull in the opposite direction, and his crude realization of it wrecked him. Another pig had walked a path in the cell he was placed in, he paced back and forth so much that one brother commented that he might walk through to the next cell under him.

Finally a comrade shouted down at a speaker who had just taken the bullhorn: "Hey man, the pig can hear everything we're talking about, we shouldn't have an open meeting, talking about this shit." For a time, things were submerged, but the question, still unresolved, bubbled. Many of us who wanted justice and were willing to pay the price and up the kitty, vowed to fight other POWs if necessary; and in many cases those who wanted to give the hostages up said that they would fight to do so. When asked what would they do if the pigs charged in, many said in effect that they would die before they would kill the hostages. We were getting close to going to war between ourselves, different groups began planning different moves to take the prisoners or to protect them. Which is not as unfortunate as the fact that the brothers who would rather die than ice three pigs were actually saying that the lives of these pigs had more worth than theirs. Black people have been conditioned to die behind any old bullshit for so long that taking those white pigs' lives in response for murders of ourselves seemed to be incomprehensible to them. A crime against God, and three other white men.

We had been following the radio reports on the rebellions. They reported that one by one the other rebellions were smashed, and that after a long delay the brothers in the Tombs had given up, letting their hostages go. Then they began reporting the situation at Branch Queens in the manner of a football game. One station began saying that the police were massed outside the building and their forces were mobilized so heavy as to have been unseen since World War Two. This was psychological warfare. The station further stated that ten Black Panthers who were awaiting trial would probably get the blame for what happened. And so on and so forth and soo bee doo bee doo. A cold silence was maintained, mostly, in Branch Queens. Although a few bursts of laughter occasionally crackled in the darkness.

Then Flim-Flam's chief executive—Lindsay—came over the radio and run down the same game on us that the slimy-bicycle-riding pig ran down on the brothers in the Tombs. A thirty-minute ultimatum for Branch Queens. Release all your hostages and there will be no reprisals. I had hoped aloud that the pigs would take for granted that no such transaction would take place and just charge in, for at that point another day of inaction was more destructive to the cause of justice than an assault on those seeking justice. To rumble then would have pulled the mass of us together in a truly revolutionary fashion. A victory—that is, to turn back the charge of the pigs— would have produced an army out of prisoners of war, who would then be drafted by their incarceration.

Now it was time to take a vote. "All right, as quietly as you can meet in the middle of your tier and starting from the fifth tier on down, give one vote for each tier. Should we turn the hostages loose or should we keep them and fight?" My only bone with the way that the voting was taken is that I think everyone should've voted individually—which would have been exact and so, fairer, more in the interest of the people. Some tiers were solidly against anything but fighting and some members of most tiers were down to fight. By giving each tier one vote those who were outnumbered on their particular tier's opinion on a sticky two-sided issue were omitted. However, many believed we should come to an understanding as soon as possible. I felt that we had more time. At the same time I hoped that we would run out of time, but really knew we wouldn't. If the half hour had run out Lindsay would have extended the time before the onrush of pigs, at least until daylight. Fifth tier—"Turn them loose." Fourth tier—"Turn them loose." Third tier—"Turn them loose." Second tier—"Fight!" The flats—"Fight." The annex—"Fight." The dormitory—"Turn them loose."

A cluster of argument formed like an electric cloud. Militant brothers shouted from the floor, "Listen brothers, we'll go along with the majority because we don't want to fight you, but the pigs are gonna fuck you up anyway!" We knew.

A few brothers still considered fighting the non-warriors. "If you're going to turn them loose, bring them on down here." The ideas about taking the hostages away from the non-warriors became a thing of the past, some non-warriors nailed the lid on the coffin of the rebellion. They packed around the hostages and covered their heads with pillows, removed the barricade, rushed them to the gate, turned the hostages over and had the gate slammed in their faces.

It was a big let-down and all the Panthers and other brothers who were down came up to the annex with us. Some were crying, everything seemed over and surely not as much came out of it as was hoped. Food was opened up and a light partying atmosphere was created for two reasons: because all of us were hungry, and to cover up the pain of losing a battle we did not have a chance to fight. I knew that there was no way I could walk down those steps and submit to the pigs. All of us Panthers knew that we were marked men, marked for murder and torture. We also felt at that time that the brothers

who'd come to the annex with us should have stayed
with the others because their lives would be in *more*
danger if they stayed with us. The explanation for the
entire sequence of events is simply "growing pains," to
those of us who believe that oppressed people *will* rise
up and seek justice, and not long from now the people's
struggle will evolve to the stage where in a similar situation the vote will be fight, fight, fight, fight, fight—and off
the pigs, physically. We begged the brothers to leave,
for what we felt then was their own good, and most of
them reluctantly did.

Then brothers began running back. Saying that the
pigs were killing different brothers down there, in the
courtyard. The pigs had lined brothers up with their
hands cuffed behind their backs and were beating them
with billy clubs, baseball bats, and ax handles. We witnessed it from the windows, and waited for some more
brothers to return. A couple of us went throughout the
building to pick up certain weapons critical to our defensive position. When our detachment came back, and still
no more brothers came up the steps, we closed the door,
jammed the lock, and barricaded the door heavily. Then
we took a large supply of food to the next floor, barricaded
the steps, and set up posts in each of the rooms on the
next two floors. Then while some of us shouted out of
the bullhorn what was happening in the prison yard, why
we were resisting, and to help us, the rest of us prepared
for battle.

The pigs jeered to cover up the voice condemning their
actions while others went about handcuffing brothers
behind their backs, making them sit cross-legged on the
ground and then beating them ruthlessly with their ax
handles, baseball bats, and billy clubs.

We were preparing to fight a week if necessary, or
even longer. Any battle up there would be a desperate

motherfucker. We knew it and the pigs knew it. We were ready to fight to the death, and take as many pigs with us as possible. All our bargaining power was released to the enemy; we now had to fight not only for our lives but for a death that would be acceptable.

We were also telling the people what was happening, explaining the crimes being carried out by the gestapo, and asking them to please contact the Black Panther Party, the Young Lords Party, Jerry Lefcourt, Charles McKinney, William Crain, Bob Bloom, Shirley Chisholm, Herman Badillo, or Minister Farrakhan.

The day stretched to noon, and thanks to a couple of true reporters the out-and-out torture in the yard came to public light and our existence was recognized. But we still continued our vigilance. A couple brothers became overly paranoid, and some made a rope that could reach to the ground in order to get out in case of a fire, but most of us would have chosen dying in the fire over climbing out of that window on a rope.

Things began to look up and that evening we heard that our release was being negotiated by our lawyers versus McGrath. We had a little bargaining power again. We watched the news and saw one of the most accurate reports that we had seen. But we continued blasting from "the golden bullhorn" and seeing familiar faces on the streets, and finally we had a meeting with our lawyers and an unharmed release in the workings, so we packed up and prepared to depart.

We left the building by way of a "cherry picker." Which is a pretty way-out way to leave any building. All power to the people. The people had saved us. They had come to our aid and we could thank them. All power to the people, we love you. Each one of us exchanged power salutes with the people, to me it was a religious experience. I saw a sister and thought, Now, I just seen a sister that looks finer than Carol. She had a red sweater on and she glowed from within. When I get out, I told myself, I'm going to get that Mickey-Fricky, hunt her down like a hound dog. I heard Hendrix, "I am gonna take you home, ain't gonna do you no harm, you got to be mine alone! . . . Foxy lady." Later I found out that it was Carol.

As the buses moved out, surrounded by a giant motorcade, what could we say but, "All power to the people." The people made the pigs act in a civilized manner. Nixon had never received an escort like the one we had. All power to the people.

Devious-snake Lindsay's evil designs had failed, his bicycle-riding through Central Park did not fool everyone. He is perfectly aware of what happened in that yard. All the committee members were tortured who didn't hold out. He didn't meet with them as he said he would, he met with his cohorts and plotted vicious reactionary plans. Lindsay is number-one pig in Flim-Flam City and to prove it he asked McGrath, his crimemate, to "investigate" the "alleged" attacks on prisoners.

It is a known fact that the pigs moved on the students of Columbia University with goals set to wreck their bodies and heads and Lindsay did nothing but appoint someone to "investigate" it. The same at Madison Square Garden, the same at Sheep Meadow, the same every time. Someone to "investigate."

Well, I've investigated Lindsay. And the only difference between Lindsay in New York and Daley in Chicago is that Lindsay is sneakier and slimier and has no national conventions to expose him. He's a deadly creep.

Well the pigs were really sorry-looking. As you know, they were out to kill us and they had told us so. Five pigs in a fit of reactionary frustration tore off their badges and at least one of them physically attacked Lindsay's "whipping boy" aide and I'm willing to bet that a whole lot of women and children were assaulted by pigs after they found out they could not get to us. And I would like to tell those women and children that they ain't got to take that shit. Move on the old man! Cut his throat, poison him, set him on fire while he's asleep. The family that gets rid of cancers together, finds out the answers together.

As the buses holding political prisoners readied to pull off, the warden and his puppet troops entered the empty warehouse; it was a very comical scene, please try to picture it: their mental state seemed to be, "Well, back to work, we might not have no inmates, boys, but we got a jail to run and a job to do." On that, the robot pigs marched into a totally unusable concentration camp. We'd left Branch Queens in no shape to store people, to hold any people in against their will. The place would have to be surrounded by pigs like it was during the rebellion. So the warehouse is out of order. This is only the beginning. We are going to have our freedom and we'll tear down the jails with bars and the jails without bars and America will be unusable for pigs and fit for people. All Power to the People.

TO: "Justice" Murtagh*

FROM: The Defendants [Lumumba Shakur, Dharuba, Curtis Powell, Cetewayo, Robert Collier, Baba Odinga, Afeni Shakur, Ali Bey Hassan, Katara, Clark Squire, Joan Bird, Lee Roper, Kinshasa]

---

* Excerpts from a statement by the defendants in the first "Panther 21" trial, addressed to the presiding judge, dated March 1, 1970.

We the defendants named by the state in the proceedings now pending before "Justice" John M. Murtagh say:

That the history of this nation has most definitely developed a dual set of social, economic, and political realities, as well as dynamics. One white, and the other black.

Let us not conveniently forget how the system of "American justice" systematically upheld the bizarre reasoning about black people in order to retain a system of slave labor. And when this became economically unnecessary, how "the great American system of justice" helped to establish and maintain social degradation and deprivation of all who were not white, and most certainly, those who were black. To be sure, the entire country had to share in this denial; to justify the inhuman treatment of other human beings, the American had to conceal from himself and others his oppression of blacks, but again the white dominant society has long had absolute power, especially over black people—so it was no difficult matter to ignore them, define them, forget them, and if they persisted, pacify or punish them.

We as a people do not exist except as victims, and to this and much more, we say, No more. For 350 years we said this in various ways. But running deep in the American psyche is the fear of the ex-slave. Those of the other reality, the dominant white culture, its institutions, had no ears to truly hear. The wax of centuries of master-slave relationship had stopped up their ears, your ears. For if our reality, the black experience in America, is invalid, then so are the institutions and social structure that contributed to its creation invalid. If you then concede it is valid (which it most definitely is), then it must be of consequence in determining what is "justice" compared to us (black people).

White citizens have grown up with the identity of an American, and have enjoyed a completely different relationship to the institutions of this nation.

Blacks are no longer the economic underpinning of the nation. But we continue to be willing, or unwilling, victims. There is a timeless quality to the unconscious which transforms yesterday into today.

In the original draft of the Declaration of Independence there was a paragraph that Thomas Jefferson intended to include in the list of grievances against King George III: "He has waged cruel war against human nature itself, violating its most sacred rights of life and liberty in the person of a distant people [African, black people], who never offended him; captivating and carrying them into slavery in another hemisphere, or to incur miserable death in their transportation thither."

This paragraph was omitted in the final document.

The years passed and our wretched plight progressively worsened, the "laws" of bondage became even more institutionalized, inculcated in the dominant culture. In order to further protect and perpetuate their domination over us, the southern states passed many repressive laws called "slave codes." For us, there was no freedom of assembly. If more than four or five slaves came together without permission from a white person, that gathering in the depraved minds of the slave masters was construed as a conspiracy. The towns and cities imposed a 9:00 P.M. curfew on us, there was no freedom of movement, a pass had to be carried by the slave whenever he was out of the presence of his master. And to enforce these ignoble laws, slave patrols, organized like militias, were composed, of armed and mounted whites. (This mentality persists to this day. Woe to the black man who is out very late in a white neighborhood; the police [white] suspect him immediately of being up to some foul deed. Even into the ghetto, the white policeman brings this mentality.)

Although slavery had been abolished in certain states, the black people who lived in those states were subjected to degrading laws which belied their so-called free status, and even worse, they were subject to kidnapping and being sold into slavery. The so-called free black man was anything but free under the "American system of justice."

Throughout this horrid epoch, a few slaves managed to escape, then more slaves. The slaveholders demanded that the runaway slave laws be enforced. They pleaded to the United States Supreme Court, and that "august" body, the most powerful judiciary body in the land, the ultimate interpreters of the Constitution, answered their plea by upholding the 1793 Fugitive Slave Act in 1842, and again in 1845, and made it more stringent yet in 1850. Now for the runaway slave escaping to the North was not enough, for the northern cities were overrun with slave-catchers.

In July 1847, Dred Scott brought suit in a Federal Court for his freedom. It took the Dred Scott case ten years to reach the "sacred" halls of the Supreme Court, and when that "prestigious" group of men spoke in March, 1857, through the voice of "Chief Justice" Roger Taney, the Court ruled that "people of African descent are not and cannot be citizens of the United States and cannot sue in any court of the United States," and that black people have "no rights which whites are bound to respect"—a classic example of the "American way of justice."

The Reconstruction Era was a time of great and unparalleled hope. It seemed as though black people were finally to be accorded equal and humane treatment when the 13th, 14th and 15th Amendments were enacted.

But terror, violence, intimidation, and murder still haunted us. The Ku Klux Klan did "their thing."

In 1866, 1871, and 1875, Congress enacted the first significant civil rights laws. They theoretically gave black people the right to equal housing, accommodations, facilities, and access to public transportation and places of public amusement. But as blacks well know and whites deny, there is a world of difference in America between theory and practice. For although the 13th, 14th, and 15th Amendments and civil rights legislation "gave" black people so-called freedom, the right of citizenship and the right to vote, the enforcement of those laws was an entirely different thing.

The Supreme Court in 1883 declared that those civil rights acts were unconstitutional. Only in 1954, after intense domestic pressure and unveiling internationally as a nation of hypocrites, the Supreme Court reversed some of its earlier, infamous decisions—not all of them—and ruled that segregated educational facilities were unconstitutional. But this ruling, like virtually every seemingly just decision for black people, was almost immediately revealed as a sham, a mere gesture to pacify us and alleviate your embarrassment, for the public schools of the nation are still overwhelmingly segregated and unequal, the result of a century of duality.

In the North, in the South, in the East and in the West, all over the country black people are accused of crimes, thrown in your jails, dragged through your courts and administered a sour dose of "American justice." We are in jail outside, and jail inside. Black people and now all poor people have been well educated in the American system of justice.

We know very well what is meant by your statement,

"This court is responsible for maintaining proper respect for the administration of criminal justice and preventing any reflection on the image of American justice." Properly translated, it simply means that the farce must go on. The image must remain intact.

In 1970, 90 per cent of the inmates of your prisons are non-white. A leading criminologist, R. R. Kornhauser of Stanford University, has noted that 80 per cent of the people now in prison were put there *illegally* according to *your* own law. (Strange that the overwhelming population is black and non-white?)

Mr. Murtagh—your record speaks for itself.

● On April 2, 1969, hordes of "police" broke down our doors, or otherwise forced entry into our homes, and ran amok. Rampaging and rummaging through our homes, they seized articles from us with wild abandon while having no search warrants. The "police" put us and our families in grave danger, nervously aiming shotguns, rifles and pistols at us and our families—even our children.

We were then kidnapped, as were some of our families. We state "kidnap" because many of us were never shown any arrest warrant, even to this day. This is illegal. This is a blatant contradiction of your own Constitution. We said nothing.

● Upon the arrest of *some* of the defendants and before the appearance of any of the defendants, New York City District Attorney Frank Hogan appeared on national radio and national television in a press conference, during which time he gave out information from an "indictment" against us in an inflammatory and provocative manner, deliberately designed to incite the people against us and to deny us even the semblance of a "fair trial." Mr. Hogan implied a lie—that we had been seized on the way to commit these alleged acts with bombs in our hands—rather than the truth—that we had no bombs and that most of us were taken out of our beds.

Subsequent to that press conference, "unidentified police sources" and "persons close to the investigation" stated falsely to the press that we, as members of the Black Panther Party, were being aided and abetted by foreign governments considered hostile to your government (i.e., Cuba and China)—that we, as Black Panther Party members, were stealing money from federal and/or state agencies and many other false wild charges, designed to heighten the public alarm against us and our Party, rather than diminish it, so as to create an atmosphere conducive to the extermination of the Black Panther Party and justify anything that might be done to us.

This unethical behavior gave, aided, and abetted further prejudicial pre-trial publicity, in direct contradiction to your law as outlined in the 14th Amendment of your Constitution of the United States. Due to this behavior alone, we are positive that we could not get a fair trial anywhere in this country. We still said nothing.

● When our attorneys learned of our arrest, they attempted to see us, as we were being held in your District Attorney's office. They were refused permission to do so. At the "arraignment" a similar request by our counsel was again refused by Mr. Charles Marks, who presided thereat. These refusals were in blatant violation of your law as outlined in the 6th and 14th Amendments of your Constitution of the United States. We continued to be silent.

● At this "arraignment" this Mr. Charles Marks, who was presiding, refused to read, explain, or give us a copy of this "indictment" against us. This is another violation of your law as outlined in the 6th and 14th Amendments

of your Constitution of the United States. Yet, we remained silent.

● Bail (ransom) was set at $100,000, which is ridicu-
lous and tantamount to no bail at all. This is another violation of your own law as outlined in the 8th and 14th
Amendments of your Constitution of the United States.
We state that this bail is not only contradictory to your
own law, but that it is also racist. When white "radical"
groups are arrested, their bails do not usually exceed
$10,000. When three Yemenites were charged with "con-
spiracy" to murder your President Nixon, and with having
the equipment to do such, their bail was $25,000; when
Minutemen in New York were arrested and charged with
a conspiracy to commit murder, the murder of 155 persons, and were arrested with bombs and guns, more than
enough to do this, bail was set at $25,000. We had no
bombs. Our bail was $100,000. We remained silent.

● At this arraignment, this Mr. Charles Marks, the
same "Judge" who is alleged to have signed the "arrest
warrants," stated in words or substance that he was accepting all of the allegations in the "indictment" against
us to be true. On subsequent hearings during April and
May 1969, concerning reduction of ransom (bail), at
which this same Mr. Marks still presided, he stated that
we were "un-American" and that the law "did not apply
to us" (sounds of history?). This does not quite show
impartiality. Yet, we said nothing.

● Our counsels have been in front of at least 35
"Judges" concerning our bail, and this attitude permeates
the "great American system of justice." All motions on
this were denied, either without comment or because
of the "seriousness" of the "charges," but *never* dealing
with the Constitutional issues involved, and it is *your*

Constitution. All of this seems to underlie "Judge" Marks' remarks. Yet, we said nothing.

● We have been treated like animals—in fact, like less than animals. On January 17, 1969, Miss Joan Bird was kidnapped, beaten, and tortured. She was punched and beaten, given the "Thumb Torture," hung upside down by the ankle from out of a third-story window of a "police precinct." On April 2-3, 1969, some of us were beaten as we were being kidnapped. From April 2, 1969, all of us were placed under constant abuse and harassment, which included twenty-four-hour lock-in, complete isolation, no library or recreation, lights kept on in our cells for twenty-four hours, physical assaults.

Our families have suffered abuse in trying to visit us, and mental anguish. One of us suffered the loss of a child because of this. Some of our families had to go on welfare because of our outrageous incarceration and ransom. We were denied mail, even from our attorneys—denied access to consult as a group with our attorneys. We have been subjected to the most onerous and barbaric of jail conditions. The objective of all this was our psychological and physical destruction during our pre-trial detention.

As even *Newsweek* magazine states, ". . . the handling of the suspects between their arrest and their trial was something less than a model of American criminal justice," and "none of it was very becoming to the state . . ." (How well we know.) All this is a blatant violation of your own law as outlined in the 8th and 14th Amendments of your own Federal Constitution. Yet, we *still* remained silent.

● You—Murtagh. You came into the case in May, 1969. You were informed of these conditions. You could have righted these blatant violations of your own law, the laws you have "sworn" to uphold. But you did not. You refused to do this—and remained silent. You tried to rush us pell-mell to trial, knowing full well that we were not, could not be, prepared. We remained silent.

We filed motions that are guaranteed to "citizens" by the 14th Amendment of your Federal Constitution. You denied them all. You denied us the right as guaranteed in your laws in the 6th and 14th Amendments of your own Constitution, to conduct a *voir dire* of the Grand Jury in these proceedings, knowing full well that they did not comprise members of our peer group. We remained silent.

You denied us a hearing with which to be confronted with the witnesses against us, as is guaranteed by your law in the 6th Amendment of your Constitution. We remained silent.

You denied us a Bill of Particulars which is guaranteed by your laws in the 6th and 14th Amendments of your Constitution. We remained silent.

Two "suspects" were kidnapped under the modification of the Fugitive Slave Act in November, 1969. You gave them no bail. (No sense pretending any more, it seems.) We remained silent.

You denied us every state and federal constitutional right, and remained silent. You substantiated Mr. Marks' "the law does not apply" to us. Yet, we remained silent.

● Lee Berry. Lee Berry is a classical example of how you and your cohorts conduct the "American System of Justice" when dealing with black people. On April 3, 1969, Lee Berry was a patient in the Veterans' Administration Hospital where he was receiving treatment as an epileptic, subject to *grand mal* seizures, which can be fatal. Lee Berry is not mentioned particularly in the "indictment." Yet, on April 3, 1969, your "police" dragged him out of the hospital. These "police" stood him up before your cohort, "Judge" Marks. Lee was "arraigned" without counsel. Bail, $100,000. He was thrown into an isolation cell in the Tombs without even a mattress. In July, 1969, he was physically attacked without provocation and without warning, while he was in a drugged stupor.

You were aware of his condition—you were quite aware. Numerous motions were in your "great court system." It took four months to even get him medication, and only in November, when he had become so ill, so progressively worse that it was frightening. He finally got consent to be transferred to Bellevue Hospital. Because of the courts' decisions under your "American system of justice," Lee Berry has had four serious operations within the last two months. Because of the courts' decisions under the Great American System of Justice at this precise moment Lee Berry is lying in the shadow of death. At the very least, your Great Court system is guilty of attempted murder, and D.A. Hogan should be named as a co-defendant. Lee Berry is our brother, and what is done to him has been done to us all. And we remained silent.

● In November, 1969, four white persons were arrested for allegedly "bombing" various sites in New York City. They were arrested allegedly with "bombs in their possession," but they were white. For three of them, bail was reduced 80 per cent in two days, because "the presumption of innocence is basic among both the statutory and constitutional principles affecting bail"—if you are white. (The political climate is such today, even this hardly matters any more if one is dissident.)

Two days after that decision, we were brought in front of you and given a superseding "indictment." We could be silent no longer. We had been insulted enough—more than enough. We had been treated with contempt, in an atmosphere of intimidation for too long.

We must reiterate—we are looking at the situation objectively. Objective reality.

At the pre-trial hearings we are confronted with a "judge" who has admitted, in fact, been indicted and arrested for, ignoring "police" graft and corruption. A "judge" who by his record shows an unblemished career of "police" favoritism and All-American racism. In your previous dealings with black people, you have shown yourself to be totally unjust, bloodthirsty, pitiless, and inhuman. We are confronted with a District Attorney machine which has shown itself to be vigilant and unswerving in its racist policies. Of the inmates convicted, 90 per cent are non-white and poor. This machine has shown itself to be unethical in its techniques and practices— even in front of our eyes—tactics which include going up and whispering to the witnesses on the stand, signaling and coaching them. We know, as *Look* magazine stated in June, 1969, "how the police corrupt the truth . . . Prosecutors and judges become their accomplices." To cite a small example: A man, a black man, was beaten to death in the Tombs in front of forty witnesses in May, 1969, and the police swore that he died of a "heart attack." Yes, we *know* what the police will swear to. All black people, poor people, know what the police will swear to. All this, together with the hostility inculcated in the dominant white culture toward anything black, is shown by you and your cohorts very well indeed. Under these conditions, and considering our stand against American racism, this is not only a challenge to us and black people, but the whole people. To relate in terms you can understand, even Racist Woodrow Wilson stated (concerning fascism): ". . . This is a challenge to all mankind; there is one choice we cannot make, we are incapable of making, we will not choose the path of submission . . . we will be, we must be as harsh as the Truth and as uncompromising as Justice—true Justice is on our side . . ." To that we say, right on!

You have implied contempt charges. We cannot conceive of how this could be possible. How can we be in contempt of a court that is in contempt of its own laws? How can you be responsible for "maintaining respect and dispersing justice," when you have dispensed with justice, and you do not maintain respect for your own Constitution? How can you expect us to respect your laws, when you do not respect them yourself? Then you have the audacity to demand respect, when you, your whole Great System of Justice, is out of order, and does not respect us, or our rights.

You have talked about our counsel inciting us. Nothing could be further from the truth. The injustices we have been accorded over the past year incite us, the injustice in these hearings incite us, racism incites us, fascism incites us, in short—when we reflect back over history, its continuation up until today, you and your courts incite us.

But we will not leave it there for you and others to distort, as some are inclined to do. There will be left no room for your courts and media to distort and misinterpret our actions. We wish for a speedy and FAIR trial, a just trial. But—we must have our "alleged" Constitutional rights. This court is in contempt of our Constitutional rights and has been for almost a year. We must have our rights first. The wrongs inflicted must be redressed. Bygones are *not* bygones. Later for that; 350 years are enough. We must clean the slate. We do not believe in your Appeal Courts (we've had experience with 350 years of appeals generally, and 35 judges specifically). So we must begin anew with a mutual understanding. When we have our Con-

stitutional guarantees redressed, we will give the court
the respect it claims to deserve—precisely the respect it
deserves.

In light of all that has been said, in view of the collu-
sion of the federal, state, and city courts, the New York
City Department of Correction, the city police, and District Attorney's office, we feel that we, as members of the
Black Panther Party, cannot receive a fair and impartial
trial without certain pre-conditions conforming to our
alleged constitutional rights. So we state the following:
we feel that the courts should follow their own federal
Constitution, and when they have failed to do so, and
continue to ignore their mistakes but persist dogmatically
to add insult to injury, those courts are in contempt of
the people. One need not be black to relate to that, but
it is often those who never experience such actions on the
part of the courts, who believe they, the courts, can
never be wrong.

Afeni Shakur

March 20, 1971

A letter to Jamala, Lil Afeni, Sekyiwa, and the unborn
baby (babies) within my womb.

First let me tell you that this book was not my idea at
all (as a matter of fact I was hardly cooperative). But
I suppose that one day you're going to wonder about all
this mess that's going on now and I just had to make sure
you understood a few things.

I've learned a lot in two years about being a woman
and it's for that reason that I want to talk to you. Joan
and I, and all the brothers in jail, are caught up in this
funny situation where everyone seems to be attacking
everyone else and we're sort of in the middle looking

dumb. I've seen a lot of people I knew and loved die in the past year or so and it's really been a struggle to remain unbitter.

February 8th when Joan and I came back to jail I was full of distrust, disappointment and disillusionment. But now the edges are rounded off a bit and I think I can understand why some things happened. I don't like most of it but I *do* understand. I've discovered what I should have known a long time ago—that change has to begin within ourselves—whether there is a revolution today or tomorrow—we still must face the problems of purging ourselves of the larceny that we have all inherited. I hope we do not pass it on to you because you are our only hope.

You must weigh our actions and decide for yourselves what was good and what was bad. It is obvious that somewhere we failed but I know it will not—it cannot end here. There is too much evilness left. I cannot get rid of my dream of peace and harmony. It is for that dream that most of us have fought—some bravely, some as cowards, some as heroes, and some as plain old crooks. Forgive us our mistakes because mostly they were mistakes which were made out of blind ignorance (sometimes arrogance). Judge us with empathy for we were (are) idealists and sometimes we're young and foolish.

I do not regret any of it—for it taught me to be something that some people will never learn—for the first time in my life I feel like a woman—beaten, battered and scarred maybe, but isn't that what wisdom is truly made of. Help me to continue to learn—only this time with a bit more grace for I am a poor example for anyone to follow because I have deviated from the revolutionary principles which I know to be correct. I wish you love.

Publisher's Note

April 2, 1969: Fifteen Panthers were arrested in a series
of raids pursuant to a twelve-count indictment
against a total of twenty-one members of the Black
Panther Party on a variety of charges ranging from
"conspiracy to commit murder" and "arson" to
"reckless endangerment" and several counts involving "possession of explosive substances." Bail
was set for *all* defendants at $100,000.

November 17, 1969: A superseding indictment com-
pounded the original indictment to include thirty
counts against all twenty-one defendants.

February 2, 1970: Pretrial hearings began in State Supreme Court at 100 Centre Street in Manhattan,
commencing the longest trial in the history of the
state and perhaps the longest trial in the history
of the United States. (The defendants were represented by Carol Lefcourt, Gerald Lefcourt, Sanford Katz, William Crain, Robert Bloom and
Charles McKinney.)

February 25, 1970: After a series of courtroom disruptions
and warnings to the defendants by State Supreme
Court Judge John M. Murtagh, pretrial hearings
were halted for an indefinite period, unprecedented in the history of the judicial system. After
a one-month recess, Judge Murtagh received into
the court's record a 24-page manifesto written by
the defendants, and pretrial hearings were resumed.

September 8, 1970: The actual trial began with the selection of the jury.

October 1, 1970: A series of prison rebellions erupted at Branch Queens Men's House of Detention and quickly spread to the Tombs in Manhattan, Brooklyn Men's House of Detention and New Queens Men's House of Detention, in an attempt to focus attention on the conditions in the state prison system, the prohibitively high bails set for crimes and the length of confinement of prisoners before they are brought to trial.

November 20, 1970: Two of the defendants were indicted on charges growing out of the October jail rebellion. Cases still pending.

February 8, 1971: Richard Moore and Michael Tabor did not appear in court and were later located in Algeria.

May 13, 1971: After nine months, the jury in the New York Panther 21 Conspiracy case returned after ninety minutes of deliberation and acquitted all thirteen* defendants on all 156 remaining counts from the previous two indictments.

---

* Three Panthers were never apprehended and brought to trial, two were severed because of age, one was severed because of illness, and two were being held in New Jersey for trial on previous charges.

Unidentified Panther 21 supporters.

Panther 21 solidarity press conference, featuring actress Ruby Dee (center).

Panther 21 courthouse rally.

Panther 21 courthouse rally.

Panther 21 courthouse rally.

Panther rank and file members in from of courthouse during trial.

Solidarity rally featuring Panther 21 codefendants Afeni Shakur, Dhoruba Bin Wahad, and Jamal Joseph.

Elbert "Big Man" Howard, one of the six founding members of the Oakland-based Black Panther Party for Self-Defense, speaking at a New York rally in defense of the Panther 21.

Dhoruba Bin Wahad and Jamal Joseph.

Afeni Shakur.

days. Part of Collier's work was building a community center on New York City's Lower East Side, in a rundown building on 9th Street and Avenue B." Such alliances, born out of political vision and practical struggle, hold valuable lessons to this day.

Even among those of the 21 who can clearly be identified as having been indicted, it is important to note that several subgroups emerged for legal and logistical reasons. Though all 21 were acquitted on all charges (and most had never before been charged with any criminal activity, nor have they since) there were essentially only thirteen who actually stood trial in the case. Thus, the list may best be broken down into five distinct categories: the base of thirteen who stood trial; three who were never captured at the time of the roundup and trial; two who were already being held in New Jersey and thus did not stand trial with the rest; two who were seventeen-year-old high school students granted youth offender status; and one who was an epileptic—separated from the rest because he was in critical condition at Bellevue Hospital at the outset of the trial.

Listed, then, in alphabetical order by chosen first name (with given or "slave" name in parenthesis) and grouped in the subgroups indicated above, the 21 were:

Thirteen standing trial: Abayama Katara (Alex McKeiver); Afeni Shakur (Alice Faye Williams); Ali Bey Hassan (John Casson); Baba Odinga (Walter Johnson); Dhoruba Bin Wahad (Richard "Dharuba," later changed to Dhoruba, Moore); Cetaweyo (Michael Tabor); Dr. Curtis Powell; Joan Bird (Byrd); Kwando Kinshasa (William King); Lumumba Shakur (Anthony Coston); Robert Collier; Shaba Om (Lee Roper); and Sundiata Acoli (Clark Squire).

Three eluded capture during NY 21 trial: Larry Mack; Mshina (Thomas Berry); and Sekou Odinga (Nathanial Burns).

Two held in New Jersey on other charges: Kuwasi Balagoon (Donald Weems); and Nine (Richard Harris).

Two granted youthful offender status: Jamal (Edward) Joseph; Lonnie Epps. One medically ill at time of trial: Mkubu (Lee Berry).

The short biographies below, including updates on all of the 21, are presented in simple alphabetical order by author's first name. Part Two will provide greater details in never-before-published reflections.

Abayama Katara (Alex McKeiver): nineteen at the time of the indictment, was president of the Afro-American History Club at Benjamin Franklin High School in Manhattan, about ready to graduate. He eventually married and raised a daughter with Safiya Bukhari, another young Panther militant who went on to join the Black Liberation Army, go underground, and ultimately get captured and imprisoned in 1975, only to escape less than two years later. Once recaptured, Bukhari served six years and, once out on parole, rose to the position of vice president of the Provisional Government of the Republic of New Afrika. She helped found the New York City Coalition to Free Mumia Abu-Jamal and cofounded, along with Herman Ferguson, the Jericho Movement to Free All Political Prisoners.

Afeni Shakur (Alice Faye Williams) is sometimes referred to as the "mother of hip-hop" because of the critical and commercial success of her son Tupac Shakur, to whom she gave birth just weeks after the acquittal of the 21. A dynamic speaker who went against the advice of some of her fellow Panther 21 cohorts in deciding to vocally defend herself in court, many credit her directly with the ultimate acquittal and dropping of all charges. Afeni was twenty-seven at the time of the indictment and had been part of the Manpower Training Program (an early vocational training effort) in the year before the trial, also working as a teaching assistant in the NYC public schools. She was a poet and a journalist, winning a citywide high school journalism contest for her research on joblessness.

Despite some difficulties in her post-Panther life, Afeni was considered a mentor and "auntie" by many figures around the Panthers. She eventually founded and led the Tupac Amaru Shakur Foundation, providing support for young people interested in the arts. Upon her passing in 2016, three former New York Panthers—Sekou Odinga, Dhoruba Bin Wahad, and Bilal Sunni Ali—collectively penned a tribute that appears on pages 563–64.

Ali Bey Hassan (John Casson): as one of the older members of the 21, Ali Bey worked for the Party "while attempting to educate the community and organize around community control issues"—according to support materials for the 21 which were published at the time of the trial. It is an apt description. He never stopped organizing and educating throughout his life—always clear about his Panther 21 affiliations and the ongoing urgent work to free all political prisoners. Described by comrades as a "true original" and a great soldier, Ali Bey succumbed to cancer in January 2010.

Cyril Innis Jr. (Bullwhip), who was appointed a Panther lieutenant working for the Bronx Ministry of Information by Zayd Shakur, became very close to Ali Bey, noting, "He was a very serious brother, and highly principled. Through his work as national coordinator of the Sundiata Acoli Freedom

Campaign, his very close relationship with Mumia Abu-Jamal and the effort to get him off death row and ultimately released, plus much else, Ali Bey inspired so many of us."

Baba Odinga (Walter Johnson) was born in Antigua in 1944. The editors of this volume have been unable to gather much information about this elder's post-Panther life.

Cetewayo (Michael Tabor Jr.) was born in Harlem on December 13, 1946, to Grace Hunter and Michael Tabor Sr. He attended the St. Aloysius Roman Catholic School on West 132nd Street and Harlem's Rice High School where he excelled in both academics and varsity athletics. Tabor joined the Black Panther Party in 1969 and took the name Cetewayo, after a nineteenth-century Zulu Warrior King. It was after he joined the Panthers that he wrote an insightful pamphlet on drug addiction called *Capitalism Plus Dope Equals Genocide* (excerpted in this special edition). According to former members, Tabor was one of the better-known spokespersons for the Panther Party and was admired for his deep voice and charismatic personality. "We loved his deep bass," recalled Bullwhip. "He reminded us of Paul Robeson."

In February of 1971, while out on bail in the 21 case, Tabor flew to Algiers with his new wife, fellow Black Panther Party member Connie Matthews, who had been the group's international coordinator. In 1972, Tabor moved to Lusaka, Zambia on a writing assignment for the Paris-based *Afrique Asie* magazine, in order to cover the African liberation movements based there. He would remain in Lusaka for the next thirty-eight years. After the death of Connie, he married Zambian national Priscilla Matanda. Tabor became a popular and respected figure in Lusaka and continued writing on politics and culture for various publications. His distinctive voice allowed him to transition into radio and for many years he hosted programs that featured jazz, African, and world music on several Lusaka radio stations. Columbia University professor and friend Melvin McCray was quoted in the *New York Times* obituary on October 23, 2010, saying Cetewayo had adamantly stated that he did not want to return to the U.S. "The old guard of African liberation movements respected him as a freedom fighter."

Dr. Curtis Powell was employed as a research biochemist at Columbia Presbyterian Medical Center at the time of his arrest, engaged in cancer research. Despite this and repeated requests and evidence from the defense, the prosecution continuously refused to address Powell as "doctor." One of the first casualties of the government-orchestrated show trial was Dr. Powell's unborn son. His wife Lena was six months pregnant at the beginning of the traumatizing ordeal, and when she gave birth prematurely due partly to the stress, the infant died shortly after birth. At age thirty-three Powell was one of the older Panther 21 members and already had a deep history in Black liberation politics. Mumia Abu-Jamal, in his book *We Want Freedom*, noted being impressed that many of the New York Panthers had converted to Islam, in part because of their relationship with and admiration of Minister Malcolm X. "Indeed," wrote Mumia, "Dr. Curtis Powell met and talked with Malcolm in Paris after his pilgrimage to Mecca."

Following the acquittal, Powell spent ten months working on viral oncology for the Public Health Research Institute of the City of New York. He worked with Dr. Mutulu Shakur as one of those first introducing acupuncture to New York, as an antidrug treatment. "Doc" moved to Lusaka, Zambia to take a position as lecturer at the University of Zambia. During his six years at the University he began his research on trypanosomiasis—a viral infection transmitted by mosquito bites that can cause Chagas disease, or sleeping sickness—that would define the rest of his professional career. In 1979, supported in part by a grant from the World Health Organization, Powell relocated to Kenya to dedicate himself to independent research on developing a potential vaccine. By 1982, he had been appointed director of the Experimental Immunity Project on Trypanosome Research and made regular trips back to the United States giving seminars at Yale, Harvard, and Columbia among others. Powell's work would lead to a major breakthrough for combating a virus previously dealt with only by aggressively limiting native mosquito populations rather than treating the disease itself. His work eventually led to the successful development of the "Powell Vaccine," which was patented in 1991.

Powell returned to live and work in New York City in the 1990s, participating in a panel at the New York Public Library Schomburg Center for Research in Black Culture commemorating the twenty-fifth anniversary of the Panther 21 acquittal. His passion for human rights and his passion for scientific advancement remained central throughout his life, along with an understanding (as he put it in a pamphlet written by fellow Panther 21 codefendant Kwando Kinshasa titled *A Brief Biography of Dr. Curtis Powell*) that "the black man will never be totally respected until Africa is respected." Powell died on June 7, 2002.

Dhoruba Bin Wahad (Richard Dharuba Moore), only twenty-four at the time of the Panther 21 trial and listed in some support materials as a "self-employed painter," was a leading member of the New York Black Panther Party and a field secretary of the BPP responsible for organizing chapters throughout the East Coast. Arrested in June 1971, shortly after all charges were dropped in the case of the 21, Dhoruba was framed as part of the illegal FBI Counter Intelligence Program (COINTELPRO) and subjected to unfair treatment and torture throughout his nineteen years in prison. During Dhoruba's incarceration, litigation on his behalf produced over 300,000 pages of COINTELPRO documentation, and upon release in 1990 he was able to bring a successful lawsuit against the New York Department of Corrections for all their wrongdoings and criminal activities. Living in both Ghana and the U.S., Dhoruba continues to write and work promoting Pan-Africanism, an uncompromising critique of imperialism and capitalism, and freedom for all political prisoners. He is coauthor—with Assata Shakur and Mumia Abu-Jamal—of *Still Black, Still Strong: Survivors of the War Against Black Revolutionaries* (Semiotext(e), 1993) and is featured in numerous books and films.

Jamal (Edward) Joseph, a junior at Evander Childs High School at the time of his arrest, recounted much of his life in and immediately after the Panthers in his autobiography, *Panther Baby: A Life of Rebellion and Reinvention* (Algonquin Books, 2012). After several incarcerations following convictions relating to Joseph's participation in the Black Liberation Army, he went on to produce various plays and performance pieces written while behind bars. Long involved in youth empowerment organizations, Joseph has been an artistic director for City Kids, the New Heritage Theatre Group, and Impact Repertory Company. A close colleague of and mentor to Tupac Shakur, Joseph is the author of *Tupac Shakur's Legacy* (Atria, 2006) and has appeared on HBO's *Def Poetry Jam* and BET's *American Gangster*. A professor at Columbia University's Graduate Film Division, Joseph received a fellowship from the Sundance Film Institute and was nominated for a 2008 Academy Award for Best Song.

Joan Bird was an outstanding graduate of Cathedral High School, studying nursing at Bronx Community College at the time of her arrest. She was also working as a teaching assistant at PS 175 when she joined the Panthers at age twenty, late in 1968. Within two months of joining, she was a target of harassment—arrested three times, beaten, and threatened by members of the NYPD. After a particularly brutal and obvious beating, and while still in custody, her arresting officers threatened that if she claimed police brutality to the chief interrogator they would "shove a gun up her cunt."

The emerging women's liberation movement paid special attention to Bird's ordeals, proclaiming in a broadside published by the Women's Committee to Defend Joan Bird that "freeing Joan not only emphasizes but also embodies our own commitment to fight those who would continue to keep us separated from our Third World sisters who are fighting for what all women want and need.... For Joan, becoming a nurse was not enough and she related to the programs initiated by the Panthers. These programs are important to all women, especially those who have experienced the physical, mental and economic oppression that comes from the lack of health care, child care, etc. Having such basic necessities allows us to pull ourselves together and begin the struggle for a better life for all human beings. Joan was jailed for her participation in this struggle."

Kwando Kinshasa (William King)—a noted educator, social psychologist, and professor emeritus of sociology in the Africana Studies Department of John Jay College of Criminal Justice of the City University of New York—cites his parents as the major influence in his life's trajectory as an activist and scholar. His father's membership in Harlem's famed all-Black 369th National Guard Regiment during World War II, and his own subsequent service with the U.S. Marines, sharpened his understanding of what he called the connections between race and the war, between "the racial riots in Harlem, the war, and my father's dedication" to the all-Black organization.

Though Kinshasa rarely discusses his involvement in the Panther 21 case, he made a major academic and activist commitment to keeping alive the memory of the 1931 case of the "Scottsboro Boys"—nine Black teenagers from Alabama accused of raping two white women, a charge so outrageous that even in the context of the U.S. South at that time simply railroading the nine was difficult. Eventually, after several trials with guilty verdicts by all-white juries, dropping of charges for four of the nine, a death sentence and extended prison terms for the others, and a massive national campaign for their freedom, the tide began to turn. Clarence Norris, the oldest of the nine and the one who was given the death penalty, went into hiding in 1946 and was not discovered for thirty years. With all the irregularities and obvious miscarriages of justice, even white supremacist Alabama governor George Wallace was forced to pardon Norris shortly after he was captured while underground. Kinshasa helped Norris tell his story in the 1998 book *The Man from Scottsboro: Clarence Norris and the Infamous 1931 Alabama Rape Trial* (McFarland, 1998). Kinshasa also led a National Endowment for the Humanities–created advisory board for the 2000 documentary *Scottsboro:*

An American Tragedy, which also won a Sundance Film Festival citation and was nominated for an Academy Award.

In addition to his work in the Scottsboro case, Dr. Kinshasa authored *Black Resistance to the Ku Klux Klan in the Wake of the Civil War* (McFarland, 2006) and chaired the John Jay College Africana Studies Department until the time of his retirement.

Kuwasi Balagoon (Donald Weems), much beloved but also misunderstood, is the sole focus of the invaluable *A Soldier's Story: Writings by a Revolutionary New Afrikan Anarchist* (Kersplebedeb, 2003). This member of the Panther 21 was already incarcerated at the time of the original roundup and indictment. A good brief summary of his life is also provided by comrade Akinyele Umoja, in his vital essay "Maroon: Kuwasi Balagoon and the Evolution of Revolutionary New Afrikan Anarchism" (*Science & Society*, April 2015). Umoja wrote:

> Black Panther Party (BPP) and Black Liberation Army (BLA) member Kuwasi Balagoon has emerged as a heroic symbol for radical anarchists and some circles of Black radicals in the United States. He is one of the most complex figures of the Black Liberation Movement. His legacy is obscured within broader Black liberation and radical circles. The evolution of his politics and his life as an open bisexual add layers of complexity to his legacy. Balagoon's political biography is a long road that includes his activism as a G.I. in the U.S. army in Germany, as a tenant organizer in Harlem, and as a member of the Harlem branch of the BPP. Documenting the political life of Kuwasi Balagoon reveals his significance as a symbol of Black and radical anarchism. Recognition of Balagoon's contribution to Black liberation will only emerge with the advance of both anti-authoritarian politics and challenges to homophobia in African-American activist circles.

Balagoon remained underground—after the Panther 21 acquittal and completing the time he was serving on other charges—only to be captured in 1981 as part of the failed October 20 Brinks expropriation. Fellow anarchist Panther and Black Liberation Army political prisoner Ashanti Alston wrote of Kuwasi:

> Risks were like the air he breathed. You breathe, you take risks. I risk, therefore I am. Kuwasi was the trickster, shape-shifter, elusive, daring, bold. . . . He could take 'em down: enemies, armored cars, while being sustained by love and loyalty, both giving and accepting. Kuwasi lived his life, his short 40

years on his own terms, outlaw terms from his personal to his political. He was in solidarity with whomever he wanted, he loved whomever he wanted, he fought on whatever terrain he landed on—whether on the streets or in the prisons.

Kuwasi Balagoon died in prison in December 1986 of AIDS-related pneumonia. The two memorials presented on pages 568–70 this book are from two of his codefendants, both still behind bars. Sundiata Acoli writes as a fellow member of the Panther 21 and David Gilbert as a participant (driver) in the Brinks expropriation. We are also pleased to present two never-before-published writings of Kuwasi's, toward the front and the back of this special edition.

Larry Mack has been near impossible to track down for decades. The following is new commentary, written especially for this book by codefendant and close friend, Sekou Odinga:

Larry Mack was more studious than many of us, a real leader. We grew up together in the same neighborhood in Jamaica, Queens, and he went to elementary school with my sister, a year younger than me. Reading wasn't really big in our community back then, but Larry always did read a lot, and didn't gang bang. He would take a subject and research it, something very few of us did before we joined the Panther Party. Although he was from the "hood," and he hung out and drank wine and did his share of fighting and carrying on, I didn't think of him as a "hood dude." His mother owned a beauty parlor. He grew up not really wanting much—he ate well, was always dressed nicely, and was always a very good student, always in the smart classes.

When we first started the Grassroots Advisory Council in Jamaica, he was part of that. But we really got close after the New York Panther 21 arrests. I was one of those who had recommended him for leadership in the Jamaica branch of the BPP. When we initially started the chapter, folks suggested that I could lead it, but I said no. I was uptown at that time. But I thought that Larry could lead it. Not only was he from the street but he was all involved in learning at that time. A lot of what we were doing in the early days was political education, and I knew that he was one of those who would be good to take in the information and then be able to pass it along and teach others; plus, he had the revolutionary zeal to stand up as a leading Panther.

When he was one of those that the state targeted as part of the Panther 21 he went underground, as I did. He was able to get in touch with some people who knew where I was, and so he was able to get in touch with me and come to where I was staying a few weeks after the arrests. From then on, we were very close. When we got the request to go to Algeria to help build the International Section, we both agreed to go and both made our way there together. When the Algerian offices were closing down we decided to come back together. On our return, we went back underground together and for the first years back—almost up until I got captured in 1981—we worked closely. But I haven't seen or heard from him since we were in jail together at the Brooklyn House of Detention back in 1982, after I was released from the hospital [Sekou was ferociously beaten and tortured upon arrest in 1981, leading to a three month hospital stay. —Ed.]. The traitor, Tyrone Rison, who was to testify against those of us in the Black Liberation Army, probably mentioned Larry in some way, which resulted in him being picked up. But Rison was not the smartest person and didn't have the best memory, and they didn't have enough on Larry to put him on trial or even hold him for long. I wish I knew how he was doing now; he was a good brother and friend.

Lonnie Epps, like Jamal Joseph, was seventeen years old at the time of his arrest, and a student at Long Island City High School. Epps turned himself in voluntarily after reading his name in a local newspaper in association with indicted Panthers; he and Joseph had their cases severed from the original New York Panther 21, as they were to be tried as youthful offenders. During a pretrial hearing on February 4, 1970, Epps was beaten by several guards and charged with felonious assault, harassment, and resisting arrest after trying to defend a Panther 21 supporter, Maryann Weissman of Youth Against War and Fascism, who yelled out, "Who Judges Your Conduct?" to the presiding state supreme court justice. Local newspapers called the court scene a "wild melee."

Lumumba Abdul Shakur was employed by the Harlem Community Housing Council at the time of his arrest. He was the lead named defendant in the 21 case. An extensive tribute to Lumumba by his close Panther friend Bilal Sunni-Ali is included in this book.

Mkubu (Lee Berry), twenty-five at the time of the arrests and a Vietnam veteran, was never technically mentioned in the Panther 21 indictments. According to support materials for the 21 produced at the time of the trial, it was "neither alleged that Berry agreed with anyone to do anything, nor that he committed any overt acts." In fact, at the time of his arrest, Berry was in the Veterans Administration hospital, suffering from severe seizures; he was considered 70 percent disabled due to service-related epilepsy. His wife recounted, "When he heard they were looking for him, he called them up and told them where he was. They went to the hospital and took him out of bed, and handcuffed him, and put him in the Tombs" (the infamous and appropriately nicknamed Manhattan House of Detention). Arraigned without any opportunity to consult with or even obtain counsel, Berry was only given partial medication during his jail time (from April 1969), subsequently suffering epileptic attacks and losing consciousness several times. For much of the trial, Berry was held at Bellevue Prison Hospital, where he was transferred in November 1969 due to medical complications and where he remained in critical condition.

Despite these "trials" and tribulations, as of the Black Panther fiftieth anniversary and the publication of this book, Lee Berry remains alive and well and riding a motorcycle.

Mshina (Thomas Berry), like Sekou Odinga and Larry Mack, escaped arrest altogether by joining the Black Panther Party International Division in Algeria.

Nine (Richard Harris) grew up in Newark at a time when gangs in that city were on the rise. Harris was directly influenced by Minister Malcolm X, whom he heard preach at the Newark Temple of the Nation of Islam. At the time of the roundup of the 21 Harris was—like his codefendant Kuwasi Balagoon— already serving time for robbery in New Jersey. Balagoon, in fact—much later in life—was convicted of attempting to break Harris out of prison. Nine passed away in prison sometime in the 1990s.

Robert Steele Collier had served as staff director of the Tompkins Square Community Center on New York's Lower East Side through the late 1960s. In recognition of his work with Black, Puerto Rican, and all lower-income peoples of that neighborhood, Manhattan Borough President Percy Sutton recommended that Collier join the Lower East Side Planning Board, and, at the time of his arrest in the Panther 21 case, the Urban Coalition was in the process of refunding the Center. After the acquittal of the 21, Collier—who always acknowledged his leadership role in founding the New York Black Panther chapter—continued his community-based work, eventually becoming assistant city assessor for the New York City Department of Finance and the project manager for the New York City Development Corporation. As a strong advocate of public health, Collier chaired the Bellevue Medical Center's Community Board, and was appointed by a federal court as Governor of the Chinatown Health Clinic's Hospital Outpatient Services department, which

Collier had helped create. As an educator, he taught at State University of New York at New Paltz, Empire State College, and elsewhere. He was treasurer of the African American Graduate Student Association and graduate advisor to the Black Student Union at Binghamton University (SUNY).

Collier settled in Poughkeepsie, New York, and passed away on February 12, 2010, at the age of seventy-three. At the time of his death, he was executive director of the Strand Community Organization to Rehabilitate the Environment (SCORE) in Kingston, New York, where he developed and implemented business strategies to assist the immediate community.

Sekou Odinga (Nathanial Burns) was a member of Malcolm X's Organization of Afro-American Unity, a founding member of the New York chapter of the Black Panther Party as well as the Black Panther International Section, and was a member of the Panther 21. A citizen of the Republic of New Afrika and combatant of the Black Liberation Army, Sekou was captured in October 1981, mercilessly tortured, and spent the following thirty-three years behind bars—a prisoner of war and political prisoner of the U.S. empire. Since his release in November 2014 he has remained a stalwart fighter for justice and for the release of all political prisoners.

Shaba Om (Lee Roper), shortly after the Panther 21 acquittal, was a key plaintiff in a movement-wide case that put security and police practices and policies on trial. Along with the War Resisters League's (WRL) Ralph DiGia, Youth International Party's legendary prankster Abbie Hoffman, several fellow Panthers, and others, the plaintiffs argued that the City of New York, its police commissioner, and the New York Police Department's Intelligence Division engaged in a systematic and historic pattern of surveillance, infiltration, and disruption of progressive, leftist, and radical political activities and groups, resulting in illegal suppression of political expression. The first-named plaintiff, Barbara Handschu, was a lawyer whose involvement in the squatter and housing rights movements got her involved in representing the Young Lords, Panthers, Chicago Seven, and others. The diversity of those involved in the case clearly revealed that government repression was not based foremost on reactions to potential political violence or armed self-defense. (At least two of the above were avowed nonviolent activists from similarly inclined organizations.) It was, rather, a proactive governmental attempt to curtail activities considered to be radically challenging to the status quo. WRL's open advocacy of draft resistance, tax resistance, and direct action civil disobedience, Hoffman's throwing dollar bills onto the floor of the New York Stock Exchange (and organizing a youth countercultural movement in general), and all the Panther activities for self-determination and independence were subject to targeted police violence.

On the heels of the initial filing of what came to be known as the "Handschu case," the U.S. Senate–based Church Committee issued its report documenting similar authoritarian practices waged against similar groups on the part of the federal government. Finally adjudicated in 1985, the Handschu decree imposed substantive and procedural guidelines upon the NYPD, to prevent future police actions designed to have "chilling effects" on First Amendment rights, unreasonable search and seizure, and the most basic of due process. While government actions along these lines may have simply (and temporarily) gone from overt to covert, there was direct pushback to the Handschu requirements after September 11, 2001. In a post-9/11 *Village Voice* feature, "The NYPD Wants to Watch You," Om noted that, among the Panther 21, he didn't think "any of us had a clue until we were brought on trial that we were infiltrated to the extent that we were." He recalled, "They had agents deep undercover," not only spying on radical groups but disrupting the activities of church groups, civic groups, social organizations. Nevertheless, a landmark 2016 decision (*Raza v. City of NY*)—based on Handschu and on recent NYPD surveillance of and illegal activities against Muslims—mandates new safeguards against police bias and unjustified investigations.

There can be little question that the Handschu and related guidelines, however weak or unenforced, grew out of a popular concern about the ways in which political dissent, especially from the likes of the Panthers, was trampled on in cases like the New York 21. That two years of trial time and money could be decided by the jury in just ninety minutes—with every single charge dropped—showed the disconnect between police and government desires and public opinion, even among non-activists and non–Panther supporters. "I was facing 365 years in prison," Om noted in conversations following the Handschu decision. "But I got nothing. The terrorists and murderers they described didn't exist."

As an organizer of the twenty-fifth anniversary commemoration of the Panther 21 acquittal, Shaba Om took care to include those Panthers still incarcerated for their work back at the height of the movement. "The United States denies the existence of political prisoners within its borders," he asserted, but in the decades since the landmark decisions it had become completely clear that "illegal methods were used to frame" those radicals who were considered dangerous to the status quo, using "gross patterns of prosecutorial misconduct, fabrication or concealment of evidence by the government during trial," and other nefarious methods of maintaining ultimate power. Overall, however, according to Om, "the acquittal of the 21 was a major political setback and embarrassment" for the establishment.

Sundiata Acoli (Clark Squire) was, at the time of his arrest in the Panther 21 case, employed as a computer operator for Data Processing International—a common-sounding job today but quite rare and reflecting a high-level skill set for 1969. Prior to that, he worked as a mathematician and computer programmer at the National Aeronautics and Space Administration (NASA) at Edwards Air Force Base in California. Energized by the civil rights campaigns of the early 1960s, and by his experiences assisting with voter registration drives during the Mississippi Freedom Summer campaign in 1964, Sundiata noted that, despite his academic and vocational success, he "couldn't be proud of survival under the system in America." Seeing so many of his community unable to thrive or even survive, and—as he put it—"aware of the subtle pressures working to force upon me the acceptance of white values, to give up more and more of being Black"—Sundiata began looking for an organization to join that would satisfy his desires to work for Black people and for liberation. After all, Sundiata noted, "I loved being Black."

In 1968, in New York City, Sundiata joined the Black Panther Party for Self-Defense, eventually rising to the position of finance minister of the Harlem branch. When a year later he was one of those arrested as part of the Panther 21, an ad hoc group of his coworkers, Computer People for Peace, raised and posted his bail. He should have been released—but was forced to spend the entire two-year pretrial preparation period behind bars, freed only at the time of the ultimate acquittal of the 21. After constant harassment and surveillance on the streets of New York, however, he went underground, and on May 2, 1973, he was ambushed by state troopers on the New Jersey Turnpike, along with his comrades Zayd Malik Shakur (Lumumba's brother) and Assata Shakur, who was later called "the soul of the Black Liberation Army." By the end of the ensuing shootout, Zayd and an officer had been killed, Assata and another officer were wounded, and Sundiata escaped, though only for two days. Following his arrest this time Sundiata was subjected to all manner of torture and mistreatment, including placement in experimental super-maximum security and sensory-deprivation federal control units, despite having never been convicted of any federal offenses.

Hollywood has reminded us that there are "hidden figures" who worked almost invisibly within NASA and other organizations to "make America great," while being treated as second-class citizens or worse. Sundiata was

among those early NASA heroes who happened to be of African descent—
only his reward has not been a Presidential Medal of Freedom or a major
motion picture but a seven-foot cell and a parole board that has instructed
him to reapply for release at age ninety-five! It is up to us to keep Sundiata
"hidden" no longer.

Assata Shakur has long spoken of Sundiata's exuberant love of the people
and of the great priority which must be placed on freeing this math genius who
turned eighty years old on January 14, 2017.

POEM FOR SUNDIATA

Assata Shakur

I remember your smile
Bright as the sun's explosion
Wide as the arms of Yemaya
Deep as a gushing well of kindness
I remember your smile

Slow like the dawn of recognition
Quick like the wit of observation
Clear as the logic of common sense
I remember your smile

Frank as a simple declaration
Bold like the taste of naked love
Wasn't no grinning or smirking or sneering
I remember your smile

Even when you were young
You had an old smile,
deep wrinkles spread across your brow

Like worn paths
Crossing familiar ground
Laugh lines descending from eyes made old
By deadly images
Laughter holding back the tears I remember your smile

Your smile is like an umbilical cord
Pulling me back, pulling us back
to a lost continent
of brown velvet faces with white incandescent teeth
radiating home, radiating peace, radiating love

Your smile
wakes me up from nightmares
turned into day-mares
Reoccurring slave-mares
In the twisted tinsel hell
They call amerikkka

When they came and they took my baby
When the milk in my breast turned to sour curds
When there was no one there to hold me
And the voices that tried to console me
Sounded like empty words
I remembered your smile

Wrote off our lives with reams of paper
Stained with filthy, greedy lies
Turned us into prison statistics
Using legalese linguistics
Regurgitating hypocritical diatribes
Like thin white vomit

In the midst of body bags
And toe tags
And the flood of black blood

In the midst of affirmative negation
And mass extermination

I remember your smile
We remember your smile
We call on your smile
We call on your smile
To give us light

They been trying to take your smile
Wipe it off your face
Like they be wiping us off this earth
But you smiled that smile in cages,
Institutionalized outrages
Twenty year hits
Like contemptuous spit
And in spite of a bitter taste
in your mouth
Your smile shines strong

All of us smile lovers
Need to set you free
We need to free your smile
That x-ray smile
Beaming rays of freedom
Unchain that smile
Unchain that smile
Set it free

We love your smile
We need your smile
Your smile is sweet enough
To melt hard hearts
Into love syrup
Sweet and sticky
as the nectar of freedom

We got to free that smile
Unchain that smile
Let it shine out
And warm us
I want to see that smile

Make children laugh
And light up a woman's eyes at midnight
We got to free that smile
That freedom smile
So we all can smile again

As noted in the article "Ride and Denied"—authored by Sundiata and appearing in this volume—he was again denied parole in 2016 after over forty years of incarceration, and despite having the New Jersey Appellate Court order the New Jersey State Parole Board to "expeditiously set conditions for parole" back in 2014. Sundiata's freedom must be part of any conscientious effort for human rights, humanitarian prison reform, or campaign against mass incarceration and police violence. Antiracist trainings or restorative justice symposia held in the USA and not mentioning the case of this still-jailed Black Panther must be vigorously questioned in terms of history, accountability, and seriousness. The Sundiata Acoli Freedom Campaign can be reached at: http://www.sundiataacoli.org/

COUNTING TO 21, PART TWO
NEW REFLECTIONS ON
MEMBERS OF THE 21

Afeni Shakur, a collective eulogy
Sekou Odinga, Dhoruba Bin Wahad, and Bilal Sunni-Ali

Afeni's passing in the year that marks the 50th anniversary of the Black Panther Party, founded in Oakland, California, is a significant sociopolitical marker in the marginalization of Black radicalism in America. Her passing as a universally recognized hip hop madonna and mother of the iconic Black rapper Tupac Shakur and daughter Sekyiwa practically obscures the formative years of her life as a Black girl from the rural South, transfigured in the Southeast Bronx into a Black teenage femme fatale and "deb" in the Bronx street set, Young Disciples/Disciples Sportsmen, as well as her transition from the harsh streets of the Southeast Bronx to the radical Black nationalism of the Black Panther Party and Black radicalism of the sixties.

Like a silent movie reel, Afeni's passing means that the Black Panthers of Afeni Shakur's generation of Black radicals, revolutionaries, and activists are etched in time by a media that portrays them as "forever young," while the conditions that nurtured their radicalism and inspired the freedom dreams of Afeni's generation are reduced to hashtag militancy and posture politics. We should not forget that she was a revolutionary leader and spokesperson for the Black Panther Party. Afeni's real historical legacy, and ultimately the celebration of her life, depends on how we, the living, perceived that life.

The name Shakur further identifies her as at one with the legacy of the extended revolutionary family of the Shakurs: Aba, Lumumba, Zayd, Mutulu, Assata.

Because Afeni was one of us, one verse in our generational bio-story, who grew to adulthood during the Cold War of white America's empire, and white supremacy's bloody domestic war on us, we not only mourn her passing but also the marginalization of her "becoming" who she was. Across America, in every major urban enclave populated by the descendants of chattel slaves, freedmen and women—a generation that would embrace Black power, Black self-determination, Black pride that would typify the civil and human rights struggles of the sixties and seventies—came of age. Now Afeni's generation's time has passed, but not the legacy of their struggles—the radical legacy of the Afeni Shakurs, Abdul Majids, Albert "Nuh" Washingtons, Zayd Shakurs. This is still accessible as long as their lives are not forgotten, as long as what made them who they became is not overlooked and ignored.

We love you, dear sister Afeni. Although you are gone you will never be forgotten.

Long live the revolutionary spirit of Afeni Shakur!

At the New York City memorial for Afeni, Sekou Odinga added: "Afeni was one of my first female heroes; I named my daughter after Afeni. . . . Afeni had a lot of people who wanted to be like her. Afeni was loved by many people, she inspired many people. She made you feel that you were special, that you mattered to her. She, like all of us, was human and had her faults. But I will always encourage young women to do the best that Afeni did. If you look for the best in Afeni, you'll find some greatness there. You'll find a whole lot of love, and you can't go wrong."

They Called Him Doc, but We Called Him Baba
Marcus Tyler Vaughn

After the 21 trial and acquittal, Dr. Curtis Powell ventured on to Africa with his wife Susan and his children Kayode, Tiassa, Taraji, and Cetywa. They first settled in Zambia and then in Nairobi, Kenya. Once there, he told all of the children they were to call him "Baba," meaning father in Swahili. Tiassa Powell would eventually return to the U.S. to become a nurse and my mother. I never knew Curtis as Doc, the revolutionary scientist, but I did know him as Baba, my grandfather. I remember him calling us from New York and saying, "How ya doin', grandson? Put Tiassa on the phone." I remember him visiting us when I was thirteen.

He walked like a man of stature and he sort of mumbled when he talked. I thought it was cool. The first time I met him, I was about three. I was his first grandchild and I suppose that made him nervous because when asked if he wanted to hold me, he replied, "I wouldn't know what to do." In best recollection of this incident, I recall that reaction as being a little "weird," but of course I loved him anyway. He was family.

Most of what I remember of Baba are the stories my family told about him. He was funny and sort of a prankster. As a youngster, he once hung his mother's pantyhose over the window like curtains, for the whole neighborhood to see! His embarrassed mother, Irene, came home to find Baba rolling on the floor with laughter.

He was a man of good sense who, though he had many college-level degrees, always respected common sense more. He would say to my mother, "A BS means 'bullshit,' an MS means 'more shit,' and a PhD means 'piled high and deep in shit.'" And most of all, Baba was intelligent. While in Kenya, he developed a cure and vaccination for African sleeping sickness.

Baba died shortly after my fourteenth birthday, in 2002, in Flushing, Queens, New York. I was very sad when he died, mostly because I felt that we did not get enough time to know each other better. Luckily, history has preserved my grandfather through his important work and the work of the New York Panthers, work that continues in these troubling times. He left behind a legacy that any young man or woman can respect, leaving with me a strong desire to do the same.

Education Update Online, 2007: Excerpt from an Interview with Dr. Kwando Kinshasa

When I became a teenager, I knew that there were a number of questions about the world, Harlem, my skin color that needed to be answered. I became acutely aware that a hostile environment awaited me beyond certain streets and avenues throughout the city. However, I am quite sure that during these early teenage years I was very much aware of and fascinated by social and political conflict and, as a result, I was determined to find a way to become as knowledgeable as possible in this regard while still in high school. During my last year of high school I became interested in history and examining how individuals or groups functioned in society from a historical perspective.

I sent a number of applications to southern African American colleges and was accepted by my first choice. Unfortunately, I could not attend due to my parents' financial status. I can still see the pained look on their faces when they informed me about our financial situation. . . .

There have been many turning points, or adjustment factors, in my life. However, an early turning point occurred in 1953 when a neighbor's nephew, Layton Brooks, visited New York City from Richmond, Virginia. During these years, much of the United States was racially separated either by de jure or de facto segregation. In southern states such as Virginia, where much of society was segregated, even a Black person's right to walk on the shady side of the street on a hot summer day was outlawed. In many southern states, if you were an African American you were required to step off the sidewalk when approaching or passing a white person.

Layton Brooks was raised in such an environment in Virginia and consequently, when he arrived in 1953 to spend the summer with his relatives, he was amazed by some of the differences in New York City.

I remember on a particular day when a group of my friends and I decided to take Layton to the movie theater on Fordham Road in the Bronx, we walked up a steep hill toward the theater. Layton suddenly jumped into the street, not once but several times, as white people approached us. When I asked him why he was doing this, he explained that this was expected "at home." We told him this was New York City, so forget all of that other racist nonsense.

As the summer went on Layton became more relaxed and truly began to enjoy himself. By summer's end, Layton returned to Virginia. Sometime that fall, my parents informed us that Layton was murdered by lynching because he refused to abide by one of Virginia's racist segregation codes. His murder, and the subsequent murder of Emmett Till in 1955, symbolized for me then and now the reality of what it means to be an African American and the responsibility that I have to combat those who would attempt to curtail or limit my right to exist and prosper. . . .

There are a number of achievements that I am proud of, however. Receiving my doctorate in sociology from New York University in 1983 is one that stands out. I was extremely fortunate to have a well-known social psychologist, Richard Sennett, as the chairman of my doctorate committee, and mentors such as sociologists Erving Goffman and Edwin Schur, and historian John Henrik Clarke as advisors on my dissertation committee. A few years later my dissertation, *Emigration vs. Assimilation: The Debate in the African American Press, 1827–1861*, was published and even now is cited as a valuable contribution to our understanding of the African American newspapers' impact on the question of Black emigration or assimilation within the American social construct.

A few years later I was introduced to Mr. Clarence Norris, the last living defendant in the infamous Scottsboro rape case of 1931. After a few conversations, he agreed to a taped interview about his experiences growing up as the oldest sibling of a sharecropping family in Georgia during the 1920s. Our interview eventually discussed those circumstances that led to his involvement in the alleged rape of two white indigent females (i.e., hobos) in March 1931, by nine black male hobos on a freight train traveling through Alabama and the subsequent infamous Scottsboro, Alabama, rape trial.

Though all of the defendants were eventually pardoned or acquitted of the charges some seventeen years later, Clarence Norris jumped parole in 1946 and lived under an assumed name until he was eventually pardoned in 1976 by the governor of Alabama, George Wallace. Mr. Norris's recollections were so inspiring that I put them into a biography entitled *The Man from Scottsboro: Clarence Norris and the Infamous 1931 Alabama Rape Trial, In His Own Words*. Recording Mr. Norris's historic recollections of the trial and his life in Georgia and Alabama as a youth was for me an important achievement due to the uniqueness of the data and the fact that these videotapes are the only detailed recollection by a Scottsboro defendant. . . .

I had several mentors at Hunter College, CUNY. From a social-historical perspective, Dr. John Henrik Clarke and Dr. Tilden LeMelle were extremely important to me. They followed each other as chairpersons of the Black Studies Department when I was an undergraduate student, and exposed the students to different ways of viewing history, particularly from the African American perspective. From Dr. Clarke I learned the importance of critical historical analysis and from Dr. LeMelle the significance of social structure, conflict, and hierarchy. I had a communications professor, Dr. Ruth Ramsay, who vigorously pushed me to improve my writing and overall communications skills. . . .

My advice to young people is not to limit a desire to understand their immediate environment. Secondly, do not rely solely upon a media-orientated or so-called virtual-reality interpretation of the world or their environment. Being there in body, spirit, and intellect helps the young social scientist to really understand the importance of what sociologist Max Weber often stressed as the "ritual regimentation of life" and the creation of the "cultural community." In this regard, I not only advise students to push themselves as much as possible toward understanding our most pressing social issues of the day, but to also seek a more critical insight into the evolutionary aspects of those issues. In this way, they will become committed to better understanding social conflict and change. I also believe that mentorship is extremely important in encouraging students to travel with me or with groups to social settings where social-political change is occurring. This is particularly important for students of African heritage who have a dire need to better understand the displacement that created the African diaspora and the ongoing evolutionary changes occurring within that realty.

Eulogy for Kuwasi Balagoon
Sundiata Acoli, December 16, 1986

Kuwasi Balagoon was a revolutionary, a rebel, a poet. And he was faithful to his calling. Once he stepped upon the revolutionary path, he remained true to the struggle for the rest of his life: fighting the good fight, staying in shape, writing poetry, and helping fallen comrades at a moment's notice, never stopping to count the cost.

He was a natural rebel—couldn't stand conformity or authority, especially an illegitimate authority. And he had the heart of a gun fighter, which he was—using all his tools in the service of Black people all his adult life.

If you ever read or heard his poem "I'm a Wild Man," you knew him, because it described him to a "T." He was wild. He knew it; we knew it; and we loved him for it, because it was his nature—and the nature of the times, in the late '60s when Black folk needed wild men. We still do today.

But now Kuwasi's gone, and the beat goes on, and we who knew and loved him can only eulogize him—and constantly scan the horizon wondering how long, how long will it be before another giant such as this comes along again.

In Memory of Kuwasi Balagoon, New Afrikan Freedom Fighter
David Gilbert, December 15, 1986

When i think of Kuwasi i think of the word "heart." No, i got that backwards. When the term "heart" comes up i think of Kuwasi, because he epitomized it so beautifully—though of course he also lived and expressed many other fine qualities. "Heart" has two distinct meanings: one is great courage; the other is great generosity. Kuwasi was an outstanding example of both.

People at this commemoration (organized by the New Afrikan People's Organization) are aware of Kuwasi's core identity as a New Afrikan freedom fighter. His political activity began as a tenant organizer in Harlem. (He was, incidentally, also part of the Harlem contingent who, bringing food and water, broke the right-wing blockade around us—when we were students holding buildings during the Columbia Strike of 1968.) Kuwasi was part of the land-mark Panther 21 case of 1969. In the same period, he was imprisoned for expropriations in New Jersey; he escaped a few years later.

It takes both daring and creativity to escape from prison. Kuwasi did that and a whole lot more: Three and a half months later, and on very short notice, he went to free a comrade being taken to a funeral under armed guard. Kuwasi was hit by a bullet yet kept moving, and he almost made it too. With a little more time for planning and preparation, he would have been successful. His second escape, about five years later, from a maximum security prison was even more impressive. That time he stayed free and active until his capture subsequent to the Nyack expropriation of October 20th, 1981.

After each of these prison escapes in the '70s, he was able to quickly establish himself in a secure and comfortable personal situation. He didn't go back for his comrade or reconnect with that unit of the Black Liberation Army (BLA) out of any personal desperation. It was purely a commitment to the struggle, to New Afrikan liberation, to freedom for all oppressed people.

When one hears of such courage and sacrifice (and here we have mentioned only a small portion of his deeds), the stereotyped image is of a stern or fierce character, perhaps with an inclination for martyrdom. But nothing could be further from Kuwasi Balagoon the person. Actually, he had an affecting ebullience, a zest for the pleasures of life, a keen appreciation for the culture and creativity of the people who lived in the ghettos and barrios. Politically he placed great stress on the need for his movement (and other revolutionary movements as well) to respond directly to the concrete needs of the people in the communities. He opposed anything he saw as hierarchy that stifled initiative from below.

Kuwasi was a poet; or, to put it better, he was a revolutionary who wrote fine poetry. He had read his poetry in the same clubs as the Last Poets way back when they were forming, and he continued to write poems in prison. Here at Auburn, he worked on drawings late at night and listened to tapes of both punk rock and jazz with great enthusiasm.

Being in prison population with Kuwasi for this past year, i got to see an additional dimension of his humanity. Prison can be depressing, especially in a period of low political consciousness. Kuwasi had a truly unique ability to make people laugh and to create a sense of community. Most jailhouse humor is either bleak or sexist. Kuwasi was able to create a healthier community humor where we'd be laughing at the authorities, or at our own foibles and pretensions. Sometimes in the yard, i could hear his whole workout crew in uproarious laughter from 50 yards away. His great spirit is not just my personal observation. Something like 100 guys have come up to tell me about it in the two days since Kuwasi died.

When a guy comes into prison with such a high-powered case and reputation—well, often the terms are: What favors can other prisoners do for him? With Kuwasi it was just the opposite. I've never seen anybody do so much for other people. I actually felt that he was accommodating to a fault. We couldn't have a half-hour political discussion in the yard without about 10 or 15 guys coming up to him to ask him for some help or favor. He always used his day off from work—even when he should have been catching up on rest—to do "personal baking" which he gave away to innumerable persons over the many weeks; he shared his commissary purchases with whoever asked. Kuwasi ran a very substantial and worthwhile political education class for several months.

Kuwasi Balagoon, a bold New Afrikan warrior with a giant heart: While we all mourn together there is something particular about the situation here at Auburn prison that puts the meaning of his life in sharp relief. The prison guards, who never had the courage to face him straight up in his life, have been obviously gloating over his death. Meanwhile, literally hundreds of prisoners are mourning him (particularly prisoners of his nation, but also a wide range of prisoners who stand up against state authority). Both sets of reactions, in their opposite ways, are tributes to Kuwasi and how he led his life. The loss is immeasurable; what he gave us is even more.

Pre-Panther Days, Summer 1965 in Newark, NJ, with Panther 21 codefendant Ali Bey Hassan (bottom center, with beret), and codefendant "Nine" Richard Harris (top left), from the collection of Ali Bey Hassan, entrusted to Cyril (Brother Bullwhip) Innis Jr.

Early New York Panther Rally (pre-21 indictments), with (l–r) Lumumba Shakur, unidentified BPP member, Zayd Shakur, unidentified BPP members, Michael Cetewayo Tabor, Debbie, Sekou Odinga, BPP member Ralph White, and Kuwasi Balagoon.

The Black Panther Party newspaper on the opening of the Panther International office in Algiers, 1970.

BPP International Solidarity, with Donald "DC" Cox, Sekou Odinga, Palestine Liberation Organization Chairman Yassir Arafat, and Eldridge Cleaver, photo taken by and from the collection of Pete O'Neal.

Sekou Odinga, PLO Chairman Yassir Arafat, and Eldridge Cleaver, photo taken by Pete O'Neal, from the collection of Kathleen Cleaver.

Panther 21 codefendants Lee Berry (Mkubu) and Thomas Berry (Mshina), circa 1968, from the collection of Marva and Lee Berry.

Marva (*in stripes*), Lee (*with "freedom" T-shirt*), and family, 2016, from the collection of Marva and Lee Berry.

Twentieth anniversary of the Panther 21 trial and
acquittal, with codefendants (left to right) Dr. Kwando
Kinshasa, Shaba Om, Robert Collier, Dhoruba Bin Wahad
(at the time, just released after nineteen years behind
bars), Ali Bey Hassan, and "Doc" Curtis Powell, May 1991,
photo by and from the collection of Roz Payne.

Dhoruba Bin Wahad, Ghana, West Africa, circa
2005, from the personal collection of Dhoruba
Bin Wahad.

Dhoruba Bin Wahad and his wife Binta, at the Masjid Sultan Ahmed, Istanbul, Turkey, circa 2014, from the personal collection of Dhoruba Bin Wahad.

déqui kioni-sadiki and Sekou Odinga, on the day he was released
on parole after more than thirty-three torturous years behind bars,
November 25, 2014, from the personal collection of Sekou Odinga and
déqui kioni-sadiki.

Jamal Joseph and Shaba Om, at the jazz brunch closing of the New York City fiftieth-anniversary celebrations of the founding of the Black Panther Party, Harlem State Office Building, November 13, 2016, photo by Matt Meyer.

Dhoruba Bin Wahad, Sekou Odinga, and Matt Meyer, circa 2016, photo by déqui kioni-sadiki.

READY TO STEP UP

LUMUMBA SHAKUR AND THE MOST NOTORIOUS BLACK PANTHERS

Bilal Sunni-Ali

I first connected with Lumumba Shakur through his mother-in-law, Mrs. Mariamne Samad, who was a strong figure in the Harlem community as a teacher of African culture. She was Muslim, based in the Lincoln townhouses. She was the founder and director of the Sankore Nubian Cultural Workshop, where we learned about West African history and Islamic history; I was in my late teens, and already a Muslim. She had twins, Sayeed and Sayeeda. Sayeeda married Lumumba. That's how I met Sayeeda and directly her husband, Lumumba, and we became good friends.

I also became close with his father, Hajji Salahdeen Shakur, who I credit with Lumumba's development and a lot of our (young people's) development. Salahdeen was a companion of Hajj Malik el Shabazz (Malcolm X), and he was demonstrating through his life a lot of things that Malcolm talked about, including being involved in Africa. Salahdeen was a merchant, traveling back and forth from Africa, bringing goods from Africa but also taking stuff from here—sneakers, jeans, etc. He was also a big supporter of the Panther Party, one of our main supporters in the community. And he was one of our main outlets for the outside world, traveling around, selling goods. That's where a lot of us began to learn firsthand the concepts of revolutionary Pan-African-ism, connecting with other people on a grassroots level.

Haji Salahudin was already moving in that international direction which the Panthers eventually took up, and he was a financial supporter of the Panther development in Algeria. He kept us in communication with a lot of forces, since he was able to travel freely as part of his business. He would keep us in touch with people in exile who were in the movement, who were living in Africa or even in Europe at that time. He was showing us that if your business is travel and the movement needs people traveling, you could combine your business with what your task in the movement is. It's not, then, a question of donating your time; you change your life so you're always developing something. I've followed in those footsteps as a musician, where I've always tried to organize the things that I do so that I accomplish more than one task at the same time. A lot of people called Salahudin *Abba*, which means "father." He was Abba to many of us, Sekou included.

Becoming strong friends with Lumumba, we were reading the same materials and felt the same way about a lot of things. We were reading the philosophy and teachings of Chairman Mao Zedong; other major books were Frantz Fanon's *Black Skin, White Masks* and *A Dying Colonialism*. At the time, it also became widespread for folks to read *The Autobiography of Malcolm X* and also *Malcolm X Speaks*, and having the connection with Lumumba's father, being directly connected to Malcolm and that history, a lot of people saw us as being in a leadership position. We were providing that leadership, but the elders that we respected and that we were related to were also directly involved in the Organization of Afro-American Unity and Muslim Mosque, Inc.—the organizations which Malcolm had founded. Folks were interested in building a Black revolutionary party, a Black liberation army, and a government for our people. The development of the Black Liberation Army (BLA) came out of the Panther Party, but there were earlier manifestations of this kind of work even before the BPP.

The building Lumumba lived in was on rent strike and we were involved with tenant organizing together even before we were involved with the Panther Party. We brought that into our work with the Panthers. Lumumba was very strong in his ability to convince people not to pay the rent but to use the rent money for the upkeep of the building. If the landlord wouldn't do it, we would do it ourselves.

Another place we did tenant organizing, after the 21 case, was in the Bronx. One time we caught people selling heroin in the buildings, and we had a policy that anyone caught selling drugs would be put out. We also had a policy of publicly dumping the substances they were selling in the street. We'd make a public spectacle out of dumping this stuff because people wouldn't believe that that's what we would do. We made sure that everybody was able to see it. People actually cried about that because they didn't think we'd actually do it. Then, when we did it, they'd stand there crying—at the lost profits and the loss of their ability to get high. We poured that shit in the gutter. No dope dealers ever challenged us on it. They more or less understood why we were doing it, that we weren't against them personally. We were just against what they did. We never caught flak from those involved in the business of drug trafficking, just from people who were using it. We had more people interested in us advising them in what should be done next—what they should do if they were not going to be able to sell dope. We had more people interested in dialoguing with us than in confronting us. We had already initiated the confrontation by taking the product and publicly destroying it.

At that time, people were interested in working together. H. Rap Brown (now Imam Jamil Al-Amin) was so well known, and many people were patterning themselves after him in what were called the "H. Rap Brown Brigades"—groups of people who were interested in stopping drug trafficking in their communities. He was very involved in publicly speaking about the problems of drugs, and he was known to speak directly to people involved in drug trafficking about what they could do for their community, how they could make money if they weren't going to be selling drugs. There were ways to make money, like developing businesses similar to Salahudin Shakur, who had worked to become an international merchant. There were more doors open through that, and a number of the people who were previously trafficking in drugs began to travel to Africa. Some people close to us began to change their whole outlook about how money could be made, doing things that could help both the grassroots economy here and in Africa even though the major economies were not in the hands of the grassroots.

I had actually joined the Panther Party, and I recruited both Lumumba and Sekou. I had gone underground in the spring of 1968, just when the Black Panther Party for Self-Defense was growing on the West Coast and beginning to recruit on the East Coast. Before the Black Panther Party for Self-Defense, organized by Huey Newton and Bobby Seale, there was a Black Panther Party in New York. We knew a lot of the earlier Panthers—between Sekou, Lumumba, and me—and wanted to pull together, just to have some talks with those who had preceded us in projecting that name. Robert Collier of the 21 was actually involved in both. Kwame Ture (then Stokely Carmichael) was involved in these earlier efforts, as was Max Stanford (Muhammad Ahmad). Stokely (Kwame) and Rap (Imam Jamil) were involved in the Lowndes County Freedom Organization of Alabama, which was the first to use the Panther symbol and name, and were part of the Student Nonviolent Coordinating Committee (SNCC), which Kwame was chairman of.

After I recruited Lumumba and Sekou, I disappeared—which had an effect on the development of the whole Party. A lot of people knew me but didn't know where I had gone. A number of us who had charges involving fire-arms just left the New York area. Some of us went to California to get a closer look at the Black Panther Party for Self-Defense and noted that it was not the same Party as what was being organized on the East Coast. In terms of being a national Black revolutionary party, they were very different. Lumumba had written articles on Black revolutionary nationalism, which were published in the Black Panther East Coast newspaper, *Right On!*. There was a lot of talk from Bobby Seale denouncing any form of nationalism. Bobby and Huey were not making a distinction between what they called cultural nationalism, and what we called revolutionary nationalism. When Bobby would say, "dem dashikis ain't gone stop no bullets," Lumumba would point out, "neither would leather jackets." What we saw as being revolutionary nationalism dated back to Mar-cus Garvey. But Bobby Seale at one time threatened to expel anyone from the Party who supported what he referred to as "Lumumba's cultural nationalist rent strike."

Lumumba and I began to see them as having major ideological differences with us. We saw them as culturally uneducated, because they denounced West African culture, and I see now that it was because they had a lot of run-ins with West Coast–based Kwanzaa founder Ron Karenga. We said that they and the whole Party needed to study African culture as well as the history of revolu-tionary nationalism. The people who they (West Coast) were calling cultural nationalists were actually from the early New York Panther group, which was started by folks close to the Revolutionary Action Movement (RAM) or who had a relationship with SNCC. Many of us looked to them as our elders and leaders. That first wave of a New York–based Black Panther Party was orga-nized in cells by that group of folks who had developed a working relationship between RAM and SNCC. To simply think of them as cultural nationalists showed a serious lack of study of ideology, and of history. The second wave, which we were a part of, was a little broader.

I remember that I was on the West Coast around the close of Huey's mur-der trial. The hype slogan at that time was "Free Huey or the Sky's the Limit." When the guilty verdict came in, the word from the BPP Central Committee was to "be cool"—that the "sky's the limit" slogan meant that we would go to the highest level of legal redress to defend our minster of defense's innocence. In New York, however, there were headlines stating "Huey Found Guilty. Panthers Keep Word," indicating that there was reportedly immediate military retaliation in response to Huey Newton's conviction.

When I came home, out of Soledad prison, in 1972, Lumumba was heavily involved in organizing the National Committee for the Defense of Political Prisoners—which brought together people interested in prisons in general and those interested in political prisoners. There were so many cases in that brief period between 1968 and 1972 that it was important to develop another organization. So many people had been arrested from the Panther Party, so much of the leadership had been attacked, that the structures were getting weak. The leading cases at that time included Sundiata Acoli (at the time Clark Squire) and Assata Shakur (JoAnne Chesimard). Another was Muhammed Ahmad, who had been arrested in 1967 along with Herman Ferguson (both were part of the RAM leadership and earlier Panthers). The development of the National Committee led to a working relationship between the BPP East Coast (Right On chapters) with the Provisional Government of the Republic of New Afrika (PG-RNA). And there were Joint Ministries in certain parts of the East Coast: Joint Ministries of Information and of Defense in New York, Boston, and Philadelphia. My late, great wife Fulani was very instrumental in developing the Republic of New Afrika 11 Defense Committee, and a series of important conferences were held—leading up to the International New Afrikan POW Solidarity Day, held in Jackson, Mississippi, I think in 1973. This was the work we were all doing, between the BPP and the RNA, which led us to head southward to New Orleans, which was considered the cultural capital of New Afrika. We went to New Orleans to work on the grassroots level, and Lumumba came to work in New Orleans following in his father's footsteps as a salesman of cultural crafts from West Africa. We had gotten involved with the New Orleans Jazz and Heritage Festival, which I'm still involved in as a vendor, and were working directly with the PG-RNA. We still pushed the National Committee and the BPP through the Joint Ministries, which is what continued to give the BPP some life in the Black communities on the East Coast and in the South.

Lumumba was supposed to make a trip to Ghana with his father, but he never did because he was killed. This was 1986. Lumumba's body was found at his next-door neighbor's house. Somebody had invaded his house, shot him. He had bullet wounds in the head and neck. There had been a wave of attacks on policemen, and there was a young man named Hasani implicated in those attacks who was killed just before Lumumba. When we went to Lumumba's just after his murder there was an article about Brother Hasani on Lumumba's pillow in his room. Someone was clearly letting us know that we were being watched, and that Lumumba's murder was tied to this young man's death as well.

The police told Lumumba's father directly: they would look into who killed his son, because (they said) they were "very good at solving murders." In fact, they added, they knew who killed the policeman in the Brinks armed robbery case, which left two officers dead. A few days later, Mutulu—who was charged as part of the conspiracy to plan Brinks and the liberation of Assata— was captured after years of being underground.

When Lumumba was killed, it was a shock to all of us—because it was generally a period of inactivity. We hadn't really been involved in very much politically or militarily. So when he was killed—especially given the police making the statement that they did and the newspaper article found on his pillow—we knew that they were making a statement to us: you could change your lifestyle and the nature of your work, but they were remembering what the focus of our work had been. They saw Lumumba and me as Black Liberation Army functionaries, whatever we were or were not doing at the time. They didn't necessarily see us as soldiers but as people involved who supported the BLA in public ways, who rallied people around the BLA. I remember we would show up at movement events and engage the crowd in chanting "All the way with the BLA." People said this was a vendetta by the police to retaliate for things that had happened to policemen over the years. When it happened, I was told by a lot of people to be careful; this was a direct warning to me as well. I was one of Lumumba's closest friends from the mid-1960s to the mid-1980s.

Lumumba Shakur will always be known as the leader of the most notorious chapter of the Black Panther Party, as a person who was anti-drug, who always supported the Black Liberation Army, and who rallied people to support liberation.

One thing which we said back in the day and still say today is: "Repression breeds resistance."

When people look at the continuation of the BLA, they often try to tie it directly to individuals who were functionaries or to those who were connected with particular shootings even decades back. But we've always said that this is not where resistance comes from—a small handful of people during a certain time period. Resistance to police murders in the 1970s was based on the fact that people responded to police repression and violence in an organized way. When there was more of an organized effort at checking police brutality— like the BPP patrols, the "policing the police" programs—and when there was more organizing in general, then the organized resistance was stronger. It could be seen and felt in many forms. If you check the newspaper accounts of those days, and the police reports, the political trials involving the BLA always had evidence of clear communiqués in which the group would take credit. One of the things some of us are considering nowadays is that some of the recent attacks may not be genuine at all but a means for police administrations to justify further repression. When communiqués would be issued after an attack on police, they would identify specific activities or violent behaviors that warranted or led to their becoming a BLA target. It was never just somebody coming with a long rifle randomly shooting uniformed police officers. Planned actions took place because of specific records and behaviors of which specific policemen were guilty in certain communities.

There hasn't been that type of response today, no communications to show any connections. Guerrilla warfare can only gain victories from particular actions and what we called armed propaganda. There will be resistance to the repression taking place today, but for us—in terms of future work—we need to look at the high number of prisoners who have been tortured by and within the U.S. I have personally challenged prosecutors and various officials to publicly present any documentation they have of a policeman ever being shot or killed by members of the Black Panther Party for Self-Defense. We must bring the U.S. before international forums, such as the Inter-American Court in Costa Rica, which is willing to take on some of these cases. We have to be legally equipped and qualified, willing and ready to step up to present them.

CONSCIOUSNESS, COMMUNITY, AND THE FUTURE

Ali Bey Hassan

Throughout the 1990s, Ali Bey Hassan worked to pen several versions of his memoir/ autobiography. The following serves as a both a review of his life and as a testimony of his priorities and hopes for future generations of revolutionaries. Written as a third-person narrative, it is published here for the first time.

Ali Bey Hassan believed that "Soul is the nucleus of a human being's self—one who rhythmically channels his or her movements into action."

Ali Bey was born Iverson Burnett on December 29, 1937, in Newark, New Jersey. He was the only child as far as he knows but was part of a large family. His parents were married, but due to circumstances beyond his control Ali Bey's father was not part of his growing-up time. His father was in Greystone Institution for fifteen years before his mother signed him out. Ali Bey was raised by his mother and members of his family.

At an early age, his mother taught him how to travel from New Jersey to New York. His childhood was typical of a young Black man growing up in the 1940s, '50s, and '60s. He learned about the streets in New York. His mother and Aunt Bea worked hard and tried to give their children the things that all children want and need: security, a safe home, and a good education.

However, when Ali Bey turned seventeen, his mother enlisted him in the U.S. Navy. Thus began Ali Bey's first real confrontations with racism—in the U.S. Navy and in America. Remember, the most recent civil rights movement was in its infancy (Rosa Parks's time). Ali Bey was not used to the "Jim Crow" laws and all they represented when he was stationed in the South (Norfolk, VA); he wasn't able to comply with the "back of the bus" laws.

Ali Bey found himself in a constant struggle, and when at last the Navy offered an early discharge he took it. This was in 1957; he had signed up for four years in 1955. When he came home to Newark after his Navy experience he applied to dental school and was told to come in for an appointment. His GI Bill would cover the tuition; the position was opening up the next day. Ali Bey showed up at the school and as the receptionist took a look at him, she told him there were no openings. While Ali Bey was standing there, a white sailor in a Navy uniform was told that the same position was open. He was dumbfounded. From that point on his consciousness was raised. At age twenty-nine he went to Harlem, New York and heard Bobby Seale of the Black Panther Party speaking on the corner of 125th Street. It was 1968.

Looking back in the 1990s, he wrote:

I immediately joined the Black Panther Party for Self-Defense. On April 2, 1969, I was arrested at 5:00 A.M. in my apartment and charged with 156 counts of conspiracy along with twenty other Panther comrades. This became known as the "Panther 21" case. At that time, it was also the longest political trial in the history of New York City and State to that date. When the actual trial took place, only thirteen Panthers stood trial. I was one of the thirteen. Each one of us was held on $100,000 bond/ransom and the case took twenty-seven months from the preliminary hearings to the verdict.

We were acquitted on Friday, May 13, 1971, on the thirteenth floor of the New York City courthouse. I was a community organizer working among the people before my capture/arrest. After the acquittal on all charges, I was remanded to New Jersey on a previous charge. I made bail, and headed back to New York to work among the people.

The Party split came down between the East and West Coast because of undercover U.S. government agents posing as Black Panthers. After spending a year and a half underground, I was recaptured in California on a fugitive warrant for allegedly shooting a police officer in New Jersey. I stood trial and was convicted.

After a long and difficult struggle, I was released on parole in 1977 to the State of Connecticut. I started working to free all political prisoners and prisoners of war in the United States. At that time, I was the National Coordinator for the Sundiata Acoli Freedom Campaign. I also worked with the MOVE family, and members of the International Concerned Family and Friends of Mumia Abu-Jamal, who was being held on Death Row in Pennsylvania at the time.

Ali Bey opened up his home to children of Panthers and to participants in the struggle whose parents were either dead, in prison, or killed in action. He made a significant contribution to building an extended family network among former Panthers, strongly committed to self-reliance. His home became a refuge for members of the struggle who needed a place to repair or recover from all the damage inflicted on them during the war on the Black community, which is still being waged by certain high government officials.

In 1998, Ali Bey organized the Norwalk Community Action Coalition, which in turn organized the first African Day Parade in the history of Norwalk, Connecticut. Towards the end of his life he placed great emphasis on developing a solid base of support for political prisoners—including economic enterprises and land so that the movement would have something to offer them when they were released. "We must become increasingly sophisticated in our efforts to educate the public about our prisoners," he noted, "changing our strategies and tactics to meet current conditions."

He had six children, twelve grandchildren, and several great-grandchildren. He believed in the African concept: the parents have the child; the village raises the child. When asked about his hopes for the movement, Ali Bey stated: "Our major task is raising the political consciousness of youth in particular. We must teach them revolutionary ideology and show them the principles of political struggle. We need to recreate trust about revolutionaries and within the community."

CAPITALISM PLUS DOPE EQUALS GENOCIDE

(EXCERPT OF THE CLASSIC 1969 PAMPHLET)

Michael "Cetewayo" Tabor

I. The Problem

The basic reason the plague of heroin cannot be stopped by the drug prevention and rehabilitation programs is that these programs, with their archaic, bourgeois Freudian approach and their unrealistic therapeutic communities, do not deal with the causes of the problem. These programs deliberately ignore or at best deal flippantly with the socio-economic origin of drug addiction. These programs sanctimoniously deny the fact that capitalist exploitation and racial oppression are the main contributing factors to drug addiction in regard to Black people. These programs were never intended to cure Black addicts. They can't even cure the white addicts they were designed for.

This fascist government defines the cause of addiction as the importation of the plague into the country by smugglers. They themselves even admit that stopping the entry of the plague is impossible. For every kilo (2.2 lbs.) of heroin they confiscate, at least 25 kilos get past customs agents. The government is well aware of the fact that even if they were able to stop the importation of heroin dope dealers and addicts would simply find another drug to take its place. The government is totally incapable of addressing itself to the true causes of drug addiction, for to do so would necessitate effecting a radical transformation of this society. The social consciousness of this society, the values, mores, and traditions would have to be altered. And this would be impossible without totally changing the way in which the means of producing social wealth is owned and distributed. Only a revolution can eliminate the plague.

Drug addiction is a monstrous symptom of the malignancy which is ravaging the social fabric of this capitalist system. Drug addiction is a social phenomenon that grows organically from the social system. Every social phenomenon that emanates from a social system that is predicated upon and driven by bitter class antagonisms that result from class exploitation must be seen from a class point of view. . . .

IV. Capitalism and Crime

Dope selling is beyond a doubt one of the most profitable capitalist undertakings. The profits from it soar into billions. Internationally and domestically the trade and distribution of heroin is ultimately controlled by the Cosa Nostra, the Mafia.

Much of the profits amassed from the drug business is used to finance so-called legitimate businesses. These legitimate businesses that are controlled by the Mafia are also used to facilitate their drug-smuggling activities. Given the fact that organized crime is a business and an ever-expanding one at that, it is constantly seeking new areas of investment to increase profits. Hence, more and more illegal profits are being channeled into legitimate businesses. Partnerships between the Mafia and "reputable businessmen" are the order of the day. There is a direct relationship between legitimate and illegitimate capitalists.

Over the years, a number of politicians and foreign ambassadors and wealthy businessmen have been arrested in this country for drug activities. Others, because of their wealth and influence, were able to avoid arrest. In the fall of 1969 it was discovered that a group of prominent New York financiers was financing an international drug smuggling operation. No indictments were handed down. Shortly after that a group of wealthy South American businessmen were arrested in a plush New York City hotel with over $10 million worth of drugs.

Given the predatory and voracious nature of the capitalist, it should come as no surprise that so-called legitimate businessmen are deeply involved in the drug trade. Capitalists are motivated by an insatiable lust for profits. They will do anything for money. The activities of organized crime and the "legitimate capitalists" are so inextricably tied up, so thoroughly interwoven, that from our vantage point any distinction made between them is purely academic.

The legitimization of the Mafia, their increased emphasis upon investing in and establishing corporations, has been accelerated by the stiffer prison sentences that are being meted out to drug profiteers. In New York this has resulted in the gradual withdrawal of the Mafia from their position of actual leadership of the New York drug trade. The New York drug trade is now dominated by Cuban exiles, many of whom were military officers and police agents in the pre-revolutionary, repressive Batista regime. They equal the Mafia in ruthlessness and greed.

These new local dope kingpins have established a broad network of international smuggling operations. They utilize the traditional trade routes and create new ones, as indicated by the increased number of Narcotics Bureau seizures of dope coming from South America.

The concept of Black Power has influenced the thinking of every segment of the Black community. It has come to mean Black control of the institutions and activities that are centered in the Black community. Black teachers demand Black community control of the ghetto schools. Black businessmen and merchants advocate the expulsion of white businessmen from the ghetto so that they can maximize their profits. Black numbers-game operators are demanding total control of the ghetto numbers operations. And Black dope dealers are demanding community control of heroin. It is a tragedy that in New York the greatest gains made in the realm of Black community control have been made by Black racketeers, numbers-game bankers and dope dealers, by the Black illegal capitalists. Prior to 1967 it was a rarity to find a Black dope dealer who handled more than 3 kilos (1 kilo equals 2.2 lbs.) of heroin at any given time. Independent Black importers were unheard of. Now, there is an entire class of Blacks who have become importers, using Mafia-supplied lists of European connections.

The extent and instant rate of profits reaped from the dope industry could arouse the envy of U.S. Steel, General Motors, and Standard Oil. From the highest level to the lowest, the profits are enormous. If the individual is sufficiently ambitious, cunning, ruthless, and vicious, he may graduate from the status of street peddler to big-time wholesaler and distributor in a short span of time.

A characteristic feature of class and racial oppression is the ruling class policy of brainwashing the oppressed into accepting their oppression. Initially, this program is carried out by viciously implanting fear into the minds and sowing the seeds of inferiority in the souls of the oppressed. But as the objective conditions and the balance of forces become more favorable for the oppressed and more averse to the oppressor, it becomes necessary for the oppressor to modify his program and adopt more subtle and devious methods to maintain his rule. The oppressor attempts to throw the oppressed psychologically off-balance by combining a policy of vicious repression with spectacular gestures of good-will and service.

Given the fact that Black people have abandoned the non-functional and ineffective tactics of the "Civil Rights" era and have now resolved to attain their long overdue liberation by any means necessary, it has become necessary for the oppressor to deploy more occupation forces into the Black colony. The oppressor, particularly in New York, realizes that this cannot be done overtly without intensifying the revolutionary fervor of the Black people in the colony. Therefore, a pretext is needed for placing more pigs in the ghetto.

And what is the pretext? It goes like this: Responsible negro community leaders have informed us, and their reports concur with police findings, that the negro community is ravaged by crime, muggings, burglaries, murders and mayhem. The streets are unsafe, business establishments are infested by armed robbers, commerce cannot function. City Hall agrees with negro residents that the main cause for this horrible situation is the dope addicts who prey on innocent people. Yes, the dope addicts are to blame for the ever-increasing crime rate. And City Hall will answer the desperate cry of negro residents for greater protection—send in more police!

That victims of the plague are responsible for most of the crimes in the Black ghettos is a fact. That Black drug addicts perpetrate most of their robberies, burglaries and thefts in the Black community against Black people cannot be denied. But before, out of desperation, we jump up and scream for more police protection, we better remember who put the plague in Harlem, Bedford Stuyvesant, and the other Black communities. We better remember who ultimately profits from the drug addiction of Black people. We better remember that the police are alien hostile troops sent into the Black colonies by the ruling class, not to protect the lives of Black people but rather to protect the economic interests and the private property of the capitalists and to make certain that Black people don't get out of place. Rockefeller and Lindsay could care less about the lives of Black people. And if we don't know by now how the police feel about us, then we are really in bad shape.

V. Pig Police

The plague could never flourish in the Black colonies if it were not for the active support of the occupation forces, the police. That narcotics arrests have increased in no way mitigates the fact that the police give dope peddlers immunity from arrest in exchange for money pay-offs.

It is, also, the practice of pig-police, especially narcotics agents, to seize a quantity of drugs from one dealer, arrest him, but only turn in a portion of the confiscated drugs for evidence. The rest is given to another dealer who sells it and gives a percentage of the profits to the narcotics agents. The pig-police also utilize informers who are dealers. In return for information they receive immunity from arrest. The police cannot solve the problem, for they are a part of the problem.

When you consider that a kilo of heroin purchased by an importer for $6,000, when cut and bagged and distributed will bring back a profit of $300,000 in a week's time, it becomes easier to understand that even if the death penalty were imposed on drug profiteers, it would not deter the trade.

The lying, devious puppets of the bourgeois ruling class, the demagogic politicians of Capitol Hill, have now passed a law which gives narcotics agents the right to crash into a person's home without knocking, on the pretext of looking for narcotics and "other evidence." This law was ostensibly passed to prevent dope dealers from destroying the dope and "other evidence." Now, anyone who thinks that this law will be confined to just suspected drug dealers is laboring under a tragic and possibly suicidal delusion. To assume that only suspected drug dealers will be affected by this law is to negate the reality of present-day America. To allow yourself to think for one moment that this law only applies to suspected drug dealers is to deny that the laws being passed, the policies being implemented, and the methods and tactics of the police have become blatantly and shamelessly fascist.

It should come as no surprise when the homes of revolutionaries and other progressive and true freedom-loving people are invaded by the police on the pretext of searching for drugs and "other evidence." A number of revolutionaries have already been imprisoned on framed-up narcotics charges. Lee Otis [Johnson] was given 30 years and Martin Sostre was sentenced to 41 years on trumped-up narcotics charges. Rest assured this policy will be intensified. We would do well to consider what kicking in a person's door in search of drugs and "other evidence" actually means. What is "other evidence"? The bourgeois, fascist law-makers have not specified what constitutes "other evidence." The No-Knock Law is an integral part of the fascist trip that this country has embarked upon.

Before, when the home of a Black person was burglarized by a drug addict, or a sister had her purse snatched, the police took all night to respond to the call, or didn't respond at all. The burglar or purse-snatcher was hardly ever caught. In most instances, when someone was arrested it was the wrong person. But when an exploiting capitalist business establishment in that very same ghetto, especially a White one, gets ripped-off, there are immediately 15 siren-wailing police cars on the set, and three dozen pigs are running up and down the street waving guns in everybody's face. And you can lay 5 to 1 odds that somebody is going to jail for it. Whether or not the arrested person perpetrated the act is irrelevant from the pigs' standpoint. The racist pig-police use Blacks as an outlet for their sadistic impulses, inadequacies, and frustrations. Now that more police have been sent in, the situation has gone from bad to worse.

VI. Revolution

The racist pig-police, the demagogic politicians and the avaricious big businessmen who control the politicians are delighted that Black youths have fallen victim to the plague. They are delighted for two reasons: one, it is economically profitable, and two, they realize that as long as they can keep our Black youths standing on the street corners "nodding" from a "shot" of heroin, they won't have to worry about us waging an effective struggle for liberation. As long as our young Black brothers and sisters are chasing the bag, as long as they are trying to cop a fix, the rule of our oppressors is secure and our hopes for freedom are dead. It is the youth who make the revolution and it is the youth who carry it out. Without our young we will never be able to forge a revolutionary force.

We are the only ones capable of eradicating the plague from our communities. It will not be an easy task. It will require tremendous effort. It will have to be a revolutionary program, a people's program.

The Black Panther Party is presently in the process of formulating a program to combat the plague. It will be controlled totally by the people. We, the people, must stamp out the plague, and we will. Dope is a form of genocide in which the victim pays to be killed.

SEIZE THE TIME!

INTENSIFY THE STRUGGLE!

DESTROY THE PLAGUE!

ALL POWER TO THE PEOPLE!

BUILDING A BRIDGE TO THE 21ST CENTURY

(EXCERPT FROM AN UNPUBLISHED LETTER)

Kuwasi Balagoon
Auburn Correctional Facility
Auburn, New York
January 24, 1984

Dear Meg,

I studied some Spanish for the first time, read a portion of a book I had laying around for a week. Ate, straightened up, made another attempt at organization and it appears that one just about succeeded. The day before, I put up some shelves; that may seem like nothing to you, but to me it's like building a bridge to the 21st Century. Maybe that's an exaggeration, but I've only succeeded in putting up shelves once before. In the Bronx, we had reefer plants in the bathroom window, and pepper plants in the living room window, somehow my measurements and patterns fell true. Before then, um, I used to fuck up putting up curtains, hanging pictures. When I was in Junior High School shop, I made a bird house that I was really proud of and took to my mom. But when she looked inside, she noticed that the nails were so long, their points stuck out throughout the interior—had a bird ever flew into it, it would have been impaled. My mum took it with good humor and kept it in the basement.

There's a guy here who opens the window in front of his cell at night, and the birds fly into his cell and stay until morning, say goodbye, and leave until the next night. There's a lot of different communication with animals. For instance, my dog house-broke herself—used to sit on my shoulder like a monkey, kill rats and line their corpses by the door, drink rum! When I lived in Rockaway, there was a family with five or six dogs that would play on the roof (!) without seeming to be the least bit pensive. The house had gables and they'd just go in and out the window, back and forth, and it always seemed amazing. They weren't circus dogs, or bred with that particularly. They didn't even seem to be terriers.

I had planned to build a geometric dome on an acre of New Afrika, to share with Chickie, so that when I wasn't busy I'd have somewhere to live that didn't cost rent and could continue to make wine and rum, and plant sugar cane in the backyard—just for that. It might seem quite ambitious, but the dome was prefabricated.

That was like an old dog learning new tricks for me, because before I escaped my personal visions were of having an estate of stone in a cold climate, where it was always foggy with an iron fence and a huge yard—grounds patrolled by mastiffs, and stables with Percherons (French draft horses). And a quiet, oak-paneled room, with chairs and a table made from single pieces of black oak, with cabinets full of cognac. And I'd picture myself sitting at the table alone, wearing a maroon, velvet robe (the floor was black oak also), inspecting an ancient bottle, pouring a good portion into a snifter that I could stick my nose into, and look over to the fireplace, yawning dogs . . . to some peace and quiet. But once out, one day I walked Chickie to the laundromat and took the dog for a walk right after—and then went back home, a little high and content until I remembered that she had cursed a guy out on the way to the laundromat. And instead of having a little time to myself, I was wondering why she was so late. So I went out to help her. Everything was OK, but I had to change my dream.

Love and Hunger,
Kuwasi

HOW COMMITTED ARE YOU?

EXCERPTS OF A TALK AT GREEN FOR ALL'S "DREAM REBORN" CONFERENCE, MEMPHIS, 2008

Afeni Shakur

I believe in the Black Panther Party; we failed because we took God out. I beg you not to do the same thing. If you take God out, you're not going anywhere except to jail. You're going to be killed, or you're going to stay angry.

I've seen many organizations and many mass movements, and it has to be something else besides "what I'm against." I've heard a lot of "what I'm against": "I don't like this, I don't like that, and I hate this." But my God, what are you for? What are you for, individually? You must make these decisions! And when you make them, be prepared for the consequences; not your sis-ter—*you!*

When I was in both the Black Panther Party and the Republic of New Afrika [where freedom is very much connected to the land and liberated terri-tory —Ed.], we said we wanted forty acres and a mule. Well how many people do you know that have forty acres and a mule? I want you to ask somebody that you know: Where is your land!? I'm talking about those folks who have two or three dollars; don't act like all of us are poor. Where are those forty acres? How committed are you to the dream, and what is that dream you're committed to?

April 4, 1968: Rev. Dr. Martin Luther King Jr. was murdered in this place. That started something in this country. April 2, 1969—363 days later—21

Black Panthers were arrested in New York City; one year later. So, the other day, I just celebrated thirty-nine years after my arrest. There is so much healing to be done in our places. And by "our," for me I mean the world. . . .

Where are the women? Where are your stories? Tell the stories! Find them stories and tell them! They don't have to be cute. If you don't do it, we will be erased. Already these young people don't know we stood mighty! Already they don't know that if it hadn't been for the women there wouldn't have been no Black Panther Party!! They already think that men did it. We've got to put an end to the lie! And if we don't do it, we can't move forward on anything.

We've got to have land. We've got to have ground. And we can't just have jobs; what else must we have? Can we please get some executive courses; there is no reason we should be talking about jobs and not talking about running companies.

We have to dream big! . . . Let's do something besides theorize!

LOOK FOR ME IN THE WHIRLWIND

(POEM-LYRICS FROM THE JAZZ INTERPRETATION)

Bilal Sunni-Ali

War is never easy
It's bound to bring on hardships.
It's bound to make you weary
Reach out for me.

And War will have us parting.
Our paths are getting distant.
We might not see each other again
Until we win

So until then
Until we win
Look for me . . . in the whirlwind
Try to see my face . . . in the whirlwind
Try to grab my hand . . . in the whirlwind
Do all you can to help your brother man through the whirlwind

(repeat second verse and interlude)

Reach out for me . . .
Reach out for me . . .
Reach out for me . . .

For VICTORY!

BLACK PANTHER PARTY PLATFORM AND PROGRAM

What We Want, What We Believe

The question of reprinting the famous "10-Point Program" of the Black Panther Party is not as easy as it might seem, just as finding the list of names that compose the Panther 21 is almost impossible, at least online. There are many links to various versions of the platform, program, and rules of the Party, but almost all of them are amalgams of several versions, and some are edited to update the language, grammar, or politics. The full, original, unedited Platform and Program, as written in October 1966, published in 1967, and used to recruit members and build chapters in the formative years, is reprinted below. There was a version revised by the Party in March 1972, and though it "cleaned up" some of the language and edited out some of the politics, it left out a crucial line, which was and remains important to many of the members of the New York Panther 21. The key sentence, foundational to the vision of a Black/New Afrikan nation, is contained in the summary of the Platform, point ten, stated as the primary objective of the Party, namely: "a United Nations–supervised plebiscite to be held throughout the black colony in which only black colonial subjects will be allowed to participate for the purpose of determining the will of black people as to their national destiny." It is this October 1966 version that we have chosen to share.

1. *We want freedom. We want power to determine the destiny of our Black Community.*
We believe that black people will not be free until we are able to determine our destiny.

2. *We want full employment for our people.*
We believe that the federal government is responsible and obligated to give every man employment or a guaranteed income. We believe that if the white American businessmen will not give full employment, then the means of production should be taken from the businessmen and placed in the community so that the people of the community can organize and employ all of its people and give a high standard of living.

3. *We want an end to the robbery by the white man of our Black Community.*
We believe that this racist government has robbed us and now we are demanding the overdue debt of forty acres and two mules. Forty acres and two mules was promised 100 years ago as restitution for slave labor and mass murder of black people. We will accept the payment as currency which will be distributed to our many communities. The Germans are now aiding the Jews in Israel for the genocide of the Jewish people. The Germans murdered six million Jews. The American racist has taken part in the slaughter of over twenty million black people; therefore, we feel that this is a modest demand that we make.

4. *We want decent housing, fit for shelter of human beings.*
We believe that if the white landlords will not give decent housing to our black community, then the housing and the land should be made into cooperatives so that our community, with government aid, can build and make decent housing for its people.

5. *We want education for our people that exposes the true nature of this decadent American society. We want education that teaches us our true history and our role in the present-day society.*
We believe in an educational system that will give to our people a knowledge of self. If a man does not have knowledge of himself and his position in society and the world, then he has little chance to relate to anything else.

6. *We want all black men to be exempt from military service.*
We believe that Black people should not be forced to fight in the military service to defend a racist government that does not protect us. We will not fight
and kill other people of color in the world who, like black people, are being
victimized by the white racist government of America. We will protect ourselves from the force and violence of the racist police and the racist military,
by whatever means necessary.

7. *We want an immediate end to police brutality and murder of black people*
We believe we can end police brutality in our black community by organizing
black self-defense groups that are dedicated to defending our black community from racist police oppression and brutality. The Second Amendment to
the Constitution of the United States gives a right to bear arms. We therefore
believe that all black people should arm themselves for self-defense.

8. *We want freedom for all black men held in federal, state, county and city prisons
and jails.*
We believe that all black people should be released from the many jails and
prisons because they have not received a fair and impartial trial.

9. *We want all black people when brought to trial to be tried in court by a jury of
their peer group or people from their black communities, as defined by the Constitution of the United States.*
We believe that the courts should follow the United States Constitution so that
black people will receive fair trials. The 14th Amendment of the U.S. Constitution gives a man a right to be tried by his peer group. A peer is a person from a
similar economic, social, religious, geographical, environmental, historical and
racial background. To do this the court will be forced to select a jury from the
black community from which the black defendant came. We have been, and
are being tried by all-white juries that have no understanding of the "average
reasoning man" of the black community.

10. *We want land, bread, housing, education, clothing, justice and peace. And as
our major political objective, a United Nations–supervised plebiscite to be held
throughout the black colony in which only black colonial subjects will be allowed
to participate for the purpose of determining the will of black people as to their
national destiny.*
When in the course of human events, it becomes necessary for one people
to dissolve the political bands which have connected them with another, and

to assume, among the powers of the earth, the separate and equal station to which the laws of nature and nature's God entitle them, a decent respect to the opinions of mankind requires that they should declare the causes which impel them to the separation.

We hold these truths to be self-evident, that all men are created equal; that they are endowed by their Creator with certain unalienable rights; that among these are life, liberty, and the pursuit of happiness. That, to secure these rights, governments are instituted among men, deriving their just powers from the consent of the governed; that, whenever any form of government becomes destructive of these ends, it is the right of the people to alter or to abolish it, and to institute a new government, laying its foundation on such principles, and organizing its powers in such form, as to them shall seem most likely to affect their safety and happiness. Prudence, indeed, will dictate that governments long established should not be changed for light and transient causes; and accordingly, all experience hath shown, that mankind are more disposed to suffer, while evils are sufferable, than to right themselves by abolishing the forms to which they are accustomed. But, when a long train of abuses and usurpations, pursuing invariably the same object, evinces a design to reduce them under absolute despotism, it is their right, it is their duty, to throw off such government, and to provide new guards for their future security.

AFTERWORD

Mumia Abu-Jamal

Sometimes a book, a really good book, is like a song.

I've always thought of songs as the closest thing to human time machines. You hear the opening chords, and it takes you back to the first moment it tickled your eardrums.

Well, *Look for Me in the Whirlwind: From the Panther 21 to 21st-Century Revolutions*, featuring a reprint of the original collective autobiography of the NY 21, is like that. To read it is to smell the odors, to see the visions, to hear the roars of 21 young Panthers—and it is as beautiful as it is wonderful.

I was a young Panther, assigned to the Ministry of Information in the Bronx. I was thrilled and honored to be in the City with brothers and sisters like Dhoruba, Afeni, Sundiata, Janet, Cyril, Ali Bey, and Shaba Om. When I first read this book, it felt like and sounded like these brothers and sisters were right there, sitting in our room in the Panther pad on Kelly Street in the Bronx, rapping with us, kicking it with us—thick with sweet, New York '60s-era slang.

I've often wondered how they did it—the 21—how they could publish a book like that, when they were in jail.

But when I read them it sounded and read as if they were just rapping; none of the words or sentences seemed written. It seemed like they were talking just to you, because they were.

Here were brothers and sisters of the Black Panther Party, facing decades in prison for trumped-up, false charges thrown on them by the state: bombing of flower gardens—you know? Seriously?

But, the fact is, the government was serious, for they were aided and abetted by the U.S. Justice Department, and then Attorney General John Mitchell who vowed to "destroy" the organization.

Happily, the Panthers took it seriously, and invited the jury to see the world from their young, rebellious eyes.

I often wonder if jurors quietly, and perhaps secretly, read the book. If so, they would've learned that the Black revolutionaries in the dock were essentially young idealists who wanted to change the world for the better.

They wanted to end the abuses heaped on all Black life by the state.

They wanted decent schools and community control of police.

They wanted hungry kids to be fed.

They wanted change.

They wanted revolution.

Like the dudes who founded America, they wanted freedom.

I remember reading the 21's accounts, and feeling that these people were just like me, just like millions of us.

At the time, Huey P. Newton and Bobby G. Seale were like gods: beautiful, Black gods clad in leather, armed to the hilt.

They didn't seem real to us, Panthers like Bullwhip and me, as we walked through the Bronx, never missing a bar, to sell our newspapers.

To read these first-person stories, to listen to them, we learned how a disparate group of Black young people came together—from the labs of NASA to the flesh-corners of Harlem—to become one. They joined because the lure of Revolution was too strong to shake. They joined because they had once heard Minister Malcolm X speak and he left a vibration of resistance in the blood. They came together because in unity there was strength.

They came together because it was the rightest thing they could think of doing. They joined because they wanted to make their lives count for something bigger than themselves.

They joined because they could do nothing else.

They joined the Black Panther Party because they could not live with themselves if they didn't.

ACKNOWLEDGMENTS

Alhamdulillah! All praise is due to God (Allah).

The authors and editors of this book wish to collectively acknowledge, first and foremost, the members of New York's Black Panther Party—both indicted in the 21 case as well as unindicted "coconspirators"—whose love of freedom and love for the people was greater than their love of the safety and comfort of inactivity. In addition, we thank Panthers and their supporters—then and now—who continue to help build the type of international movements we need to end all interconnected empires, oppressions, and injustices which plague the people and the planet.

We call out in appreciation, sadness, and rage those former Panthers who have recently passed on to the ancestors while still imprisoned—behind bars and behind enemy lines in a war the imperial superpower neither acknowledges nor admits to. These include but are not limited to Bashir Hameed, Nuh Abdul Qayyum (Washington), Abdul Majid, Teddy Jah Heath . . . and former Panther 21 members Baba Odinga, Kuwasi Balagoon, and Richard Harris (aka "Nine"). Fellow freedoms fighters who were killed in the course of the struggle also include fellow Panther 21 member Lumumba Shakur, as well as Zayd Malik Shakur, Twyman Myers, and many others.

Sekou Odinga adds: I bear witness that there is no God but God (Allah), and I bear witness that Prophet Muhammad is His Prophet and slave servant! I must acknowledge first that whatever I do, have done, or will do is only by permission of Allah, Lord of the world Creator of everything.

Next I want to acknowledge my wife, my love, my partner déqui, whose love, help, and support is always there for me. I want to thank the mothers of my children who helped keep me connected to them throughout my thirty-three years of internment in the political gulags of the u.s.a. And much love to my children, Zainot, Shadia, Malik, Anochi, Dadaji, Hasheem, Kaltish, Meisha, Yafeu, Sundiata, Muhammad, and their beautiful children and grands, who continue to give me so much love and support.

I also want to acknowledge Al Hajj Solidin Shakur (Aba) and the Shakur family—of which I am one—who were there with me every step of my early political life. Especially my brother Lumumba, whose courage, love, and commitment to our people always inspired me, as it continues to do.

We owe a debt to our fallen comrades that only can be paid by our continued struggle to liberate our people here in bowels of the world's most oppressive government. We must not forget our prisoners of war and political prisoners (POWs/PPs) left behind the prison walls. Their freedom must remain first and foremost in our struggles.

Last but defiantly not least, I want to acknowledge the person who did the most to aid me in gaining my freedom, Brother Hassan (Anthony Linnen), jailhouse lawyer extraordinaire.

Dhoruba Bin Wahad offers acknowledgements to Tanaquil Jones, Elizabeth Fink, Robert Boyle, and Robert Bloom, "without whom my freedom from captivity would have remained 'freedom dreams.'" He acknowledges his wife and family: Binta Dieng Bin Wahad, Mujahid Bin Wahad, Saif'uddin Bin Wahad, and Dhoruba Moore. He would also like to acknowledge his elder sons, wherever they are at in the hinterland of the American Empire: Tarik ibn Dhoruba Bin Wahad and Mustafa ibn Dhoruba Bin Wahad. "Their births while in captivity inspired my life in my bleakest hours of isolation." Dhoruba sends his revolutionary love to the comrades of the BPP and soldiers of the BLA—especially those who lost their lives in the struggle—who answered the Call of our Generation to defend the weak and demand justice.

Editor **déqui kioni-sadiki** gives thanks to the Creator for blessing her with the breath of life to be able to engage in this work of challenging the power structure's denial about the existence of u.s.-held POWs/PPs. She gives thanks to the Ancestors for strengthening her resolve, lifting her Spirit, and for the great example and legacy of Black Resistance they leave behind. She gives thanks to our fallen, imprisoned, and exiled members of the BPP/BLA and their families, to whom we owe a debt of gratitude that can never be paid, and to the countless named and unnamed Black womyn, men, and youth who lend their skills, time, talent, and lives to Struggle. She gives thanks to the children—those she's birthed and those of her Heart—for reminding her that everything depends on our preparing for the next seven generations. She gives thanks to her sistas Deb Ingram, Yaa Asantewa Nzingha, Valerie Haynes, and her brother Norman "Mogadishu" Coward, for their days and nights of putting in the work to Free 'em all. And most especially, déqui gives thanks to "myLove, myFriend, myBrother"—Sekou—"for enriching my life with bountiful Love, inspiration, commitment, strength, solidarity, support, and for reminding me just how beautiful Struggle is. May the Spirit of the Black Panther Party continue on for generations to come! All Power to the People!"

Editor **Matt Meyer** adds his thanks—first and foremost—to his mentor-colleague-comrades Sister déqui, Sekou, Dhoruba, and Jamal. "It has been and continues to be an honor, a pleasure, and a profound education, to serve, take leadership, join in accountable solidarity, and hopefully be of service. The lessons and legacy of the Black Panther Party and Black Liberation Movement (for all people) are many, varied, and still to be fully understood, and i have been blessed to have exemplary teachers and cohorts."

Meyer further appreciates the support and guidance of his grassroots collective, Resistance in Brooklyn (RnB), as well as Craig, Ramsey, Jonathan, and Steven from PM Press, and the incomparable designer/artist Josh MacPhee. We thank Emory Douglas for reuse of his art on the cover. The content of this book would not be as rich without the commentary, advice, and many contributions of Imam Jamil Al-Amin, Mumia Abu-Jamal, Shaba Om, Bilal Sunni-Ali, Cyril Innis Jr. (Brother Bullwhip), and Marcus Tyler Vaughn; the images in the book are largely the work and generous contributions of photographer-activists Stephen Shames and David Fenton. A special thank you to Lily Constantinople is deserved, for her assistance in work on the photos. Another is due to Kathleen Cleaver for also digging up and contributing some never-before-published images. Cleaver was also joined by Melina Abdullah, Frida Berrigan, and Johanna Fernandez in contributing prepublication endorsements of this special edition.

Essential copyediting of the manuscript was provided by Steve Bloom, whose commitment to accuracy is only exceeded by his commitment to the freedom of our incarcerated political prisoners. Other supporters who discussed early versions of this project, helped contact key contributors, gave insight into a factual point or two, and/or looked over versions of the manuscript along the way include: Carlito Rovira, Tanaquil Jones, Heidi Boghosian, Marva Berry, Imam Khalil of North Carolina, and El Hajj Mauri' Saalakhan. Special thanks to early mentors, who made their mark and have now made the transition: Kwame Ture, Luis Nieves Falcón, Bill Sutherland, Mawina Sowa Koyate; and to ongoing teachers Bob Brown, David Gilbert, Oscar Lopez Rivera, and all U.S. political prisoners. Finally, special shout-outs to Michael, Molly, and life-partner/confidant/best friend/comrade Meg Starr, who remind me daily of the many reasons one must both fight for real victories and hold onto hope.

AUTHOR/EDITOR BIOGRAPHIES

Sekou Odinga was a member of Malcolm X's Organization of Afro-American Unity, a founding member of the New York chapter of the Black Panther Party as well as the Black Panther International Section, and was a member of the Panther 21. A citizen of the Republic of New Afrika and combatant of the Black Liberation Army, Sekou was captured in October 1981, mercilessly tortured, and spent the following thirty-three years behind bars—a prisoner of war and political prisoner of the U.S. empire. Since his release in November 2014, he has remained a stalwart fighter for justice and for the release of all political prisoners.

Dhoruba Bin Wahad was a leading member of the New York Black Panther Party, a Field Secretary of the BPP responsible for organizing chapters throughout the East Coast, and a member of the Panther 21. Arrested in June 1971, he was framed as part of the illegal FBI Counter Intelligence Program (COINTELPRO) and subjected to unfair treatment and torture during his nineteen years in prison. During Dhoruba's incarceration, litigation on his behalf produced over three hundred thousand pages of COINTELPRO documentation, and upon release in 1990 he was able to bring a successful lawsuit against the New York Department of Corrections for all their wrongdoings and criminal activities. Living in both Ghana and the U.S., Dhoruba, an uncompromising critic of imperialism and capitalism, continues to write and work promoting freedom for all political prisoners and revolutionary Pan-Africanism.

déqui kioni-sadiki is the chair of the Malcolm X Commemoration Committee, and was a leader of the Sekou Odinga Defense Committee, which waged a successful campaign for the release of her husband. A tireless coalition builder and organizer, déqui is a radio producer of the weekly show "Where We Live" on WBAI Radio, Pacifica; an educator with the NYC Department of Education; and a member of the Jericho Movement to Free All Political Prisoners.

Matt Meyer is a New York City–based educator, organizer, and author who serves as War Resisters International Africa Support Network Coordinator, and who represents the International Peace Research Association at the United Nations Economic and Social Council. A former draft registration resister, Meyer's extensive human rights work has included support for all political prisoners and prisoners of conscience, solidarity with Puerto Rico and the Black Liberation Movement, and membership on Board of Directors of the A.J. Muste Memorial Institute.

INDEX

Page numbers in *italic* refer to illustrations. "Passim" (literally "scattered") indicates intermittent discussion of a topic over a cluster of pages.

Abdul Hakeem, Adam. *See* Davis, Larry
Abdul Qayyum, Nuh. *See* Washington, Albert "Nuh"
Abu-Jamal, Mumia, 32, 70, 547, 548, 589, 607–8; *Still Black, Still Strong,* 549
Acoli, Sundiata (Clark Squire), xi–xii, 12, 23, 35, 68, 122, 421–22, 556–58, 583; arrests, 22, 116, 120–1, 336, 474, 557; "Brief History of the Black Panther Party," 79–84; childhood, 223–26, 278–80; civil rights movement, 421; on college education, 299; dual life, 466; employment, 329–32, 336, 383, 466, 556–57; eulogy for Balagoon, 568; on Harlem ca. 1956, 259–61; Mexico, 383–84; Panther role, 557; parole denial, 29–30, 37–40, 562;

"Parole 2016: Ride and Denied," 37–40; "Truth Is a Virus," 7–9; "Senses of Freedom," 85–86; "Updated History of the New Afrikan Prison Struggle," 41–83. *See also* Sundiata Acoli Freedom Campaign
Adams, Red, 66
Addonizio, Hugh, 53
Africa, 47, 87, 88, 89, 126–28 passim; Bin Wahad in, 102, 549, *575*; Curtis Powell in, 401–402, 548; exiles in, 71. *See also* Algeria; Ghana; Zambia
Africa, Delbert, 66
Africa, Ramona, 70
African American police officers. *See* Black police officers
African American press. *See* Black press
Ahmad, Muhammad (Max Stanford), 52, 56, 581, 583

Aiyetoro, Adjoa, 67, 69

Alabama, 66, 106n2, 581–82; Birmingham church bombing, 428. *See also* Scottsboro case

Al-Amin, Jamil Abdullah (H. Rap Brown), xiii–xvi, 32, 56, 131, 132, 438, 467, 581

Alderson Women's Penitentiary. *See* Federal Prison Camp, Alderson

Alfred 2X, 59

Algeria, 87–91 passim, 463, 470, 532, 547, 552–53, 554, *572*, 580

Ali, Bilal Sunni. *See* Sunni-Ali, Bilal

Ali Hassan, Muhammad (Albert Dickens), 53, 65, 69

Allen, Bruce, 102

Alston, Ashanti, 551–52

American Indians. *See* Native Americans

Amsterdam News, 445

Annandale Reformatory for Boys, 339

Anarchist Black Cross Federation, 74

anarchists, 14, 74, 551

Angola Prison, 44–45

Arafat, Yassir, *573*

assassinations, 24, 25, 59, 66, 73, 74, 113, 116, 125; James Shabazz, 65; Lumumba Shakur, 13, 71, 583–84; Malcolm, 54; Meredith, 54; MLK, 16, 57, 599; Robert Webb, 115

Attica Correctional Facility, New York, 45, 57, 64–65, 354–55, 412

Auburn Correction Facility, New York, 43, 45, 569, 570

Autobiography of Malcolm X, 336, 414, 422, 467, 580

automobile theft, 309, 337, 338, 360, 415

Balagoon, Kuwasi, 14, 23, 32, 69, 437–38, 551–52; arrest, 22; childhood, 201–6, 255–56, 272–74; community organizing, 425–28; death, 552; employment, 324, 335–36; escapes, 569; eulogies, 568–70; incarceration, 494–515; international travels, 290–93; letters, 597–98;

"Lock Step," 10; military service, 368–72, 390; Panthers, 438–39; reading, 438

Baldwin, James, 394, 422

bank robbery, 53, 69, 120

Baraka, Amiri (LeRoi Jones), 56, 452, 501

Barcelona, 391–92

Barksdale, David, 58

Barron, Charles, 95

basketball, 239–40, 241, 245, 246

Batelli, Neil, 74

Bay, Robert, 99

bean pie, 410, 501–2

Bell, Herman, 32, 65, 122

Benjamin X, 433

Bennett, Fred, 100, 115

Bennitt, Roseland, 543, 544

Benton, Roger, 44–45

Berry, Lee, 22, 524–25, 553–54, *572*, *574*

Berry, Marva, *574*

Berry, Thomas, 22, 545, 554, *572*, *574*

Bey Hassan, Ali, 23, 340–42, 546–47, *571*, *575*, 587–89; arrests, 22, 340–41, 588; birth and childhood, 186–89, 254–55, 293, 374–75, 587; "Consciousness, Community, and the Future," 587–89; Cuba, 383; employment, 301–2, 321, 341; higher education, 588; Islam, 416–17; marriage, 416; military service, 301, 383, 375–79, 588; on Newark rebellion, 256–57; Panthers, 439–40, 546, 588; on quitting school, 296–97

Binetti, Nicholas, 100, 101, 102

Bin Wahad, Binta, *576*

Bin Wahad, Dhoruba, 12, 98–102 passim, *140*, *149*, 321–24, 548–49, *578*, 613–14; Afeni Shakur eulogy, 563–64; Algeria, 532; arrests and charges, 22, 23, 101; "Assata Shakur," 103–23; childhood, 193, 235–36, 261–62, 311–13; conviction reversal, 30, 102,

122–23; demonstrations, *539*, *541*; employment, 322, 323; father of 192–94, 237; gangs, 311–13, 359; Ghana, 102, 549, *575*; incarceration, 30, 100, 549; Istanbul, *576*; "The Last of the Loud," 95–96; military service, 322, 359–60; "New Age Imperialism," 125–28; Panthers, 12, 457, 461, 464; release, 67; trials, 102; at twentieth anniversary reunion, *575*; "Urban Police Repression," 97–102; Youth House incarceration, 339–40

Bird, Joan, 14, 22, *140*, 549–50; arrests, 473–76, 523, 549; childhood, 262–63, 270–71; employment, 342–43, 475, 549; higher education, 299, 473, 475, 549; incarceration, 462, 485–94, 528, 529; Panthers, 471–78

Black police officers, 257–58

Black Guerrilla Family (BGF), 62–63 passim

Black Liberation Army (BLA), 26, 65–69 passim, 91, 116–21 passim, 546, 555, 584–85; Balagoon, 569; Jamal Joseph, 549; Panther roots, 580

Black Lives Matter, 12, 26, 136, 138

Black Man's Liberation Army, 431–32

Black Men's Movement Against Crack, 70

Black Panther, 81, 83, 110n9, 113, 453, *572*

Black Panther Party (BPP), 54–56, 79–84, 104–20 passim, 166, 583; Abu-Jamal, 607; Acoli, 557; Afeni Shakur, 455–63, 599–600; Algeria, 87–91 passim, 463, 470, 532, 547, 552–53, 554, *572*, 580; Baba Odinga, 465; Balagoon, 438–39; Bey Hassan, 439–50, 588; Bin Wahad, 12, 457, 461, 464; Bird, 471–78; Cleaver-Newton split, 114–15; Collier, 470–71, 581; community

programs, 30–31, 55–56, 133, 134, 138, 465, 470; community programs (breakfast), 109, 133, 470, 472; community programs (health-related), 134, 470, 477; drugs, 596; East-West divide, 582, 588; Fenton photos, *533–42*; founding, 54, 79, 106; funds, 90; Illinois, 17, 112; infiltrators, 110, 399–400, 451, 556; International Section, 87–89, 116, 470; Jamal Joseph, 131–39 passim, 467–70; Katara, 440–50; Los Angeles, 60, 110; Lumumba Shakur, 463–65, 581; Mack, 552; Om, 452–55; organizations patterned after, 74, 137; police patrols, 107, 116, 135, 584; Powell, 450–52; Sacramento demonstration, 107–8, 116, 453, 456, 467; Shames photos, *140–54*; South, 59, 583; Sunni-Ali, 581; 10-Point Program, 54–55, 107, 137, 463, 603–6; Zayd Shakur 116, 544, 546. *See also* New York 21

Black Power movement, 54, 129, 131, 132

Black press, 445, 566–67. See also *Black Panther*

Black prisoners, statistics on, 44, 45, 60, 72, 75, 77

Black Rage (Grier and Cobbs), 191

Bloods (gang), 63

Bloom, Robert, 23, 513, 531

Bolton, Mathias, 74

Boston, Cynthia. *See* Sunni-Ali, Iya Fulani

Bottom, Anthony. *See* Muntaqim, Jalil

Bowen, Joseph, 32

boycotts, 48

Boyle, Robert, 67, 610

boys' reformatories. *See* reformatories

breaking and entering. *See* burglary

Brims (gang), 61, 63

Brinks robbery attempt, Nyack, New York, October 20, 1981, 551, 552, 569, 584

Brooks, Layton, 566
Brothers, David, 79, 98
Brown, Henry "Sha Sha," 65, 120n18
Brown, H. Rap. *See* Al-Amin, Jamil
    Abdullah (H. Rap Brown)
Brown v. Board of Education, 47
Bukhari, Safiya, 65, 120n18, 546
Bureau of Special Services, NYPD. *See*
    New York City Police Department:
    Bureau of Special Services (BSS)
burglary, 310–11, 325, 360
Burnett, Iverson. *See* Bey Hassan, Ali
Burns, Nathaniel. *See* Odinga, Sekou
Butler, Sam, 469
Byrd, Joan. *See* Bird, Joan
Byrd, Rosemary, 543

California Institution for Men, Chino,
    63
California legislation, 74, 107–8, 116
Carmichael, Stokely. *See* Ture, Kwame
    (Stokely Carmichael)
Carnegie Hall, 262, 263–64
Carr, James, 58, 61, 91
Carson, Sonny, 440
Carter, Alprentice "Bunchy," 60–61, 91
Carter, Lateefah, 70
Casson, John. *See* Bey Hassan, Ali
Castro, Fidel, 397
Catholic schools, 270–71, 547
Causey, Clarence, 62
cavity searches, 487
Central Harlem Committee for Self-De-
    fense, 428
Central Intelligence Agency (CIA), 47,
    57, 72, 74
Central State College, 51–52
Cetewayo. *See* Tabor, Michael
    "Cetewayo"
Challenge (organization), 51
Chaplains (gang), 345–49 passim
Chesimard, JoAnne. *See* Shakur, Assata
Chicago, 16, 17, 66, 67, 72–73, 112;
    gangs, 58, 64
Chicago conspiracy trial, 16, 120, 555

Chimurenga, Coltrane (Randolph
    Simms), 70
Chino Prison. *See* California Institution
    for Men, Chino
Church Committee. *See* U.S. Senate:
    Church Committee
Christmas, William, 62
CIA. *See* Central Intelligence Agency
    (CIA)
civil rights movement, 48–52 passim
Clarence 13X (Clarence Smith), 52–53,
    59
Clark, John Andaliwa, 66
Clark, Mark, 17, 112, 476
Clarke, John Henrik, 566, 567
Clay, Omowale, 70
Cleaver, Eldridge, 82, 87, 90, 114, 470,
    573; New York, 457, 458
Cleaver, Kathleen, 87, 129–37 passim,
    446
Clinton, Bill, 74, 122
Clutchette, John, 62
cocaine, 70, 71, 74–75, 238–40, 251–52,
    253
Codd, Michael, 100
COINTELPRO, 21–30 passim, 58, 61,
    65, 67, 82, 91, 108–9, 114–16; Bin
    Wahad and, 12, 30, 67, 549; New
    York operations, 2, 98, 99; scope,
    136
Cold War, 105, 126
college education. *See* higher education
Collier, Robert, 23, 554–55, 575; arrests,
    22, 424; birth and childhood,
    174–75, 235, 275–76; community
    organizing, 422–25, 545, 554; con-
    spiracy case (1965), 400; CORE
    work, 303; Cuba, 396–400 passim;
    death, 555; employment, 302, 342,
    399, 422–23; gangs, 313–15, 470;
    higher education, 302–3; military
    service, 342, 362–68; Panthers,
    470–71, 581; Young Lords and, 544
Collins, Ella, 433
Coltrane, John, 452, 453, 454–55

Columbia University, 428, 514, 569
Computer People for Peace, 557
Comstock Prison, New York, 351–54, 409, 428–31
Congressional Black Caucus, 75, 76
Congress of Racial Equality (CORE), 51, 52, 303
Connor, Bull, 181, 256, 446
conspiracy charges, 1, 23, 56, 69, 70, 89, 100, 584
constitutional rights. See U.S. Constitution
control unit prisons, 67, 72
convict labor, 43–46 passim, 77
Cooper, Edwin, 100, 101, 102
CORE. See Congress of Racial Equality (CORE)
Corntop, William, 349–50
Coston, Anthony. See Shakur, Lumumba
Coston, James F. See Shakur, Salahudin (James Coston)
Coston, James F., Jr. See Shakur, Zayd Malik
Cox, Donald ("D.C."), 58, 87, 88, 573
crack cocaine, 70, 71, 74–75
Crain, William, 23, 531
criminal charges: conspiracy. See conspiracy charges
CRIPs (gang), 61–63 passim
Crockett, George, 59
Cruse, Harold, 51
Cuba, 15, 69, 108, 114, 383, 387, 389, 451; Collier visit, 396–400 passim
Curry, Thomas, 100, 101, 102

Daughtry, Herbert, 95
Davis, Angela, 62
Davis, Larry, 70
December 12th Movement, 71, 73
Declaration of Independence, 517
Dee, Ruby, 534
Del Rio, James, 59
demonstrations, 52, 71, 425–27, 502, 533–41; antiwar, 16; NAACP, 105n1; Panthers (Sacramento),

107–8, 116, 453, 456, 467; prison, 60, 62
Detroit, 50, 56–57, 58–59
Dickens, Albert. See Ali Hassan, Muhammad (Albert Dickens)
DiGia, Ralph, 555
Disciples (Chicago gang). See Gangster Disciples
Disciples (New York City gang), 296, 307, 458, 563
Dostoevsky, Fyodor, 480
Dred Scott case, 518
drinking, 221–22, 290, 294, 310, 313, 321, 329, 374
drugs, 56, 237–54 passim, 333, 342, 455, 591–96; CIA and, 57; in schools, 291, 297; selling of, 326, 361, 406, 414, 452, 592–95 passim. See also cocaine; heroin; marijuana
Drumgo, Fleeta, 62

Eastern State Penitentiary, Philadelphia, 42–43
education, formal. See schooling
Edward, Cleveland, 61
Egypt, 88
Emancipation Proclamation, 43
Emigration vs. Assimilation: The Debate in the African American Press, 1827–1861 (Kinshasa), 566–67
England, 366–68, 392
Epps, Lonnie, 22, 553
escapes from prison. See prison escapes and escape attempts
Evans, Ahmed (Fred), 57

Families Against Mandatory Minimums (FAMM), 75
Fanon, Frantz, 451, 580
Farrakhan, Louis, 74, 513
FBI, 24, 399, 451; NYPD and, 97–102 passim. See also COINTELPRO
Federal Prison Camp, Alderson, 41, 67
Fenton, David, 533–42
Ferguson, Herman, 56, 71, 73, 546, 583

Fifteenth Amendment, 518, 519
fights and fighting, 286; gangs, 307–8,
    313, 315, 318, 344–49 passim; in
    military, 363–64, 371, 373, 377;
    in prison, 339, 344–49 passim; in
    school, 280, 290; with police, 427
Fink, Elizabeth, 67, 610
Fire Department of the City of New
    York, 423
Five Percenters, 52–53, 59, 290, 415–16
Flagg, Louis S., 344
football, 286–87, 355
Ford, Joudon, 443, 459
Fourteenth Amendment, 518, 519, 522,
    524, 605
Franklin, C.L., 58–59
Freeman, Donald, 51, 52
free stores, 423–24
Fugitive Slave Act, 518, 524
Fula, Yaasmyn, 139
Fula, Yafeu Akiyele. See Yaki Kadafi
Fuller, Chaka, 59

gambling, 326
gangs, 57–64 passim, 117, 307–18
    passim; New Jersey, 308–10; New
    York City, 161–62, 236, 243, 249,
    296, 307, 458
Gangster Disciples, 58, 64
Garvey, Marcus, 19, 46, 108, 130, 582
George Jackson Brigade, 66
Germany, 365–66, 369
Ghana, 49, 71, 102, 549, 575, 583
Gilbert, David, 552, 568–70
Grass Root Front, 433
Gray, Jesse, 426, 427, 428
Great Meadow Correctional Facility. See
    Comstock Prison, New York
Green, Woody, 66, 120
Guatemala, 385, 387–89
Guevara, Ernesto "Che," 33, 395
gun rights and gun control, 107–8,
    116–17, 605

Hakeem, Adam Abdul. See Larry Davis
Hakim, Abdul, 416
Hameed, Bashir, 32, 69, 122, 609
Hampton, Carl, 59
Hampton, Fred, 17, 91, 112, 131, 132,
    136, 476
Hampton, Fred, Jr., 72–73
Handschu case, 555–56
Harlem Hospital, New York City, 173,
    464
Harris, Richard, 22, 23, 337–39, 571;
    Annandale Reformatory, 339; Black
    Man's Liberation Army, 431–32;
    childhood, 189–90; death, 554;
    employment, 360; gangs, 309–10;
    Malcolm X and, 407–8; military
    service, 361; reading, 407–8;
    robbery and burglary, 325
Hassan, Ali Bey. See Bey Hassan, Ali
Hayes, Robert Seth, 32, 122
health care, 134, 175, 462, 477
Heath, Teddy "Jah," 32, 122
heroin, 46, 162, 237, 241–54 passim,
    291, 317, 325, 591–96 passim; Five
    Percenters and, 416; Mafia and, 47,
    592; Om and, 454; public destruc-
    tion of, 580–81
Hibbit, Alfred, 59
higher education, 292, 299–300, 302,
    333, 393, 473, 565–67 passim
High School of Performing Arts, New
    York City, 293–96, 308
Hilliard, David, 90
Hoffman, Abbie, 555
Hogan, Frank, 450, 464, 485, 507, 520,
    525
homosexuality in prison, 336, 352–53
Hoover, J. Edgar, 21–31 passim, 55;
    New York City operations, 99–101
    passim, 119
Hoover, Larry, 64
hospitals, 175, 464, 477
Houston, 59
Howard, Elbert "Big Man," 540
Huggins, Ericka, 134

Huggins, John, 91
Hunter College, 567

Imarisha, Walidah, 7–9
Indians, American. *See* Native
    Americans
infiltrators and infiltration, 110,
    399–400, 451, 556
Innis, Cyril, Jr. ("Bullwhip"), 546;
    "Counting to 21," 543–58
international law, 33, 42, 585
international travel, 87–89, 365–67,
    383–2
Islam, 49, 50, 68, 73, 341, 405–17, 548,
    556
Istanbul, *576*

Jackson, Alexander, 182–85 passim,
    206–10 passim
Jackson, Anna, 182–85 passim, 206–7
Jackson, George, 62, 64
Jackson, Jonathan, 62
Jackson, Mississippi, 66
Jefferson, Thomas, 517
Jericho Movement to Free All Political
    Prisoners, 546
ji Jaga, Geronimo, 58, 65, 66, 67, 73,
    116, 123, 544
Johnson, Lee Otis, 59, 595
Johnson, Lyndon, 111, 426
Johnson, Walter. *See* Odinga, Baba
    (Walter Johnson)
Johnson, William Roger Edward. *See*
    Sunni-Ali, Bilal
Jones, LeRoi. *See* Baraka, Amiri (LeRoi
    Jones)
Jones, Waverly, 100, 101
Joseph, Jamal (Edward), 13, 30, 89, 100,
    141, 142, 151, 549; Afeni Shakur me-
    morial, 95; arrest, 22; childhood,
    182–86, 206–10, 233–35, 290–92,
    415–16, 467; demonstrations, *539,*
    541; Five Percenters, 290, 415–16;
    incarceration, 549; "Man-child
    in Revolution Land," 129–39;

Panthers, 132–39 passim, 467–70;
    Panthers' fiftieth anniversary, *578*
Joseph, Jamal, Jr., 134, 138
Joseph, Pauline, 101–2

Kansas City, Missouri, 73, 88
Karenga, Ron (Maulana), 582
Katara, Abayama (Alex McKeiver), 22,
    23, 545–46; birth and childhood,
    178–81, 214–15, 219–21, 274–75;
    employment, 440; gangs, 310–11;
    high school, 297, 298, 445–46,
    545; Panthers, 440–50; on police,
    257–59
Katz, Sanford, 23, 531
Kelly, Yvette, 70
Kennedy, John F., 52
killing by police, 32, 59, 73, 91, 92, 118,
    120, 136–37; Chicago, 17, 112,
    136, 476; lists, 58, 65–66; New
    York City, 119, 264
killing of police, 55, 58–59, 70, 100–102
    passim, 584, 585
King, Christopher. *See* Toure, Kazi
King, Martin Luther, Jr., 21, 50, 129,
    132, 214–15, 394; Kuwasi Bala-
    goon view, 255–56; Lumumba
    Shakur view, 405; in Memphis, 57,
    599; in SCLC, 49; Vietnam War
    denunciation, 105
King, William. *See* Kinshasa, Kwando
Kinshasa, Kwando, 2, 23, 431, 550–51,
    565–68, *575;* arrest, 22; on becom-
    ing a revolutionary, 437; childhood,
    198–201, 213–17 passim, 223,
    231–32, 263–65, 270, 287–88, 315;
    Emigration vs. Assimilation, 566–67;
    gangs, 315; high school, 565;
    higher education, 566, 567; *Man
    from Scottsboro,* 550, 567; military
    service, 216, 362, 372–74, 384–89
kioni-sadiki, déqui, 21–33, *577,* 614
Kornhauser, Ruth R., 520
Ku Klux Klan, 105n1, 217
Kunstler, William, 23

Laborde, Anthony. *See* Majid, Abdul
Law Enforcement Group (LEG), 444
lead poisoning, 468
Lefcourt, Carol, 531
Lefcourt, Gerald, 23, 513, 531
LeMelle, Tilden, 567
libraries, 399, 407, 490, 548
Lincoln Hospital, New York City, 464
Lindsay, John, 497, 508, 510, 514
Little, Joan, 66
Los Angeles, 60–66 passim, 110, 544
Louisiana State Penitentiary. *See* Angola
    Prison
Lower East Side, New York City,
    422–24, 470–71, 554
Lowery, Joseph E., 48
Lowndes County Freedom Organiza-
    tion, 106n2, 581–82
Luciano, Lucky, 47
lumpenproletariat, 83
Lumumba, Chokwe, 69, 71
lynchings, 214, 566

Mack, Larry, 14, 22, 87–90 passim, 433,
    552–53
Mafia, 46–47, 325
Magee, Ruchell Cinque, 56
Majid, Abdul, 32, 33, 122
Malcolm X, 50–51, 56, 165–66, 405–17
    passim, 421–22, 431–33 passim,
    465, 548, 608; assassination, 110,
    132, 432–33; *Autobiography of
    Malcolm X*, 336, 414, 422, 467,
    580; Curtis Powell and, 394–95,
    405, 548; FBI and, 21; Gene
    Roberts and, 110; influence on
    Balagoon, 438; internationalism,
    112; on jail, 480–81, 494; Sala-
    hudin Shakur and, 409–10, 579;
    on tokenism, 48; on travel, 384;
    tributes, 446; view of March on
    Washington, 52, 255; "you were
    born in prison," 118
Malcolm X Commemoration Commit-
    tee, 73

*The Man from Scottsboro: Clarence Norris
    and the Infamous 1932 Rape Trial*
    (Kinshasa), 550, 567
Mao Zedong, 139, 438, 580
Marcello, Warren, 65
March on Washington, 1963, 52, 255
marijuana, 75, 83, 192, 194, 243, 290,
    324, 328–29; Afeni Shakur view,
    253; Lee Otis Johnson conviction,
    59; "roogie," 406, 414
Marion Prison. *See* U.S. Penitentiary,
    Marion
Marks, Charles, 521, 522, 523, 525
Mason, Ila, *143*
Matanda, Priscilla, 547
Matthews, Connie, 100, *148*, 547
McClain, James, 62
McCormack, John, 428
McCray, Melvin, 547
McGinnis, Paul D., 429, 430
McGrath, George F., 497, 502, 508, 513
McKeiver, Alex. *See* Katara, Abayama
    (Alex McKeiver)
McKinney, Charles, 23, 513, 531
McVeigh, Timothy, 73–74
media, 68, 81, 453, 471, 479, 567; New
    York 21 case, 520, 523, 526. *See also*
    black press; radio; television
Media, Pennsylvania, FBI break-in,
    1971, 24
Memphis, 57, 66
Mexicans and Mexico, 41, 113, 278,
    383–84, 388n
Meyer, Matt, 11–19, 543–58, *578*, 614
Meyers, Twyman, 66, 120
military service, 200–201, 359–79, 550;
    Balagoon, 368–72; Bey Hassan,
    301, 383, 588; Bin Wahad, 322,
    359–60; Collier, 342, 362–68;
    Harris, 360–61; Kinshasa, 216, 362,
    372–74, 384–89, 550; Powell, 293
Miller, Alvin "Jug," 61
Mississippi, 44, 45, 54, 66, 165, 363,
    421, 557, 583
Mitchell, John, 608

Mkubu. *See* Berry, Lee
Montgomery bus boycott, 48
Moore, Richard. *See* Bin Wahad,
    Dhoruba
Moorish Science Temple of America
    (MST), 49
MOVE (organization), 66, 70, 589
Mshina. *See* Berry, Thomas
Muhammad, Elijah, 49–53, passim, 68,
    406–7, 416
Muhammad Speaks, 414, 415, 416
Mulford Act (California), 107–8
Munsell, Alex, 400–401
Muntaqim, Jalil, 32, 65, 68, 73, 122
Murtagh, John M., 515, 523–24, 532
music, 187, 193, 263–64, 327, 394, 405,
    507; in jail, 504, 569; jazz, 452, 453,
    454–55, 569
Muslim Mosque, Inc., 580
Muslims. *See* Islam; Nation of Islam
Mussolini, Benito, 46

NAACP. *See* National Association
    for the Advancement of Colored
    People (NAACP)
Naehle, Henry, 97
Napier, Sam, 91, 115
National Aeronautics and Space Admin-
    istration (NASA), 383, 557
National Association for the Advance-
    ment of Colored People (NAACP),
    51, 52, 105–6n1; Jamal Joseph and,
    130, 134, 135, 208–9
National Committee for the Defense of
    Political Prisoners, 583
National Committee to Combat Fascism
    (NCCF), 110, 113, 114
nationalism, 80, 402, 452, 582
National Rifle Association (NRA), 107
Nation of Islam (NOI), 49–53 passim,
    59, 65, 68, 71, 74. See also *Muham-
    mad Speaks*
Native Americans, 136, 218, 223
Negroes with Guns (Williams), 105–6n1
Nelson, Aki, 412

New Afrikan Independence Movement
    (NAIM), 57, 69, 71, 73
New Afrikan Liberation Front, 73
New Afrikan People's Organization
    (NAPO), 41, 71, 73, 568
Newark, New Jersey, 53, 65; Bey Hassan
    in, 186–89 passim, 341, 587; Black
    Man's Liberation Army, 431–32;
    gangs, 308–10; Harris in, 189,
    308–10; rebellion of 1967, 256–57
New Black Panther Party, 137
New Haven, Connecticut, 65, 99, 120,
    472, 476
New Jersey Anarchist Black Cross, 74
New Jersey State Parole Board, 562
"Newkill" (FBI-NYPD operation),
    100–102 passim, 119, 120, 121
New Libya Movement (Cleveland), 57
New Orleans, 13, 48–49, 59, 65, 71, 583
Newton, Huey P., 55, 82, 99–100, 114,
    132, 446; death, 71; Executive Man-
    date #1, 453; FBI on, 99–100, 115;
    Panthers founding, 54, 79; Sekou
    Odinga on, 90–91; trial, 582–83
New World Nation of Islam (NWI),
    53–54, 65, 69
New York City Department of Parks and
    Recreation, 422–23
New York City Fire Department. *See*
    Fire Department of the City of New
    York
New York City Police Department
    (NYPD), 97–102 passim, 119;
    Bureau of Special Services (BSS),
    2, 53, 59, 97–101 passim, 110, 450;
    Handschu case, 555–56
New York 8 case, 70
New York State Parole Board, 346, 411
New York State prisons, 53. *See also* At-
    tica Correctional Facility; Auburn
    Correctional Facility; Comstock
    Prison, New York; Woodbourne
    Correctional Facility
New York 21 case, 1–3, 89–92, 110, 465,
    469, 476–81 passim, 502, 543–58;

charges, 1, 23, 89; demonstrations, 502, *533–41*; infiltrators and, 110, 451, 556; statement from defendants, 515–28; timeline, 531–32. *See also* trial (New York 21)

New York Women's House of Detention. *See* Women's House of Detention, New York City

Nieves, Albert, 543, 544

Nine. *See* Harris, Richard

Nixon, Richard, 100–101, 112, 119, 478

Nolen, W.L., 61–62

Norris, Clarence, 550, 567

Norwalk, Connecticut, 589

Nyack, New York, robbery attempt, October 20, 1981. *See* Brinks robbery attempt, Nyack, New York, October 20, 1981

OAAU. *See* Organization of Afro-American Unity (OAAU)

Oakland, 64, 106, 107, 463; NYPD in, 98, 114n10

Obama, Barack, 103–4

Odinga, Baba (Walter Johnson), 22, 23, 57–58, 547; arrest, 465–66; childhood, 195–99, 226–30, 276, 280–85; employment, 465; gang leader, 57; Panthers, 465

Odinga, Sekou, 12, 22, 30, 73, 459–63 passim, 555, *578*, 613; Afeni Shakur memorial and eulogy, 95, 563–64; Algeria, 87–91 passim, 463; Arafat and, *573*; arrests, 461, 553; incarceration, 411, 553; Lumumba Shakur and, 290, 318, 411, 413, 414, 433; on Mack, 552–53; marriage and children, 414; Panthers, 581; release, *577*; Salahudin Shakur and, 580; son of, 139; "Still Believing in Land and Independence," 87–94; torture of, 69

Office of Strategic Services (OSS), 47

Ogbar, Jeffrey, 544

Oklahoma City Federal Building bombing, 73–74

Olugbala, Kakuyan. *See* Meyers, Twyman

Om, Shaba, 1–3, 23, 555–56, *575*, *578*; arrest, 22; birth and childhood, 171–73, 221–23, 232–33, 285–87, 324, 361–62; employment, 329; high school, 326, 329; Islam and, 414–15, 454; Panthers, 452–55; renaming, 454–55

O'Neal, Pete, 32, 88

O'Neal, William, 17

Organization of Afro-American Unity (OAAU), 165, 421–22, 432–33, 465, 580

Palestinians, 87, 88, 114, *573*

Panama, 385–87

Panther 21 case. *See* New York 21 case

Paris, 393–96

Paterson, Dolores, 543

Pean, Colette, 70

penitentiary concept, 42–43

Pennywell, Ron, 463

Performing Arts High School, New York City. *See* High School of Performing Arts, New York City

Philadelphia, 66, 70, 190–91, 275, 315–17 passim

Phillips, Joseph A., 458

Piagentini, Joseph, 100, 101

"pig" (word), 441

pimping, 327–28, 452, 453

Pinell, Hugo, 66

Plummer, Viola, 70

police killings. *See* killing by police; killing of police

Powell, Curtis, 22, 23, 332–35, 464, 479–81, *575*; Africa, 401–402, 564, 565; arrest, 333, 479–80; childhood, 175–77, 292–93; on "conspiracy," 300–301; death, 548, 565; employment, 333–35, 450, 547, 548; eulogy by grandson, 564–65; higher education, 299–300, 333, 393, 401, 450, 565; incarceration,

480; on Islam and Muslims, 405;
medical research, 334, 547, 548,
565; military service, 293; Panthers, 450–52; Paris, 393–96
Powell, Tiassa, 564, 565
Powell, William, 62
Pratt, Geronimo. See ji Jaga, Geronimo
Pratt, Sandra, 66
prison escapes and escape attempts, 69,
92, 546, 554, 569; Assata Shakur,
12, 103
prison homosexuality. See homosexuality in prison
prison rebellions, 349, 411, 429–31
passim, 496–515, 532
prison labor. See convict labor
prison statistics, 68–69, 71–72, 74, 77
prisons, California. See California Institution for Men, Chino; Soledad
Prison
prisons, control unit. See control unit
prisons
prisons, early history, 42–44
prisons, federal. See Federal Prison
Camp, Alderson; U.S. Penitentiary,
Marion
prisons, Louisiana. See Angola Prison
prisons, New York State. See New York
State prisons
prisons, Pennsylvania. See Eastern State
Penitentiary, Philadelphia
prisons, women's. See women's prisons
Project Rescue, 425, 426
prostitution, 264, 383. See also pimping
protests. See demonstrations
Puerto Ricans, 41, 122, 307–8, 312, 323,
544; incarceration, 346, 349, 351.
See also Young Lords

Qayyum, Nuh Abdul. See Washington,
Albert "Nuh"
Queens 17 case, 438
Quiñones, Raymond, 543, 544

racial segregation. See segregation
radio, 70, 440, 445, 547
RAM. See Revolutionary Action Movement (RAM)
Ramparts, 453
rape accusation, 204–5. See also Scottsboro case
rats, 425–26, 468
Raza v. City of New York, 556
rebellions, riots, etc. See riots and
uprisings
reformatories, 57, 339
religion, 176, 405. See also Islam
rent strikes, 441, 442, 580
Republic of New Afrika (RNA), 56–57,
66, 546, 555
Republic of New Libya, 57
Revolutionary Action Movement
(RAM), 51–52, 56, 582; Queens 17
case, 438
Richardson, Fred, 544
Richard X, 422
Ricks, Willie, 54
Right On!, 582
riots and uprisings, 134, 135, 255,
256–57. See also prison rebellions
Rison, Tyrone, 553
robbery, 251, 309, 324, 325, 337, 338,
360. See also bank robbery; Brinks
robbery attempt, October 20, 1981
Robinson, Zontini, 428
Rockefeller, Nelson, 64, 65
Rogers, J.A.: From "Superman" to Man,
298
Roper, Lee. See Om, Shaba
Rovira, Carlito, 544–45
Russell, Harold, 120

St. Louis, 65
Samad, Mariamne 579
Samad, Sayeeda, 413–14, 579
Sanchez, Tony, 425
Sanders, Beulah, 464
San Francisco, 63–64, 106, 109
Sauer, Kenneth, 101, 102

Sayles, James. *See* Shanna, Atiba
school desegregation, 47–48
schooling, 269–303, 308, 547, 565. *See also* higher education
Sciascia, Leonardo, 47
SCLC. *See* Southern Christian Leadership Conference (SCLC)
Scottsboro case, 550–51, 567
SDS. *See* Students for a Democratic Society (SDS)
Seale, Bobby, 16, 79, 82, 120, 131, 132, 133, 467; arrest, 476; incarceration, 469; nationalism and, 582; New York, 439, 455–57, 588; Sacramento demonstration, 453
search and seizure, 110, 556, 595. *See also* cavity searches
Second Amendment, 116–17, 605
Seedman, Albert, 101
segregation, 378, 379; childhood experiences of, 205, 215–16, 223, 269, 278; in military, 364, 376–77; in prison, 354–55. *See also* school desegregation
self-defense, 80, 107, 115, 257, 421, 422
Senate: Church Committee. *See* U.S. Senate: Church Committee
sexual harassment of women, 487, 488
Shabazz, James 3X, 53, 65, 433
Shakur, Afeni, 5–6, 13, 89, 136, 139, 405–7, 455–63, 546; arrest, 22, 465; birth and childhood, 181–82, 217–18, 230–31, 271–72, demonstrations, *539, 542*; employment, 546; eulogy, 563–64; gangs, 307–8; high school, 293–96, 308; "How Committed Are You," 599–600; incarceration, 485, 486, 490; letter to family, 528–29; Lumumba Shakur and, 460–62; memorial, 95–96; Panthers, 455–63, 599–600; trial, 23; view of drugs, 252–54
Shakur, Assata, 11, 12, 32, 41, 120, *145*, 557, 583; at Alderson, 67; Cuba, 15, 69, 103, 108, 121; escape, 69,

92, 121; "it is our duty," 15; "Poem for Sundiata," 559–62; shooting and capture of, 116, 120–21, 557; *Still Black, Still Strong,* 549
Shakur, Lumumba, 13, 23, 57–58, 79, 123, 343–55, 553, 579–84 passim; Afeni Shakur and, 460–62; arrests, 22, 343, 461, 464–65, 474; childhood, 190–92, 213, 218–19, 269, 275–77 passim, 290; death, 13, 71, 583–84; gangs, 57, 315–17; grandfather of, 257; Grass Root Front, 433; high school, 298; incarceration, 344–55, 408–13, 428–31, 432; Islam, 408–14 passim, 432; Malcolm X and, 408–14 passim, 432–33; marriages and children, 413–14; Panthers, 463–65, 468; reading, 353–54, 580; renaming, 413; Sekou Odinga and, 290, 318, 411, 413, 414, 433; stuttering, 269, 275
Shakur, Mariyama, *146, 147*
Shakur, Mutulu, 13, 32, 73, 548
Shakur, Salahudin (James Coston), *146, 147*, 190, 191–92, 409–10, 579–80
Shakur, Tupac, 13, 139, 549, 563
Shakur, Zayd Malik, 66, *150*, 479; childhood, 213, 218–19, 277; death, 13, 116, 120–21, 557; Panthers, 116, 544, 546; renaming, 413
Shames, Stephen, *140–54*
Shanna, Atiba, 66, 68
Shoatz, Russell "Maroon," 32, 65, 122
sickle cell anemia, 134
Sixth Amendment, 524
slavery, 43, 118, 283, 517, 518
slogans, 54, 71, 111, 582
Smith, Clarence. *See* Clarence 13X (Clarence Smith)
SNCC. *See* Student Nonviolent Coordinating Committee (SNCC)
Soanes, Kennie, 543
Soledad Prison, 61–62
solitary confinement, 412, 544
Sostre, Martin, 595

Southern Christian Leadership Conference (SCLC), 48–49, 50, 52
Spain, 390–92
Spofford Youth House, 339–40
sports, 286–87, 351, 355. *See also* basketball
Squire, Clark. *See* Acoli, Sundiata (Clark Squire)
Stanford, Max. *See* Ahmad, Muhammad (Max Stanford)
Students for a Democratic Society (SDS), 51, 136
Student Nonviolent Coordinating Committee (SNCC), 50, 51, 52, 54, 446, 450, 582
suicide, 336, 480
Sundiata Acoli Freedom Campaign, 73, 546–47, 562
Sunni-Ali, Bilal, 463, 563–64; "Look for Me in the Whirlwind," 601; "Ready to Step Up," 579–85
Sunni-Ali, Iya Fulani, 583
Supreme Court, U.S. *See* U.S. Supreme Court
Sutton, Percy, 554
Sweden, 299, 300, 401, 479

Tabor, Michael "Cetewayo," 100, *142*, 461, 464, 547; Algeria, 14, 88, 90, 532, 547; arrest, 22; birth, 175; "Capitalism Plus Dope Equals Genocide," 591–96; childhood, 237–52; Connie Matthews and, *148*, 547; drug use, 237–52; high school, 248, 547; Innis (Bullwhip) on, 547; renaming, 547
Taney, Roger, 518
Taylor, Donald, 66
Taylor, Robert "R.T.", 70
television, 76, 81–84 passim, 130–31, 134, 135, 202
Ten-Point Program. *See* Black Panther Party: 10-Point Program
"terrorist" label, 103–4, 108, 121–23 passim

theft, 291, 415. *See also* automobile theft; burglary; robbery
Thirteenth Amendment, 518, 519
Thomas, Edgar, 293
Thompson, Edward, 344
Till, Emmett, 566
Todd, Cheryl, 66
tokenism, 48
Tompkins Square Community Center, 423, 424, 470, 554
torture, 69, 103–4, 585
Toure, Kazi, 70
traitors, 553
travel, international. *See* international travel
trial (New York 21), 1, 22–23, 79–100, 543–48 passim, 553–56 passim, 588; Afeni Shakur, 13, 458; protests and supporters, *146–47*, *152–53*, *533–41*; verdict, 25. *See also* New York 21 case: statement from defendants
Trotsky, Leon, 481
Ture, Kwame (Stokely Carmichael), 54, 56, 129, 132, 581–82

Uganisha, Shiriki, 73
Umoja, Akinyele, 551
United Federation of Teachers (UFT), 439, 446
United Freedom Front (UFF), 70
United Nations, 55, 603–4, 605; Commission on Human Rights, 67–68
university education. *See* higher education
U.S. Congress, 519; demonstrations, 425–27. *See also* Congressional Black Caucus; Fugitive Slave Act
U.S. Constitution, 527, 528. *See also* Fifteenth Amendment; Fourteenth Amendment; Second Amendment; Sixth Amendment; Thirteenth Amendment
U.S. Penitentiary, Marion, 41, 67, 72
U.S. Senate: Church Committee, 24, 25, 26, 109, 555 56

U.S. Supreme Court, 47–48, 518, 519

Vaughn, Marcus Tyler, 564–65
Vierra, Rafael, 59
Vietnam War, 16, 61, 105, 111, 135
Virgin Islands, 66

Wallace, George, 181, 567
Wareham, Roger, 70
War on Drugs, 27, 74–78 passim
War on Poverty, 111–12
War Resisters League (WRL), 555
Washington, Albert "Nuh," 32, 65, 122
Washington, James, 53
Washington, Raymond, 61
Waters, Maxine, 75–76
Weather Underground, 90
Webb, Robert, 115
Weber, Max, 567
Weems, Donald. See Balagoon, Kuwasi
Weissman, Maryann, 553
Wells, Warren, 32
White, Anthony Kimu, 66, 120
White, Ralph, 97
Williams, Aki, 412
Williams, Alice Faye. See Shakur, Afeni
Williams, Jeral Wayne. See Shakur,
     Mutulu
Williams, Robert, 105–6n1, 438
Williams, Sharon, 543, 544
Wilson, Woodrow, 526–27
wiretapping, 99, 110, 115, 136, 478
Wolf, Paul, 97–102
women, sexual harassment of. See sexual
     harassment of women
Women's Committee to Defend Joan
     Bird, 550
Women's House of Detention, New York
     City, 475, 476, 485–94
women's prisons, 41, 67
Wood, Raymond ("Ray Woodall"), 399
Woodbourne Correctional Facility,
     344–50
Woods, Dessie, 66
World War II, 46, 47, 187, 198–99, 200

X, Benjamin. See Benjamin X
X, Malcolm. See Malcolm X
X, Richard. See Richard X

Yaki Kadafi, 139
Yaki Yakubu, Owusu. See Shanna, Atiba
York, James D. See Hameed, Bashir
Young Lords, 113, 136, 502, 544–45,
     554, 555
Youth Against War and Fascism, 553
Youth House, New York City. See Spof-
     ford Youth House
Youth International Party (Yippies), 555

Zambia, 547, 548, 564
zip guns, 307, 309

Let Freedom Ring

A Collection of Documents from the Movements to Free U.S. Political Prisoners

Edited by Matt Meyer

Foreword by Adolfo Pérez Esquivel

Afterwords by Ashanti Alston and Lynne Stewart

$37.95
ISBN: 978-1-60486-035-1
912 pages • 6 by 9

Let Freedom Ring presents a two-decade sweep of essays, analyses, histories, interviews, resolutions, People's Tribunal verdicts, and poems by and about the scores of U.S. political prisoners and the campaigns to safeguard their rights and secure their freedom. In addition to an extensive section on the campaign to free death-row journalist Mumia Abu-Jamal, represented here are the radical movements that have most challenged the U.S. empire from within: Black Panthers and other Black liberation fighters, Puerto Rican independentistas, Indigenous sovereignty activists, white anti-imperialists, environmental and animal rights militants, Arab and Muslim activists, Iraq war resisters, and others. Contributors in and out of prison detail the repressive methods—from long-term isolation to sensory deprivation to politically inspired parole denial—used to attack these freedom fighters, some still caged after 30+ years. This invaluable resource guide offers inspiring stories of the creative, and sometimes winning, strategies to bring them home.

Contributors include: Mumia Abu-Jamal, Dan Berger, Dhoruba Bin-Wahad, Bob Lederer, Terry Bisson, Laura Whitehorn, Safiya Bukhari, The San Francisco 8, Angela Davis, Bo Brown, Bill Dunne, Jalil Muntaqim, Susie Day, Luis Nieves Falcón, Ninotchka Rosca, Meg Starr, Assata Shakur, Jill Soffiyah Elijah, Jan Susler, Chrystos, Jose Lopez, Leonard Peltier, Marilyn Buck, Oscar López Rivera, Sundiata Acoli, Ramona Africa, Linda Thurston, Desmond Tutu, Mairead Corrigan Maguire and many more.

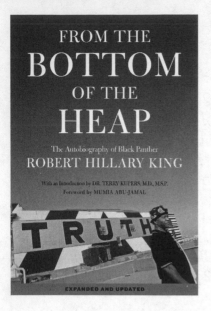

From the Bottom of the Heap
The Autobiography of Black Panther Robert Hillary King

Robert Hillary King
Introduction by Terry Kupers
Foreword by Mumia Abu-Jamal
$19.95
ISBN: 978-1-60486-575-2
272 pages • 6 by 9

In 1970, a jury convicted Robert Hillary King of a crime he did not commit and sentenced him to 35 years in prison. He became a member of the Black Panther Party while in Angola State Penitentiary, successfully organizing prisoners to improve conditions. In return, prison authorities beat him, starved him, and gave him life without parole after framing him for a second crime. He was thrown into solitary confinement, where he remained in a six-by-nine-foot cell for 29 years as one of the Angola 3. In 2001, the state grudgingly acknowledged his innocence and set him free. This is his story.

It begins at the beginning: born black, born poor, born in Louisiana in 1942, King journeyed to Chicago as a hobo at the age of 15. He married and had a child, and briefly pursued a semi-pro boxing career to help provide for his family. Just a teenager when he entered the Louisiana penal system for the first time, King tells of his attempts to break out of this system, and his persistent pursuit of justice where there is none.

Yet this remains a story of inspiration and courage, and the triumph of the human spirit. The conditions in Angola almost defy description, yet King never gave up his humanity, or the work towards justice for all prisoners that he continues to do today. *From the Bottom of the Heap*, so simply and humbly told, strips bare the economic and social injustices inherent in our society, while continuing to be a powerful literary testimony to our own strength and capacity to overcome. The paperback edition includes additional writings from Robert King and an update on the case of the Angola 3.

PM Press was founded at the end of 2007 by a small collection of folks with decades of publishing, media, and organizing experience. PM Press co-conspirators have published and distributed hundreds of books, pamphlets, CDs, and DVDs. Members of PM have founded enduring book fairs, spearheaded victorious tenant organizing campaigns, and worked closely with bookstores, academic conferences, and even rock bands to deliver political and challenging ideas to all walks of life. We're old enough to know what we're doing and young enough to know what's at stake.

We seek to create radical and stimulating fiction and non-fiction books, pamphlets, T-shirts, visual and audio materials to entertain, educate, and inspire you. We aim to distribute these through every available channel with every available technology—whether that means you are seeing anarchist classics at our bookfair stalls; reading our latest vegan cookbook at the café; downloading geeky fiction e-books; or digging new music and timely videos from our website.

PM Press is always on the lookout for talented and skilled volunteers, artists, activists, and writers to work with. If you have a great idea for a project or can contribute in some way, please get in touch.

PM Press
PO Box 23912
Oakland CA 94623
510-658-3906
www.pmpress.org

FRIENDS OF PM

These are indisputably momentous times—the financial system is melting down globally and the Empire is stumbling. Now more than ever there is a vital need for radical ideas.

In the many years since its founding—and on a mere shoestring—PM Press has risen to the formidable challenge of publishing and distributing knowledge and entertainment for the struggles ahead. With hundreds of releases to date, we have published an impressive and stimulating array of literature, art, music, politics, and culture. Using every available medium, we've succeeded in connecting those hungry for ideas and information to those putting them into practice.

Friends of PM allows you to directly help impact, amplify, and revitalize the discourse and actions of radical writers, filmmakers, and artists. It provides us with a stable foundation from which we can build upon our early successes and provides a much-needed subsidy for the materials that can't necessarily pay their own way. You can help make that happen—and receive every new title automatically delivered to your door once a month—by joining as a Friend of PM Press. And, we'll throw in a free T-shirt when you sign up.

Here are your options:
- $30 a month: Get all books and pamphlets plus 50% discount on all webstore purchases
- $40 a month: Get all PM Press releases (including CDs and DVDs) plus 50% discount on all webstore purchases
- $100 a month: Superstar—Everything plus PM merchandise, free downloads, and 50% discount on all webstore purchases

For those who can't afford $30 or more a month, we have Sustainer Rates at $15, $10, and $5. Sustainers get a free PM Press T-shirt and a 50% discount on all purchases from our website.

Your Visa or Mastercard will be billed once a month, until you tell us to stop. Or until our efforts succeed in bringing the revolution around. Or the financial meltdown of Capital makes plastic redundant. Whichever comes first.